Please return to :
Ellen Denison
145 E. Hereford
Gladstone, Or.
655-3032

Psychology for a Changing World

Psychology for a Changing World

IDELLA M. EVANS, Ph.D.

PATRICIA A. SMITH, Ph.D.

JOHN WILEY & SONS, INC.

New York • London • Sydney • Toronto

Library of Congress Catalog Card Number: 72–110167

SBN 471   24870   3

Printed in the United States of America

10 9 8 7 6 5 4 3 2 1

To our teachers, students, clients, and patients who have made the study and practice of psychology a deeply rewarding experience.

Preface

This book is designed to introduce beginning college students to the rapidly developing field of psychology in a way that will make the subject an important and meaningful part of their general education. The book is intended for use as an introductory text for a one term course in general psychology. It has been written especially to meet the needs of students in career preparation programs at the college level who want to know how to apply principles of behavioral science to problems of everyday living.

Topical areas have been carefully selected to involve students with current developments in psychology that are of significance to their lives and to increase their awareness of the benefits resulting from the scientific study of behavior. Greater emphasis has been placed on practical applications than upon theoretical material or preparation for more advanced study of psychology. The text has been written in the belief that the study of psychology can be meaningful in the lives of all persons whatever their individual directions may be.

Special effort has been made to present fundamental principles in clear and concise terms that are readable, understandable, and applicable, but without oversimplification. The presentation of basic concepts has been planned to permit instructors freedom and flexibility in supplementing the text in class lectures, discussions, or demonstrations according to the needs and goals of their own class situation. Technical vocabulary has been kept at a minimum without sacrificing key concepts. The importance of research has been stressed by the selection of relevant and timely studies in areas of popular concern.

Organization of content enables the student to begin by developing a scientific frame of reference for understanding behavior. The first chapter introduces psychology as the science of behavior, both animal and human, and emphasizes areas of application, methods, and special problems of behavioral study. What psychologists do is illustrated by introducing actual individuals in the fields of industrial, clinical, and school psychology and viewing a typical day in their professional lives.

Beginning with perception, the physical bases of behavior are presented with emphasis on the psychological significance of biological characteristics that permit and limit behavioral expression. The beginnings of human life and the relative contributions of heredity, maturation, and environment are explored in preparation for the chapter on learning. The topics of motivation and emotion are treated from a humanist viewpoint.

Understanding individual differences, their nature, development, importance, and methods of assessment, leads into an examination of personality with an emphasis upon the development of the self concept. Life tasks are presented in terms of the demands that social living imposes upon individuals as they strive to realize their potentialities. Times of crisis or periods of difficulty familiar to most persons are considered with an analysis of their problem elements to aid the student in effective handling of these crises in his own experience.

The chapter on emotional and mental illness follows the descriptive framework of the World Health Organization and emphasizes the importance of early recognition and help seeking. Concrete suggestions about community treatment resources are included. Mental health is presented as more than the absence of illness and stresses actualizing potentialities. Normality is examined in terms of a national study of mental health and the role of religion in mental health is considered. The individual as a member of various groups and the processes of these groups are explored, followed by a discussion of some of the problems in group living.

The final chapter explores some of the scientific and technological developments that are changing the social environment and influencing the psychological experiences and opportunities of individuals.

The case history materials used to illustrate various points throughout the book are taken from the clinical and counseling experiences of the authors. Summaries and suggestions for additional reading accompany each chapter and a glossary of terms is included at the end of the book.

We are most appreciative of the efforts of the following psychologists in academic settings who reviewed the manuscript in various stages of development and made valuable suggestions about content and clarity: Ronald Murdoff, San Joaquin Delta College, Stockton, California; Suzanne Adams, Merritt College, Oakland, California; Frank Blume, San Bernardino Valley College, San Bernardino, California; Arthur Freeman, Rockland Community College, Suffern, New York; E. Stewart Trebbe, West Valley College, Campbell, California; and M. A. Treynor, University Community and Technical College,

Toledo, Ohio. Grateful acknowledgement is also made to Dr. Gloria Lee Hutchins for the material on the development of motor and athletic skills. A special thank you is due our typists, Miss Aletha W. Landry and Mrs. Pat Keeley, for their diligent efforts in the preparation of the manuscript.

IDELLA M. EVANS, PH.D.
PATRICIA A. SMITH, PH.D.

San Jose, California
February 1970

Photo Credits for Chapter Opening Photos

Chapter 1   by Jim Sargent

Chapter 2   Bridget Riley. *Current*, 1964; Collection, the Museum of Modern Art, New York. Philip C. Johnson Fund

Chapter 3   by Jim Sargent

Chapter 4   by Ken Heyman

Chapter 5   by Ron Tunison

Chapter 6   by Ken Heyman

Chapter 7   by Anne Zane Shanks

Chapter 8   by Bullaty-Lomeo

Chapter 9   This picture, "The Story of My Life," was painted in pastels by one of the patients whose illness is described in the chapter. For reasons of confidentiality, the identity of the artist is withheld. Photo by George Engel.

Chapter 10 by Wayne Gravning

Chapter 11 by Bob Adelman

Chapter 12 by Ken Heyman

Contents

Psychology in Action

"Man Goes Berserk in Crowded Bus: Injures Four"

"Computer Error Grounds All Local Air Traffic Despite Clear Skies"

"Riot Over Curriculum Cancels All Classes"

"New Bridge Open Increases Commuter Load by 30,000 a Day"

"V.D. Outbreak Closes Local High School"

These are imaginary headlines, but you have probably seen real ones which carry the same stories . . . frustrated people; destructive people; more people; expanding technology and shifting standards. We are living in an exciting, but troubling age of anxiety. Change and upheaval in standards and values surround us. The guidelines of past generations are of no help to us as we seek to find our way in an ever-changing world. Personal meaning and a sense of identity are hard to find. Improved conditions of health and longer span of life, urbanization, industrial automation, population explosion, racial unrest, and the threat of nuclear warfare confront us with serious personal and social issues to resolve. Mankind is searching for new and more effective ways to come closer to one another. For these and other human problems we turn to psychology and the social sciences for help and understanding.

WHAT IS PSYCHOLOGY?

Psychology is a subject of increasing interest and concern in our modern complex society. Public awareness has been heightened by movies, television, and the popular press. Although psychology was established as an independent science less than one hundred years ago (1879), its subject matter has been a concern of philosophers and scholars for many centuries. Typical questions for speculation were: What are the functions of the human mind? Where does the mind come from and how does it develop or change? How is mind related to the body? Do animals possess minds? How is mind related to the brain? What is the role of the brain in governing behavior? How do the sense organs and the brain contribute to our perception of the world? How is the soul related to the mind? What causes mental disorders? To what extent is man a product of his culture? How is individual behavior influenced by groups? What are the best methods for raising children? How can we develop and structure the environment to make it possible for the inborn potentialities of individuals to be realized? What is human nature and what are its limitations and potentials?

The psychology of today represents a stage in the history of man's inquiry into the nature of man. Prior to the nineteenth century the study of the mind belonged to philosophy, and the study of the body was considered an appropriate subject for anatomy and physiology. The body, as something apart from the mind, was seen as an objective phenomenon, directly observable, and subject to the same general laws that governed other physical matter. The idea of mind and body as separate is no longer considered accurate, although it still persists in popular thought in such expressions as "mind over matter." Both mind and body are combined and interrelated in those expressions of the individual which we call *behavior*. Thoughts, dreams, and wishes, while we cannot see them, are as much a part of an individual, and as expressive of him, as are his acts of walking, talking, or eating. Psychology began as the study of mind, but, as with all branches of modern science, new discoveries and improved methods of inquiry have advanced our understanding of man and the world, until it has evolved into a science of behavior. The term *behavior* is broadly applied to a wide range of activities, including observable action; conscious processes of sensing, feeling, thinking; and unconscious processes within the biological organism which are not directly observable.

Psychology, then, is the study of behavior for the purpose of understanding. We will be examining not only what people do, but also why they do it, what satisfactions or obstacles they find, and why they change. To understand behavior we will need to know something about the physical body—its inherited capacities, how it functions to make behavior possible, its growth and development, and its potentials for change. We will look at the processes of learning which bring changes to behavior as a result of the experiences people have and the training they receive. We will want to know about motives, needs, and wishes that set behavior in motion and propel it forward. Finally, we will look at social and environmental forces that create crises for people and shape their behavior as they make responses to events around them.

Although psychology is a relatively young science, it is rapidly growing in knowledge and expanding its areas of application. The information psychology offers is not limited in its usefulness to just those in the profession. Anyone who comes in contact with people can utilize psychological information to his benefit. Understanding human behavior can help us to do a better job as a student, employee, supervisor, marriage partner, parent, and citizen.

PSYCHOLOGY AS A PROFESSION

What do psychologists do? Many people have the mistaken notion that psychologists are bearded geniuses with an intense gaze in their eyes who can read minds or predict the future. The really outstanding characteristic of the men and women attracted to the profession of psychology is their interest in understanding and helping other people. The life work of a psychologist involves the application of knowledge developed through research to problems of individual and group behavior. Psychologists work closely with members of other professions including physicians, teachers, lawyers, social workers, engineers, clergymen, nurses, policemen, biochemists, physiologists, sociologists, and business and industrial personnel.

There are approximately thirty thousand psychologists in the United States, about a third of whom are employed by colleges and universities. Federal, state, and local governments make up the second largest group of employers. Public school systems rank third, followed by nonprofit organizations and private industry. There is a growing number of psychologists who are self-employed in therapeutic and consultation activities full time, but most of the practicing psychologists in this country are affiliated with some educational institution, medical facility, governmental agency, or industrial research organization.

The major professional organization for psychologists in this country is the American Psychological Association, founded in 1892. The APA is organized into divisions which represent the major areas of special interest to the members. If you look at the divisions of the APA listed in Table 1-1 you will see that the profession reflects a wide range of interests and application to human problems.

Areas of Specialization

Because psychology has application to all fields of human activity and developments occur so rapidly, psychologists cannot expect to be expert in all areas of the subject. As the profession grows and matures new areas of specialization emerge and develop, although there is still a great deal of overlap in what psychologists do. To give an overview of the profession we will briefly describe the major areas of current specialization.

Clinical psychology is the most popular area of specialization within psychology today. Clinical psychologists engage in the prevention and treatment of emotional and mental disorders (see Chapter 9) by working with individuals

Table 1-1. Divisions of the American Psychological Association[a]

> General Psychology
> Teaching of Psychology
> Experimental Psychology
> Evaluation and Measurement
> Physiological and Comparative Psychology
> Developmental Psychology
> Personality and Social Psychology
> Society for the Psychological Study of Social Issues
> Psychology and the Arts
> Clinical Psychology
> Consulting Psychology
> Industrial Psychology
> Educational Psychology
> School Psychology
> Counseling Psychology
> Psychologists in Public Service
> Military Psychology
> Maturity and Old Age
> Society of Engineering Psychologists
> Psychological Aspects of Disability
> Consumer Psychology
> Philosophical Psychology
> Experimental Analysis of Behavior
> History of Psychology
> Community Psychology
> Psychopharmacology
> Psychotherapy
> Psychological Hypnosis
> State Psychological Association Affairs

[a]Source: American Psychological Association, 1969.

and small groups who have personal social, emotional, and behavior problems. The clinical psychologist, in addition to training in treatment methods, has special skills in research and the use of psychological testing instruments. The clinical psychologist provides therapy for individuals, families or groups; determines specific behavior problems through interviewing or testing techniques, gives in-service training for other staff members; offers consultations, community education, or organization services; and provides leadership for mental health program development and evaluation. Many clinical psychologists today are involved in community mental health programs aimed at prevention of illness through better understanding of the causes and improvement of opportunities for healthy development within the community.

Closely related to the clinical field is the specialty of *counseling*. Together these two specialties account for half of all psychologists in our country. Counseling psychologists are primarily concerned with behavior adaptation and the adjustment of individuals to their environment. Counseling psychologists work in vocational guidance, rehabilitation, educational planning, marriage counseling, and community mental health programs. The training and supervision of many elementary and secondary school counselors, classroom teachers, clergymen, law enforcement personnel (especially juvenile workers), and state employment service counselors is a responsibility of counseling psychologists. Both clinical and counseling psychologists are interested in behavior adaptation so that all potentials of the individual may be realized.

Industrial psychologists are the highest paid, on the average, of all psychologists. They comprise about 8 percent of psychologists but they are in increasing demand. They may be employed by industry or government, but frequently they are members of independent groups who sell their services to many different industries. The problems for which industrial psychologists are called upon for service in a given industry may include excessive turnover, absenteeism, inefficiency, or accidents. They may set up a personnel selection and training program to enable a firm to obtain better qualified employees and increase productivity, or help with the selection and appraisal of potential management personnel. Management training courses are frequently offered by industrial psychology firms. Understanding human relations is an important part of industrial management which poses many challenges for the psychologist in industry. Labor–management disputes, poor morale, and breakdown of communication between workers and supervisors are common problems dealt with by the industrial psychologist. Industrial psychologists are also called upon to study complex man–machine systems and to investigate such factors as the arrangement of equipment and work space, designing of tools and equipment, and the prevention of industrial accidents.

Social psychologists study the impact of community and social forces on individual and group behavior and adjustment. Group dynamics, social interaction, delinquency, illegal behavior, and problems of prejudice are among the concerns of the social psychologist. Polling techniques for measuring public opinion, attitudes, and beliefs have become well-known as methods of understanding and predicting group behavior. Some of the newer developments in social psychology include methods for modification of group attitudes to reduce intergroup tension as in congested neighborhoods.

Social psychologists have been increasingly involved in the analysis of propaganda, counterpropaganda, and all aspects of psychological warfare. Social psychology has been applied to business problems with remarkable benefits. Market research includes the testing of products for manufacturers and testing the effectiveness of different advertising techniques in magazines, radio, and television.

Educational psychologists specialize in problems of learning and achievement. They are concerned with the psychological aspects of training, remedial and special education, and school psychology. Recent developments in automated or programmed instruction have attracted many psychologists to this specialty. Research in this new educational technique is still in its infancy, but those who are active in the field are convinced that it will have a dramatic effect upon education in the future.

School psychology has emerged as a separate specialty quite rapidly in the past 20 years. School psychologists usually work in the elementary and secondary schools where they have an opportunity to help children whose problems interfere with their education. The school psychologist emphasizes early detection of learning and behavior problems as the most effective way to prevent later personal and social disability.

Experimental psychology is perhaps one of the least known, but oldest of the special fields of the profession. The experimental psychologist is a research specialist whose efforts to develop theory and make application of newly discovered information has established psychology as a science. The experimentalist works with humans and animals as research subjects and may be found in universities, industry, and government settings. Laboratories for the experimental study of learning, motivation, sensation, perception, and motor skills have become common in the military services and space-age industries. One of the important fields of experimental interest is psychopharmacology, the study of drugs and other chemical agents that produce change in the behavior of living organisms. Working with biochemists, physiologists, and pharmacists, the experimental psychologist conducts research to study the effects of drugs on animals and humans. Psychopharmacology is particularly challenging to the psychologists who work in this area of research because of the potential contributions to be made to the treatment and prevention of human suffering.

What Psychologists Do

It is not very likely that any two psychologists function in exactly the same way even though they may be working toward the same goals and using the same skills. Rather than describe typical functions, let us give you a personal introduction to some psychologists by looking in on them engaged in a typical day's work.

Dr. Milton K. Davis is an industrial psychologist in Portland, Oregon. He is not nationally famous but he is probably typical of many members of the Division of Industrial Psychology of the American Psychological Association. Dr. Davis is a graduate of Reed College. He earned his Ph.D. at Purdue University where he worked as a graduate assistant and a research fellow during graduate school. He is an Associate Professor at Portland State College and has an independent private practice on a part-time basis.

Early in the morning we would find Dr. Davis teaching Industrial Psychology and Personnel Management to a class of psychology majors at the college. After classes he spends an hour in his office at school where he talks with students regarding their research projects for which he is advisor. He is interrupted by a phone call from a colleague who talks over some minor revisions in a research paper they have cosponsored and are submitting for publication.

At noon Dr. Davis meets with a group of power company executives in a downtown restaurant. Over lunch they discuss the final plans for a management development course he has helped to plan and will conduct for their company. This course is designed to help prepare supervisors and managers for positions of higher responsibility.

Dr. Davis reaches his private office in the early afternoon to look over his mail and messages. He dictates a letter agreeing to appear as a speaker for the Personnel Management Association on the topic of "Employee Attitudes and Automation." He phones a computer center to check on results of his market research project, which measures attitudes of the public toward a new labor-saving device which is not yet on the market. The company's promotional staff is anxious for the results. He scans some notes from his clinical associate and dictates the report of an executive appraisal on a young junior executive trainee he interviewed yesterday.

The secretary interrupts; a client is here by appointment. He will spend the next hour talking with the new owner of a chain of variety stores about streamlining their advertising program.

His next client is a job applicant who is seeking a position as an airplane salesman. After interviewing the man Dr. Davis selects some interest and aptitude tests from his files and takes the man into an adjoining room where he will not be interrupted during the testing. Dr. Davis handles the personnel selection for a number of small companies that do not have their own personnel departments.

Dr. Davis spends the next few minutes with his assistant examining the results of data collected for a morale study in another industry. He organizes the findings, outlines the work to be done and thus concludes another busy day.

Dr. Thomas N. Weide is a clinical psychologist in San Jose, California. He is a graduate of the University of Kentucky and holds a Ph.D. from Stanford University. He took advanced clinical training as a U.S. Public Health Service Fellow and served his clinical internship in the Veteran's Administration. He has been a staff member at the Santa Clara County Mental Health Center for a number of years and he has a part-time private practice.

We join Dr. Weide in the morning as he is coming out of his adult therapy group meeting. This is an open women's group which has been meeting at the same time each week for six years. He calls it an open group because the individual women have attended for varying lengths of time from a few weeks to four years. As members of the group improve and no longer need to attend, new members are added and the group continues.

Dr. Weide stops in his office to take phone calls between appointments. He takes a call from a juvenile probation worker and gives him a verbal report of the psychological examination of a 10-year-old boy who has been setting fires in his neighborhood. He discusses the results and recommendations with the probation officer and tells him that a written report to the court has been prepared.

We follow Dr. Weide to the conference room where he participates in a case conference regarding a 12-year-old girl who refuses to go to school and who appears to be beyond control by her parents. Discussing the case with Dr. Weide are the school psychologist, the Public Health Nurse, the Public Welfare caseworker, the staff psychiatrist, and the staff social worker, all of whom are involved in working with the girl and her family. They meet to consider the child's problems and to plan how they can work together to help the family avoid a major crisis and also give the child the help she needs.

For the next hour Dr. Weide is with two postdoctoral psychology trainees whose work he is supervising. We later can observe through a one-way mirror as Dr. Weide engages a 7-year-old girl in play therapy. Children this young are often unable to tell their feelings or to discuss problems with a therapist, so they are encouraged to act out their feelings in a play situation with the therapist's help. At the end of the hour Dr. Weide discusses the treatment session with the two trainees.

Dr. Weide returns to his office for a brief chat with the Health Educator regarding a series of educational programs they are planning for a parent–teacher group in the community. His next appointment is with a very disturbed adolescent boy whose mother has committed suicide.

Dr. Weide joins other members of the staff for lunch while they discuss suggested additions to the professional library. After lunch he leaves the clinic and drives to one of the local high schools. He talks with the assistant superintendent about personnel problems and meets with the school psychologist. The rest of this afternoon Dr. Weide will meet with individual school counselors to discuss particularly difficult problems in the students they are counseling. This consultation activity helps school counselors to increase their professional skills and prevents problems from becoming so serious that students have to be referred to an outside agency.

Dr. Weide will visit other schools on other days of the week on a regular basis throughout the school year. This consultation service to the schools is provided without cost as a part of the program of the county mental health center. One afternoon of each week Dr. Weide goes to the state hospital where he is participating in an exchange program of professional staffs. These exchange programs between treatment agencies bring new people and ideas into agency functioning and keep the participating professionals aware and informed of community problems.

Miss Mary Callantine is a school psychologist in Lansingburgh, New York. She is a graduate of the University of Montana and has a master's degree in psychology from the University of Oregon. Following advanced graduate study at Syracuse University she became a school psychologist.

Miss Callantine's day begins in her combination office and playroom in one of the five schools where she works. By choice, she concentrates most of her efforts on a relatively few children who present serious learning and behavior problems in school. The children with whom she chooses to work intensively are selected on the basis of her contacts with teachers, counselors, and administrators in her district. One of these, an emotionally disturbed first-grade girl, is seen for an individual session in the playroom where the child is accompanied by several imaginary cats. The little girl projects her feelings, fears, and frustrations onto the cats and uses them to communicate with the psychologist. With patience and acceptance Miss Callantine works toward helping this child gain better understanding and acceptance of herself. Frequent contacts with parents and teachers are also part of the work in this case.

The next child to see Miss Callantine is a socially maladjusted third-grade boy who is a show-off in the classroom and on the playground. In this case the psychologist's efforts are directed toward helping the boy build confidence in himself and find more socially acceptable ways of gaining the attention he needs.

A succession of children presenting a wide range of problems are seen for individual half-hour sessions throughout the day. Some are poor readers with normal intelligence who have special learning problems, others are overly active and aggressive in the classroom, and a few are shy, withdrawn youngsters who seem to prefer daydreaming to class participation.

Between appointments Miss Callantine takes phone calls from parents, counselors, public health nurses, welfare caseworkers, juvenile probation officers, and other professionals in the community who are also working with families in her school district.

Some of the children Miss Callantine sees are referred by their teachers for individual diagnostic evaluation to determine the nature and extent of their learning disabilities and for recommendations regarding necessary remedial help. Individual testing and observation by the psychologist is often requested by teachers who need help to decide whether a child is just lazy or really does not have the ability to do his work.

Miss Callantine works closely with the Director of Pupil Personnel Services who is responsible for developing programs to meet the special needs of all children who have physical, mental, or emotional handicaps that interfere with their education.

PSYCHOLOGY AS A SCIENCE

Is psychology really a science? This is a question often asked by the beginning student. How does psychology differ from observation and common sense? Most people feel confident that they have a fair amount of understanding of human nature based on their experience and observation of other people and their knowledge of their own feelings. Nearly everyone has a set of beliefs and opinions about human behavior but not everyone can agree on what the facts really are. Some of the commonly held notions that have been subjected to

Table 1-2. How Accurate are your Observations?

Self test: Mark each statement true or false.
(Check your answers on page 24)*

---

1. Highly intelligent people are more apt to become mentally ill than are people of average intelligence.

2. Slow learners remember what they learn better than fast learners.

3. People who threaten suicide are not apt to actually commit suicide.

4. Competition is instinctive in human nature.

5. Alcohol in small doses is a stimulant to clear thinking.

6. Intelligent people form most of their opinions by a process of logical learning.

7. The most important factor in job satisfaction is salary.

8. Punishment is more effective than reward in teaching children to behave properly.

9. Personality is largely determined by heredity.

10. Mental telepathy is a well-established fact.

11. Gifted children are usually weak, sickly, and unpopular with their classmates.

12. People who seek help from psychologists must have something seriously wrong with them.

---

scientific study are listed in Table 1-2. On the basis of your own observations, which of these statements are true? At the end of the chapter you will find the correct answers based on scientific evidence.

Psychology is a science because systematic methods are employed to collect information about the phenomenon, behavior, which is studied; then hypotheses are formed and tested and general laws or theories are constructed on the basis of the observed findings. In having a defined area of subject matter and approaching its study in systematic ways, psychology is like the other sciences. The difficulty for most people in thinking of psychology as a science involves the degree of certainty or absoluteness with which its principles can be applied. Most of the principles and laws of psychology are relative and not absolute, and in this sense psychology is a science in process rather than a completed science. But what science in the twentieth century can be said to be complete and its laws absolutely certain? As new methods of measurement, recording, detection, isolation, and observation become available, all sciences are required to reevaluate and reinterpret findings that were once thought to be certain and complete.

How many absolute laws of any phenomenon really exist? The law of gravity in physics is not an absolute but a relative law. "What goes up must come down" is neither a certainty nor equally applicable to all forms of matter. If some things go up far enough in the atmosphere above the earth they may disintegrate and never return. Space exploration might be simpler if the law of gravity were an absolute certainty as it was thought to be a few years ago. Psychology also shares the goal of all sciences which is to achieve sufficient understanding of its subject matter to be able to predict it. Psychology has the same difficulty as the other sciences in discovering laws for prediction. For instance, we know that intelligence is related to learning ability, and we know that a person with high average intelligence should be able to complete a high-school education. However, this prediction is relative, because an individual's motivation, economic level, personal values, health, and other factors may facilitate or may interfere with the expression of his potential.

Psychology is the science that systematically studies and attempts to explain observable behavior and its relationship to external events in the environment, but it must also study the unseen mental processes within the individual that are both causes and effects of behavior. Because the human individual is so complex and capable of such a wide range of activities, psychologists have had to develop different techniques to study his behavior. New methods of psychological investigation are continually being sought and old methods improved. Some of the ways in which psychologists study behavior include the experimental method, observation, tests and measurements, survey techniques, and clinical methods.

Experimental Methods

The goal of the experimental method in natural science is to determine cause-and-effect relationships, or in other words, to answer questions of "what will happen if—?". Usually the experimenter begins with some ideas, or *hypotheses*, about the behavior and its expected outcome. He designs an experiment in order to answer certain specific questions or to confirm (or reject) his hypothesis. Some hypotheses which have been tested by psychologists using experimental methods include: (*a*) reward is more effective than punishment in habit-training situations; (*b*) certain drugs (LSD and others) can produce distorted sense perceptions; (*c*) amount of alcohol in the blood stream directly effects reaction time; (*d*) tension and anxiety reduce learning efficiency; and (*e*) efficiency of production workers can be increased by minor changes in working conditions.

The procedure of experimental methods involves the control, manipulation, and measurement of experimental variables. A *variable* is anything that can vary and take on different value, for example, height, weight, response time, errors, attitudes, and opinions. There are two kinds of variables in an experiment, called independent and dependent. Their relationship is shown in Figure 1-1.

The *independent variable* is the one selected by the experimenter to be manipulated because it is presumed to cause change in the dependent variable. The independent variable is usually some stimulus (S) factor. A *stimulus* is any object, event, energy or energy change that creates a response in an organism. It is usual in illustrations or tables of results to give the independent variable on the horizontal axis or abscissa.

The *dependent* variable is the outcome we are studying and attempting to predict. It corresponds to the effect or results obtained. The dependent variable is usually a response (R) factor. A *response* is any internal or external activity

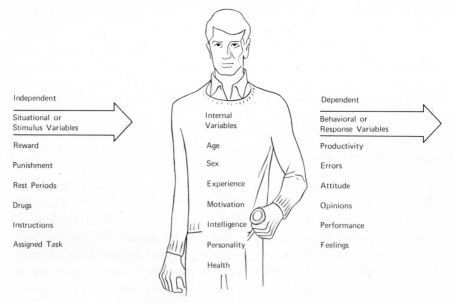

Figure 1-1.   The relationship of variables in psychological experiments.

of the organism. The dependent variable is typically shown on the vertical axis or ordinate of illustrations or tables of results.

To the extent that all the related conditions are actually controlled, it can be presumed that the independent variable has been the cause of the observed outcome. Where cause-and-effect relationships can be demonstrated, accuracy in prediction is possible. The conditions which must be controlled are all those factors except the independent variable which could possibly cause the results obtained to occur. Since it may not always be possible to identify the many conditions which could be operating to cause the results obtained, the investigator controls as many as he can be aware of and calls the others "chance." Chance to the scientist is not capricious fate but the action of important, but unknown, factors that operate as causes to produce certain effects. To the extent that the investigator can control the conditions of the study, chance factors are reduced and observed outcomes may be more certainly related to the treatment administered. For example, what is the effect on production of a 15-minute break in an 8-hour factory work day? The 15-minute break is a treatment to be studied and changes in productivity or output is the outcome to be observed. What are the conditions to be controlled that might also cause changes in productivity besides a 15-minute break? We might consider the time of the day or the day of the week, the nature of the work and the nature of the worker, the way the break is introduced, whether the break is voluntary or compulsory, and the way the break is used as all potentially important conditions to control.

Equating of Groups. To further aid objectivity and add to the certainty of findings it is desirable that two subject groups be employed. One group, called the *experimental* group, receives the treatment under study (independent variable). The second group, called the *control* group, does not receive the experimental treatment. For example, in our study of the effect of rest breaks on productivity, two groups of workers should be identified; one group (experimental) to have the rest break and the second (control) to continue without a rest break. In all other respects the groups should be as equal as possible; same ages, ability, length of time with the company, etc. Both groups should be measured in the same way on the dependent variable (productivity) so that differences in their performance, if any, can be related to the experimental treatment. Equality of groups whether animal or human is very hard to insure especially if the problem under study is quite complex and other studies have failed to identify significant factors. It is common to equate or match groups for factors like age, sex, experience, ability, and any other special characteristics one believes may be important. If the groups perform at different levels on the dependent variable it may mean the experimental treatment produced the difference in response. If care is taken to equate groups then differences in performance are due to something other than differences in the groups.

Observing the conditions outlined above will not guarantee accuracy, objectivity, and certainty in experimental studies, but they will greatly reduce the probability that chance factors are operating. Findings thus demonstrated become reliable steppingstones to further understanding of the problem.

Observational Methods

Casual or Incidental Observation. This is a method of study common to everyone and might be simply described as "people watching." In our interactions with others, whether with familiar people or strangers, we do much casual observing and often are impressed by the many similarities as well as differences which behavior displays. Some of our better understandings of ourselves and others have come by casual observation. We are not looking for anything in particular but we note and remember what we see and later may repeat it in our own behavior, or avoid it as the case may be. This method of gathering information is random, not systematic, and often more meaningful in retrospect (after the event) than it is in prospect (before the event). For these reasons accurate predictions of behavior from casual observation are not likely to develop.

Casual observation has an additional problem that limits its effectiveness called the "single incident error." As you casually observe, your attention is focused upon an event in progress. You are not usually aware or concerned about how the event developed or what may be its eventual outcome. It is like viewing a portion of a movie, you see a scene or two but you do not know the beginning or the end. You make your evaluations from that which you see and conclude the rest. Behavior in its totality is never suspended in time, it changes as it occurs in response to ever-changing circumstances. If you can view behavior from its beginning it never looks overall as it might look at a given moment. How often have you met or observed someone who seems very unpleasant and perhaps to be avoided whom you later decide is a very fine and pleasant person? In these instances you generally discover that your first poor impression of this person was based on his behavior in a particular situation at the moment you began to notice him. The single incident which brings us information of the moment does not tell us what has gone before and we may conclude too quickly from very limited information. Casual observation is valuable in that it often raises questions that can be subjected to research.

Controlled Observation. Observing children at play is one of the best ways of studying their behavior. Keeping accurate records of repeated observations of the same child or group of children over a period of time in the same situation, or in a variety of situations, will often reveal behavior patterns that would not be known from casual observation. Recording the actions, speech, gestures, and physical reactions can be made more precise and objective by using cameras and tape recorders or by having more than one observer take notes. If controlled observation is used as a means of scientific study the behavior that is sampled must be precisely defined and the observations must be quite exact.

Controlled observation of children in nursery schools has been the source of valuable insights into the personality development of preschool children. The patterns of normal development to be discussed in later chapters are based on the controlled observation of a large number of different children in particular situations. This method permits comparisons to be made between boys and girls or between children of different ages and backgrounds. Some other uses of controlled observation include studying reactions to stress, effects of discipline, interaction in groups, and emotional developments. Observation of children through a one-way mirror is used to observe their resistance to temptation. The child has been left alone in a room full of toys and has promised not to touch anything until the examiner returns. We can observe how different children will respond in this situation and by comparing our observations to other characteristics of the children we can determine which factors are related to self-control.

Field-Study Methods. The observation of behavior in its naturally occurring settings is called field study. No attempt is made to control the behavior or the situation, but rather observation is made of the behavior as it occurs. Field study has been used to investigate social development of individuals in cultures different from our own. Subgroups of our own society, such as delinquent youth gangs, have been studied by this method. Unlike casual or controlled observation, the field-study technique permits an analysis of environmental as well as individual factors in behavior while the behavior is in progress. Field studies have given us much information about human nature in terms of characteristics common to all people. It has been found, for example, that in some cultures competition is an unknown trait. Many traits that we think of as basic to human nature such as aggressiveness and acquisitiveness have been shown by field study to be reflections of the culture rather than universal human characteristics.

Tests and Measurements

Since human abilities and potentials for behavior and learning cannot be observed directly, they must be inferred from the behavior we can observe. We can set up a situation in which a sample of behavior can be observed (a standardized task with set instructions), record the individual's performance in some systematic way (scoring), and then compare these results with the performance of other individuals and groups. Performance on psychological tests can be used to predict behavior in situations that call for the same kind of functions as that measured by the test. Interests, abilities, aptitudes, and personality traits such as dominance–submission can be studied by psychological tests.

The college entrance examinations you took when you started college are an example of how testing is used to predict and control behavior. The entrance test consists of a number of tasks or problems related to different areas of learning. The results are scores which are compared to some later condition such as earned grade-point average. If we find that students whose scores fall below a certain point on the entrance exams have a high percentage of failure and those whose scores fall above a certain point have a high percentage of success we can predict outcome in college on the basis of extreme scores. This information can be useful in a limited way, for if we look more closely we find that some low-scoring students succeed and some high-scoring students fail. Tests cannot predict with absolute certainty because of all the variables within the individual and the situation. By careful analysis of test results it can be shown that a low-scoring student's chances of success can be increased by the addition of certain remedial courses. The tests can thus be used to aid a student in planning his future education with greater assurance of success.

Tests and measurement of human behavior have found widespread practical use in our highly complex society where it is desirable to be able to predict and control outcomes. In the study of behavior you will find that most of the psychological factors (learning, motivation, and emotion) and psychological characteristics (intelligence and personality) cannot be observed directly, but must rely on the development of accurate tests and measurements if we are to be able to understand, predict, and control behavior. Testing will be discussed in greater detail in Chapter 6.

Survey Techniques

Sometimes it is not possible or desirable to spend the time that field studies require to get information about the behavior of groups. The survey technique permits us to get information from many persons at a time and relatively quickly. In surveys the questionnaire or interview are the principal techniques for collecting information. The group of persons to be studied are identified and then a representative sample of the group is selected for the interviewing or questionnaire. The responses of all individuals are pooled and generalizations are made to make predictions for the entire group. Attitudes, values, needs, motivations, and typical reactions to common experiences are some of the human behaviors that can be studied by survey techniques. The Kinsey report on sexual behavior, political opinion polls used to predict election results, and the reaction of television audiences to advertisers' products are examples of how survey techniques are used to understand and predict behavior.

Clinical Methods

Clinical methods focus on the understanding of a single individual, usually through case study. The past history and present life circumstances are explored in an effort to discover causes and develop solutions to problems the individual is facing. Clinical methods are used mainly by clinical, counseling, and school psychologists.

Among the procedures included are interviewing, psychological tests, information-gathering from other persons who know the individual, securing existing records of his past performance, and integrating findings of current physical and social functioning. The result is a vast amount of information about a single person which can be used to aid his adjustment. Case study stresses the uniqueness of the individual as well as his life experience and his reactions to it.

Study of the single case cannot be used to make generalizations about other persons. However, if one examines the details of many case studies of a given kind of problem behavior, sometimes certain themes can be detected. For example, case studies of underachievers suggest the early appearance of this behavior in school performance and a general lack of intellectual stimulation in the home environment. This suggests that an experimental study could be done using intellectual stimulation as an independent variable and achievement as the dependent variable. In terms of our earlier discussion, how could these variables be specified and measured and what conditions would have to be controlled in such a study? Themes from individual case studies have been a productive source of ideas for experimental investigations of behavior.

SPECIAL PROBLEMS IN BEHAVIOR STUDY

The methods of psychology for collecting information just described may make it seem that the study of behavior is fairly easy. As consumers of psychological information we should be aware that there are some problems besides time, money, and talent that make behavior study difficult. Some of these problems are due to the very complexity of behavior, some are due to the fact that there is still much to learn about the nature of human behavior, and some are due to the attitudes of individuals and society about behavioral study.

Variables of behavior are often hard to specify, define, and measure. Consider the behavior we call love and think of the many ways it can be defined: love of country (patriotism), love of friends (familial), love of children (parental), love of spouse (conjugal), romantic love, and love of people. No one would deny that love, however defined, is a very important part of behavior both as an activator and a goal toward which much behavior is directed. Let us agree for a moment that parental love means the love a parent has for his child or children. That is a simple definition and now how to measure it? We might try measuring parental love by what the parent gives the child (care, attention, and material things) or what the parent withholds (anger, scoldings, and pain), but each of these raises added problems of definition and measurement. What units could be employed to scale love from greater to lesser amounts? Could we use the minutes or hours involved when a person says he is showing love by any of a variety of ways? Or could we use the minutes and hours a person says he feels loved regardless of how much others say they are offering? Obviously we have a problem and a solution satisfactory to all eludes us. What happens most often is that the investigator defines the problem for study, love, in a particular way; for example, "parental love is for the purpose of this study defined as more than 10 hours of companionship with the child as an individual a week," and then proceeds from there. We have discovered important information with this approach but also at times have missed the very essence of what we were trying to study. The choice seems to be that some behavior at this time must be studied in rather dissected units or not studied at all. The more specific we get in defining behavioral variables, the less application our information has. As a result, it is more common for psychological information to be expressed in generalities rather than specifics. With progress in methods of measurement and scaling these problems are being handled more effectively but they are still very real and limiting.

The critical variable may not be recognizable. A question of some social as well as individual concern involves the relationship between groups of differing races or national origins and intelligence. This seems a straightforward problem. Are people of differing races or of differing national origins the same or different in their levels of intelligence? The determination of race or national origins as well as the measurement of intelligence are quite complex in themselves, but let us assume for a moment that we can accurately assess these conditions. We find people of various races and people of various national origins and give them all an intelligence test and note the differences, if any, that occur. This was the approach taken to this problem for years. Differences were always observed and always attributed to the racial and national differences. This seems a very straightforward answer to the question. In recent years, however, we have discovered a missing and more important variable to account for differences in intelligence test performance in racial and national groups. The missing variable is socioeconomic level. When representatives of different races or of different national groups are equated for their socioeconomic level, we find differences in their intelligence test performances to be much smaller than previously believed and of less significance. As the science of psychology gains in knowledge and understanding, new information about "old" problems comes to our attention.

Sociocultural taboos and values. The study of behavior at any given time is limited by the prevailing system of social values and the prohibitions or taboos of the society. Our society has been very repressive in matters relating to sexual behavior and research on this subject has been difficult because of these social attitudes. While research on sexuality is more common today than 50 years ago it is still an area of inquiry that is subject to much criticism and censure. The topic of death and the study of mourning is also subject to cultural taboo. In our society we prefer not to confront the subject of death and interest in the subject may be called indelicate or morbid. Death is a part of existence, just as birth, and it is possible that many of our fears of death could be alleviated if they could be explored. There has been an increasing negative public attitude developing about the use of psychological tests to gain information about behavior. Criticism has included charges that psychological tests invade the privacy of the individual, are used unfairly to "label" individuals and exclude them from opportunities, and are poorly developed instruments. These criticisms make people suspicious and fearful of psychological tests even when they are used carefully by skilled persons. There is a need to improve the quality and use of psychological tests and such improvement is the continuing concern of many psychologists. Public attitudes, however, can greatly limit or eliminate methods of behavioral study.

Availability of Human Subjects. Despite great popular appeal for psychological information it is often difficult to find persons willing to serve as subjects for psychological research. Reluctance to participate can sometimes be overcome by inducements of money, special privileges, or the opportunity to take part in an unusually interesting experiment. However, subjects whose motives are other than voluntary and spontaneous participation introduce additional variables into experiments. There are real differences between people who can be motivated by money, privilege, or curiosity and those who cannot. These differences must be recognized and equated for in the groups used in experiments. The most frequently studied group in American psychology is the college student. College students differ from the general population in many ways of advantage including youth, ability, education, health, cultural experiences, and opportunity. Findings of studies based on groups of college subjects may bear limited, if at times any, generalization to persons in the larger population. Why is there reluctance to be involved in psychological study? Factors of time, convenience, and interest are undoubtedly involved. Fear seems also to be an important consideration. Fear of self-revelation in a strange setting, fear of self-discovery, and fear of control and manipulation by someone else are usually involved. The problem of obtaining human subjects could be reduced if the public could be made more aware that psychologists who do research, like those that give treatment services, are guided by ethical standards and practices designed to protect the public and promote good health.

Use of Animals. Some people think psychology is more concerned with monkeys, dogs, cats, and rats than it is with people. This is not true. Psychology is interested in the study of all living organisms because they provide information about the evolution of behavior. There are ethical reasons why the study of animals is sometimes preferred to the study of humans and these deal with the health, safety, and comfort of the subjects. Animals are also more available for research than humans and there are some other advantages to using them as subjects. Species differences throughout the animal kingdom in terms of biological structure and behavioral function are fairly well-detailed and understood. This permits a degree of generalization from study of one animal species to another within rather clear limits. Use of lower animals also permits the investigator to "breed for effect," i.e., to mate animals in order to study particular problems such as the relative contribution of heredity and environment in learning a specific behavior. The gestation periods tend to be shorter for animals of lesser biological complexity. The rat gestation period is only 4 weeks and the investigator does not wait long for an answer to a question involving breeding effects. Another advantage to using lower animals is their comparative biological simplicity. When one is studying a simple behavior, like maze learning, a simple organism is preferable for drawing conclusions about treatments or conditions imposed in the experiment and the behavioral outcome observed.

SUMMARY

This chapter has introduced psychology in its perspective as a dynamic modern science which seeks to understand human behavior and help solve the human problems we face in our rapidly changing world. Contemporary psychology represents the current stage in the history of man's inquiry into the nature of man. This inquiry has evolved into a science of behavior. The term behavior is broadly applied to a wide range of activities which characterize living organisms, both animal and human.

Psychology is a rapidly growing profession with many practical applications in modern life. About half of today's psychologists are engaged in teaching and research directed toward increasing our knowledge and understanding of behavioral principles. The other half of the profession is involved in applying the knowledge we now have to the treatment and prevention of human problems. The areas in which psychologists specialize include clinical, counseling, industrial, social, educational, and school psychology.

Psychology is a science because it applies a variety of scientific procedures to the study of behavior in an effort to discover the principles or laws which enable us to understand, predict, and control behavior. The systematic methods used by psychologists include the experimental method, controlled observation, tests and measurements, survey techniques, and clinical methods. Special problems are associated with the study of behavior. These include the complexity of behavior, the stage of our knowledge at any given time, public attitudes, and the use of human and animal subjects for research.

Behavior results from the interaction of mental and physical processes. In the next chapter we will study the physical foundations of behavior and their significance to psychology.

*Note: All of the statements in Table 1-2 Self Test are false.

SUGGESTIONS FOR FURTHER READING

Anastasi, A., *Fields of Applied Psychology*, New York, McGraw-Hill, 1964. An introduction to personnel and industrial psychology, human engineering, consumer psychology, clinical and counseling psychology, and discussion of the contribution of psychology to education, law, and medicine.

Charney, Nicholas H. (Ed.), *Readings in Psychology Today*, Del Mar, Calif., CRM Books, 1969. A selection of 69 articles, with full color illustrations, that is representative of the wide range of contemporary psychological thought, controversial issues, and problems of human behavior in today's world.

Coopersmith, Stanley (Ed.), *Frontiers of Psychological Research*, San Francisco, Calif., Freeman, 1966. A selection of illustrated research reports on topics of contemporary interest in psychology.

Ross, F. and Lockman, R. F., *A Career in Psychology*, Washington, D.C., American Psychological Association, 1963. An illustrated pamphlet that describes what psychologists do and tells where to find out more about the preparation for and opportunities in the profession.

Schultz, Duane P., *A History of Modern Psychology*, New York, Academic Press, 1969. A brief account of the development of psychology in its first century as a science, showing how new approaches to the study of behavior have emerged.

Watson, Robert I., *The Great Psychologists* (2nd ed.), Philadelphia, Pa., Lippincott, 1968. A history of psychology based on the lives and work of the people who have been most influential in its development.

Physical Foundations
of Behavior

How do we become aware of the world around us and how do we establish and maintain our contact with it? What processes enable us to make sense out of the mass of energy that surrounds us in various forms of light, sound, heat, pressure, and movement? How can we recognize the familiar and identify the unfamiliar? How can we understand reality and develop control of the environment? The remarkable advantages mankind enjoys over other species of life have been attributed primarily to his greater brain development. By the application of intellect to technological problems man has devised ingenious mechanical means to overcome his natural physical limitations. As a consequence man alone can travel faster than the speed of sound, can live in depths of water or heights of atmosphere, and communicate directly in moments with others of his species around the globe. Perhaps it is the many wonders created by the mind that lead us to associate behavior with mind functions separate from the underlying processes of our physical bodies. Yet all behavior, including mind functions, is but an expression of the physical response capacity of the body.

Most of our mechanical marvels are designed to make our interactions with the world at a distance more efficient. It is in our immediate contacts with the world that we become aware of our dependence on our physical bodies for action and reaction potentials. We are responsive to stimuli from the external world which includes other persons and we are responsive to stimuli produced within our own bodies. It is not the presence of stimuli, however, but our capacity to be responsive to them that distinguishes our behavior from that of other species. How do we receive, process, and act upon the information that comes to us from our external and internal environment?

PERCEPTION

Have you ever had the experience of driving along the highway and seeing a dead dog in the road ahead of you? Then as you came closer and slowed down you found that it was not a dead dog at all but a rumpled piece of paper? At one moment there is no doubt in your mind that what you see is a dog, but a few minutes later you know that you are not looking at a dog but a piece of paper. The fact is you did not *see* a dog but you did *perceive* a dog. We are continually seeking to identify and make sense out of the objects in our environment. The process is rapid and somewhat automatic. We often jump to conclusions based on insufficient evidence and, as in the case of the nonexistent dog, we are sometimes incorrect. This process through which we become aware of our environment by organizing and interpreting the evidence of our senses is called *perception.* Our perceptions are usually made without any deliberate effort and we do so whether we think about it or not. Perception is a process over which we usually exert little or no conscious control. Perception influences our entire image of the world around us including all of the things we see and hear. Our perception also influences our behavior toward other people. We do not perceive the world as a confused jumble of miscellaneous sights and sounds, but we tend to organize input from the environment into meaningful patterns.

Selection and Organization

The most elementary stage in perception is the emergence of awareness of detail. From the whole range of stimuli which impinge upon our senses we select certain factors and focus on them so that they stand out from the rest of the generalized background of events. This is called *figure–ground perception.* From earliest awareness and throughout our lives we know and we organize all our experience in terms of figure and ground. In Figure 2-1 we see an example of figure–ground relationships.

Most people will perceive the drawing in Figure 2-1 as a white vase against a dark background. However, it can also be perceived as two faces in profile against a white background. Whether we see the faces or the vase depends upon how we want to perceptually organize the experience. We can see both faces

Figure 2-1.   Do you see this as a vase or as two faces?

and the vase in Figure 2-1 only if we shift the elements perceptually, allowing first one and then the other to become the figure. Otherwise, Figure 2-1 appears to be only a simple design. Notice that you cannot perceive both the faces and the vase at one time. When you perceive the faces the vase fades out as the background. The tendency to perceive the environment in terms of figure and ground seems to be an innate characteristic of humans. The process of perception then is the selection of certain details from the environment which we organize into figures so that the rest of the environment becomes a generalized background for the figure.

The outline of a figure that separates it from the ground is called *contour*. To perceive a figure we do not need to see the complete uninterrupted contour. If part of the contour is missing our perceptual processes fill it in. Notice in Figure 2-2 that you are able to recognize the figures for what they are even though part of the contour is missing. This process of filling in the gaps in contour is called *closure*. While the process of selecting and organizing the environment into meaningful units is common to all people we do not all experience the world in the same way. What we experience through our perceptual processes depends upon a variety of factors.

Experience

Perception is highly dependent upon experience. The first significance an infant attaches to his perception is probably emotional. All events for the infant are either satisfying or unsatisfying. The tastes, smells, sights, sounds, touches, and other happenings that fill, comfort, soothe, or relieve are satisfying and pleasant. Those sensations that stick, jar, chafe, surprise, and leave empty or alone are unsatisfying and unpleasant. As persons and events occur and recur in the experience of the infant they begin to be distinguished from one another, then recognized, remembered, and looked for or avoided, in terms of their satisfying or unsatisfying potential. Associations are gradually being formed within the nervous system between events that happen outside the body and the results they create within the body.

It is not instinct that binds the child to the mother in love. It is the faithful performance of a warm, relaxed, tender, and satisfying object that the infant responds to and seeks and later perceives as "mother." Whoever will be these things to the child, be it male or female, biological or adopted parent, young or old in years, will become for the child the object of trust, regard, and affection.

With increased experience and maturation the significance of things perceived

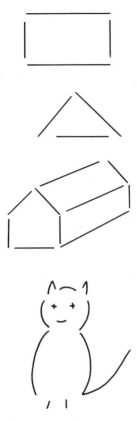

Figure 2-2. Examples of closure, the process by which you recognize a form even though you see only part of its outline.

will be extended from the emotional to include awareness of usefulness. A child soon learns that chairs are to sit on, spoons are to eat with, and stairs are to climb. Later perceptual distinctions will be made on the basis of color, form, and number. As the child experiences his world and orders it perceptually he learns that many objects remain stable and he develops a sense of constancy about them.

It is due to the characteristic of *perceptual constancy* that a familiar object retains its size, shape, color, and brightness regardless of the conditions under which we view it. Things which are far away from us should be seen as smaller. Objects viewed at dusk should appear drab in color and lacking brightness, and one object in front of another should hide the second from view. That is how things should be in terms of the effect of the physical stimuli upon our senses under the given environmental conditions. Because of constancy that is not how things are for us perceptually. A new red wagon half-hidden by a tree and viewed at dusk from a porch some distance away is still perceived as bright red and a complete wagon of its own familiar size. Constancy permits us to perceive objects as we have come to know them and not as they appear under changing environmental conditions. We might look at the Empire State Building from the sidewalk in front of it, from an airplane above it or from an automobile up the street from it and in each case it will look different but we will still perceive it as the same building. In Figure 2-3 we see an example of the way experience has taught us to order the events of our environment.

Since experience is vital to perceptual growth, an environment that is deficient in objects can delay or impair perceptual skills. Project Head Start, one of the programs of the war on poverty, is an attempt to provide a stimulating environ-

The above pattern is usually perceived
as a curved line and a straight line
thus:

But it can be seen as two lines, each
with a straight and curved portion
thus:

Principle of Continuity: Stimulus elements
tend to be grouped together into a
continuous sequence.

Figure 2-3.   Examples of perceptual
patterning.

ment for children from homes that lack such opportunity. In a Head Start class children can see, touch, manipulate, and learn the uses for many objects that most of us take for granted in our homes. Through field trips the Head Start class can experience places and events that their own families cannot provide and may not have experienced themselves. The contact and thus the experience these programs provide give the children a head start on the perceptual growth that will be needed for their continued intellectual development in school.

Needs

Have you ever noticed how many restaurant signs you see as you are driving along the highway when you are hungry? Or have you noticed how much brighter the motel signs look than any other signs when you are tired from traveling? The loss of a friend leaves a bigger gap in the life of a person who has few friends. The failing grade on a report seems bigger and stands out more for the student who needs to achieve. Advertising makes its appeal to our needs, especially our social needs to be liked, admired, and included, and our needs for self-esteem. Our need states also operate to prevent our perceiving some things. Things we don't like and are afraid of, or things that remind us of unpleasant events, or those that interfere with our progress toward a current goal are perceptually avoided even though stimuli for them are all around us.

Conditions of need or deprivation within the individual from time to time will alter his perceptions. The need state may be physiological (hunger, thirst, fatigue, or pain relief) or it may be social (companionship, prestige, or status). Needs may be related to self-esteem (security, attention, or achievement) or any combination of these. We perceive what we need and our perception of a needed object is often distorted by the intensity of our need.

Experiments with distorted rooms reveal that the way in which we perceive the size and even the shape of others is greatly influenced by our emotional relationship to them. In a series of experiments designed to measure the degree to which emotional feeling of one person toward another may modify that person's image of the other, Wittreich (1959) found that newly married couples reported less distortion in the appearance of their partners than in a controlled group of strangers although the distortion in both cases was exactly the same.

Attention

Have you ever noticed how a group of people can witness the same event and report quite different experiences as to what happened? It is the perceptual differences among people that make eyewitness testimony so unreliable. For

Figure 2-4. The Ames room, used to study perception, is constructed to give false perceptual cues. Notice how the person appears larger as he moves from one side of the room to the other. The room actually is smaller on one side, giving the impression that the man has changed size. (Photo by William Vandivert with permission of Scientific American.)

example, three people enter a hotel lobby late in the evening where an unmasked gunman is holding up the desk clerk. The gunman takes the money from the clerk, turns and walks past the three people into the darkness of the night. The clerk and the three guests all give differing accounts of the gunman; his looks, his clothes, in which direction he went when he left the building. The same stimuli were present in the situation for all the people but their perceptions were different. Why? They were different individuals, each with his unique past experience, his current need state, and present focus of attention. Some perceived very accurately what the others did not perceive at all, but no one of them could give a complete account. The clerk perceived clearly the gun that threatened his life. One of the guests who was tired from traveling noticed the gunman but did not notice what he was doing. Another guest was carrying a lot of money and his attention was upon ways for his own escape. The other guest had been robbed a few weeks earlier under similar circumstances and he turned his attention away from the present scene to a remembrance of the past event.

When we are at attention or attending to an object or event we are focusing our consciousness upon it. Attention narrows the range of perception to the object of interest and obscures the presence of other objects or events. How long we can attend, our *attention span*, differs among individuals depending upon their age, intelligence, health, and past experience. The attention span also varies within each individual depending on his current need state.

There are some characteristics in the stimuli themselves that can command our attention. Great *intensity* of size, sound, brightness, odor, or other aspects of a stimulus will direct our attention to it. The *repetition* of a stimulus will draw our attention, and any *change* in a stimulus will be attended. A stimulus which *contrasts* in some way from the things around it will capture attention because it stands out more. Advertising makes wide use of these stimulus characteristics: intensity, repetition, change, and contrast, to focus our attention upon a product, and then appeals to our need states to purchase the product.

Perceptual differences help us to understand why even members of the same family who grow up in the same general home atmosphere experience the home life differently. In whatever way the home life is perceived by the family members, their own reactions to it are developed, and the memories that they retain of it may be quite different.

Illusions

Strange as it may seem, many of the things we think we see, hear, and enjoy in the world do not really exist, at least not in the way we believe they exist. Distortions of experience that are quite common among people are called *illusions*. An illusion is a misinterpretation of the relationship that exists between stimuli when they are experienced in other than their usual settings.

Motion pictures are based on an illusion of movement. The pictures do not really move. They are simply a series of still pictures like snapshops which are flashed on the screen at the rate of about 20 per second. We fill in the gaps so that what we perceive is continuous movement. This phenomenon is called the *stroboscopic effect*. The stroboscopic effect occurs when separate stimuli are presented in rapid succession one after the other so that there is an illusion of movement. Another example of this is in the neon sign where light bulbs are flashed one after another in rapid succession so that the appearance of movement, which is an illusion, can be seen. Apparent motion is produced by the rapid succession of images that are actually stationary but so compelling are the expectancies developed from past experience that even when we are told the details we cannot overcome the illusionary effect.

Illusions result because our past experience with stimuli, especially in terms of their constancy, leads us to expect certain relationships between them. These *expectancies* from past experience are carried over into new situations and are the basis of our interpretation as well as the conditions that actually prevail in the new situation. As a consequence our perceptions are in error. Not all illusions are bad; they are simply perceptual errors, many of which serve useful and entertaining purposes. Figure 2-5 shows some of the more common visual illusions. Modern op art is a development in which the illusion of movement is created in a stationary picture, as shown in the illustration at the beginning of this chapter.

Extrasensory Perception

Have you ever had the experience where you were about to call a friend and at that precise moment the friend called you? How do you explain this? Is it pure coincidence? Extrasensory perception, or ESP as it is commonly called, refers to the possibility that perceptual activity is not limited to the known senses. ESP has become a subject of great fascination to some scientists. The name itself "extrasensory" has placed these phenomena, which include telepathy, clair-voyance, and movement of objects by mental energy, outside the boundary of recognized sensory events. Perhaps there is some other mysterious sense which allows people to send and receive thoughts (mental telepathy), or to gain some awareness of objects and events which are not within the range of our ordinary senses (clairvoyance), or to influence the movement of physical objects without actually contacting them physically (psychokinesis).

Whatever its cause, ESP does happen to people and it happens with some frequency, if we can accept the reports of those who say they have had such experience. There has been an emphasis given to the ESP experiences that have negative or unfortunate aspects such as forewarnings of the injury or death of a loved one. This negative emphasis may be obscuring many other instances of the phenomena with more positive but less dramatic aspects. Much that we call luck or hunch may have ESP significance.

In terms of our discussion in Chapter 1 of the requirements for an experimental

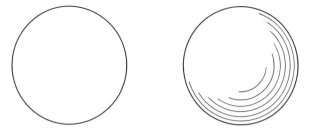

A. The use of shading creates the illusion
    of a three-dimensional ball in a flat circle.

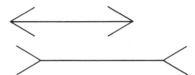

B. The Muller N Lyer Illusion: The two horizontal
    lines are exactly the same length.

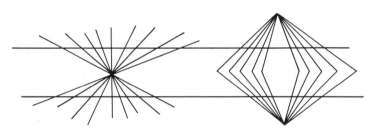

C. Hering's Illusion: The horizontal lines are
    parallel.

Figure 2-5.   Some common illusions.

study, it can be said of ESP that the variables are difficult to specify. Specifications of the variables must include sorting out and isolating enough instances of the phenomena to make identification possible. Lacking specification, the variables also cannot be measured or controlled with the precision needed to demonstrate them and gain understanding of their operation. This does not mean that ESP is impossible. As psychology advances in development of methods for stimulus detection and recording, the factors involved in ESP may be isolated for observation. We can speculate and wonder if ESP is caused by some presently unknown form of physical energy. Another possibility may be that ESP is a known energy form that occurs outside the usual limits of human sensitivity to persons of special acuity. Some tissues of the body as yet not identified may have receptor functions for ESP stimuli, or perhaps ESP is a result of overlap between different receptors in the sensory system.

The leading American researcher of the ESP phenomena is Dr. Joseph B. Rhine of Duke University and he has written extensively on his work (Rhine and Brier, 1968). At this time we can say that ESP phenomena do not lend themselves to systematic scientific study and understanding. However, the science of psychology is still too new to dismiss a topic like ESP without making a more serious effort to bring it within our understanding.

We have seen how our awareness of the world develops through perception. Let us turn now to the basic processes which enable us to become aware of the world and to act upon it. The essential features of body organization and functioning might be compared to *an energy system* with *input, distribution*, and *output* mechanisms. The input mechanisms that receive stimulus energy from the environment and convert it to neural energy for use by the body are the specialized organs of sense or the *receptors*. The distribution of neural energy within the body, its routing to appropriate organs, and its interpretation for meaning and use, is accomplished by the central and involuntary nervous systems, or the *connectors*. The return of energy to the environment in the many forms of response called behavior is achieved through neural action upon muscles or glands called the *effectors*. These elements, receptors of the senses, connectors of the nervous system, and effectors of muscles and glands, provide us with experience and the means to express ourselves behaviorally.

THE RECEPTORS

Our Senses

We tend to take the functioning of our sense organs for granted being more concerned with the experience we enjoy from their functioning. We have seen how the process of perception gives meaning and interpretation to the information received through the senses. The stimulation and arousal of a sense organ is the process of *sensation*. Let us look at the sensory system and see how it operates to help us experience the environment.

The nature and location of the receptors for each sense, the appropriate stimulus to arouse the sense, and the qualities of the sensory experience as well as the area of brain where the information is referred for perceptual processing are shown in Table 2-1. From Table 2-1 we can see that our senses respond to different kinds of stimuli. More important, in terms of the variety of experience available to us, the receptors respond differently to different aspects of their appropriate stimulus. Vision and hearing, for example, both depend upon wave energy. Light and sound waves differ in their length (frequency), height (amplitude), and their patterns of overlap (complexity). The receptors for vision which are photosensitive cells on the retina of each eye receive differences in the length of the light wave as color sensations, differences in the height of the light wave as brightness, and differences in the overlap pattern of light waves as purity. All of our visual experiences depend upon the receptor cells reacting differently to different aspects of their appropriate stimulus, but we do not see all of the electromagnetic wave energy that is available in the physical world. Our receptor cells are limited in the length and height range of light waves to which they can be responsive. We call this range the *visible spectrum.*

The sense of hearing also depends upon wave energy, more specifically, alternations of pressure created by molecules in vibration. Sound waves differ in their length, height, and pattern of overlap. Our hearing receptors are sensitive hair cells inside the tiny organ of Corti in our inner ear. The receptors for hearing receive differences in the length of the sound waves as pitch sensation, differences in the height of the sound waves as loudness, and differences in the overlap of sound waves as timbre or purity. The receptors for hearing, like those of vision, are not sensitive to all the sound-wave energy available in the world around us, but only to a limited range called the *audible spectrum.* The pleasure of a hi-fi set is that it enables us to enjoy both longer and shorter length of sound waves, hence greater variations in pitch. The hi-fi set is not more sensitive to wavelengths than our hearing receptors are but it can mechanically control loudness. By varying the loudness or height of a sound wave those pitches (length) at the extremes of the audible spectrum are more easily detected by our receptors and hence more fully enjoyed. No amount of increased loudness, however, can bring within our range those lengths of sound waves outside the audible spectrum.

The receptors for the sense of taste respond to four basic qualities: bitter, sweet, sour, and salt. All of our experiences of taste and flavor are combinations of these four basic qualities and an interaction effect with the sense of smell. We can appreciate the contribution of smell to taste sensations when we have a cold. A cold dulls our smell receptors leaving us only the taste receptors to

Table 2-1. The Sensory System

Sense	Nature of receptors	Location of receptors	Appropriate stimulus	Qualities of sensory experience	Brain area
Vision	Photosensitive cells called rods and cones	At center and edge of retina	Electromagnetic waves differing in Length Height Complexity	Color Brightness Purity	Occipital lobe
Hearing (Auditory)	Hair cells	Organ of Corti on basilar membrane inside cochlea of inner ear	Alternations in air pressure differing in Length Height Complexity	Pitch Loudness Timbre	Temporal lobe
Taste (Gustatory)	Cells clustered in buds	On tongue mostly at sides and back	Substances in chemical form	Bitter Sweet Sour Salt	Parietal lobe
Smell (Olfactory)	Hair cells	High in the nasal cavity to right and left of air passages	Substances in chemical or gaseous form	Indefinite	Olfactory bulb

Table 2-1. The Sensory System

Sense	Nature of receptors	Location of receptors	Appropriate stimulus	Qualities of sensory experience	Brain area
Skin (Cutaneous)	Hair cells and free nerve endings	Mostly skin surface with some fewer on internal organs	Any intense stimulus Temperature changes and chemical solutions Pressure	Pain Cold; warm Touch	Parietal lobe
Kinesthesis	Hair cells and free nerve endings	Muscles, tendons, and joints	Stretch, pressure, and contraction movements	Position and location	Parietal lobe
Equilibrium	Hair cells and tiny stones called otoliths	Semicircular canals and vestibular sacs of inner ear	Body movements and rotation	Location and balance	Cerebellum

experience flavor. It can be demonstrated with humans that if the subject is blindfolded and the nasal passages blocked by cotton pads he cannot tell the difference between slices of onion, potato, and apple placed in the mouth and eaten.

The sense of smell is one of the least understood senses of man in terms of the nature of the stimulus and the quality of the sensory experience. A promising new theory suggests that molecules of different size and shape in the stimulus find their counterparts in the receptor cells for smell in the nasal cavity and resulting "fit" gives rise to seven primary smell sensation of odors (Amoore et al., 1964). The seven primary odors include musky (moss), camphoraceous (moth repellent), peppermint (mint candy), ethereal (dry-cleaning fluid), floral (roses), pungent (vinegar), and putrid (rotten egg). Presumably combination effects occur between these primary odors giving greater variety to our sensations of smell.

Pain, touch (pressure), cold and warm (temperature) all belong to our skin or cutaneous sense. The distribution of the receptors for these cutaneous senses is not the same over all parts of the body nor do they occur in equal numbers. There are more pain receptors than touch and more touch receptors than cold or warm. The receptors for pain are the only ones in the whole sensory system that can be aroused by *any* stimulus of great intensity regardless of what form the stimulus energy takes. A loud sound, a sharp odor, a bright light, and heavy pressure can all arouse the pain response. Touch or pressure sensitivity is greater on mobile parts of the body such as lips and fingers than on immobile parts such as the back. Our receptors for cold and warm respond to variations in temperature above and below the temperature of the skin (about 90 degrees Fahrenheit). At skin temperature there is a psychological zero point and it is degrees of difference above and below this point that results in temperature sensations. There are no receptors for the experience we call hot. Rather it appears that the sensation of hot results from the simultaneous arousal of cold and warm receptors. This probably accounts for the chilling sensation that often accompanies a scalding experience such as putting your hand under a faucet of very hot water.

Kinesthesis and equilibrium are the senses which provide us with continuous information about the location and action of our limbs and our position in space. When a limb "goes to sleep" cramped circulation has dulled the kinesthetic receptors in the muscles, tendons, or joints and we get no sensory information. Our experience is one of no control over the limb. As we shake the limb, stamp it, or rub it vigorously to restore sensation we are giving stimulation to pain and touch receptors in the area and may experience a "pins and needles" or even painful sensation.

Kinesthesis and equilibrium together with the sense of vision provide us with the necessary information to locomote or get around in space efficiently. Sometimes the information we get from these three senses is contradictory. Alcohol intoxication causes pressure changes in the blood that stimulate the receptors for equilibrium in the inner ear and make us feel in motion when our visual and kinesthetic senses tell us otherwise. Some carnival rides moving up, down, and sideways rapidly furnish varying stimulation to the receptors of vision, kinesthesis, and equilibrium. The result of such contradictory sensory information is dizziness and disorientation often accompanied by nausea which is called *vertigo*.

Thresholds

The minimum amount of stimulus energy that is required to activate a sense organ sufficiently for an awareness of sensation to occur is called the *absolute threshold* or *limen*. Thresholds vary with each sense and for each individual and they are influenced by existing surrounding conditions of the environment. In general terms, however, absolute threshold levels for human sensitivity have been defined (Mueller, 1965). In Table 2-2 are some examples of sensory stimulation required for the detection of the sensory experience to occur.

Sensory receptors can be aroused at energy levels below the threshold of awareness and this is called *subliminal* stimulation. We can receive and act upon

Table 2-2. Samples of Sensory Stimulation Required for Detection[a]

Sense	Detection of sensation
Vision	A candle flame seen at 30 miles on a dark clear night
Hearing	The tick of a watch under quiet conditions at 20 feet
Taste	One teaspoon of sugar in 2 gallons of water
Smell	One drop of perfume diffused into the entire volume of a 3-room apartment
Touch	The wing of a bee falling on your cheek from a distance of about 4/10 of an inch

[a]Adapted from Galanter (1962).

information supplied by subliminal arousal but we are not aware of the presence and operation of the stimulus. There has been some concern that subliminal stimulation might be used inappropriately for advertising or propaganda purposes. The variations of threshold levels among persons and the dependence of threshold levels upon conditions in the immediate surroundings make it highly improbable that this technique could be used for large-scale exploitation. Subliminal stimulation is of greater interest to the scientist in the laboratory studying sensory processes than it is of any value to the manipulator in the market place. We are more vulnerable to persuasion techniques that play upon our needs, wishes, motives, and fears than we are to techniques designed to arouse our receptors at subliminal levels.

Sensory Adaptation

We have all had the experience of walking into a dark room and within a few seconds being able to see quite well. You have also noticed the seeming disappearance of background music in a store after you have been there for a while. This change in our sensory responsiveness is called *sensory adaptation* and it is a familiar experience. If we enter a room with strong odors we are keenly aware of the smell stimuli, but as we remain in the room we notice the odors less and less and then not at all. The level of stimulus energy in the room has not changed but our smell threshold has shifted to a higher level, thereby reducing our sensitivity.

While stimulus energy at threshold level is required to activate a sense organ, continuous stimulation results in a reduction of sensitivity. If it were not for sensory adaptation, the receptors in our senses would be overwhelmed by the stimulus energy present in our environment. Yet sensory adaptation occurs so gradually that we are usually not aware of the gaps or changes in our sensory experiences. Other examples are the feeling of traveling slowly when in fact you are exceeding the speed limit or the ability to speak over the noisy engine of an airplane.

Energy Conversion

What happens when you see the color red? A series of wavelengths reaches the eye. When the appropriate kind and required level of stimulus energy reaches a receptor the specialized cells of the receptor change the physical stimulus energy into neural energy. No environmental stimulus energy, as such, enters the body beyond the receptors cells. That is, the series of wavelengths ends at the eye. All stimulus energy is changed at the receptor cells in the eye to energy in nerve cells which then stimulate other cells and the fibers of the nervous system. In the form of neural impulses, the sensory information is routed to the brain. In the brain, both the place where the neural impulses are received and the pattern of neural impulses are used to identify and locate the sensation. The result is a sensation of the color red. Only certain fibers go to certain areas of the brain so that specific sensations are localized in specific areas of the brain.

Hallucinations

Sensory experiences that occur in the absence of any physical stimulus are called *hallucinations*. These false sensory experiences can occur for a variety of reasons. If the areas of the brain are stimulated by electrical current, hallucinations may result because the experience on the brain is similar to that of the neural impulses from the receptors. Excessive amounts of drugs and alcohol can cause hallucinations by altering the chemical balance within the nervous system and generating impulses like those that ordinarily come from the receptors. Some forms of emotional and mental illness are characterized by hallucinations. These hallucinations may be but symptoms of disturbed mind functions or the product of chemical changes in the nervous system resulting from the emotional or mental illness. In studies concerned with the effects of sensory deprived environments, where the individual is isolated from all sources of physical energy, hallucinations are a commonly reported occurrence (Heron, 1961). Such environments exist where individuals are placed in solitary confinement as in laboratory studies of conditions for space travel. These findings suggest that the brain needs sensory stimulation. If the stimulation is not provided by external physical energy activating receptors it may be provided internally, probably by chemical action upon the nervous system.

Our receptors of sense serve us by bringing us in contact with the external world in ways both useful and enjoyable. They are limited, however, by the range of environmental stimuli to which they are responsive. The receptors serve us by providing an important source of the excitation needed to stimulate the brain. In the absence of receptor activity stimulation of sensory areas of the brain by mechanical or chemical means gives rise to distortions of sensation called hallucinations. The receptors have done their work when they receive physical energy from the environment and convert it to neural energy. The conduction, processing, and interpretation of neural energy are the tasks which our nervous systems are uniquely designed to accomplish and we turn to these next.

THE CONNECTORS

Neurons and Nerves

Billions of tiny cells called *neurons* make up the vast network of information receiving and processing that we call the nervous system. Neurons differ in their shape and size depending upon where they are in the body, but they are alike in having three essential parts. The center of a neuron is a cell body having a nucleus and other cell material. Extending from the cell body in one direction are several branchlike processes called dendrites. Extending from the cell body in the other direction is a long single process called an axon. Information in the form of a neural impulse is received by dendrites, passes through the cell body, and goes out across the axon of the neuron. Neurons do not make direct connection with one another but are separated by a tiny gap called the synapse. Neural impulses from the axon of one neuron cross the synapse to the dendrites of another neuron and the process continues until the impulses reach their appropriate places in the body. The synapse is not just an empty space, but a junction at which a chemical exchange occurs that serves to block, change, or continue the direction of the neural impulse.

Nerves are bundles of neurons bound together as in a cable. *Sensory nerves* include all those neurons bringing information from the receptors. *Motor nerves* include all those neurons that carry information to the effectors (muscles and glands). The neural impulse has both electrical and chemical properties and for this reason is described as being electrochemical in nature. As few as 10 and as many as 1,000 neural impulses may travel along the nerve in a second, depending upon which nerve is involved and the nature of the stimulus. The rate at which a neural impulse may travel can be as slow as 2 feet per second or as fast as 300 feet per second. A neuron and a synapse are the basic elements of the nervous system. The complex interaction of millions of these simple elements constitute the nervous system of an organism. This nervous system is organized into units for easier understanding. The *central nervous system* consists of the brain and the spinal cord. The *peripheral nervous system* is made up of nerve fibers going to and from the central nervous system. The peripheral nervous system is further divided into two parts. One is called the *voluntary* nervous system and the other the *autonomic* system. The voluntary nervous system is composed of fibers connecting the receptors such as the eye, the ear, and the skin with the central nervous system and conducting the impulses to the muscles involved in voluntary movements such as walking or talking. The autonomic nervous system connects with the glands, muscles, and internal organs over which we have no conscious control.

The Central Nervous System

The function of the central nervous system, the brain and the spinal cord, is to integrate and make the various parts of the body work together. The nervous system functions at three levels of complexity. At the first level, the simple involuntary processes, such as reflexes, are made possible for the most part by connections in the spinal cord and the brain stem, located at the top of the spinal cord or base of the brain. If you tap a person below the kneecap with a rubber mallet his leg will swing out. This illustrates the reflex action of a *sensory motor arc*. What actually happens is that the skin receptors pick up the sensation, the sensory neuron carries the information to the spinal cord where the connector neurons convey it to a motor neuron running back to the muscle which is then innervated and the action takes place. This level of nervous system function goes on without our conscious control.

At the second level, more complex processes such as standing, walking, breathing, and carrying out well-coordinated voluntary movements are organized. These processes are dependent upon parts of the brain itself as well as the spinal cord. Figure 2-6 shows the cross-section of the brain as though it had been cut down the middle from front to back. Notice that the largest part of the brain is the *cerebrum*. When we consider the brains of animals as compared with those of man, we find that going up the evolutionary scale, the difference is that with the higher animals a larger part of the brain, proportionately, is cerebral cortex or outer covering of the cerebral hemisphere.

The third level of functioning is concerned with the complex interaction that takes place in the *cortex* or outer covering of the two halves of the cerebrum. The cerebral cortex is the location for such complex processes as learning, thinking, and most of the higher mental processes, although it is quite likely that they are dependent upon the rest of the brain as well. In Table 2-3 the different parts of the brain are listed and their functions described.

As we look down on the top of the brain we are looking at the cerebrum which appears to be divided into two halves. Each of these halves of the cerebrum

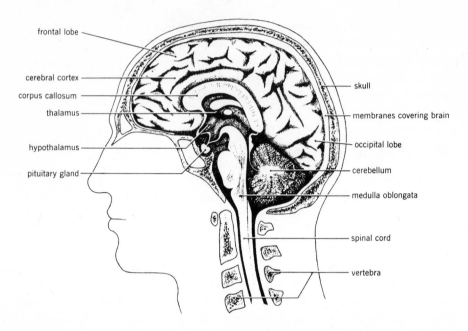

frontal lobe

cerebral cortex

corpus callosum

thalamus

hypothalamus

pituitary gland

skull

membranes covering brain

occipital lobe

cerebellum

medulla oblongata

spinal cord

vertebra

Figure 2-6.   A midline cross-section of the human brain. (After Schifferes, 1960.)

is called a *cerebral hemisphere*. The projection of neural impulses to the lobes of the hemisphere occurs in a very systematic way. The principle of organization is called *contralateral dominance* or opposite-side dominance. This means that the sensory and motor functions on one side of the body are processed by the hemisphere on the opposite side of the body. Thus the lobes of your right hemisphere receive sensations and control movement on the left side of your body and vice versa. Individuals who have suffered strokes in one cerebral hemisphere sometimes show a paralysis on the other side of the face or in the limbs on the other side of the body.

You may wonder how the activities of the two sides of our body are integrated and coordinated. Some of it is done by a portion of the hindbrain called the *cerebellum* which can be seen in Figure 2-6. Coordination between the two hemispheres, however, seems to depend upon the stalklike structure between the hemispheres called the *corpus callosum* which is also illustrated in Figure 2-6. For many years it was believed that the corpus callosum served only the mechanical purpose of holding the hemispheres together. Recent studies indicate that its primary purpose is to integrate sensory and motor neural impulses between the two hemispheres. Investigation with individuals whose illness or injury has necessitated cutting through the corpus callosum has produced some new information about the functioning of the brain (Sperry, 1964). Individuals who have had the split-brain operation seem to function normally but behave as if they have two separate brains. This does not mean that they become twice as smart or that they have two personalities like Dr. Jekyll and Mr. Hyde, but it does mean that they receive sensations, carry out activities, and find solutions to problems independently in each hemisphere at the same time. Such a person could accurately be described as one whose right side does not know what his left side is doing. The younger the patient is when severance of the hemispheres occurs the less is the effect on his behavior. The split-brain individual must learn other ways to integrate and coordinate his movements. The operation seems to have less effect upon habitual motor behavior than it does upon such functions as perception, learning language, and sensation.

Most of our behavior is controlled by the sensory and motor areas of the cerebral cortex. Numerous studies have been done to determine exactly which areas of the brain handle the functions of sight, sound, touch, and action. Within the last two decades attention has been turned to ways in which we can determine such things as the pleasure centers in the brain (Olds, 1956). By implanting electrodes in various parts of the brain in large numbers of animals it has been possible to determine which areas when stimulated give the animal pain or discomfort and which areas give him pleasure or a desirable feeling. Certain centers of the brain have been termed reward centers, particularly the hypothalamus, because electrical stimulation of some of these regions appears to be more rewarding to animals than an ordinary satisfier such as food (Olds and Olds, 1963). For example, hungry rats ran faster to reach the electrical stimulator than they did to reach food and, in fact, the hungry animals often ignored available food in favor of the pleasure of stimulating themselves electrically. Some rats with electrodes in these places of the brain stimulated themselves as much as 2,000 times an hour for 24 consecutive hours. Similar experiments have been carried out to determine what parts of the brain cause an animal to experience fear and anger.

As science moves toward better understanding of the complex functioning of the brain and nervous system new avenues of treating behavior disabilities are opened to us. For example, drugs have recently been developed to act specifically on the hypothalamus or reward center of the brain. Chemical stimulation of this area tends to produce behavioral changes in persons with emotional disorders.

Table 2-3. Brain Parts and Their Functions

Part	Function
Cerebrum (cerebral cortex and cerebral hemispheres)	Sensation–perception, thinking, remembering, learning, consciousness, and voluntary activities
Thalamus	Receiving center for many sensory impulses on way to specific areas in cerebral hemispheres
Hypothalamus	Control center for involuntary nervous system, biochemical processes of the body, emotional responses, and motivated behavior
Reticular arousal system	A routing center for neural impulses to and from the cerebrum but less specific in this function than the thalmus. A generalized arousal system important to wake–sleep cycle
Medulla oblongata	Regulates vital functions such as heart rate, breathing, circulation, and digestion
Cerebellum	Regulates muscular tonus and coordination, body balance, and equilibrium

The Peripheral Nervous System

On each side of our head there are 12 nerves having sensory and motor functions. These are called *cranial nerves* and they include the nerves for smell, sight, hearing, taste, facial muscles, and teeth. From the top to the bottom of the spinal cord there are 31 pairs of nerves called *spinal nerves*. One of each pair is the sensory nerve and the other of the pair is the motor nerve. Sensory nerves bring information from the sense organs and distant areas of the body to the brain, and the motor nerves carry action information from the brain to the various parts of the body.

What would life be like if we had to consciously think about making our heart beat, digesting our food, and breathing? We would probably get little else done and we would find these life-sustaining tasks very tedious employment. The *involuntary nervous system* of our body regulates many of these life functions for us and in addition plays an important part in our emotions.

This nervous system is sometimes called the *autonomic*, meaning independent or self-regulating. It does function independently of our attention and con-sciousness, but it is not independent of the central nervous system. The in-voluntary system is primarily a motor nerve system receiving neural impulses from the central nervous system that result in movement or activity of the effectors of the muscles and glands. The neural impulses from the central system reach the involuntary system at synapses near, but outside of, the brain and spinal cord. The location of the synapses outside the brain and spinal cord probably led early observers to conclude that this was a separate, independent system. The involuntary nervous system is like a trunk line on a major rail system having its own track and terminal points. The two parts of the autonomic nervous system, the *parasympathetic* and the *sympathetic* nerves, and the areas and organs of the body they serve are illustrated in Figure 2-7.

In general, the parasympathetic division acts to conserve and store body energy and resources, while the sympathetic division acts to expend body energy and resources at the time when we are excited or feel threatened by danger. All the behavioral expressions that are associated with emotion—tears, blushing, sweating, heavy or shallow breathing, heart pounding or skipping, hair standing on end—are the result of neural impulses from the involuntary system acting upon particular muscles, organs, or glands. Whatever the demands of the changing circumstances of your life, your body adapts and responds quickly without thought, through the functioning of the autonomic nervous system. The rush of adrenalin to the blood of an athlete competing in an event is a sympathetic function. Sexual excitement in the human is a parasympathetic function and sexual release (orgasm) is a sympathetic function. The emptying of bowel and bladder is a parasympathetic function and retention of their contents is a sympathetic one. Table 2-4 shows the functions of the two divisions of the involuntary nervous system.

The regulation of bowel and bladder by the involuntary nervous system occurs in response to organ conditions and emotional states and should not be confused with toilet-training. The process of toilet-training consists of bringing under the direct control of the central nervous system, by the development of conscious thought and habit, that which is naturally an involuntary nervous system function. A child cannot be toilet-trained until he is old enough to exert voluntary control and acquire habits of proper elimination. Such maturity does not occur all at once and success is intermingled with failure or accidents throughout childhood. Emotional upsets at any time in life may be accompanied by wetting and soiling incidents as the involuntary nervous system acts to meet the needs of the body in a stress situation.

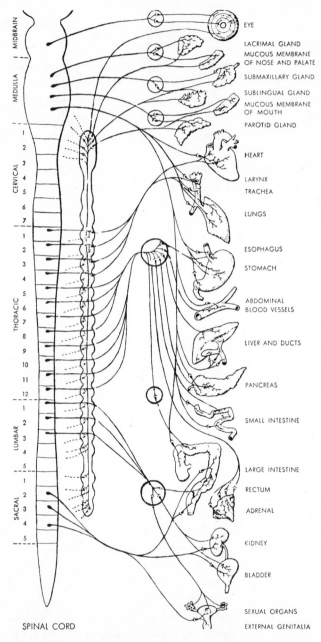

Figure 2-7. The autonomic nervous system is represented by this diagram. Notice that the parasympathetic branches arise from the brain and sacral vertebrae and the sympathetic branches arise from the thoracic and lumbar vertebrae. (From *The Physiology of Fear and Anger* by D. H. Funkenstein. Copyright 1955 by Scientific American, Inc. All rights reserved.)

Table 2-4. Functions of the Involuntary Nervous System

Organ	Sympathetic division	Parasympathetic division
Eye		
Pupil	Dilation (open)	Constriction (close)
Ciliary muscle		
of eyeball	Relaxation	Tension
Lungs		
Bronchi	Dilation	Constriction
Heart		
Beat	Increase rate	Decrease rate
Blood vessels	Dilation	Constriction
Skin		
Hair	Erection	None
Blood vessels	Constriction	None
Glands		
Tear	(Doubtful)	Secretion
Salivary	Retention	Secretion
Sweat	Secretion	None
Adrenal	Secretion	None
Digestive		
Stomach	Retention	Secretion
Pancreas	None	Secretion
Liver	Releases sugar	Sugar retention
Elimination		
Intestine	Bowel retention	Release of bowel
Kidney	Secretion	None
Bladder	Urine retention	Release of urine
Reproduction		
Male	Ejaculation	Erection
Female	Orgasm	Excitement

Some elderly people whose brain centers are affected by the deterioriation of aging find voluntary control hard to maintain and they too experience accidents. Anyone who has waited too long in meeting his elimination needs experiences a great sense of urgency. That urgency is the insistence of the involuntary nervous system to meet body needs.

Some children learn to exert conscious control over breathing and thereby frighten and control their parents. When the breath is held by brain control it will ultimately lead to unconsciousness as the brain loses oxygen supply. When unconsciousness occurs brain control is lost and the breathing function is restored by the involuntary nervous system just as it happens when we are asleep. The child who is permitted to hold his breath until he is unconscious generally learns not to repeat the experience.

THE EFFECTORS

The nervous system carries neural impulses from the sensory receptors to the brain where they are interpreted in the process called perception. After a stimulus event is perceived, action information is carried from the brain by the nervous system to the *effectors*. The effectors are the muscles and glands of the body. These are the mechanisms by which we respond and express ourselves in behavior.

The Muscles

Muscles are of three types: voluntary, involuntary, and cardiac. The *voluntary* muscles are activated by the central nervous system and are under the conscious control of the cerebrum. Voluntary muscles move our head, face, neck, shoulders, arms, hands, fingers, trunk, legs, feet, and toes. By contraction or relaxation in the muscles, movements such as reaching, raising, lowering, bending, rotating, and manipulation are possible.

The *involuntary* muscles are activated by the autonomic nervous system without voluntary control by us. Action of the involuntary muscles regulates the internal organs of the abdomen to accomplish digestive and eliminative functions. Involuntary muscles are also found in the skin, blood vessels, glands, and eyes causing these to constrict or close and to dilate or open. The involuntary muscles serve protective functions by conserving or expending body resources as our life circumstances require.

The third type of muscles, *cardiac* muscles, control the action of the heart. The cardiac muscles are activated by the central nervous system and some by action of the involuntary nervous system. The heart is a very complex muscle which is different from any other muscle tissue in the body.

The Glands

Some of the glands of our body have ducts or tubes by which their products are secreted directly into body cavities or under the surfaces of the skin. These ducts are called *exocrine*. Tears, saliva, and sweat are some of the products of exocrine glands. The mammary glands that secrete milk for the newborn and some of the internal glands whose secretions are needed in digestion are also exocrine glands.

There is another system of glands within our body that does not have ducts but secretes its products directly into the blood stream. These ductless glands belong to what is called the *endocrine* system. Products of endocrine gland secretion are called *hormones*. The endocrine glands function under control of neural impulses from the involuntary nervous system. The location, functions, and some consequences of malfunctioning of the endocrine glands are shown in Table 2-5.

The endocrine gland system is vitally important to our behavior because its hormones affect our appearance, growth, and development. They affect our general activity level, reproductive capacity, and they help us to maintain the biochemical balance needed to sustain life. The pituitary gland secretes many hormones that regulate the functioning of the other glands in the endocrine system and for this reason it is called the "master gland." Over- or under-production of the pituitary growth hormone causes gigantism or dwarfism. The pituitary secretes a hormone that regulates carbohydrate metabolism and too little of this hormone is a factor in the condition called obesity. Water balance in body tissues, blood circulation, and stimulation of involuntary muscles are also controlled by pituitary hormones. The growth of the sexual organs and their functioning for reproductive purposes depend upon hormones from the pituitary gland as well as hormones from the ovaries or testes glands. Glandular deficiencies are related to some types of mental retardation as we shall see in Chapter 6. The location of the endocrine glands in the body is shown in Figure 2-8.

Most of the hormones secreted by the endocrine glands can now be produced synthetically in the chemical laboratory. Thus it is possible to regulate metabolism and prevent the conditions associated with glandular deficiency. Study Table 2-5 and consider the many implications of the proper functioning of the endocrine glands. Behaviorally, it matters a great deal how we appear in size and figure, how energetic we feel, and the condition of our health, in terms of the way other people feel about us and treat us, and how we feel about ourselves (Figure 2-9).

DRUGS AND BEHAVIOR

The use of drugs to produce altered states of consciousness, to reduce pain, and to stimulate perception, is as old as the recorded history of civilization, but the

Table 2-5. The Endocrine Gland System and Functions

Gland	Location	Function	Underproduction of hormone	Overproduction of hormone
Pituitary	At the base of the brain	Stimulates activity in all other endocrine glands; Growth hormone	Restricts output of hormones from other specific glands; Dwarfism	Increases output of hormones from other specific glands; Gigantism
Pineal	Above and in front of the pituitary	Sexual maturation	Delayed sexual development	Early sexual development
Thyroid	In the throat beside the larynx	Metabolism; weight and activity level	Retarded physical and mental growth; weight gain	Hyperactivity; excitability; weight loss
Parathyroid	Two on each side behind the thyroid	Maintain calcium and phosphorus balance	Tetanus and convulsions	Calcium is dissolved from bones causing them to be soft and misshapened
Pancreas	In the abdomen behind the stomach	Regulate sugar metabolism	Diabetes	Excessive hunger, general weakness, and fatigue
Adrenal	One on each side over each kidney	Maintains water balance in tissues; salt and carbohydrate metabolism; sexual development and emotional excitation	Reduces blood volume and other body fluids; delays sexual development; anemia; extreme weakness and sluggishness	Early sexual development; excessive body hair and increased fatty tissue

Table 2-5. The Endocrine Gland System and Functions

Gland	Location	Function	Underproduction of hormone	Overproduction of hormone
Gonads				
Ovaries	One on each side of uterus in lower abdominal cavity	Sexual activity; production of eggs; development of secondary sex characteristics; preparation of uterus for pregnancy; important to onset of labor	Low sexual activity level; delayed sexual growth and development; infertility or miscarriage	Early sexual development and increased sexual activity
Testes	In the scrotum on external body surface of the pubic area	Sexual activity; production of sperm; development of secondary sex characteristics	Low sexual activity level; delayed sexual growth and development; infertility	Early sexual development and increased sexual activity

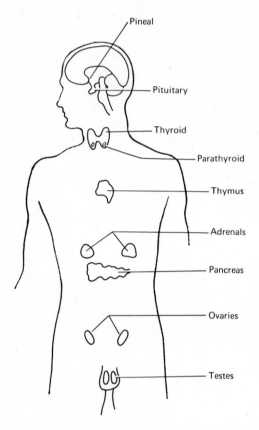

Figure 2-8.   Location of the endocrine glands.

scientific study of relationships between chemical substances and behavior is a fairly recent development. It was not until the early 1950's that psychopharmacology emerged as a scientific discipline, made possible by advances in biochemistry, neurophysiology, endocrinology, pharmacology, and the behavioral sciences. Psychopharmacology includes many areas of research concerning: (a) the effects of specific drugs on normal and abnormal behavior in animals and humans; (b) the relationships between certain chemicals, brain mechanisms, and behavior; (c) the development of drugs or chemical agents that will alter the psychological or behavioral aspects of biological systems; and (d) the long-range effects of continued drug use and its withdrawal.

Drugs which are known to act on the central nervous system are called psychoactive, psychotropic, or psychopharmacologic, to indicate the interaction between the drug and the psychological characteristics of the organism. At least 500 drugs are now known to have important psychopharmacologic effects (Miller, 1968). Some of the drugs are used to produce a general increase in activity and some aim for slowing down the activity level; other drugs are more specific in their action and are used to reduce anxiety, combat depression, induce muscle relaxation, prevent fatigue, and treat the symptoms of mental and emotional illness.

Figure 2-9.   Pituitary gland deficiency accounts for the size of this couple. The tiny bride, 25 years old, is only 40 inches tall and the groom, 41, is 60 inches tall. (Photo by Jim Sargent.)

Virtually all psychoactive drugs have some unwanted, irrelevant actions which are known as "side effects" or adverse reactions. In many instances these are minor irritations: dryness of the mouth, nasal stuffiness, weakness, tremors, blurred vision, skin rashes, and weight gain or loss. Adverse reactions which are more serious include changes in blood pressure, liver function, constipation and urination difficulties, allergic conditions, asthma attacks, convulsions, and hallucinations. Some of the psychoactive drugs are known to aggravate existing conditions like jaundice, hepatitis, glaucoma, hypertension, thyroid malfunctioning, and heart trouble. Sometimes the undesirable side effects can be reduced by adjusting the dose level and in some cases another drug must be used to counteract side effects. Individuals respond differently to the drugs so that side effects and adverse reactions are difficult to predict. The following material is reported by the National Institute of Mental Health (1968).

Stimulants and Antidepressants

Stimulants to the central nervous system are used to combat fatigue, sleepiness, and appetite. Stimulants act to release the chemical substance found in nerve endings (norepinephrine) and concentrate it in the higher centers of the brain. The result is an increase in metabolism, heart rate, and blood pressure. Usually, they act rapidly to produce feelings of mental alertness, confidence, and a sense of well-being, followed by a letdown and mild depression when the drug effect wears off. Overdoses of stimulants cause one to be jittery, irritable, and tense, and very heavy doses can cause a temporary mental disturbance accompanied by auditory and visual hallucinations. Abrupt withdrawal of stimulant drugs drugs by heavy users can result in serious mental depression.

The most commonly used stimulants are the amphetamines (Benzedrine, Dexedrine, Methedrine), known in slang terms as "bennies," "pep pills," and "speed." Stimulant drugs are usually ingested and taken into the blood stream through the stomach, but they can be taken in liquid form by injection into a vein for faster effects. This practice is known by drug abusers as "speeding."

Although stimulant drugs do not produce physical dependence or addiction, the body does develop a tolerance for these drugs, so that increasingly larger doses are required to feel the effects. People who use stimulant drugs for mental or emotional reasons can develop a psychological dependence on drugs that becomes a habitual pattern of behavior. The danger in habitual use of stimulants is their ability to disguise fatigue and symptoms of physical illness. The drugs can drive a person to exert himself beyond what his body can endure and cause him to ignore the symptoms of physical illness.

A more powerful group of drugs used to combat depression in pathological cases has been developed recently and is still the subject of much research. In contrast to the stimulants, which increase the production of hormones in the brain, these psychic energizers affect the brain's metabolism by inhibiting the production of those substances which cause the hormones to be used up. The monoamine oxidase (MAO) inhibitors are examples of this class of drugs. Another potent group of antidepressant drugs acts to prevent the process of brain hormones being normally reabsorbed into the neurons.

The effects of stimulant and antidepressant drugs on the functions of perception, attention, learning, memory, creativity, and personality characteristics is an exciting and challenging subject for experimental study, but one in which the risks are great. Several factors have been found to influence drug action in addition to those factors associated with the drug itself. It is a common observation that when people consume too much alcohol some of them become hostile and aggressive while others become docile and complacent. You can observe how different amounts of alcohol produce intoxication for different people and for the same person at different times. The same factors that influence an individual's reactions to alcohol tend to influence his reactions to psychoactive drugs. Thus drug action depends in part on the genetic and physiological characteristics of the organism and in part on the behavioral and psychological characteristics of the person to whom the drug is administered.

Sedatives and Tranquilizers

Sedatives include a large group of drugs used to relax the central nervous system and produce depression of both sensory and motor functions. The best-known and most widely used sedatives are the barbiturates, commonly called "barbs" and "goof balls," in slang terms. Barbiturates depress the action of the nerves, skeletal muscles, and heart muscle, resulting in lowered blood pressure, slower heart rate and breathing, and slower reactions and responses. Mild doses aid relaxation; higher doses cause confusion, slurred speech, staggering, inability to concentrate (resembling alcohol intoxication), and an overdose can cause death.

Barbiturates tend to increase the effects of alcohol, and the combination is particularly dangerous. Barbiturates are a frequent cause of automobile accidents and accidental poison deaths, and they are among the most common methods used to commit suicide.

People who take barbiturates regularly soon find that the body needs increasingly higher doses to produce the same effect, and they become physically addicted to the drug. When it is discontinued suddenly the person will experience withdrawal symptoms (nausea, cramps, convulsions, and delerium) and in some cases sudden death results. Withdrawal from any addicting drug should be accomplished gradually over several weeks with reduced successive doses, until the body can return to normal.

Tranquilizers act selectively on certain parts of the brain to control emotions, and modify abnormal behavior. They are useful in the treatment of mental illness, because they help to reduce anxiety, tension, confusion, agitation, and hallucinations. The precise effects of these new drugs on the brain are still under investigation and not completely understood, but they appear to modify the metabolism of the brain to change the interpretation of information from the senses.

In the treatment of abnormal behavior tranquilizers are often combined with antidepressants to treat both the anxiety and depression. Extreme caution should be used in combining psychoactive drugs because of the adverse reactions and side effects associated with the drugs.

Narcotics

The term narcotic is used to identify those pain-relieving drugs derived from opium, such as morphine, heroin, codeine, and other synthetic drugs which are known to produce physical addiction. Narcotic drugs are more strictly regulated by law than other drugs because of the danger of addiction and the seriousness of the effects they produce.

Narcotics depress those areas of the brain that control perception of pain, hunger, thirst, and the sex drive, leaving the person with a false sense of well-being. The drugs first produce a reduction of tension, relief from worry and fears, followed by a period of inactivity and stupor. Tolerance develops fairly rapidly and increasing doses are needed regularly to maintain the person. When a person who is addicted to narcotics suddenly stops taking the drugs he suffers serious withdrawal symptoms (perspiring, trembling, chills, nausea, and severe cramps in legs and abdomen) within 18 hours after the drug is discontinued. Because the narcotic addict is insensitive to hunger he is usually suffering from malnutrition and is in a weakened physical condition.

Cases of terminal illness in which the pain is incurable and unbearable clearly indicate the need for narcotic drugs as a last resort. The use of such dangerous drugs for "kicks" or as a means to escape facing one's problems often has more serious consequences. Most authorities agree that the drugs do not directly produce criminal behavior but that narcotic addicts resort to crime in order to support the habit. Some progress is being made in the development of new drugs to help decrease the addict's need for narcotics but there remains a great deal to be known about these drugs.

Hallucinogens

Substances capable of producing symptoms in normal subjects resembling those of psychotic or mentally ill patients are called hallucinogens. These drugs have not been subjected to sufficient scientific research to determine exactly how they act on the nervous system to produce the effects that have been reported. Hallucinogens are not legally used, except for research, although many of them have been widely used in the past and some are enjoying illegal popularity today.

Marijuana, also known as pot, tea, grass, weed, or Mary Jane, is a drug found in the leaves and flowers of the ancient Indian hemp plant. When it is smoked, chewed, drunk, or eaten it quickly enters the blood stream and begins to affect the brain and nervous system within 15 minutes. The range of effects reported by users can vary from excitement to depression or there may be no mood change at all. Many people report a distorted sense of time and distance. A few minutes may seem like hours and things that are near seem to be far away. Taken in higher strengths, marijuana may cause hallucinations, distorted images, and increased intensity of sights, colors, and sounds.

The immediate physical reactions of marijuana include increased heart rate, lowered body temperature, and changes in blood sugar levels. The long-range effects of continued marijuana use are not yet known. Within the past few years scientists have been able to isolate the active ingredient in marijuana and produce it in pure form called tetrahydrocannibinol (THC). This new development will enable researchers to study the drug with greater precision than was possible before THC was discovered.

Marijuana is classified legally, but not chemically, as a narcotic. The body does not become physically dependent on continuing use of marijuana, and sudden withdrawal does not produce physical symptoms. The National Institute of Mental Health (1968) reported a study of narcotic addicts that indicated over 80 percent had previously used marijuana, but we have no accurate records of the numbers of people who use marijuana and do not go on to the stronger drugs. Many people share the opinion of those who claim that marijuana is less harmful than alcohol and should therefore be legalized.

A powerful chemical, lysergic acid diethylamide (LSD), has recently become the subject of widespread research and illegal use. The average dose, amounting to a mere speck, produces a peculiar mental reaction which lasts 8 to 10 hours. The most noticeable physical effects produced by LSD are increases in heart rate, pulse, blood pressure, and body temperature, followed by perspiration, trembling, chills, irregular breathing, nausea, and loss of appetite. The drug is not physically addicting and produces no withdrawal symptoms.

People who have taken LSD report a variety of effects, sometimes different at different times in the same person. Controlled laboratory studies have been unable to predict individual responses. Users of LSD describe their experiences with it in terms of "good trips" or "bad trips."

One of the most common reactions reported by LSD-users is the ability to experience opposite feelings at the same time. They are happy and sad, relaxed and tense, depressed and elated at once. Many users feel a loss of the sense of self and some kind of mystical or spiritual experience in which they feel they can fly or float through the air or become a part of the surroundings. Sights, sounds, tastes, smells, and feelings seem more acute and merge together so that colors have a taste and music is a color. Experiments with animals suggest that the normal filtering out and screening functions in the brain are blocked by LSD, causing a flood of unselected sights and sounds to reach the higher centers. This overload of sensory information could explain why it is so difficult for chronic LSD-users to concentrate or to think clearly.

The strange confusion of sensations the LSD-user experiences tend to recur at unpredictable times even months after he has stopped taking LSD. These "flashbacks" are said to be very frightening, and in some cases lead to serious emotional problems.

Some other less well-known hallucinogens include peyote, mescaline, psilocybin, DMT, and STP. The National Institute of Mental Health has the only legal supply of LSD in the United States and it is currently conducting and supporting numerous research studies designed to find out more about the mind-altering drugs (Figure 2-10).

SUMMARY

Awareness of the world around us and our interaction with it depends upon the functioning of our physical bodies. All behavior, including mind functions, is but an expression of the physical response capacity of the body. In our immediate contacts with the world we become aware of our dependence upon the physical body for action and reaction potentials.

Perception is the process through which we become aware of our environment

Figure 2-10.   These paintings were produced by an LSD user at different times during the course of psychotherapy. Can you see the message in the lower right picture? Look for the words LSD, ACID, and HELP. (Photo by Sharon Wright.)

by organizing and interpreting the evidence of our senses. Perception influences our understanding of the world and our behavior toward other people. Perception involves the selection and organization of stimuli in terms of figure and ground relationships. What we experience through our perceptual processes depends upon maturation, learning, needs, and the characteristics of the stimuli that command our attention.

Illusions are distortions of experience that are common among people, as a result of past experience and expectation. The illusion of movement seen in motion pictures is called stroboscopic effect. Extrasensory perception, including telepathy, clairvoyance, and psychokinesis, has been neither proven nor disproved.

The essential features of body organization and functioning have been compared with an energy system having input, distribution, and output mechanisms. The input is the system of receptors of sense, without which there could be no experience of the external environment. Threshold levels of stimulus energy necessary to activate a sense organ have been defined. Sensory adaptation prevents us from being overwhelmed by the vast amount of stimulus energy present in the environment. The receptors pick up stimulus energy from the environment and convert it to neural energy so that it can be distributed and processed by the connectors or nervous system.

The central nervous system, consisting of the brain and spinal cord, is connected to the receptors and the effectors by means of nerve fibers which make up the peripheral nervous system. This system is further divided into voluntary and involuntary systems. The involuntary or autonomic system has both sympathetic and parasympathetic functions. The nervous system acts as distributor of neural energy from the receptors to the brain and on to the effectors. Without the connectors there would be no awareness or giving meaning to sensation.

The output mechanisms or effectors are the muscles and glands of the body. Without the effectors there could be no action or expression of what has been sensed and understood.

The organization of our bodies into specialized mechanisms for reception, distribution, and output of energy *makes* behavior possible, and the functioning of these mechanisms *is* behavior.

The use of chemical substances or drugs known to act on the central nervous system has generated widespread interest in recent years. At least 500 psychoactive drugs are presently available, all of which have some undesirable side effects. Stimulants and antidepressants act as psychic energizers; sedatives and tranquilizers are useful in reducing anxiety and treating mental illness; narcotics depress brain activity to reduce suffering and pain; and the hallucinogens alter perception of the environment in different ways.

We turn next to the conception of the new individual, his potentials and limitations. How do the factors of heredity, environment, maturation, and learning function to shape the individual into the person he will become?

SUGGESTIONS FOR FURTHER READING

Landauer, T. K., *Readings in Physiological Psychology*, New York, McGraw-Hill, 1967.
Reports of current research covering a wide range of studies concerning the bodily basis of behavior.

Nowlis, Helen, *Drugs on the College Campus*, New York, Doubleday, 1969. An informative handbook of information about the current situation with regard to student use of drugs.

Segall, M. H., Campbell, D. T., and Herskovits, M. J., *The Influence of Culture on Visual Perception*, New York, Bobbs-Merrill, 1966. Shows how bodily processes are influenced by social and psychological factors.

Tart, Charles T. (Ed.), *Altered States of Consciousness*, New York, Wiley, 1969. A selection of readings by leading authorities on hypnosis, drugs, dreams, meditation, and other means by which consciousness can be altered.

Ungerleider, J. T. (Ed.), *The Problems and Prospects of L.S.D.*, Springfield, Ill., Charles C. Thomas, 1968. A panel of five authorities in the field discuss the history and current use of LSD, its effects, and prospects for future use.

Shaping the Individual

The conception, growth, and development of a new individual are not just biological events, but have significant psychological and social aspects too. An understanding of behavior requires an appreciation of the origins of a new life and the influences that give it shape. These influences are present at conception and begin to operate immediately although their importance may not be immediately realized.

The parents who conceive the new individual contribute the hereditary potentials that will fix the limits of the child's capacities for growth and determine his race, sex, intelligence, appearance, and many special aptitudes. The life circumstances of the parents, their national origins, occupation, social class, and educational backgrounds will create limits for the child in terms of his early experiences and social opportunities. The relationship of the parents to each other, their feelings about the conception of the child, their readiness to assume responsibility for the care of the child, their attitudes about life and how it should be lived will all operate to create psychological limits within which the child must grow. This combination of biological, social, and psychological influences will determine what the child is like, how he is treated, how he will come to feel about himself, how he will in turn treat others, and how his life is valued. The value placed upon each new life changes in time the nature of society. The feeling of responsibility each member of society has for one another, the kind of laws considered necessary to protect the individual, the variety of services provided to ensure realization of individual potentials, and even the use of natural resources reflect the value placed by society upon a new life. As we examine the biological details of the origin of a new life let us keep in focus their psychological and social implications (Figure 3-1).

CONCEPTION TO BIRTH

Conception

Conception occurs as a result of sexual intercourse when the sex cell of the male (sperm) unites with the sex cell of the female (egg). The sex cells are produced in the testes of the male and the ovaries of the female. At puberty, hormone changes in the endocrine gland system initiate the production of the sex cells. The beginning of puberty, or adolescence, usually occurs between 13 and 15 years for males and 12 and 14 years for females.

The sperm of the male has a flat, oval-shaped cell body and a long taillike process. The cell body of the sperm is about 1/5000 of an inch in size and con-

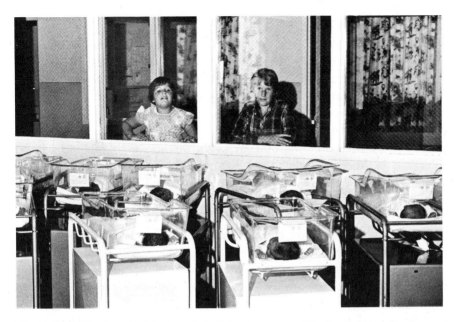

Figure 3-1.   Newborn babies in a hospital nursery are alike in their helplessness and dependency, but their differences in hereditary potentials are already determined and will become more evident as they develop and mature. (Photo by Jim Sargent.)

tains a nucleus with cell material and one-half or 23 of the hereditary carriers called *chromosomes* that are necessary for reproduction. During sexual activity millions of sperm suspended in a fluid called *semen,* are ejaculated from the penis as a function of the involuntary nervous system. Sperm cannot live outside the body, but if deposited in the female have a life span from 2 to 5 days depending upon their vitality and the chemical conditions in the female body. Suspended in the semen the sperm move by the whiplash action of the tail process at a rate of about 3–6 inches per hour. The number of sperm produced, and their vitality depends upon the general health of the body and the health of the endocrine gland system in particular. Only one sperm is needed to fertilize an egg cell, but of the millions of sperm present in each ejaculation even one may not survive to reach the egg cell.

The egg cell is much larger than the sperm being about 1/180 of an inch in size and round in appearance. The egg cell consists mostly of nutritive material and has a nucleus with 23 chromosomes. The life span of an egg cell is very short, lasting usually for only a few hours and probably never more than

2 days. Normally, the ovaries alternate in producing one egg cell a month beginning at puberty and continuing until about age 45–50 years when the reproductive capacity of the female stops with the process called *menopause*.

The discharge of an egg cell from the ovary is controlled by a number of endocrine gland hormones as part of a regularly occurring process called the *menstrual cycle*. It takes, on the average, about 28 days to complete the menstrual cycle. The menstrual cycle includes: (*a*) the discharge of an egg cell from an ovary and its movement toward the uterus (ovulation); (*b*) the buildup of blood and tissues in the walls of the uterus in preparation for a fertilized egg; (*c*) the discharge of the accumulated blood tissue from the uterus when the egg has not been fertilized (menstruation); and (*d*) the return of the uterus to a resting and restored condition before the next ovulation. Health factors in the female, especially those involving the endocrine glands, can alter or stop the menstrual cycle and impair the vitality of the egg cell.

In Figure 3-2 are illustrated the reproductive organs of the female. The egg cell is discharged from the ovary to the oviduct and moves downward toward the uterus. The sperm cells deposited in the vagina of the female during sexual intercourse move upward through the uterus toward the egg cell. The sex cells generally meet somewhere in the oviduct.

When the nucleus of a sperm cell that has penetrated the egg joins with the nucleus of the egg cell the full number of the chromosomes (46) needed for reproduction are joined and *conception* occurs. Changes in the membrane around a fertilized egg cell will prevent other sperm from entering it. The fertilized egg will continue its movement to the uterus where it will attach itself to the uterine wall. The presence of a fertilized egg in the uterus is accompanied by special hormone action that will prevent the menstrual cycle continuing and will aid further buildup in uterine tissues. The growth and development of the single-celled fertilized egg to the millions of specialized cells that make up the newborn infant will require about 270 days or 9–9½ months.

Sex Determination

Whether a person is a male or a female is one of the most important factors influencing his personality development and adjustment. In our society the opportunities available to us, the demands others make upon us, and the aspirations we develop for ourselves differ for males and females. This most important form of our psychological and social identity is determined at conception by the sperm cell.

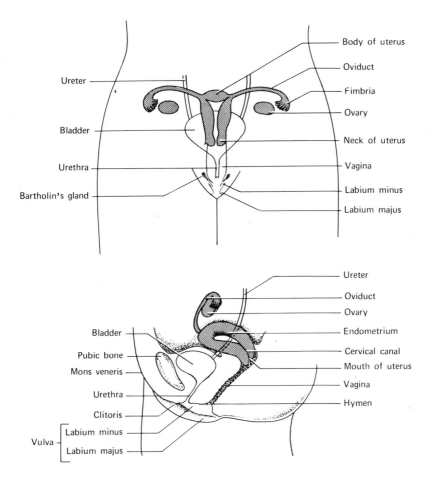

Figure 3-2. Diagram of the female reproductive organs. (After Shifferes, 1960.)

The factor for sex type is carried by the chromosomes in the sex cells of the parents. Some sperm cells carry an X factor for sex and other sperm cells carry a Y factor for sex. All egg cells carry only an X factor for sex. If a sperm cell carrying a Y factor for sex fertilizes the egg cell then the pattern XY occurs and we call this *male*. If a sperm cell carrying an X factor for sex fertilizes the egg cell then the pattern XX occurs and we call this *female*.

Every male has an XY pattern for sex and the sperm cells he produces should be about equal in carrying either an X or a Y factor for sex. The chances, however, that a man will conceive a male or a female child are not exactly 50:50. Age, health, and hereditary considerations in the parents influence a tendency to conceive more children of one sex than the other. The sperm cells that carry the Y factor for maleness are smaller and have less vitality than the sperm cells that carry the X factor, but they move faster and have a greater chance of reaching the egg cell. The number of males born exceeds females by a ratio of about 106:100. Since more males than females perish during the period of pregnancy we can assume the ratio of conception favors males even more than the ratio of births would indicate.

Multiple Births

When more than one egg cell is produced and fertilized then multiple conceptions occur resulting in multiple births. Two egg cells fertilized by two sperm cells produce individuals called *fraternal twins*. Fraternal twins need not be anything alike since they result from the union of different sex cells and the hereditary potentials each receive can be quite different. Similarly, 3, 4, 5, or more egg cells may be produced and fertilized by separate sperm cells resulting in fraternal triplets, quadruplets, and quintuplets. Endocrine gland changes, hereditary factors, and more recently the use of fertility drugs seem involved in the cases where more than one egg cell is produced at a time.

Sometimes, a single egg cell that has been fertilized by a single sperm cell cleaves or separates soon after fertilization and produces two individuals who are exactly alike called *identical twins*. Because identical twins come from a single fertilization the hereditary potentials that each possesses are the same and they are biologically alike. The reasons for the separation of the single fertilized egg are not well understood, but it can happen more than once and produce identical triplets, quadruplets, quintuplets, or more from the single fertilization.

When a single, fertilized egg fails to complete a cleavage it has started, individuals called *siamese twins* are produced. Siamese twins may be joined on the body surface or may share vital internal organs. The possibility for surgical separation of siamese twins depends upon how they are joined.

Children born in multiples have been objects of special public interest and present special problems. Biologically, the size, health, and survival chances for individuals born in multiples are poorer than those for single births. The personal and social resources of the parents, whatever they may be, must be extended further to care for more than one child born at a time. Providing for the psychological adjustment of children born in multiples requires particular attention to ensure that each grows in an appreciation and awareness of his own identity. There is an unfortunate idea that all children born together must be alike. We have seen that only where the individuals are the result of the fertilization of a single egg by a single sperm are they biologically alike. The effect of the environment may cause differences to appear even in identical twins. Individuals who are fraternal twins, triplets, quadruplets, etc. need not be anything alike and expectations that they will perform alike puts them at a great disadvantage.

Prenatal Development

The first two weeks after conception are called the period of the *zygote* or fertilized egg. A rapid process of cell division, specialization, and multiplication goes on during this period. The new individual as well as supporting tissues of placenta, umbilical cord, and amnion sac with fluid (bag of waters) are being formed from the cells of the *zygote*.

The fluid of the amnion sac protects the delicate tissues of the child as they are formed and cushions the child from movements of the mother's body. The placenta is a network of blood vessels and membranes attached to the wall of the uterus on one side and the umbilical cord on the other side. Materials from the mother's blood system needed to serve the nourishment and respiration needs of the developing child pass through the placenta to the blood vessels of the umbilical cord to the blood system of the child. Waste materials from the child are carried by the blood vessels of the umbilical cord through the placenta to be eliminated by the blood system of the mother.

The connection of the mother and child's blood systems is not direct, but across the tissue barrier of the placenta. The placenta is not selective of materials that pass through it and from the mother will come oxygen, nutrients, and hormones as well as viruses, antibodies, and allergens. The life of the developing child depends upon the maintenance of the mother in a condition of good health and nourishment. The mother's use of *toxic* substances that reduce the oxygen level of her blood (tobacco, alcohol, drugs) can impair or suffocate the tissues of the child as they are forming. The absence of vitamin, mineral, and chemical substances in the mother's blood deprive the child of needed nutrients.

A question of great concern has been what effect emotional or mental conditions of the mother during pregnancy have upon the developing child. The answer must be found in the chemical changes of the mother's blood caused by such conditions. If the mother by reason of her emotional state is using alcohol, sedatives, or addicting drugs, then the child may suffer toxic poisoning. The child can be addicted in the uretus by the mother's use of addicting drugs and have to be withdrawn if he survives their effect. The emotional state of the mother may cause overproduction of some hormones in her body such as adrenalin and these enter the blood system of the child. Chemical changes in the mother's blood from disturbances in the functioning of her nervous system are other sources of infiltration of the child's blood system. The possibilities are many, but always limited to chemical factors in the blood exchanged through the placenta. The effect of this exchange may be seen in the child after birth as unusual excitability or sensitivity (Ottinger and Simmons, 1964). We will consider other potential risks to the child in the later discussion.

From 2 weeks to 2 months after conception is the period of the *embryo*. During this period all the essential anatomy of the child will be started. The brain, heart, and liver are the first organs to be formed and are especially vulnerable to injury or infiltration of the blood by deadly substances. If the mother contracts the German measles (*Rubella*) during these first months of the pregnancy, the virus of the disease in her blood passes through the placenta to the child's blood damaging especially the tiny brain cells of the embryo. The heart begins to beat during this period at first irregularly and then more evenly. The liver of the embryo begins to manufacture its own red blood cells. The limbs begin to appear as budlike structures and may be stunted in their budding stage if the mother is using the drug *thalidomide* during this time.

At the end of the embryonic period the head, eyes, nose, and mouth are nearly completed including even tiny buds for the milk (or baby) teeth. The limbs are completed and fingers and toes are detailed to about the first joint. The spinal cord is completed although the skeleton is made up of cartilage rather than bone cells. If the embryo is removed from the uterus it cannot survive, but there is no biological question that it is anything but a human being.

Beginning with the third month after conception until the time of birth is the period of the *fetus* or young one. During this period bone tissue will replace cartilage in the skeleton, all the anatomical details will be finished, the developing child will make his first movements, and there will be a rapid increase in size and weight. In Table 3-1 some of the growth changes of the prenatal child and special events that mark his progress in development are reported.

The early momements of the fetus are slight stirrings, rather gross and jerky. As growth continues, however, integration of movements develops and reflex patterns such as grasping, swallowing, and sucking will appear. The *reflex pattern* is the simplest form of nervous system organization and involves very limited chains of neurons that respond automatically to highly specific stimuli.

Table 3-1. Growth Changes of the Prenatal Child[a]

Time from conception	Length	Weight	Progress in development
4 weeks	Microscopic	Microscopic	Heart beats, blood forming
8 weeks	1 inch	Less than 1 ounce	All essential anatomy has been initiated
12 weeks	3 inches	1 ounce	Sex can be determined
16 weeks	6 inches	4 ounces	Reflex action movements
20 weeks	10 inches	$\frac{1}{2}$ pound	Mother feels movements and activity of fetus
24 weeks	12 inches	$1\frac{1}{4}$ pounds	Can open and close eyes; liver and kidneys are beginning to function; fetus may "hiccup"
28 weeks	15 inches	$2\frac{1}{2}$ pounds	All anatomy and physiology completed but still too small to survive
32 weeks	$16\frac{1}{2}$ inches	4 pounds	If born at this time has about 50–50 chance for survival
36 weeks	18–20 inches	6–8 pounds	Birth at this time or after, survival should be assured

[a]Adapted from Stone and Church (1957).

Examples of reflex movements of the fetus include the opening and closing of the mouth when the lip area is stimulated, stroking the sole of the foot will cause the toes to fan out and the leg to be pulled up and away. The fetus makes some independent movements such as rotating the head, turning the trunk of his body, and extending or contracting his limbs. These early movement patterns represent progress in the development of the neural and muscular systems of the individual before birth.

Birth

The prenatal period ends with the birth of the child. Hormone changes in the mother's endocrine glands will start the strong contractions of uterine and abdominal muscles called *labor*. The increasing weight and size of the fetus stretches the uterus to its maximum size and is an additional factor in the readiness of the mother's body for birth. The child must leave the protected environment of the uterus where all his needs have been immediately met and he has been insulated from many forms of stimulation.

At birth the child is biologically an independent being and he must accomplish respiration, digestion, and elimination by the functioning of his own body. The world of the newborn is full of unfamiliar sensations of light, sound, odors, tastes, textures, surfaces, and changes of position. The senses of the newborn are ready to function, but not with equal sensitivity. Smell, taste, and touch are well developed, but hearing, vision, and especially pain are not. All reflexive movements are present at or shortly after birth including grasping, blinking, sneezing, yawning, sucking, swallowing, and the knee jerk.

Psychologically, the newborn and the world of events around him are one and the same. He is without a sense of self or *ego*. He does not know the relationship between events that occur outside his body and the events they create within his body. He may kick his foot on the bar of his crib feeling the hurt and enjoying the sound and not know he is causing either. His awareness of himself, *me*, as distinct from other persons and objects around him will develop very slowly beginning sometime after the second month when his visual system is better integrated. The emotional responses of the newborn are very general forms of excitement and not until the third month can infant expressions of satisfaction or distress be well distinguished.

Socially, the newborn is a helpless and dependent being. His biological capacities permit him to utilize what others do for him but he can do nothing in his own behalf to meet his needs. Other people acquire meaning for him as their activities result in satisfying or unsatisfying states within him. The mother of the newborn is usually the most constant social stimulus in his world. The nature of the interaction between the mother and the child sets a pattern for the child's later responses and shapes what has been called the *basic sense of trust* (Erikson, 1968).

A recent research study compared the behavior of children raised in institutions until about 2 years of age and then placed in foster or adoptive homes with a group of children of the same age raised entirely in their own homes. The investigators' report indicates that the children who spent their infancy in institutions showed improved general health and appearance, increased activity, and quickly learned self-care habits after placement in a home setting. However, the institutionalized children showed deficiencies in language and thought development, difficulty in self-control and expression of feelings, less curiosity and imagination, and a reluctance to turn to adults for help or comfort when things did not go well for them (Provence and Lipton, 1963).

It would seem that the child whose early experiences give him the impression that this world is a safe, good, and pleasant place to be reaches out to it with curiosity and his explorations enrich his experience. The good feeling the child has about the world includes other persons and he feels safe in going to them for help and comfort. The child whose early experiences make him doubtful or fearful of this world does not wish to reach out to it and he limits the experiences he can have. When things go wrong for him the child with a negative world view gives up and withdraws into himself and the presence of other people does not help or comfort him.

HEREDITY

Chromosomes and Genes

The basic mechanisms of heredity are threadlike structures called *chromosomes* that contain thousands of smaller units called *genes*. Heredity is the means by which the species characteristics are transmitted from one generation of off-spring to another. The study of the hereditary process is called *genetics*. The promise contained in the union of the sperm and egg cells is the production of a human being whose behavioral capacities will be expressed through his biological structure. Many cells of the body contain chromosomes, but only those that are found in the nucleus of the sex cells affect human heredity.

At conception the new individual receives 23 chromosomes from each of his parents and these 46 chromosomes with their thousands of genes represent all of his hereditary potentials. Variations from the 46 chromosome pattern in humans are associated with developmental defects. Mongoloidism, for example, a type of mental retardation, seems to result from the presence of an extra chromosome. The functioning of genes to create a new person is accomplished by a complex chemical coding process. Basic to the genetic code are two nucleic acid compounds, abbreviated DNA and RNA. The way the code works and the biochemical processes involved are still not well understood, but progress is being made and it is expected that it may someday be possible to control the functioning of the genes (Crick, 1963). The genes that parents contribute to the child depend upon the genes they have received from their own parents and how these are combined in the chromosomes of their sex cells.

Dominance and Recession

Some genes work in pairs to create a given characteristic such as color vision and in these instances one gene of the pair must come from each parent. Other characteristics such as skin color result from the combined action of many genes and the pattern of contribution of each parent is more complex. Genes that work in pairs can be described as dominant, recessive, or a combination of both (hybrid).

A *dominant* gene, when it is present, will appear in the physical makeup of the person. Color vision is a dominant gene trait. The capital letter is used to indicate a dominant gene and so for normal color vision let us use the letter C. A *recessive* gene is one that can be present in the genetic makeup of the person, but by itself cannot be expressed in the physical makeup. The only time a recessive gene can be expressed in physical makeup is when it is paired with another recessive gene for the same trait. Color blindness is a recessive gene trait. The recessive gene is indicated by the small letter and so for color blindness let us use the small letter c.

A person who receives a dominant gene for color vision from one parent and a recessive gene for color blindness from the other parent is a genetic *hybrid* and has the pattern Cc. The hybrid always shows the dominant trait in his own physical makeup. In this case he has normal color vision. But, the hybrid is carrying the recessive gene too and may pass it along to his offspring. These relationships are illustrated in Figure 3-3.

Most humans are probably genetic hybrids for most paired gene traits. During the nineteenth century, an Austrian monk named Gregor Mendel

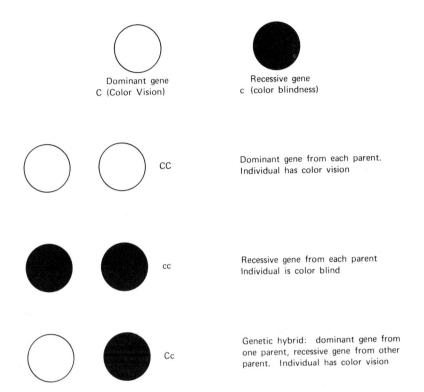

Figure 3-3.   Dominant and recessive gene pairs.

demonstrated that mating of genetic hybrids would produce the recessive trait in an offspring 1 in 4 times of mating. However, Mendel's work was done with garden pea plants under controlled conditions of mating. Mendel's probabilities are useful, but not binding, when humans are concerned. The recessive trait may be present in a human family for generations but never appear in the physical makeup of the offspring.

It should be clear that the idea of dominant or recessive is concerned with whether a trait will or will not show in the physical makeup. Dominant genes are not necessarily better genes than are recessives. Dominant genes also do not necessarily occur in greater number than do recessive genes. Finally, dominant genes are not necessarily normal and recessive genes abnormal. In Table 3-2 are reported some of the dominant–recessive gene patterns constituting various human traits. It is apparent from Table 3-2 that categories like better–worse, most–few, normal–abnormal, cannot be used to describe either dominant or

Table 3-2. Dominant and Recessive Patterns in Human Traits

Dominant trait	Recessive trait
Skin pigmentation or color	Albinism (lack of skin color)
Blood types A, B, AB	Blood type O
Curly hair	Straight hair
Dwarfed limbs	Proportioned limbs
Color vision	Color blindness
Extra fingers, toes	10 fingers and toes
Rh positive factor	Rh negative factor
Brown eyes	Blue or grey eyes
Hazel or green eyes	
Baldness in males	Baldness in females
Blood-clotting factors	Hemophilia
White hair patch	Hair color even

recessive genes as a group. We all display a variety of dominant and recessive gene traits and are fortunate because of it.

Birth Defects

Approximately 250,000 of the four million American babies born each year have important birth defects. About 20 percent of these defects are attributed to heredity, another 20 percent are caused by environmental factors during pregnancy, and the remaining 60 percent are thought to result from chromosomal abnormalities (Stock, 1969). In recent years scientists have been studying the effects of numerous substances (including fungicides, pesticides, artificial sweeteners, caffeine, and LSD) that are suspected of causing gene mutations and damage to the chromosomes.

One condition based on genetic factors that may have serious consequences in the early development of the child is the Rh blood factor, so-named because it was first observed in the Rhesus monkey. The Rh-positive factor is a dominant genetic trait and the Rh-negative factor is the recessive. When Rh+ blood is mixed with Rh− blood, antibodies are formed that destroy the red blood cells. The blood type and associated factors are determined at conception.

Difficulty arises when the mother is Rh− and the child is Rh+. Some of the Rh+ factors in the child's blood pass through the placenta to the mother's blood system. The mother's body forms antibodies to fight the foreign Rh+ factors. The antibodies in her blood pass through the placenta to the smaller blood system of the child destroying the red blood cells and the tissues that depend on them. The danger is usually not great with the first pregnancy, as it takes time for the mother's system to become sensitized and develop antibodies. The risk grows, however, with additional pregnancies. The child may suffer organ damage, especially to the brain, or may not survive at all. Where the Rh incompatibility is known, transfusions to replace the entire blood volume of the child at birth may forestall developmental injury. If the mother is Rh+ and the child Rh− no problems arise. Young women who know they are Rh− blood type should consult their physicians about new desensitization treatment procedures that have been developed.

Within the past decade new techniques have been developed to study the 1500 or more recognized gene defects, at least 30 of which can be identified by analysis of the amniotic fluid. Birth defects that affect metabolism and have serious consequences of development can often be detected by screening tests performed on newborn infants. An example of this kind of screening concerns the disease called PKU, an abbreviation for *phenylketonuria*. PKU is a metabolic disorder that prevents full utilization of food proteins and the buildup in the blood of a chemical substance that disturbs brain and nervous system functioning. Children with PKU disorder show severe mental retardation, hyperactive and destructive behavior patterns, and epileptic-type seizures.

The PKU condition is a recessive genetic trait and each parent contributes one recessive gene. A urine test shortly after birth has proved a valuable screening device followed by a laboratory blood study for definitive diagnosis. PKU can be controlled by careful diet management so early identification of PKU babies can prevent its serious effects. Even older children who show PKU damage have been aided by diet control, but nothing can be done to restore damage already completed. Many states have made PKU screening a mandatory hospital procedure for the newborn. Parents should consult their physician for certainty of the screening procedure when their child is born.

The processes involved in heredity are being closely studied by geneticists, biochemists, and other scientists. The prospect that the genetic code will be known and subject to systematic change raises great hope, but also great concern. Biologically, the manipulation of the genetic code may make possible the substitution of healthy for defective factors and future generations may not need to fear the "gamble of the genes." In the future, parents may go to genetic counseling centers to plan the characteristics of the children they feel they can best provide for. Most human traits are not easily separated into good and bad, however, and society itself could change if some human traits were given preference and others were systematically eliminated.

A number of studies are being done to determine the effects of LSD on chromosomes but the evidence is not conclusive to date. Laboratory studies report chromosomal changes in tissue cultures with LSD, and they warn that the observed changes in the chromosomes of people who have taken LSD may cause abnormalities in their offspring. Some birth defects have been reported in newborn infants whose mothers admitted using LSD but the facts so far available have not established a direct cause-and-effect relationship between LSD and birth defects.

The possibility of a relationship between a particular chromosomal abnormality and criminal behavior has stirred interest in recent years, following the finding that the frequency of XYY males in a prison hospital population was significantly higher than in the general population (Montagu, 1968). We must bear in mind when reading results such as this, that few laboratories are equipped to do chromosome studies on a large scale, so that most current studies are based on limited samples.

The process of the genes, chromosomes, or heredity should not be interpreted as the equivalent of fate or predestination. The genetic code carries certain potentials that can influence but not determine the outcome. The potentials are there at the time of conception, but their development depends upon the interaction between the inherited genes and the environment to which they are exposed, including the other genes with which they come in contact.

What is Inherited?

Most human characteristics are a product of the interaction between heredity and environment. Heredity is mainly responsible for determining physical differences in skin color, body build, shape and color of eyes, hair color and texture, shape of nose, and blood type. Beyond these physical features which are evident at birth, heredity influences the potential limits of an individual's capacity for intelligence and other traits which we will discuss in Chapter 6.

In the past humans were classified on the basis of physical characteristics into three broad groups called races. These were the Mongoloid or "yellow race," the Negroid or "black race," and the Caucasian or "white race." In modern times the "races" have become so intermingled that the differences within each group are greater than the differences between groups. Many years of scientific study have failed to establish proof of the superiority of one race over another. Racial differences apply only to physical appearances, but, unfortunately, these apparent differences constitute an important factor in determining how people are treated in our society. Group differences, where they do exist, are more closely related to environmental differences than they are to hereditary differences.

Most human infants at birth are quite similar psychologically. They are dependent and incapable of self-help, and their behavior is very limited. Their differences are mainly in *potentiality*. The adults they will become will be profoundly dissimilar because of the limits of their hereditary potentials *and* because of the opportunities they will have to develop these potentials. Some of their inborn potentialities will be actualized but many of their potentialities may never be realized. Heredity and environment do not function as independent influences. Unfavorable surroundings make it impossible for even the most gifted individuals to realize or actualize their potentialities, and even the best environment cannot enable an individual to actualize potentialities he does not possess. The problem is that we do not know in advance what the potentials may be for any given person and we must wait for them to develop. We do know that it is only in a favorable environment that the inborn potentialities of any individual can be actualized. This fact has important implications for everyone.

MATURATION

The hereditary potentials do not appear as fully developed traits at any given time. They must wait upon a process of systematic growth change called *maturation*. Maturation requires an environment that will permit growth to occur and to be expressed. Environments lacking in needed forms of nourishment and stimulation or which contain harmful agents can delay, retard, or prevent maturation. The environment should not be thought of in physical terms only. Adequate diet, shelter, safety, and sanitation are required for maturation, but so too are psychological and social factors.

Every individual has a natural tendency to grow, and each one has his own distinctive rate and pattern of growth. We do not expect every child to be at exactly the same point of growth at the same calendar age. However, maturation occurs in systematic ways and within broad limits we can predict the growth process.

Rate of Maturation

Maturation for most human characteristics follows rather clearly defined stages. The developmental periods of the prenatal child (zygote, embryo, fetus) are maturational stages. After birth, the maturational stages are usually divided into infancy, childhood, adolescence, and adulthood. The rate for physical maturation is usually expressed in terms of growth *norms*. Norms are average time periods, based upon information from large samples of individuals, when we can usually expect certain behavior to appear.

Rates for psychological and social maturation are somewhat harder to express because they depend upon so many complex relationships and experiences. A helpful way to think about psychological and social maturation is in terms of the tasks the individual must accomplish at each stage of development in order to be ready for the opportunities and challenges of later developmental stages (Havighurst, 1953). In Chapter 7 we will consider psychological and social maturation in terms of the life tasks that the individual must accomplish for healthy development. In this chapter we will be primarily concerned with physical maturation.

In Table 3-3 are reported some average times, based upon growth norms, when many important human behaviors appear in development. No person should be expected to be average in all these respects, for his particular hereditary potentials and the circumstances of his environment may cause some behaviors to appear early and others to be somewhat later. Even within the individual, physical growth is uneven in various body systems. The brain grows rapidly in size during the prenatal period and continues to do so until about age 6 years after which changes of size are very small. The skeleton will reach half its adult size within 3 years, after which skeletal growth will be slow until adolescence when rapid growth begins again. The permanent teeth do not begin to appear until about age 6 years and then one or two are added each year until adolescence. The last teeth to develop, the so-called "wisdom" teeth, will not appear until about age 17 or 18 years. The sexual organs change very little from birth through childhood and then as adolescence approaches, change both in size and capacity for function occurs rapidly. With so many body systems growing at uneven rates in peaks and spurts we sometimes fail to see that growth is really an orderly process. Some systems are delayed as others important to their function are completed and rate of maturation follows a particular pattern.

Pattern of Maturation

Simple to Complex. We have seen biologically how a single, fertilized egg cell becomes billions of specialized cells forming different tissues and organs

Table 3-3. Typical Ages for Appearance of Developmental Behavior [a]

Behavior	Age
On stomach, holds chin up	3–4 weeks
Following object with eyes	4–5 weeks
Babbles to self or in response to familiar objects	4–6 weeks
Makes sounds to indicate distress	1 month
Smiles	2 months
On stomach, holds head and chin up	$2\frac{1}{2}$ months
Makes sounds and expressions of delight	3 months
Sits with support	4 months
Rotates head	4 months
Grasps at objects with either hand	6 months
Bounces when held under arms	6 months
Holds trunk erect, sits alone	7 months
Moves objects from hand-to-hand	7 months
Puts sounds together and repeats them	8 months
Stands with support	9 months
Leans forward to reach and regains upright posture	9 months
Imitates sounds made by others	9–10 months
Maintains balance when turning from side-to-side	10 months
Creeps	10 months
Pulls himself to knees	10 months
Walks when led	11–12 months
Says one or two words	12 months
Climbs stairs	13 months
Stands alone	14 months
Walks alone	15 months
Extends arm and hand to assist dressing	15 months
Indicates is wet or soiled	15 months
Holds cup	15 months
Scribbles with pencil, crayon	15 months
Can unzip zippers	18 months
Responds to simple commands	18 months
Can hold and fill a spoon with much spilling	18 months
Identifies 1 or 2 objects by pointing	18 months
Can carry out simple commands	21 months
Begins to tell toilet needs	21 months
Helps with own dressing	24 months
Uses words in simple sentences	24 months

[a]Adapted from Gesell, et al. (1940).

(e.g., receptors) to serve complex behavioral functions (sensation–perception). Language behavior will begin with assorted grunts and sounds, gradually achieving complex speech patterns. Growth and the behavior made possible by growth begins in simple structure and form and changes toward greater complexity.

System Integration. Tissues and organs that first appear as independent structures are integrated into larger systems. The ductless glands appear separately during the prenatal period but eventually function as parts of the endocrine system. Growth in the visual and motor systems makes possible increased eye–hand coordination, a skill that is necessary for developing reading readiness. After puberty, the endocrine glands and the nervous system through their integrated activity accomplish the reproductive function.

Directions of Growth. Growth proceeds at different rates all over the body but follows two principal directions: from head to toe, and from the center out to the extremes. At birth, the head is about one-half the total body size and the legs about one-third. The head of the adult, however, will represent about one-tenth of body size and the legs about one-half. Behaviorally, the child will be able to lift his head first, then he can hold up his trunk to sit, then he can hold up his body to stand, and finally he will walk. The head and trunk appear first in prenatal life, then the limbs appear as buds and finally hands with fingers and feet with toes are detailed. Behaviorally, the first movements of the arms are very gross, then the child is able to reach, then to grasp objects, and finally to manipulate objects with fine finger dexterity.

If we keep these three principles of maturational pattern in mind we can recognize the systematic changes of growth and the increased behavioral capacity as growth proceeds.

Effect of Training

A question of great interest has been what effect, if any, does early practice and training have upon skills that depend upon maturation. The question is really complex, since heredity and environment cause the maturational pattern to be somewhat different for each individual. We do have, however, in cases of identical twins, a chance to study this question because identical twins have the same hereditary potentials and they experience the environment with the same capacities.

Such a study has been reported using identical twin girls about 1 year of age testing the effect of training upon the maturation of several motor skills including stair-climbing (Gesell and Thompson, 1929). One twin (T) was given 6 weeks of daily practice in stair-climbing and showed some gain in skill during this training period. The other twin (C) received a 2-week training experience in stair-climbing after the longer training period of the first twin (T) was finished. When the twins were measured 10 weeks after the study began there was no difference in their level of performance for the stair-climbing skill. Twin T had received three times as much training as Twin C, but Twin C was older when her training started and she was able to profit equally as much.

Later studies involving other skills have generally supported the conclusion that behavior dependent upon maturation is not appreciably improved by early or intense training. The effort required to train a child in a particular behavior before maturation occurs does not seem justified in terms of the level of performance observed at a later time. Parents would do well to use growth norms as the basis for determining probable readiness when considering training the child for skill development. All skills require the opportunity to be expressed and when maturationally ready do show improvement with practice. The child's interests are probably better served when his environment provides him opportunity to express his growth progress and offers him help as it is needed, rather than attempting to train him ahead of his own rate of development.

ENVIRONMENT

As a new human being you were born *with* your hereditary potentials and limitations *into* a set of surroundings and conditions with which you must continuously interact from birth until death. Those factors in the world around you which influence your growth, behavior, and realization of potentialities are all included in the term *environment*. To understand how the forces of heredity and environment interact in shaping the individual, let us first identify those surroundings and conditions that constitute environment.

Physical Environment

Everything in the world around you that you can know about through your sense organs—seeing, hearing, tasting, touching, smelling, feeling—exerts some influence on your development as an individual. Both before and after birth, hereditary potentialities can unfold only if the environment is favorable. You will recall from Chapter 2 that the development of perception, basic to intellectual growth, requires opportunity for a variety of experiences with objects

Figure 3-4. Contrast the physical environment surrounding the children in these two pictures. How is their growth and development affected by their different environments? (Photos by Jim Sargent.)

and events. The development of any skill or talent is contingent upon an opportunity to learn through experience. The environment must provide that opportunity.

The capacity for speech depends upon maturation of body tissues, but language develops in response to stimulation from the environment. What a child learns to say, and the language he will use, depends upon what is available for him to imitate in his environment. It has been shown that existing social class differences affect the kind and amount of vocabulary children acquire, and this, in turn, alters the capacity for learning and thinking (Bernstein, 1958).

It is easy to see how the home where you live, the neighborhood where you play, the school where you learn, the community where you grow up all play an important part in determining the extent to which you are able to realize your potentialities. An environment that is enriched and stimulating will excite a child's curiosity and offer interesting and challenging opportunities to explore and learn. Fresh air, sunshine, good diet, room to play, and a comfortable home are important, not only for physical well-being, but for good mental attitudes. A child for whom reality consists of poverty, hunger, physical discomfort, danger, displacement, diseases, and deprivation is so defeated by his physical surroundings that he usually lacks the necessary incentive to take advantage of what few opportunities he does have.

In a detailed study which sparked the "War on Poverty," it was estimated that between 40 and 50 million Americans, or about one-fourth of the population, were living in poverty. Poverty was defined in terms of "those who are denied the minimal levels of health, housing, food, and education that our present stage of scientific knowledge specifies as necessary for life as it is now lived in the United States" (Harrington, 1963, p. 175). People who live in slums, ghettos, and rural poverty areas are at a serious physical disadvantage, suffering more chronic diseases with less possibility of treatment, and more mental and emotional problems than any other segment of American society.

Another large segment of the "underprivileged" has been identified as "above poverty but short of minimum requirements for a modestly comfortable level of living," by the Conference of Economic Progress. Using this definition of "deprivation" it was estimated that almost half the population of the United States in 1963 was living in poverty or deprivation (Macdonald, 1963). Since then some steps have been taken to provide better housing and employment opportunities for the poor, but progress has not been fast enough to prevent outbreaks of violence in areas where poverty and deprivation prevail. We cannot know the extent of human potential that is never realized because of the lack of opportunity in the environment.

Psychological Environment

Psychological environment includes those attitudes, expectations, and feelings people express toward one another. Since humans are so dependent upon one another, the feelings or *emotional climate* generated by feelings can exert an important influence on individuals. The first experience of the individual with the psychological environment occurs in the home and later in the classroom, on the job, and in the community.

A home atmosphere of parental acceptance leads to the development of self-confidence and respect in children. A home atmosphere filled with conflict between family members or rejection leads to insecurity, rebellion, and anxiety in children. Studies have shown that in families where children are controlled

Figure 3-5.   What can you tell about the emotional climate of this classroon and how it will influence the individuals in this class? (Photo by Dave Bellak, San Jose State College.)

by strict, authoritarian rule the children become either obedient and conforming or rebellious and nonconforming. In contrast, the more permissive family atmosphere tends to result in children who are more creative, original, self-reliant, spontaneous, and considerate of others. Harsh, punitive treatment often results in hostile, aggressive children.

Even within the same family the psychological environment is somewhat different for each person. Parents usually have greater expectations for their first-born child than they do for later children. Perhaps this is because parents are a little less secure, a little more strict, and give the first child more responsibility. As a result, first-born children tend to be more dominating, independent, serious, and studious than their younger brothers and sisters.

The importance of psychological climate in community life is reflected in the social treatment of various groups. The Mexican–American population, a large minority group in our country, has experienced the subtle forces of an unfavorable psychological climate. Living mostly in the southwest and western United States, the Mexican–Americans do not have the same history of segregation and discrimination that characterized treatment of black Americans. However, they have a different cultural heritage of values, customs, and the Spanish language. For many of these people English is a second language which must be learned. Many Mexican–Americans feel that our school systems regard their children as inferior or retarded on the basis of their language difficulty.

In a United States civil rights hearing, conducted in December, 1968, school administrators admitted that junior-high-school counselors tended to guide Mexican–American students into predominantly vocational high schools rather than to encourage them to choose college preparatory schools. The limited expectations of school authorities for Mexican–American youth have operated to limit their opportunities and their expectations for themselves.

Social Structure

In spite of the American ideal of democratic equality it is no secret that American society is characterized by distinctions between people based on social class or prestige level of families. Class boundaries are not rigidly enforced, and *upward mobility* (improvement of social status) can be achieved by individual effort. Realistically, however, it is often extremely difficult for a person to improve his social status and to rise above the social class to which he was born. Barriers to upward mobility are part of the social structure and thus part of the environment or reality around us.

Figure 3-6. This Project to Excite Potential (PEP) helps to bridge the gap between different socioeconomic classes. PEP introduced young people from disadvantaged urban areas to the culture of a rural private college. (Photo courtesy of Skidmore College.)

Social class in the United States today is defined mainly in terms of the amount and source of income, education, occupation, and family status. The smallest class, in numbers about 1 or 2 percent of the population, is the upper class or the elite group which is comparable to the aristocracy in most other countries. Inherited wealth has been in the family for several generations as in the case of such prominent families as the Kennedys, Roosevelts, Rockefellers, Fords, and Hearsts. The lower-upper class is made up of equally wealthy families but they have less social prestige because the family's wealth has been acquired in the last generation or two, and thus they lack a history of social prominence. Income in the upper classes comes from investments rather than salaries or wages.

The middle class in our society includes the broad range of occupations from white-collar workers with low salaries to business and professional people with considerable education and high salaries. This is often further defined as lower-middle class and upper-middle class on the basis of living standards. The middle classes generally regard success in terms of upward mobility as highly desirable.

The largest social class in our society, making up about 50 percent of the population, is regarded as the working class. This group includes those skilled and semiskilled wage earners who are more stable and less concerned with social status than the lower-middle class. Working-class people, particularly those represented by labor unions, often earn more money and have less education than middle class, but their opportunities for social advancement are more limited. The truck driver with less than a high-school education may earn more money than a bank clerk with a college education but the difference is that the bank clerk expects to become an executive while the truck driver expects to continue driving trucks.

The lower class, including unskilled and seasonal workers, tends to be more transient, migratory, and less stable than any other group in our society. Inadequacies in the physical and psychological environment of people born into the lower class in our society make it difficult, and sometimes impossible, for them to realize their potentialities.

Psychological results of social class membership are quite profound. Members of different social classes tend to differ in their views of the world as a result of the amount and kinds of education, travel, and entertainment they experience. They also differ in political and economic attitudes, child-rearing practices, and ideas of correct and proper behavior. Religious beliefs and practices, values and ideals, are all related to the subculture of one's social class within the broad social structure of society.

The position and role or function an individual serves within a society determines the pattern of privileges and obligations that influence his behavior. Within any social class the roles of mother, father, teacher, doctor, policeman, neighbor, landlord, student, barber, banker, salesman, lawyer, mechanic, clergyman, and many others are assigned positions of relative importance or social prestige. Very often external factors such as neighborhood, furniture, automobiles, clothes, jewelry, and other material possessions become extremely important as symbols of successful upward mobility.

Changes in social structure come about very slowly. Some societies are more rigidly structured than ours and some are less so, but all human societies are characterized by some sort of class structure. It is important to recognize those factors within the social structure that are influential in shaping the individual.

Cultural Heritage

Culture refers to the training you get because of your membership in a certain human society. The society's attitudes, beliefs, customs, and traditions are handed down from each generation to the next, not through the biological mechanisms of heredity, but through environmental pressures and expectations. Ideal patterns of conduct, standards of behavior, habitual life plans, accepted beliefs that have become customs and traditions are all part of your *cultural heritage*. When you conform to the culture patterns of your society you gain recognition, acceptance, and approval. When you do not conform you may be subjected to ridicule, rejection, and even punishment. Your cultural heritage consists of those indirect forces from the environment that help to shape you into the person you will become.

The American cultural pattern is different in several ways from other societies existing in today's world. It sets certain ideals and expectations which are sometimes in conflict and difficult to resolve. Our cultural heritage in America stresses competition: we teach our children to be self-reliant, to stand on their own feet and get ahead, to seek status, prestige, and power. We uphold the democratic ideal that hard work and individual effort are the best ways to get ahead.

Our cultural heritage stresses faith in material progress: technological advances have greater value than humanitarian goals (the scientist has higher prestige than the minister), as we strive for greater mastery over the environment. We teach fair play and stress the principle that honesty is the best policy, but a child soon learns that being tactful is often better than being completely honest and straightforward. Our culture teaches us to value human life by making it a crime punishable by death or life imprisonment, to kill another person. Yet in times of war it becomes a duty to kill our fellow man.

American culture includes a predetermined life plan which goes something like this: an individual must overcome his dependency, develop basic skills, learn how to behave appropriately, choose educational and occupational goals, prepare for work, select a mate, raise a family, and be a good citizen. Environmental pressures operate to enforce conformity to this cultural pattern although a wide latitude of individual behavior is tolerated within this general plan.

The life tasks imposed on the members of an organized society are examined in greater detail in Chapter 7.

INTERACTION OF FORCES

Which human characteristics are inherited and which ones are acquired as a result of forces from the environment? This question is frequently asked by the beginning student of human behavior and for many years it was the subject of heated controversy and extensive scientific study. Recent developments in the science of genetics have made it possible to resolve the conflict by demonstrating the fact that *all* human characteristics are a result of the complex interaction of heredity and environment through time.

When a human being is conceived, it has the proper genes to determine the production of a body with arms, legs, head, hair, face, eyes, and all other essential features of a human infant. However, it must have the proper environment in the mother's uterus in order to develop into a new individual. If the genes are defective the organism that develops may not be normal (stillborn, blind, crippled, or deformed), and if the prenatal environment does not supply the necessary physical and chemical materials the growing organism may be defective in spite of its hereditary potentials carried by the genes.

The interaction of hereditary potential and environmental forces begins with conception and continues until death. Any combination of genes without the proper environment cannot produce an organism, and no environment can produce an organism without the necessary hereditary potential. This principle also applies to the physical and psychological characteristics a human individual develops over a period of time. To illustrate how hereditary and environmental forces interact through time let us consider some examples.

German measles is a fairly common and rather mild disease for most humans, including pregnant women, but it can be severely damaging to an unborn child. Blindness, deafness, mental retardation, and a number of other defects are associated with this disease. The kind of defect a child will suffer depends upon the stage of development of the embryo at the time of the mother's measles. If the embryo is at the stage when eyes are developing, a defect in the structure of the eyes may result; if the ears are developing at the time of the mother's illness the child's hearing may be defective, and so on. Toxic substances in the mother's bloodstream are part of the environment that influences the developing embryo.

The interaction of heredity and environment is most obvious in the behavior of minority groups in this country during the past decade. Consider, for example, a potentially brilliant black youth living in Newark, New Jersey at the time of the ghetto outburst in 1967. At that time Newark was 62 percent nonwhite in population and the unemployment rate was three times that of the national average (Hayden, 1967). If our bright young man was employed at all, he was likely to have a less skilled and less secure job than he would have held had his hereditary potentials included a white skin. Because of his capacity for greater accomplishment than the environment allowed, he would be more inclined to be dissatisfied with conditions which were oppressive for himself and for his fellow human beings. If he joined his neighbors in an organized protest against unfair conditions and economic deprivation, he could easily become the victim of antiriot measures by police or be one of the 1400 people arrested in the rebellion. The interaction of this young man's hereditary potentials and his environmental influences will continue to determine his characteristics as his personality develops over his lifetime.

SUMMARY

Many of the forces that shape the individual are present at conception and begin to operate immediately. Not only the hereditary potentials, but life circumstances of the parents, and their feelings about the new child-to-be, will influence what the new individual will be like.

Conception occurs when the nucleus of a sperm cell joins with the nucleus of an egg cell and the 46 chromosomes needed for reproduction are joined in a single cell. This single cell develops into the millions of specialized cells that constitute a newborn infant in about 270 days. The factor for sex type of the child is carried in the chromosomes. When more than one egg cell is fertilized multiple births may result. Fraternal twins result from two different cells, but when only one cell is fertilized and splits into two soon after conception identical twins are produced. If the cell is only partially split the result may be siamese twins.

During the prenatal period (from conception to birth) the growing individual is highly susceptible to influence by any changes in the blood chemistry of his mother. By the time an infant is born he has developed reflexes and has matured enough to function as a biologically independent being, although he is quite helpless and dependent on others for satisfaction of his needs.

Heredity is the means by which certain characteristics are transmitted from one generation to another. The 23 chromosomes in the nucleus of the sex cells contain thousands of smaller units called genes which function in complex ways to create specific characteristics. Two conditions based on genetic factors that may have serious consequences for a newborn child are the Rh blood factor and the metabolic disorder called PKU. Heredity sets the limits and determines potentialities but environmental factors are instrumental in determining how much of one's potentiality will become actual.

Maturation is the systematic process of growth change in which hereditary potentials develop within a favorable environment. Maturation follows rather clearly defined stages at a rate that varies with individuals. The pattern of growth is from simple to complex, from head to toe, and from center to edge as the maturing organism achieves integration. Skills that are dependent upon maturation are not appreciably improved by early or intense training.

Environment includes all those forces outside the individual himself that influence his growth, development, behavior, and realization of potentialities. The physical environment provides opportunities and sets limits on the variety of experiences available to an individual. Psychological environment includes those feelings, attitudes, and expectations of other people that create an emotional climate or atmosphere within which an individual must live and learn.

The social structure of society is an influential part of the environment. Social class in the United States today is defined in terms of income, education, occupation, and family status. Social classes differ in their views of the world, political and economic attitudes, child-rearing practices, and standards of behavior.

Cultural heritage refers to those ideals and accepted beliefs that have become customs and traditions handed down from each generation to the next through environmental pressures and expectations. The American cultural pattern stresses competition, independence, faith in material progress, and a predetermined life plan. Some of our cultural ideals appear to be in conflict with each other, causing difficult problems for individuals to resolve.

The interaction of heredity, maturation, and environment is continuous from conception until death, shaping the individual into the person he is. We do not inherit behavior patterns, except for simple reflexes, but we do inherit the capacity to learn. How and what we learn is the subject of the next chapter.

SUGGESTIONS FOR FURTHER READING

Brackbill, Yvonne and Thompson, George C., *Behavior in Infancy and Early Childhood*, New York, Free Press, 1967. A book of readings selected from the wide range of studies and observations of young humans.

Deutsch, Martin, *The Disadvantaged Child*, New York, Basic Books, 1967. Studies of the psychological and social environments of disadvantaged children and their effects on development and learning.

Deutsch, Martin, Katz, Irwin, and Jensen, Arthur R., *Social Class, Race and Psychological Development*, New York, Holt, Rinehart and Winston, 1968. A review of research dealing with the relative contributions of heredity and environment and their bearings on the issues of social class and racial differences.

Gale, Raymond F., *Developmental Behavior: A Humanistic Approach*, New York, Macmillan, 1969. The major concerns of human growth and development are seen as parts of the total developmental process of an individual.

Spuhler, J. N. (Ed.), *Genetic Diversity and Human Behavior*, Chicago, Ill., Aldine, 1967. Reports of recent studies dealing with new behaviors and pathologies linked to genetic abnormalities.

How We Change and Adapt through Learning

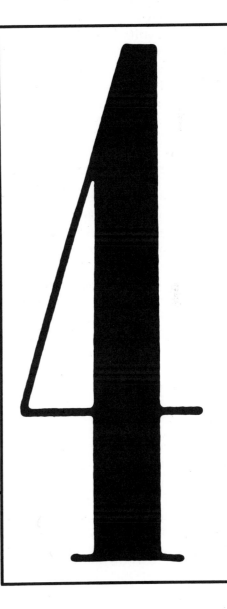

We have seen how people differ from one another both in terms of hereditary potentials and in opportunity to realize their inborn potentialities. The process by which self-awareness and actualization takes place is called learning. Most human infants behave in similar ways in response to their environment at first, but the older they get the more their behavior changes and becomes individually characteristic of them. Learning is the process by which behavior is changed as a result of experience. Heredity sets the limits of our capacity to learn; a supportive environment permits the maturation necessary for learning; and experience provides the exposure, stimulation, training, and practice that determines what we learn. All our skills, knowledge, attitudes, opinions, ideals, and values are a result of learning. We learn to become what we are, and with learning we are able to change and adjust to the world around us. In the science of behavior the study of learning occupies a position of central importance.

HOW LEARNING TAKES PLACE

Exactly how does learning occur? We have some theories but we have very few proven facts about the internal processes that make learning possible. We know that the changes in behavior we call learning depend upon association and some kind of connection in the brain and nervous system, but the actual biochemical nature of the learning process remains a challenge for future scientific investigators. At the present time our understanding of how learning occurs is based primarily on the study of events that happen outside the individual and his responses to them. However, since learning is a process which we can observe in part, it can be studied without complete understanding of its structural basis.

Conditioning

Much of what we learn is acquired through a process called *conditioning*. Habits are behaviors that are learned by conditioning and can occur without our necessarily being aware of it. The strength of our conditioned learnings is such that we may find it hard, at times almost impossible, to behave in any other way.

Conditioning depends upon the formation of associations between stimuli and responses. A *stimulus* (S) is any object, event, energy, or energy change that produces a response. Stimuli may be external such as other people, physical objects, or forms of physical energy (light and sound waves). Stimuli may be internal, from within our own body, such as neural impulses, glandular functions, or states of physical need (hunger, thirst, rest). A *response* (R) is any activity of an organism. Human responses may take the form of neural, muscular, or glandular action and be expressed in activities like thinking, talking, or crying.

The associations between stimuli and responses that become conditioned may occur quite incidentally or as a result of deliberate effort. However they first occur, these associations become fixed and gain strength through a process of *reinforcement*.

Reinforcement, to be effective, must be repeated and have some reward value. The number of times a reinforcement must be repeated before conditioned learning occurs will vary greatly depending upon what is being learned. The reward value of a reinforcement may consist of obtaining something we want (toys, money, or praise) or it may consist of avoiding something we do not want (pain, punishment, or ridicule).

The Russian physiologist, Ivan Pavlov, conducting research with dogs, observed and reported the first, or *classical*, form of conditioned learning. Pavlov's experiment began by placing food powder in the mouth of a dog causing the dog to salivate. Salivating when food is placed in the mouth is not a learned response for dogs or humans but a natural reflex action. Pavlov then introduced a new stimulus. Just before putting the food in the dog's mouth a bell was sounded. When these events, bell ringing and food in the mouth, had been repeated a number of times the dog eventually began to salivate at the sound of the bell alone. The dog had learned a new association between a bell ringing and food in the mouth (stimuli) and would salivate (response) to either (Figure 4-1).

This new learning Pavlov called *conditional* to distinguish it as something acquired and not naturally present in behavior (Pavlov, 1903. 1927). Neither dogs nor humans salivate naturally to the sound of bells. Classical conditioning is really a process of stimulus substitution. Some new stimulus (a bell) which ordinarily will not produce a given response (salivation) is associated with a stimulus (food in mouth) that can produce that response and in time comes to substitute for it. The elements of classical conditioning are illustrated in Figure 4-2. What was the reinforcement that made this conditioned association between stimuli and response possible? The reinforcement was the food in the mouth (reward) and the repeated pairings of the bell sounding before the food was given.

After the dog had been conditioned to the sound of the bell Pavlov observed

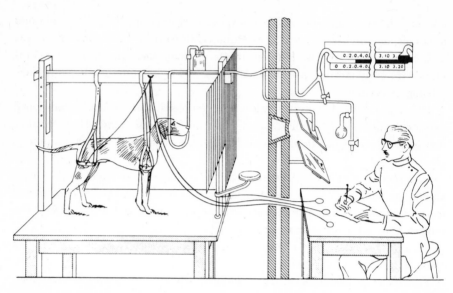

Figure 4-1.　Diagram showing Pavlov's dog and the apparatus used to demonstrate classical conditioning. (Pavlov, 1928.)

that other sounds of similar tone would also cause the dog to salivate. Pavlov called this spreading of the association to other similar stimuli the principle of *generalization*. Not only could the dog learn to respond to a new stimulus (bell), but he would respond to other new stimuli like it (buzzer or gong). Finally, Pavlov observed that if the sound of the bell or other new stimuli was not followed at some time by food in the mouth (reinforcement), the dog would salivate less and less and then not at all. What had been learned could be unlearned. Pavlov called this the principle of *extinction*, the disappearance of a conditioned response when reinforcement was not given.

Many human behaviors are learned by conditioning of the classical type. The development of language behavior is one such conditioned learning. The sounds the child makes in the presence of an object (mother) or event (being fed) become associated with these stimuli. As these sounds are repeated they are gradually shaped into words and are effective in helping the child express and meet his needs (reinforcement).

Most of our fears are acquired by conditioning. Watson and Rayner (1920) demonstrated how an infant could learn to fear a white rat if it was presented to him just before a loud, sudden noise was made. Fear and unpleasant emotional feelings are the natural response to loud, sudden noises. The sound which caused the child to be afraid was associated by the child with the white rat. When the child saw the rat again, in the absence of the loud noise, he showed signs of fear and emotional distress. The investigators observed that the child also showed fear of other white, furry objects (generalization) such as a towel, a toy, and a man's beard. Extinction of the child's fear was accomplished by presenting the rat many times in the absence of loud, sudden noises and by a process of *reconditioning*. The reconditioning was done by pairing the feared object (rat) with stimuli that already had safe and pleasant associations (mother, feeding time).

We rarely recognize the origin of our acquired fears because most of them are conditioned in childhood by the incidental pairing of stimuli. Our *preference* responses are acquired in the same way. The stimuli present when we feel safe, happy, and comfortable become associated with our good feeling and we like them and seek them. A child's attachment to a particular object (blanket, toy)

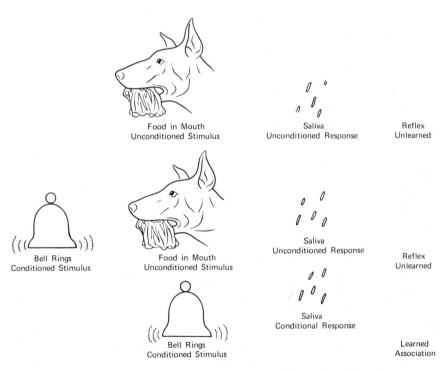

Figure 4-2.   Diagram showing the elements of classical conditioning.

like his attachment to persons (mother, father) is a conditioned preference response.

A child treated badly by his parents develops negative associations to them. These attitudes may generalize to other adults (teachers, employers). The strength of these negative attitudes about adults may be so strong that when others try to treat him well he will act in ways to provoke them. If they retaliate by treating him badly (as his parents did) they reinforce his negative response. This may account for the obvious fact that punishment does not seem to reform criminal personalities. Punishment only reinforces already negative attitudes. Society might realize greater value from its penal institutions if extinction and reconditioning programs were substituted for confinement and punishment. In recent years we have seen a trend in this direction.

Another kind of conditioning involving similar principles was observed and reported by the American psychologist, B. F. Skinner. This kind of conditioning is called *operant.* Operant conditioning begins with some response that the organism makes that leads to a satisfying state of affairs. This satisfying state of affairs is the reinforcement because it causes the behavior to be repeated.

Skinner's original experiments were done with rats (Skinner, 1938). A rat was placed in a box with a lever and a food tray. At first, the rat explored the box, sniffed at the lever and food tray, and engaged in many random activities. Eventually by some means, usually accidental, the rat depressed the lever and when he did a food pellet was dropped in the tray. After this sequence of events, lever press and appearance of food, the rat began to press the lever rapidly and continued to do so for long periods of time even though he got no more food. Skinner called this operant conditioned learning. The rat had formed an association between his response (operation of lever) and a satisfying state of affairs (appearance of food). The animal repeating the lever-pressing behavior was evidence of the learned association because it had shown little interest in the lever until pressing it was followed by the appearance of the food. The elements of operant conditioning are illustrated in Figure 4-3. You use operant conditioning when you teach a dog to do "tricks." When the animal makes a response in the desired direction (sitting up or rolling over) you reinforce it with food or praise and the animal repeats the behavior.

Classical conditioning is an association between a natural stimulus and a new or substitute stimulus. Operant conditioning is an association between a response and the stimuli events that follow it. Like the classical form, operant conditioned learning will generalize from the stimuli present in the learning situation to other stimuli that are similar. Operant conditioning, unlike classical,

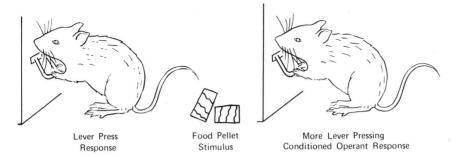

Lever Press
Response

Food Pellet
Stimulus

More Lever Pressing
Conditioned Operant Response

Figure 4-3.   Diagram showing the elements of operant conditioning.

requires very little reinforcement. The rat continued to press the lever many times for only the one food pellet. For this reason, operant conditioned behavior is very difficult to extinguish. Operant conditioning also has wider application to visible behavior than the classical form because it shapes responses. Salivation is still salivation whether it is in response to food in the mouth or to a bell ringing. Classical conditioning is therefore limited to only those responses that are made naturally to some stimulus. Lever-pressing is a response that rats do not make naturally to any stimulus. Lever-pressing by rats is a new response, a novel behavior. Operant conditioning is a method of learning new responses in animals and humans.

Examples of operant conditioning in human behavior are numerous. One example is easily seen in slot-machine behavior. People put money into and pull the handle on a slot machine until they are broke or their arms become too painful to move, for some very irregular reinforcement of a few coins. Addiction to alcohol or drugs can be understood by operant conditioning. Some people under the influence of alcohol or drugs experience a sense of power, security, or confidence that they otherwise lack. In order to maintain this satisfying state of affairs they continue to use alcohol or drugs. You cannot tell an alcoholic or drug addict that this behavior is not good for them because they know how it makes them *feel*. How they feel is the reinforcement for their behavior. To alter addicted behavior learned by operant conditioning the reinforcement must be withheld or new associations for the response (feeling bad rather than good) must be formed.

Skinner has applied the techniques of operant conditioning to the development of teaching machines. The child's correct responses on a teaching machine are reinforced by words or signs of praise and an opportunity to go on to newer, more challenging material. Incorrect responses on teaching machines are followed by a statement as to why the response is not correct and another approach is made to the same material. Figures 4-4 and 4-5 illustrate some of the new teaching machines that have proven to be highly efficient tools for learning.

Classical and operant conditioning are considered elementary learning methods because they can occur with little or no awareness or effort on the part of an individual. While elementary in form, your conditioned responses are of great significance to your lives because they shape many of your attitudes, emotions, and social behavior.

Conditioning is an important learning process but it does not provide an adequate explanation for all learning. You do not merely respond to your external environment, but you learn how to deal with your environment in

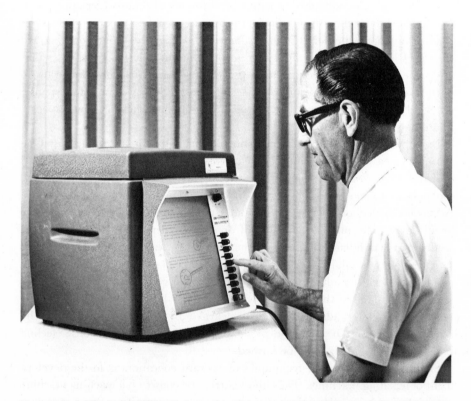

Figure 4-4. The "Auto-Tutor" shown here is one type of teaching machine that makes use of the principles of conditioning. (Photo by Shirley I. Fisher.)

Figure 4-5.   Another type of teaching machine which is highly efficient in the teaching of language skills to handicapped people. (New York State Mental Hygiene photo by Julian Belin.)

terms of past experience. We humans are not only the subjects of conditioning but we are problem-solvers as well.

Problem-Solving

Problem-solving differs from conditioning in that it requires some effort on the part of an individual if learning is to occur. The basic method used in problem solving is called "trial and error." When you are faced with a problem you wish to solve, you must try several possible solutions before you find one that will solve the problem, you are using the trial-and-error method. This method of learning is characterized by recognizing a problem, varying the approach to the problem, attempting solutions, discarding errors, and repeating efforts that are closer to a successful solution. Like conditioning, trial-and-error learning involves reinforcement. Efforts that seem to bring you closer to success are reinforcing and will be repeated while errors or faulty solutions will be eliminated.

Problem-solving may be aided by help from other people. Guidance by a more experienced person can help you to recognize potentially successful approaches to problem-solving and reduce the time and effort spent on errors. The actual learning is an individual process, but it can be aided by guidance to help develop understanding and increase awareness of possibilities.

The experience you gain from problem-solving makes future problem-solving easier because you are able to make use of what you have previously learned to avoid making the same mistakes again. In a sense, you learn how to learn by learning. You develop learning *sets* or expectations. Study habits are a form of learning set. The more you study the better you get at studying.

The more experience you have in learning the more learning sets you develop. What happens is that you learn to apply certain hypotheses to the solving of new problems on the basis of what has been successful for you in the past. Much of our behavior becomes habitual in this way, and sometimes these learning sets get in the way of new learning. You can miss a simple, easier solution to a problem by relying too much on your old habitual pattern of approach. Older people often become very rigid in their thinking and find it difficult to accept new ways of doing things. Flexibility is important in problem-solving in order to avoid missing the shortcuts and overcomplicating your problems.

Imitation and Identification

We learn a great deal by copying the behavior of other people. When you are faced with an unfamiliar stress situation you will usually look around to see what others are doing and act accordingly. Sometimes this occurs without our conscious awareness and at other times it is deliberate. Children imitate the behavior of people they see on television and in movies. They also learn by imitating parents and trying to be like them. Younger children imitate older ones in both acceptable and unacceptable behavior. A considerable amount of children's play is imitative in nature, dramatizing the roles they have observed in others. The different dialects in the same language are learned by imitation of the speech of the people with whom we associate.

The people children choose to imitate are very important to them, because they are the models that children pattern themselves after. Your children not only copy your behavior and try to act like you, but they try to look like you, think like you, and feel like you because they respect and admire you. Children learn to share the attitudes, opinions, and preferences of their parents through this process of identification beginning in early childhood. Later, in adolescence, we see a changing trend toward peer group identification and the young person learns by imitating others in his own age group (Figure 4-6).

Figure 4-6.   Young children usually love to play "grown up" and to imitate adults as we see with this "little lady" who has won the prize for halloween costumes. (Photo by Jim Sargent.)

Use of Symbols

Conditioning, trial and error, and imitation characterize animal as well as human learning. The method that is unique to man involves manipulation of symbols. A symbol is something that stands for something else. One of the important symbol systems we learn is language. This *verbal symbol system* is made up of letters of the alphabet combined into words.

Some symbols are very specific, such as the word "dog," and others are more general, such as the word "animal." The symbols that are more general

Figure 4-7. Symbolic learning, illustrated here, provides a child the basic tools he must have to succeed in school. (New York State Mental Hygiene photo by Julian Belin.)

and refer to a group of objects, operations, or relationships are called *concepts*. "Tables," "chairs," "beds" are word symbols of familiar objects. "Furniture" is a word symbol, but it is also a concept because it stands for a group of objects (tables, chairs, beds). "Uncle" is a word symbol that is also a concept of relationship standing for all brothers of one's mother or father. The word symbol "mix" is also a concept of operation because it means to put everything together in combination. The ability to use symbols and concepts makes our thought processes rapid and efficient.

The intellectual learning of childhood is a gradual task of acquiring symbols, concepts, and their meanings. The first concepts to be acquired are for objects (shoe, bird), then for spatial forms (circle, square), next probably colors, and later for numbers (Heidbreder et al., 1948). This early symbolic learning is achieved by ages 5–7 years. What has not been achieved at the time of school entry will probably be mastered in the first year or two of school. These first symbolic learnings become the basis from which our ability to deal with complex ideas develops.

There are other symbol systems in our experience. Numbers and their operational signs ($+$, $-$, $\times$, $\div$) are symbols. Music has a symbol system (staff, bar, and flats) and so does art (religious forms, flag). There are symbols of everyday use such as traffic signs, operational signs, directional signs, and danger signs that add safety and efficiency to our lives. Finally, there is a motor symbol system we call *nonverbal cues*. The nonverbal cues are familiar gestures, expressions, and postures that we have learned through experience mean particular ideas or emotions without anything being said. The raised eyebrow, the clenched fist, the thunb down, the slumped shoulder or hung head all convey their message.

Symbols to be useful must convey meaning and their meaning must be understood. Musical symbols mean nothing to a person who does not read notes. Symbols are learned by conditioning, by trial and error, and by formal instruction. Symbols are the shorthand of thought because they stand for something else. Using symbols we can think about the objects (chair, book), operations (lift, push), or relationships (north, south) they stand for without these things being present. Symbols make it possible to recall things from the past or imagine them in the future. How limited our thought processes would be if the only time we could think about a thing was when it was present.

WHAT WE LEARN

Almost all human behavior is learned. Even those relatively simple patterns of unlearned reflex behavior can be modified by learning. As we grow and develop from the helpless dependency of infancy toward the mature responsibility of adulthood we are continually learning new ways to satisfy our own needs in harmony with the changing demands of our environment. We learn what our potentialities are and how to make them become actual. We learn who we are and what we are, what we can do, and what we can be. We learn to become more competent in dealing with our surroundings by acquiring basic skills which prepare us for more complex learning. We learn physical, emotional, social, and intellectual behavior at the same time, and we will see how all this learning influences the development of our self-concept.

Motor Skills

Motor learning involves increased integration and coordination of nervous and muscular systems. The child's ability to feed himself with a spoon requires his control over large and small muscles of the head, trunk, arm, and hand, integration of neural impulses for these muscle actions, and eye–hand coordination.

Some motor learning, as we have seen, begins even before birth. The movements of the child in the uterus are the beginnings of motor patterns that will be refined with greater precision and behavioral significance after birth. Motor learning is rapid during infancy and childhood, reaches its peak during adolescence, and tapers off in adulthood. In Table 4-1 are reported some of the components of motor learning and examples of their expression in early and later behavior. There are many forms of motor behavior that involve more than a single component including, for example, marksmanship, reading, swimming, and gymnastics.

Most of our motor learnings are acquired by trial and error. Activities like walking, handwriting, playing a musical instrument, driving a car, and using utensils and other tools are learned by trial and error. Sport and recreational skills such as golf, swimming, dancing, bowling, and skating are mastered only after much trial and error. We are reinforced as we attempt these motor learnings by the progress we make in our efforts. We also receive reinforcement in the greater freedom, enjoyment, or approval that mastery of these skills provide.

Locomotor skills are dependent on neuromuscular maturation. When a child has reached the required maturational level he will begin to walk and further practice will bring improvement and finally success. Marked improvements in other motor skills such as reaching, grasping, self-feeding, and handling objects will also be expected by the end of his second year. Learning to walk is an important milestone in a child's life because it affects all other aspects of his development. Walking enables the child to explore the world around him and to increase his contact with people and with things. The young child's ability to walk will create some problems for his parents because his ability to get into mischief will be ahead of his judgment or awareness of danger. The child who has just learned to walk, run, and climb is a high risk for accidents.

After a child has learned to walk alone his progress in other motor skills will depend more on opportunity than it did previously. Most children can learn to run, jump, climb, skate, swim, and throw a ball by the time they are 5 years

Table 4-1. Components of Motor Learning and Behavioral Samples[a]

Component	Early behavior	Later behavior
Locomotor (trunk and legs)	Creeping Crawling Walking Running Jumping	Dancing Marching (drill team) Skating Speed and distance running Soccer and other sports
Manual (arm and hand)	Reaching Pulling Lifting Holding Guiding Throwing Catching	Building trades Large mechanical operation Large machine repair Cooking Golf and baseball
Manipulation (hand and finger)	Grasping Guiding Rotating Placing Pressing	Typewriter, telegraph, keypunch operation Musical instrument operation Assembly tasks Fine repair (jewelry) Sewing Sculpture
Graphic (eye and hand)	Centering Sizing Copying Creating	Painting Handwriting Printing Drawing Drafting and design Arts and crafts
Verbal (lips and tongue)	Talking Singing	Broadcasting Public speaking Political activity Dramatic arts Teaching Vocal skills
Expressive (face, limbs, and trunk)	Posture Gestures Smiling Laughing	Social skills Dramatic arts Modern dance

[a]G. L. Hutchins (1967).

old, if given the opportunity and encouragement. Motor skills are also important in such activities as drawing, writing, dancing, and playing a musical instrument.

As motor skills become well-established children tend to combine physical activities with social and intellectual activities. The acquisition of satisfactory motor abilities is very important to the social adjustment of children, and even more so for boys than for girls. Speed, strength, coordination, and endurance in motor activities will usually enhance a child's social status and acceptability among his peers (age mates). Children with serious deficiencies in motor skills often suffer social rejection and psychological maladjustment.

From early childhood into the adult years an individual's self-concept is influenced by his perception of his body, his strength, control, and skill in physical activities. Motor achievement is probably less important to adults in today's highly complex society than in the past, but it still plays a crucial role in the psychological development of children.

Emotional Behavior

Emotional behavior has at least four different aspects: (*a*) physiological changes in heart rate, respiration, and glandular secretions; (*b*) distinct patterns of central nervous system activity; (*c*) the kind of overt behavior that is labeled emotional, including smiling, crying, and thrashing about; and (*d*) subjective feelings of love, fear, anger, etc. which are sometimes called *affect*.

The young infant will respond with intense emotional behavior to pain, loud noises, and loss of support (being dropped), on the basis of reflex action. The experiment with the child and the white rat already cited shows how fear can be conditioned to a previously neutral stimulus. Other emotional behavior is likewise acquired by conditioning. As a child grows older he learns to recognize and describe his feelings in the terms used by the people around him. He learns how to express and how to control emotional behavior. Emotions will be discussed more fully in Chapter 5.

Social Learning

Before an infant is 2 years old he begins to recognize the demands of socialization. Parents begin to impose restrictions on his behavior and he must learn to act in accord with what is socially acceptable. One of the first major sources of frustration to the child is toilet-training. He has to learn bowel and bladder control and to take responsibility for his own care in this regard. Experts agree that toilet-training should not be started before the child's neuromuscular development is mature enough that he can understand what is expected of him and can communicate his needs. Bowel control is learned much more easily after the child is 18–20 months old, although recent studies indicate that most mothers begin bowel training at between 9 and 14 months (Mussen, Conger, and Kagan, 1969). Research suggests that toilet-training which is too severe or started too early may be responsible for later personality and behavior problems. The child's concept of himself and his self-esteem are learned as a result of his interaction with his social environment. It is obvious that the child who is shamed, punished, and rejected for his failures in toilet-training is more apt to develop feelings of unworthiness and inferiority.

Socialization of the child includes training in eating habits, table manners, cleanliness, temper control, and sharing with others. Social growth is quite rapid during the preschool years as children progress from solitary play to cooperative play with their peers.

We use trial and error in our social learning as we develop relationships with others and practice social roles. One advantage of participation in extra-curricular school activities is the opportunity we have to try out new roles and their responsibilities. Social codes of etiquette and manners are learned by trial and error and by imitation. One can read books on the social graces, but a satisfying performance results only after practice in a social situation.

Social learning involves the development of complex relationships with other persons that have affectional, friendship, authority, occupational, and other importance. Social learning also includes an understanding and capacity to perform certain expected behaviors called *roles*. Among the more important social roles we learn are the masculine–feminine, marital, parental, and occupational. Social learning in terms of relationships and roles is essential to mastery of the life tasks (Chapter 7) and successful personality adjustment.

Social learning begins at birth with the family as models; later, extensions of these models are found in the school, neighborhood, and world-at-large. Social learning continues for most people throughout their lives. As we and the world around us change we have to learn new relationships and roles.

Language and Intellectual Learning

Language refers to the set of symbols humans use to communicate with each other. Language skills include the ability to speak, to write, to read, and to understand the meaning of what is being said. Children who fail to develop language skills are seriously handicapped in modern social living. The ability to benefit from formal education is dependent upon the achievement of basic language skills in early childhoods.

An infant uses cries, grunts, and other sounds to communicate with others long before he has any use of words. He also uses gestures, pointing, reaching, and bodily movements to indicate acceptance or rejection. Language development tends to parallel motor development in its dependence on maturation, but only for the production of speech sounds. The child begins to babble at about the same time he is able to sit alone, and he usually speaks his first word at about the time he is first able to stand alone. The development of speech also depends on the development of teeth. The child's ability to understand words and sentences will initially be much greater than his ability to produce words. The child can usually understand more than he can express. A child's early progress in speech formation is related to emotional factors, particularly to the affection and attention he receives from adults (Jersild, 1960).

When a child has mastered verbal communication and has attained adequate emotional maturity he is ready to begin school. The first few years of school place great emphasis on developing language skills. Maturation is again crucial to the child's readiness for reading and writing. Girls tend to mature somewhat faster than boys in the first six years and they have fewer problems with speech and reading. Reading readiness is based in part upon the ability to recognize similarities and differences in language forms and the capacity for attention and concentration.

Another type of learning is intellectual, the capacity to deal with increasingly complex ideas and relationships. Intellectual learning is dependent upon language development and reading skills. The basic components of thought are words, symbols, ideas, and relationships. The child will learn first to say numbers and then to understand ideas of oneness, twoness, etc. Later, he will learn operations like addition, subtraction, multiplication, and finally he will be able to work with a complex thought system like algebra. In Table 4-2 are reported some of the intellectual skills expected of individuals at different ages of development.

For many persons intellectual learning is confined to the years of school attendance. Formal education, however, is not the only means by which intellectual learning can occur, just as it is no guarantee that it will occur. All kinds of learning are limited by the capacity of the individual to profit from his experience. This capacity we call *intelligence* and, as we will see in Chapter 6, individuals differ in how much of this trait they possess. Some people do not

Table 4-2. Intellectual Skills Typical at Different Ages[a]

Skill	Age level (years)
Follows simple instructions (give, put, take, hold)	2
Executes simple eye–hand tasks (sort, stack)	3
Understands general relationships (likeness, differentness, opposites)	4
Understands simple categories (defines objects by use "to eat" or class "clothes")	5
Understands numbers and simple number operations (oneness, twoness; add, subtract)	6
Understands subtle relationships (absurdities, analogies)	7
Recognizes and recalls parts of whole situations (can give details of story heard)	8
Uses words and numbers purposefully (makes rhymes, makes change)	9
Understands complex ideas (finds reasons, gives explanations)	10

[a]Adapted from Terman and Merrill (1960).

benefit as much from formal educational experience as do others but they may learn a great deal by more informal and immediate experiences.

Trial and error is a common method of intellectual learning. We do not always see immediately what the teacher is trying to illustrate. We must search in our past experience for a similar relationship or try a new approach of our own to grasp the idea. Reading and spelling are intellectual skills achieved largely through trial and error. The scientist puzzled by the outcome of his experiment uses trial and error to find a satisfactory solution.

Just as the various kinds of learning are not independent of intelligence they are also not independent of one another. Motor and intellectual learning must develop closely together to make skills like reading and writing possible. Much social learning begins in childhood through participation in play and games and these skills depend on motor and intellectual development. The activities of adult life, (for example, the performance of the occupational role) will require motor, social, and intellectual learning.

Conscience and Moral Values

Conscience is made up of the moral ideas, standards, and values by which a person judges right from wrong and holds himself obligated to think, feel, and act in accordance with his knowledge of right and wrong. Conscience is also called *superego* and is described as that part of the personality which exerts control over the impulses. As soon as a child is able to understand the meaning of "do" and "don't," he begins to learn moral standards and to develop concepts of right and wrong. When a child who has done something he knows is wrong experiences a feeling of guilt instead of a fear of punishment his conscience has started to function.

Moral standards are learned by the process of imitation and identification. As the child strives to make himself as much like his parents as possible he accepts the parental standards and values as his own in order to strengthen his identification with them. Once he has learned right from wrong and accepted these standards as his own, the child feels guilty or disapproving of himself whenever he does something for which he believes his parents would punish him or disapprove of him. Thus, the values of his parents become *internalized* (taken into the self) as a part of the child's personality through the process of identification.

There is a close relationship between the child's development of moral values and his concept of self. The child is usually confronted with *"don't"* do this or that many times before he begins to learn what sorts of things he should *do*. If his behavior meets with disapproval and is regarded as bad most of the time he may begin to consider himself as a person who is all bad. When he begins to learn what he ought to do and should do he begins to formulate ideals and aspirations which can cause him guilt if he is unable to live up to them.

The young child's moral judgments and values are determined by his parents' influence at first, but with increasing age the influence of parents declines. His concept of his own "ideal self" and his conscience begin to take shape in the preschool years. He learns to value honesty, kindness, loyalty, fair play, respect for human life and the property of others, as well as the particular values of his family and his social group. The way in which an individual uses or interprets these moral values in his own daily living determines his character.

Character development is a complex process because the growing child is repeatedly confronted with conflicting impulses and influences. What his parents preach and what they practice may not be the same, or the child may find that what he is taught at home is in conflict with what he learns at school. Each generation tends to modify the interpretation of good and bad behavior and to demand less restraint.

The child who develops a consistent set of moral standards has the advantage of avoiding indecision, and will not be caught in a situation of having to decide what he should or should not do as each opportunity for action presents itself. As he grows older his values are helpful in planning for the future and setting desirable goals to work toward.

By the time an individual reaches adolescence his conscience is fairly well-developed, and he is faced with the problems of shifting standards. There may be a conflict between the standards of parents and peers and a choice must be made as to whose acceptance and approval he needs most. Generally speaking, there is a shift of values from the strict, literal, idealistic interpretation of childhood to a more flexible, practical, realistic value system of adulthood. For example, the child may have been taught to accept without qualification the principle that "honesty is the best policy," and he may give his honest opinion about anything without regard for the feelings of others. After he discovers the value of tact in social relations and develops greater sensitivity to people's feelings, this principle may be modified. He will emphasize the positive and withhold the negative or damaging truth in the interest of kindness. Standards for moral conduct and religious beliefs tend to become more abstract and less literal during the adolescent years.

Self-Concept

The infant's first awareness of self occurs when he learns to distinguish his own body from the rest of his surroundings. By the process of touching, pushing, pulling, and pinching, the infant learns the limits of his own physical self as different from the rest of the world. Throughout life our *body image* or how we feel about our physical being is an important part of our *self-concept*.

Within the first few months of life an infant learns to distinguish persons from things. He finds that things do not respond to his needs but persons do. Soon he learns that not all people are the same, some are more responsive to him than others, and some (his mother in particular) are more important to him than others. As he learns what other people expect of him he tries to behave in a way that will win their approval. While the young child is learning all the demands and expectations of the environment he is also developing an awareness of the kind of person he is. Thus the *self-concept* begins as a product of social learning in early childhood.

The self-concept of a child takes shape in response to the rewards and punishments or the approval and disapproval he gets from people who are important to him. If his parents frequently praise and admire him, the child tends to regard himself as praiseworthy and admirable, and he develops a positive self-concept or feeling of self-worth and adequacy. If, on the other hand, his parents more frequently reprimand him, show disapproval, or emphasize his shortcomings, the child will develop feelings of inadequacy, unworthiness, and inferiority, which result in a negative self-concept. If people treat him as a bad child and expect him to behave badly, a child will usually fulfill these expectations because he will learn to regard himself as a bad child. A child's sense of personal worth is a direct result of the way he is treated, judged, and valued by others.

As the young child grows and matures he becomes more aware of himself as an individual and more conscious of the appraisals made of him by others. He also makes his own comparisons of the way he is treated and the way other children are treated. By the time a child enters school he usually has a fairly well-developed self-concept as a result of his awareness of how other people respond to him and evaluate him. As his social contacts increase the child's self-concept is modified, and it continues to change as a result of experience and learning new things about the self in relation to others and the environment.

The self-concept is always subject to change and modification although it becomes less so with advancing age. As our self-concept develops we seek ways to protect it and to enhance it. We develop characteristic ways of defending ourselves against situations that threaten damage to our self-concept or to our self-esteem. For example, we tend to like people who support and confirm our concept of self and we are drawn toward groups whose members and activities contribute to our self-concept in a positive way.

Ego Defenses

Another term for self-concept that has become common in popular usage is *ego*. A person whose ego is strong has a positive self-concept. A person whose ego is weak has a negative self-concept. People are called egotistical when they have an exaggerated sense of self-worth and are self-centered in their behavior. However weak or strong your ego may be you develop mechanisms to protect it from damage and loss of strength. We call these mechanisms the *ego defenses* and they are acquired through learning and experience. When you are faced with problem situations that you cannot solve, your progress toward goals and the satisfaction of your needs are blocked and you feel frustrated. Frustration threatens the ego and generates anxiety because of the potential loss to your self-esteem when you cannot master the problems you face.

It is important that you develop some ego defenses to deal with frustration, but it is also important to be aware of these defenses. The ego defenses can function both consciously and unconsciously and it is possible to rely on them too much. The ego defenses serve to maintain self-respect and self-confidence when you encounter difficult adjustments. However, the ego defenses also enable you to avoid responsibility for your failures and thus limit your ability to face reality. Let us examine some of the more common mechanisms of ego defense.

Rationalization is a process of making up socially acceptable reasons or explanations to substitute for real reasons when you encounter failure, frustration, or threats to your self-esteem. Rationalization is the giving of good reasons rather than real reasons. All of us rationalize to some extent to make ourselves feel better or to appear better to ourselves or to other persons important to us. For example, the student who fails the college entrance exam may rationalize that he did not really want to go to that college anyway. The man fired from his job for poor performance may rationalize that the job was really beneath him, did not inspire his best efforts, and he was intending to look for a better job. The player who does not make the team may rationalize that the coach did not like him, rather than accept the fact that he lacked the needed ability. Some people rationalize failures by feeling that fate is against them or that they are victims of circumstances beyond their control.

Projection is the process of unconsciously attributing to others those qualities which you cannot accept or tolerate in yourself. The person who feels angry and hostile toward authority may perceive authority figures as hostile toward him. Or, he may see other people as hostile toward authority and criticize them for it while denying these same feelings within himself.

Compensation is the process of making up for feelings of inadequacy in one area by developing superior competency in some other area. The student who seeks to find recognition in athletics but fails may turn his efforts toward music, art, or drama. If he has the ability to excel in one of these areas it will serve to compensate him for his frustration in sports. The student who cannot excel in academic studies may compensate by learning social skills and becoming popular. Many people compensate for feelings of social inadequacy by developing unusual hobbies or skills in which there is little competition for attention. Collecting rare or unusual items such as coins, stamps, books, bottles, buttons, and antiques are popular hobbies that provide status and enhance the ego.

Parents who try to compensate for their own failures by pushing their children into unwanted accomplishments often create problems for their children unless the children have similar interests and goals. Another undesirable form of compensation is found in delinquency and criminal behavior. The boy who fails to gain status and recognition in socially acceptable ways may turn to antisocial and aggressive acts to gain attention and acceptance in the delinquent group.

Identification is the process of deriving ego strength from association with another person or group of persons. We have already seen how the child's identification with parents enhances his self-esteem and provides him with moral values. Identification with your family and other groups helps provide status and a feeling of personal worth. Identification is usually a healthy defense unless the individual neglects his own development because of the satisfaction he gets from identification with others.

Withdrawal is the process of escaping frustration by refusing to face it. When people withdraw into daydreams they are defending themselves from anxiety by diverting their attention away from reality. This is not always harmful if it does not become a habit or a way of life. Sometimes the temporary retreat into fantasy or daydreams can provide a new source of energy or a new plan of attack on a difficult problem.

Some people withdraw from the stress and anxiety of everyday life by developing illnesses. They do not really make themselves ill but they become overly sensitive to minor physical disturbances that most people would usually disregard. Lack of interest in life and apathy may also be symptoms of withdrawal tendencies.

Regression is the process of reverting to earlier, less mature forms of behavior in response to frustration and conflict. The most common example of regression is illustrated by the child of 3 or 4 years who reverts to infantile behavior patterns when a new baby is introduced into the family. The older child may compete with the baby for his mother's attention by frequent crying, crawling, and wetting himself even though he has learned to walk and has been toilet-trained. Baby talk in an older child is another frequent form of regressive behavior. Adults of any age may defend themselves against anxiety by regression to an earlier more successful period in their lives. For example, the threat of divorce may cause an adult to revert to irresponsible, adolescent behavior patterns.

Repression is the process by which painful and anxiety-producing ideas and experiences are forgotten or blocked from conscious awareness. Repression is the most harmful of the defense mechanisms because though kept from conscious awareness, repressed thoughts and feelings continue to influence behavior. Repression of thoughts, feelings, or painful experiences contributes to the development of phobias, compulsions, and other emotional and mental illnesses described in Chapter 9. Children should not be taught to repress feelings and forget fears, but rather they should be helped to recognize their needs and find socially acceptable ways to satisfy them.

Whether the defenses just described will function as a help or a hindrance to the ego will depend upon how they are used and how much they are relied upon for all adjustment needs. For the immature and inexperienced person, the ego defenses provide protection and security until they can be replaced by genuine confidence and resourcefulness resulting from personal growth. When the ego defenses are used habitually to deny or avoid the real nature of problems or prevent the person from developing other approaches to problem solution they cease to be helpful and may be very damaging. Mental health requires that we recognize the needs of our ego to be defended and evaluate our use of the ego defense mechanisms. If you find you are typically defending your ego you may need help in discovering why it is so weak. The ego defenses will only protect the ego, they cannot strengthen it. Ego strength develops from facing problems and learning effective ways to master them.

LEARNING AND ADJUSTMENT

When we speak of *adjustment* in psychology we are referring to the continuous process of interaction between the individual and his environment including other people. Adjustment then means change in behavior as required to conform to the cultural or social demands of our environment. In our society we are expected to put aside childish ways or wishes and conform to standards of adulthood as we grow older. Sometimes we may be able to change our environment to better suit our needs or capacities. Job change may occur in order to obtain more money, better working conditions, or an opportunity to be with people we feel more comfortable with and enjoy. This process of interaction, of give-and-take, between the person and his environment goes on continuously throughout life. No one is ever adjusted at any point in life as a final and absolute quality. Change in adjustment will occur as the circumstances of life change and whether a person is well- or poorly adjusted can only be determined from one time to another.

Rather than think of adjustment as good or bad, it is more helpful to think of it as *adaptive* or *maladaptive*. Adaptive adjustment will be behavior that meets the demands of the situation, will not create new problems for the individual, and will permit other behavioral functioning to continue without disruption. Adjustment that is maladaptive will fail to meet the demands of the situation, or create added problems, or disrupt other behaviors of the individual, or all of these things. A person who aspires to be a success in a competitive field of activity such as the entertainment world may ruin his health (added problem) and neglect his family and friends (disrupted other functioning) before he discovers he does not have enough talent to succeed (inability to meet demands of the situation). His behavior is maladaptive. Even if he should succeed as an entertainer, his neglect of himself and his social relationships are still maladaptive. Adjustment then is not simply success or lack of success, but a matter of behavioral adaptation to meet a variety of needs.

What kind of an adjustment a person will make in response to changing circumstances will depend upon several factors. These factors will include his response capacities, his perception of the situation, his motivation for change, and the nature of the situation. Let us look at these more closely.

Response Capacities

Adjustment of any kind, adaptive or maladaptive, will always reflect the response capacities of the individual. These capacities, such as intelligence, special abilities, aptitudes, physical characteristics, and other traits will be determined in part by heredity. The potentials for response set by heredity must wait upon the orderly growth processes we call maturation before they can be realized. The more favorable the environment in which one grows the more likely will his full potentials for response be realized. Finally, the response capacities will be shaped by experiences of learning. If opportunities for the development of response capacities have not been provided or if the learning experiences have been faulty the potentials for response will be diminished. Behaviorally, for purpose of adjustment, the individual can never do more than he is capable of doing. He may, however, do less and to understand why he may do less we need to consider the other factors that determine adjustment.

Perception of Situation

Perception, as we learned in Chapter 2, is an individual intellectual process of giving meaning to your experiences. The way you perceive a situation is, so far as you are concerned, the way the situation is. The individual will respond to his perceptions of situations and these may not be consistent at all with objective reality (or the situations as seen by most persons). Faulty perception may lead to poor adjustment in a number of ways. The individual may not recognize that change in his behavior is necessary. In the case of the individual aspiring to be a success as an entertainer many events may indicate quite clearly that he lacks enough talent to succeed. Yet, he perceives himself as able and he persists in spite of any encouragement. His subjective reality based on his own perceptions of his ability is inconsistent with the objective reality of other people's perceptions of him. Another way perception can alter adjustment is when only part, rather than the whole, of a situation is perceived. Tom's coworkers tell him he is going to be fired if he continues to be late for work. Tom, however, perceives his boss as a friendly, lenient, person who does not care about a few minutes here or there. Tom's dismissal for lateness may come as a complete surprise to him. He may have perceived his boss accurately as a friendly, lenient person who does not care personally about a few minutes here or there. He has failed to perceive the whole situation, however, in that the morale of the work group requires everyone to be treated alike and habitual tardiness is grounds for dismissal. Tom probably could change his tardy behavior, but he perceived no need to do so. You will engage your capacities for response in a situation only as you perceive it necessary to do so. Still, you may do less than you are able to do for yet another reason.

Motivation for Change

Motivation refers to the goals toward which behavior is directed. When these goals are important or vital, behavior will usually be more intense and show a greater variety of approaches to obtain the goals. (Motivation will be discussed at greater length in Chapter 5.)

You will engage your response capacities in as many ways as you can according to how important your goals are to you and what difference you perceive your efforts will make. Tom, who lost his job for lateness, might have been more responsive to the warnings of his coworkers if he had desperately needed his job to provide for his survival needs. The individual who wanted to be an entertainer persisted in his maladaptive behavior because he placed his personal goals of mastery and achievement above his goals for survival (physical health) or social relationships (family and friends) and failed to perceive that all his efforts could not make up for a lack of sufficient talent. There are times, however, when we are motivated to change, perceive what changes are needed, and have the capacity to make these changes, but adaptive change is not possible.

Nature of the Situation

Some situations do not permit adaptive change. These situations typically are of the *interpersonal* variety, involving relationships to other persons. As you interact with others over some period of time they develop attitudes and expectancies about you that limit your behavior in relation to them. These attitudes and expectancies may be positive or negative, but they are always restrictive.

The child who has done well in school is expected by parents, teachers, and classmates to continue to do well. Over time, however, school may have less and less meaning to this individual in terms of his life goals. If the individual performs at a lower level of achievement (A to C), it will be interpreted by others as a "bad" change and pressures may be exerted upon the individual to regain his "lost" level of performance. The boy who grows up in a slum neighborhood may recognize that petty stealing, swearing, and school truancy are not the way to achieve what he wants of life. Yet, the only companions he has live by some code of the street, and his continued association with them demands that his behavior be like theirs. The family member who has always assumed responsibilities, financial and otherwise, for other members of the family may be viewed as "selfish" when he or she decides to marry and no longer has time or resources except for his or her own home. The girl who grows up in a small town, rather plain and uninteresting as an adolescent may continue to be considered a "poor date" even though with maturity she becomes pretty or beautiful and interesting by any ordinary standards.

People expect that what you have been you will continue to be. As your needs for their approval, acceptance, and companionship dictate, you try to meet their expectations. The more you meet their expectations, the less you become what you could or might be, and the more you become what you were. Adaptive changes in adjustment require, at times, a removal from a given situation in order that change in a new direction may occur.

Adjustment then is a process of change in ourselves, in others, or in the environment. To say that a person is well-adjusted does not mean he has solved all his problems or that he has no problems. It does mean that he has *learned* how to handle his problems as they arise in an adaptive way and he is ready to meet new problems as they arise.

EFFICIENCY IN LEARNING

From a practical standpoint, most students would like to know how they can get the most possible good from the least possible time spent in studying. Teachers are also interested in finding the most favorable conditions for learning to take place. Psychologists have devoted a great deal of time and effort to the study of learning and how to manage it for the greatest efficiency. We will summarize here some of the findings in hopes that the student will be able to put them to practical use.

Motivation

The old adage, "you can lead a horse to water but you cannot make him drink," holds very true for learning of an intellectual nature. Most people are strongly motivated to learn some things and less strongly motivated to learn others. When you are really interested and want or need to learn you find that it is easy to pay close attention and thus easier to learn. If you are reading a textbook that you are not very interested in reading your mind will wander and you may read several pages without knowing what you have read. What can you do to control your attention? If you can somehow relate the subject matter to your needs and motives you will find that your attention is sharper and learning is easier. Thus the study of a foreign language becomes easier if the student keeps reminding himself that he may want to travel or even spend some time living and working in a foreign country whose language he is learning. Sometimes it is difficult to study for the required courses in college that are not directly related to your major interest. If you are able to recognize your motives for taking any course you can usually see how it serves to satisfy some particular need you have and it becomes easier to focus your attention on it. The most successful teachers are those who are able to relate their subject matter to the needs of their students.

Feedback

Feedback means knowledge of results or keeping informed about how well the learning process is going. Feedback helps the learning process because it enables a student to correct mistakes quickly and to avoid building on faulty premises. The major advantage of teaching machines is that they provide immediate feedback. As soon as a student responds the machine lets him know if he is right or wrong and he is able to correct himself before bad habits are acquired.

Feedback also stimulates attention and serves as a reinforcement in the learning process. The main reason for giving frequent quizzes during a course of study is to give the student some feedback or knowledge of how well his learning is progressing. By studying the results of an examination you can see how you stand and find where you need more effort while there is still time to fill in the gaps and avoid faulty learning.

Reward and Punishment

The most frequently used tool in the management of learning is reward. Babies are rewarded for each new accomplishment by the attention and approval of their parents. Older children are rewarded with gifts and promises as well as approval. Even college students are rewarded with grades, honors, recognition, and diplomas as well as the rewards their parents give. All these external rewards are really bribes provided by other people but they can still be effective and useful in motivating an individual to learn. Many adults find themselves happier and more successful because of learning they accomplished primarily to satisfy the demands or fulfill the expectations of their parents. Some college students find it helpful to establish a system of rewards and punishments which they grant and impose upon themselves—like promising yourself a new sweater if you get a good grade on a term paper, or not turning on the television until you have all your assignments completed.

Another group of rewards, which are usually more effective, are called *intrinsic* or internal rewards. Intrinsic rewards are pleasant feelings you get from the satisfaction of proving to yourself that you can do what you set out to do. If you have ever observed a baby learning to walk you have seen the experience of utter joy he feels when he is finally able to succeed in mastering that skill. If you can set certain goals for yourself in terms of tasks to be mastered you will usually find that learning becomes intrinsically rewarding as you meet your own standards of perfection.

In most learning situations both external and internal rewards help to stimulate interest, direct attention, and increase motivation. Learning to play a musical instrument, overhaul an engine, or discuss political issues can be a source of inner satisfaction as well as praise and recognition from your friends. Sometimes it is possible to learn about subject matter that does not especially interest you simply to prove to yourself that you can succeed in whatever you make up your mind to do.

Punishment seems to be somewhat less effective than reward in managing learning although it is difficult to separate the two. Failure to earn a desired reward can serve as a punishment in many instances. The guilt feelings you suffer for lack of accomplishment serve as an intrinsic punishment, and the poor grades are external punishment.

Good Study Habits

We cannot overemphasize the importance of developing good study habits for successful adjustment in college. It is not uncommon for intelligent, capable students to fail in college because they have not learned enough self-discipline to apply themselves to the task of studying. At the risk of belaboring the obvious, let us summarize some of the ways we have found that successful college students differ from unsuccessful ones.

1. Class participation. Students who get the best grades are those who not only attend class regularly but who ask questions and enter into class discussion. Even in classes too large for discussion the college professor usually allows time for questions in class or he will answer them after class. Most students in college take notes and try to summarize the main points in each lecture. If you do miss a class, it is a good idea to get the class notes from another student, and be sure you understand what material was covered.

2. Study time. One of the common mistakes college students make is not allowing enough time for preparation outside class. The full-time academic load of 15 hours a week in class is based on the assumption that the full-time student will have 30 hours a week for study outside class. Most college courses are geared to the expectation that an average student needs two hours of preparation for each class hour, although some students need to spend more time and some can get by with less.

Students who average 3 hours a day in classes and spend five or six hours a day in study time have much greater success than those who have the same classes but spend 25 or 30 hours in study on the weekends. Research has shown that short distributed periods of study are more efficient than the same amount of time in one long period. If you have to mass your study time into long periods it helps to break it up by using 1 hour for one subject and then changing to another. The most efficient way to schedule time for study is to plan for short periods distributed throughout the day each day. The poorest students are those who put off doing any preparation until the night before an exam. Successful students usually try to plan a time and place for study periods and hold themselves to their study schedule just as they do their class schedule.

3. Use of textbooks. Instructors select certain textbooks for their courses because they feel that the books will provide the student with enough background information to prepare him for the course. Students who study the assigned reading material in advance of the class are better prepared to participate in class and benefit from what the instructor has to offer. The instructor sets the pace and guides the learning process not only by his leadership in class but by his selection of textbooks and assignments of supplementary reading. Students who feel that perfect class attendance excuses them from reading or vice versa seldom succeed in college.

The most effective way to study a textbook chapter for most students is to follow these five steps: (*a*) Skim over the chapter, reading introduction and summary, noting headings and illustrations, to get a general idea of what is being covered; (*b*) Read the entire chapter and underline the main points in each paragraph; (*c*) Review the chapter noting points you have underlined and making sure you understand what you have read; (*d*) Test yourself by writing down what you can remember or try to recite to yourself or someone else; and (*e*) Review again to see what you have missed and clarify any parts on which you were in doubt.

4. Recitation. Students who study together and recite to each other are at an advantage over those who study alone, although it is possible to recite to yourself while studying. Recitation aids learning by making the material more meaningful as you rephrase it in your own words and relate it to what you already know. It also provides a form of feedback to let you know your strong points and weak spots. Many outstanding students will tell you that their most valuable study technique is getting together with classmates in small informal groups to discuss subject matter, exchange ideas, and share feelings about their courses.

SUMMARY

Learning is defined as the process by which behavior is changed as a result of experience. What we learn is determined by hereditary potentials, environmental opportunities, and individual experiences. Learning enables us to change and adapt to the world around us.

Learning takes place by conditioning, problem-solving, imitation and identification, and by the use of symbols. Conditioning occurs as a result of associations between stimuli and responses being established and strengthened by reinforcement. Classical conditioning occurs when a natural stimulus is associated with a substitute stimulus to produce a natural response. Operant conditioning is an association between a response and the events that follow it which are rewarding or satisfying. Conditioning can occur without awareness or effort by an individual.

Problem-solving requires recognition of a problem and effort to try different approaches until successful solutions are found. Problem-solving can be aided or hindered by the development of learning sets.

Children imitate people they respect and admire and try to pattern themselves after these models. By identification with parents children learn to share their attitudes, opinions, and preferences.

The use of symbols enables man to learn about complex ideas and to communicate them more efficiently.

Almost all human behavior is learned. Motor learning begins before birth and is dependent on neuromuscular maturation. As motor skills are learned the physical activities are combined with social and intellectual activities. Socialization includes habit training, development of relationships with other people, and learning expected behavior patterns or roles. Intellectual development depends on learning language skills. Adequacy as an adult requires motor, social, and intellectual learning, all of which are interdependent on each other, and contribute to the growth of self.

Conscience is learned by the process of internalizing moral values and setting standards of right and wrong by which an individual judges himself and his behavior. Character development includes the concept of ideal self and the way a person uses his moral values to guide his life.

Self-concept begins with body image and develops as the result of social learning. Self-concept is also called ego and the characteristic ways we learn to protect our self-concept are called ego defenses. Some of the more common ego defense mechanisms are rationalization, projection, compensation, identification, withdrawal, regression, and repression. The ego defenses can be a help or a hindrance depending on how they are used.

Adjustment refers to the interaction of an individual and his environment in which he must learn how to satisfy his own needs in harmony with the cultural and social demands of his society. Adjustment may be adaptive or maladaptive but it represents some degree of behavioral change. The factors that limit and determine adjustment at any time include response capacities, perception of the situation, motivation for change, and the nature of the situation.

Efficiency in learning, particularly in an academic setting can be improved by motivation, feedback, reward and punishment, and good study habits. Reward may be intrinsic or extrinsic but in either case it is more effective than punishment. Successful college students differ from unsuccessful ones in several ways, including class participation, study time, use of textbooks, and recitation.

We have seen how learning makes adaptation possible in terms of external pressures and internal needs. We turn next to the considerations of needs and motives that provide the push behind behavior and answer the question—why?

SUGGESTIONS FOR FURTHER READING

Deese, J. E. and Hulse, S., *Psychology of Learning* (3rd ed.), New York, McGraw-Hill, 1967. A comprehensive text covering both human and animal learning from conditioning to complex concept learning.

Gelfand, Donna (Ed.), *Social Learning in Childhood*, Belmont, Calif., Brooks-Cole, 1969. A practical guide for effective child-rearing practices based on research studies of the development and modification of children's behavior.

Holt, John, *How Children Learn*, New York, Putnam, 1967. Stresses the human component in education and points out the need for better methods of developing individual potentials.

Lindgren, Henry Clay, *The Psychology of College Success*, New York, Wiley, 1969. Shows the student how college can be used to experience self-discovery and self-development as well as academic success.

Slamecka, Norman J. (Ed.), *Human Learning and Memory*, New York, Oxford University Press, 1967. A collection of classical and modern research reports in the field of human learning.

Why We Behave
As We Do

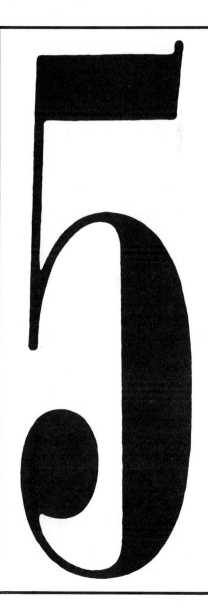

If you ask a number of different students why they are in college you will get a number of different answers: to satisfy parents, to get a better paying job, to avoid being drafted, to find a husband, to improve social status, to learn more about life, and many more reasons. If a stranger came to your door and offered you a gift you would normally assume that he had some motive; he might be trying to sell you something, he could be a new neighbor who wants to get acquainted, or he may be there for some other reason. You would probably wonder what his motive was and try to find out. We generally assume that all behavior is purposeful or that it is directed toward some goal. *Motivation* is the term used to describe the *push behind behavior* that directs action toward certain goals.

Why does one student stay up all night studying for an exam and go to any lengths, even to cheat, in order to excel in college, while another student acts as if he does not care whether he passes or fails? Both students are motivated to attend college but one is more highly motivated than the other to achieve success. Motivation in this instance refers to the *relative energy* that is put into reaching the goal.

Motivation refers to the internal conditions that arouse, sustain, and direct behavior in response to situations and objects in the environment. Several theories have been advanced to explain human motivation and no one theory has yet achieved universal acceptance. In this text we will see how the push behind behavior can result from the interaction of biological drives, emotional needs, and social motives, functioning as an integrated motivational system.

If we think of man as an organism of the animal kingdom whose primary motivation is self-preservation and perpetuating his species we see that there are certain conditions necessary for survival. If we perceive man as a dynamic force interacting with his environment and realizing his potentialities, we recognize a second order of needs which are conditions necessary for growth and development. If we regard man as a spiritual being, in unity with the universe, contributing to the progress of humanity, we are aware of a third order of conditions which are necessary for fulfillment. These three aspects of motivation do not function separately but are integrated into a complex system. Figure 5-1 summarizes the three orders of an integrated motivational system.

BIOLOGICAL DRIVES

Complex living organisms, including man, are composed of millions of cells which form the tissues and organ systems of the body. All activity and func-

BIOLOGICAL DRIVES ⟶ SURVIVAL ⟶ SELF PRESERVATION

1	hunger thirst oxygen sleep sex	homeostasis responsiveness perception pain avoidance stress tolerance	Man as an organism of the animal kingdom maintaining self and perpetuating his species

EMOTIONAL NEEDS ⟶ DEVELOPMENT ⟶ SELF ACTUALIZATION

2	security independence control achievement recognition	trust freedom responsibility confidence identity	Man as a dynamic force interacting with his environment, realizing his potentialities

SOCIAL MOTIVES ⟶ FULFILLMENT ⟶ SELF INTEGRATION

3	knowledge meaning expression unity humanism	understanding appreciation creativity relatedness faith	Man as a spiritual being in unity with the universe, contributing to the progress of humanity

Figure 5-1. An integrated motivational system.

tioning of the cells depend upon biochemical materials such as oxygen, food, water, vitamins, and minerals being taken in from the environment as well as the chemical substances produced within the body—hormones and enzymes, for example (see Chapter 2). The overall process of maintaining the chemical balance or equilibrium in the body tissues is called *homeostasis*. Whenever this balance is disturbed by a lack or deficiency in some chemical a *tissue need* results. The term *drive* refers to the state of tension and activity that is aroused by these needs and directed toward regaining homeostasis. Thirst is an example of a drive based on the tissue need for water.

There is no doubt that human behavior is motivated by the biological drives and that prolonged failure to satisfy these basic physical needs will result in death. However, the satisfaction of physical needs and reduction of biological drives in the human are greatly influenced by social learning and experience.

Hunger and Thirst

Whenever the body tissues are in need of food or water a state of tension is aroused which we learn to recognize and describe as feelings of hunger or thirst. These feelings are regulated by the nervous system in the hypothalamus (see Chapter 2) where the specific bodily needs are interpreted as special appetites. A tissue need for protein, for example, will cause a person to seek meat or fish in preference to other foods, and a deficiency of vitamin C will cause one to crave oranges or other foods high in that vitamin, because he has learned that these foods will satisfy his needs or specific hungers. Studies of infants and young children who were permitted to choose what they wanted to eat from a variety of foods have demonstrated that, over a period of time, even young infants will select a well-balanced diet. Through the process of trial and error they soon learn to identify by taste and smell which of the foods will satisfy their needs.

We can easily recognize the fact that failure to satisfy the hunger drive results in malnutrition and weakened physical strength, but what effect does an inadequate diet have on the personality and behavior of individuals? Experience has shown that men can survive total fasting for several weeks if they have water. After a few days without food, hunger pangs are greatly diminished, with less effect on behavior than prolonged semistarvation produces. When some food, but not a sufficient amount, is available, the hunger drive tends to dominate behavior and influence personality.

An experiment with conscientious objectors who volunteered for a year-long study of the effects of semistarvation was conducted near the end of World War II (Guetzkow and Bowman, 1946). Striking personality changes occurred in the men as a result of semistarvation but they did not persist after the men were returned to a normal diet. The outstanding characteristic of the half-starved men was apathy. There was a decrease in sociability, loss of sense of humor, and inability to display affection. The men became nervous, irritable, tactless, and short-tempered. They lost interest in their personal appearance and developed feelings of inferiority and depression. Their conversations, interests, activities, and daydreams all centered on food, in fact they became so preoccupied with food that they were unable to concentrate on anything else. Sexual urges decreased markedly and were slow to return during the recovery phase with normal diet. The men became very interested in such subjects as dietetics, agriculture, and frozen food processing. Some gave serious consideration to changing their occupations to become cooks, bakers, or food handlers.

Eating and drinking are basically the means of satisfying biological drives, but they also serve other purposes. Why do you join your friends in having a beer even if you are not thirsty? Why do you eat a piece of your favorite pie after a big meal when you are not really hungry? Under what circumstances might you be able to eat raw liver or kidney? Social learning influences what we eat and drink, how and when we do it, and sometimes motivates eating and drinking behavior without regard for biological drives. The vast differences in the manner in which people satisfy their hunger and thirst drives as a result of different social learning are illustrated in Figure 5-2.

In our society social activities often involve eating and drinking together. Overweight is a common problem for people who like to be sociable and do not want to risk offending others by refusing food when it is offered. The treatment of people with drinking problems is seriously complicated by the fact that their entire range of social and recreational activities usually involves drinking. Giving up social drinking or overeating may necessitate major changes in a person's way of life.

Figure 5-2. This Japanese child experiences the same hunger drive as American children but her eating behavior is quite different because of social learning. (Photo by Shirley I. Fisher.)

Excessive overeating is frequently associated with emotional tension and feelings of insecurity. For some people eating becomes a pleasurable activity that is substituted for other desirable and unavailable pleasures. People who develop a compulsive desire to eat more than is necessary to satisfy hunger are often sexually frustrated or insecure and fearful of being rejected in personal relationships.

Many of the adjustment problems of children that come to the attention of psychologists are associated with eating behavior. Children who refuse food as an attention-gaining device can be very disturbing to their parents. If a child succeeds in controlling parents by this tactic it may become such a well-established habit pattern that in later years he will actually be unable to eat or keep food on his stomach when faced with frustration. In some families meal times are associated with antagonism, frustration, and tension because the children are severely nagged about table manners or are sent away hungry as a means of punishment, or the family meal becomes a battleground for family conflict. Unfavorable conditions in the home associated with eating often result in eating problems. Children need an atmosphere of emotional security in which to satisfy their food hunger.

Rest and Sleep

The need for rest and the need for sleep are related but not identical. You can rest without sleeping but you seldom sleep without resting. Whenever you exercise your muscles you become aware of feelings of fatigue and the need for rest. Fatigue resulting from physical exertion is simply relieved by rest, but fatigue that results from worry, boredom, frustration, and emotional tension is not dispelled so easily, if at all. Some people are chronically exhausted regardless of how much rest they get.

The steady contraction of a muscle without periods of rest will result in such extreme fatigue that it becomes painful. It is probable that tension headaches are caused by sustained muscle contractions in the same way that eyestrain is caused by continued exertion of eye muscles. Ruch (1965) has suggested that the chronic feelings of fatigue common to neurotics may be the result of constant muscle tension even though the muscles are not being used in active exercise.

Sleep is a form of temporary isolation from the environment that provides the body with rest. During sleep you are in a lowered state of consciousness and your awareness of environmental stimuli is greatly restricted. Sleep is controlled by a mechanism in the brain which, if damaged, can cause a person to sleep excessively. Removal of the sleep centers from the brains of animals will cause them to remain awake and active until they die of exhaustion.

Worry and emotional turmoil can interfere with sleep by causing a person to stay awake longer, wake up frequently, sleep "lighter," or all of these. The fact that some people sleep more deeply than others has been verified by measures of heart rate, respiration, body temperature, brain waves, and rapid eye movements during sleep. Light sleepers show more anxiety and conflict on personality tests than deep sleepers (Zimmerman, 1968).

Although sleep is a biological need, it is readily influenced by emotional and social learning. Sleep patterns are learned behaviors that have become habitual. People train themselves to function on a schedule that best suits their own needs. Some people are more efficient early in the morning after a period of sleep and others function better late at night. Some individuals learn to sleep long hours to escape boredom or to avoid facing problems.

Under normal conditions most people spend about one-third of their lives sleeping. Whether this much sleep is necessary or not has been the subject of extensive research. The amount of sleep an individual requires seems to vary with the demands of his life circumstances. You probably know from your own experience how much easier it is to stay up and awake late at night if you are enjoying yourself than it is if you are doing some unpleasant work. In a recent study of the sleep patterns of normal volunteers, Tune (1968) found that adults average slightly less than 8 hours sleep in 24 hours, and that the duration of sleep decreased between the ages of 20 and 50, after which it increased. Women in this study tended to sleep less than men and to have more sleep disturbances.

One basic element in so called "brain-washing techniques" is prolonged deprivation of sleep. Studies have shown that judgment, reasoning, and problem-solving ability become seriously impaired after 24–30 hours without sleep, although simple tasks can be performed with only slight losses in efficiency for as long as 100 hours without sleep (Clark et al., 1946).

Other Survival Needs

The need for oxygen is so easily satisfied that we are usually unaware of the breathing drive. The importance of a continuous supply of oxygen to the brain is probably greater than the need for food. Brain damage occurs when the supply of oxygen is cut off for as short a time as 1 minute. Temporary asphyxiation at birth is known to result in mental retardation, epileptic seizures, and paralysis. Some high-altitude flyers and some skin divers who try to conserve their oxygen have been found to suffer permanent brain damage as a result.

Temperature regulation is another biological drive related to survival needs. Except for extremes of climate the human body is able to maintain its temperature at about 98.6 degrees by the complex mechanisms of the autonomic nervous system. Yet a considerable amount of human effort is spent on clothing, houses, heating and cooling systems, and special appliances designed to keep the body at a comfortable temperature.

The elimination of bodily waste materials is basically a biological drive, similar to breathing in its control by the autonomic nervous system. In humans, however, it is brought under voluntary control through learning. Because society sets standards to regulate and restrict the time, place, and manner in which these drives can be satisfied they are often a source of conflict and may lead to personality problems.

The Sex Drive

Unlike the other biological drives, the sex drive does not have to be satisfied for the individual to survive, although it is essential to the survival of a species. In lower animals the sex drive appears to be a purely biological process functioning in much the same way as hunger or thirst. For most organisms, sexual behavior is unlearned and is dependent upon the hormone cycle of the female of the species. Removal of the ovaries or testes will diminish or eliminate the sex drive in lower animals but not in humans. In humans, both male and female, sexual desires and responses are much less dependent upon hormones and purely biological processes than they are on emotions, experience, and learning.

Most infants show an interest and curiosity about their bodies and can be observed touching and examining all parts of it, including their sexual organs. These early interests and exploratory actions have no sexual significance until the youngster has learned the social meaning of his behavior. The parents' attitudes toward sex and the ways they handle the child's curiosity influence the way a child feels about the sexual parts of himself. Parents communicate their attitudes toward sex to the child by what they say and what they do not say. By refusing to discuss sex or answer a child's questions, parents can convey the impression that sex is wrong or bad and the child is left to seek information from less desirable sources.

Physiological changes in the body that occur at the time of puberty result in an increased level of sexual drive and a maturation of the sexual organs for reproduction. How a youth will react to the changes of puberty and the ways in which he will express and control sexual urges depends upon the social learning experiences he has had. Important to his social learning experiences are the values, morals, and expectations of his family and social class group.

Kinsey and his associates have reported on sexual behavior patterns in a large sample of males and females (1948, 1953). Males appear to reach their maximum sexual peak in their late teens and the intensity of their sexual drive begins to decline in their early twenties. The intensity of the sexual drive for males seems related to the age of adolescence. In general, the earlier adolescence begins the more sexually active the boy will be in his youth and in later life. The intensity of the sexual drive for females develops more slowly from the time of adolescence and continues to increase until about age 30 after which it remains fairly constant.

The difference in the peak times of sexual drive intensity for males and females has important implications for social and personal adjustment. Males experience their greatest intensity of sex drive during the years when they are still in school and not ordinarily financially secure. Early marriage with economic hardships or else the continued financial support of parents are possible solutions. Early marriage, however, will find the female not yet at the height of her sexual drive intensity and this may result in problems of marital adjustment for the couple.

Other solutions include premarital intercourse experiences and masturbation. The Kinsey studies found that 83 percent of males in their sample and 50 percent of females had had premarital intercourse experiences. Premarital intercourse contributes to social problems of venereal disease, illegitimate births, and illegal abortions and these in turn create serious problems of adjustment for the individuals concerned. Masturbation was found in the Kinsey studies to be a common experience for 92 percent of the males and 62 percent of the females. Masturbation seems to generate strong feelings of guilt, loss of self-esteem, and anxiety about possible impairment of sexual capacity. Feelings of guilt and loss of self-esteem as a result of masturbation reflect attitudes that have been socially conditioned rather than any inevitable psychological consequence of the act itself. There is no evidence that masturbation in itself will cause mental illness. Fears that masturbation will impair sexual capacity or sexual enjoyment are also apparently groundless.

Masters and Johnson (1966) have reported a study of sexual behavior in humans using techniques of direct observation and physical measurement. They have found that there are wide individual differences in the duration and intensity of physical reactions to sexual stimulation. Women, however, can maintain their experience of sexual climax (orgasm) relatively longer and repeat it sooner if restimulated than men. They also report that the size of a male's penis is not related to his effectiveness as a sexual partner and is not related in any consistent way with his body build, both of which are common misconceptions. Aging does not necessarily reduce sexual capacity or effectiveness. Important factors in the maintenance of effective sexuality into the advancing years are the opportunity in the life experience for regular and consistent sexual expression and continued good health.

In previous generations society imposed so many limitations on the satisfaction of sexual needs that many people suffered from inadequate sex education, prudish attitudes, guilt feelings, and overemphasis on sexual conflicts. At the present time, sexual taboos are weaker than ever before and opportunities for sexual gratification are more easily found. With the new sexual freedom, the problems people bring to psychotherapists today are less often centered around guilt feelings or social expectations and more often involve feelings that sexual behavior is an empty and meaningless experience. One reason people may find sexual behavior empty and meaningless is that they emphasize one aspect of sexuality over other and equally important aspects. Human sexual behavior satisfies a biological drive but it occurs in a social and psychological context. It finds its greatest social approval in marriage and family life. It finds its greatest psychological satisfaction in a sincere, mutual, and meaningful relationship with another person.

Satisfaction of the first-order needs or biological drives in harmony with the demands and limitations of the environment in which we live will accomplish the goal of self-preservation. It is of primary importance to maintain our equilibrium or homeostasis in order to perceive reality and be responsive to it. As we learn how to avoid pain and to tolerate stress we recognize that we are biological organisms of the animal kingdom with very primitive needs which must be met if we are to survive. However, it would be a serious oversimplification to assume that all human behavior is directed toward the satisfaction of basic biological needs. Emotional needs also motivate behavior and their satisfaction is necessary for the development and enhancement of the self as an individual.

EMOTIONAL NEEDS

Emotions are like drives in that they represent a physiological state of disturbed equilibrium, but they differ from biological drives in three ways: (*a*) they are aroused by external stimuli rather than tissue needs; (*b*) they depend upon the significance of the situation to the individual; and (*c*) they usually occur in situations where there is no habitual response. Emotions are experienced as feelings (sometimes called affect) like anger, joy, fear, love, distrust, and confidence. When someone insults you, you may react with feelings of anger, fear, surprise, disappointment, rejection, indifference, or some other feeling, depending upon the significance you put on the person and the situation. Your reaction to being insulted will be influenced by your feelings and how you have learned to express and control them. You will recall from Chapter 4 that emotional responses are learned by imitation, conditioning, and understanding.

The physiological indicators of disturbed equilibrium that accompany strong emotional states or intense emotional experiences may be summarized as follows (Lindsley, 1951):

1. Electrical conductance of the skin increases with the degree of emotional arousal of an individual.
2. Increased blood pressure and heart rate and changes in blood chemistry accompany changes in emotional states.
3. Faster and more shallow breathing are characteristic of intense emotional experience.
4. Lowered skin temperature is related to continued emotional stress and sweating of the skin is common.
5. Salivary glands stop secreting during emotional reactions.
6. Muscle tension and tremor occur in emotional states.
7. Other bodily functions which are controlled by the autonomic nervous system are temporarily disrupted during emotional states.

The physiological changes associated with emotional disturbance, if continued for a prolonged period of time, can result in physical as well as emotional and mental illness (see Chapter 9).

Development of the self and full realization of individual potentialities depends upon forming satisfying emotional relationships with significant other people. It is in our interpersonal relationships that we are able to enrich our lives beyond the level of mere need reduction.

The personality and behavior disorders we see in adults can frequently be traced back to the failure to satisfy the basic emotional needs in childhood. As we mature from infantile dependency to adult independence, we never outgrow the need for meaningful interpersonal relationships and close affectional ties. The basic emotional needs or conditions necessary for development include security, independence, control, achievement, and recognition.

Security

Emotional security is a feeling of being loved and accepted, feeling protected, and a feeling of belonging. The feeling of emotional security or lack of it comes from the way a child is treated by the people who are important to him.

A child's first experience with interpersonal relationships begins within his own family. The infant's relationship with his mother is probably the most crucial one in his life, because it lays the foundation for later affectional ties with his friends, spouse, and children. The child's need for love and affection must be satisfied before he can feel emotionally secure. A secure child feels unqualified acceptance by parents, that is, he knows that he is loved just for himself, regardless of what he is or does. If a child's relationship with his mother is emotionally satisfying he will be able to relate to others affectionately. Lack of motherly love and affection can generate insecurity in a child which in turn can prevent his ever satisfying the need for acceptance.

Numerous studies have reported the high rate of illness and death among infants physically well cared for in institutions but deprived of those close affectional contacts that we call "mothering." Reports from English nurseries for evacuees, war orphans, and displaced children all stress the need for mothering and the severe personality problems that stem from failure to satisfy their basic affectional needs. The degree and kind of emotional difficulties experienced in later life were found to be related to duration of stay in an institution, amount of parental interest shown in the children, and age at the time of institutionalization and foster home placements (Spitz, 1945, 1949; Goldfarb, 1943, 1945).

Children who lack the security of feeling loved may carry their unmet needs into adult life, craving love and affection, but being unable to give of themselves in return. When this happens the person appears selfish and demanding and tends to drive people away from him. It is trite but true of love and affection that one cannot give to others that which has never been given to him.

The importance of a child's early experience within his family cannot be overemphasized. The problems he encounters later in adolescence and adult life and the way he handles them will reflect the nature of his affectional ties in infancy and early childhood. The capacity to give love develops slowly and only after the child has learned to accept love. Erich Fromm (1956) observes, "The affirmation of one's own life, happiness, growth, freedom, is rooted in one's capacity to love." Some of the problems created by the inability to love are illustrated in the following case.

Janet was a young woman in her middle twenties when she first sought help for a continuous problem of broken love relationships. She was very attractive in appearance and had considerable personal charm. Beginning about age 15 she had been involved in a series of love affairs which always ended badly. She was sexually promiscuous between affairs but tried, when she thought she was in love, to be faithful. She felt no guilt about her sexual behaviors because she believed as long as she was not cheating someone she loved she was free to do as she pleased. Her difficulties always began when she felt she was in love. She would smother the object of her love with her attentions and try to monopolize him in an exclusive relationship. Usually outgoing and social, when she was in love she became very withdrawn and seclusive and did not want to go with her lover to any social affairs.

Janet's history revealed that she had been raised by a very immature and insecure mother. Her mother frequently neglected her and rejected the child's emotional needs for affection. Janet's father was apparently a warm and spontaneous person but he left the home for service when she was 5 and died in combat. When Janet fell in love with someone she demanded a constant display of his affection and reassurance that he loved her. She would provoke her sweetheart in every way possible to be sure that his love was real and genuine. Sometimes she would tell him of her sexual adventures to see if he could love her in spite of such behavior. With others, she would flaunt their religious faith or their occupational interests. When one after the other became fed up with her behavior and dropped her, Janet always interpreted it as evidence that they didn't "really care." Her problem was that the more she loved someone the more she tormented him. As a consequence, when her boy friends dropped her she felt a great sense of loss as well as a feeling of being unloved.

It was after a particularly intense involvement of this kind that she sought help. Over a period of several months Janet began to gain some insight into her behavior. Sexuality for her was a substitute for the stroking, caressing, affection she had not received enough of in infancy. It was a means to receive the very basic touch contact that the child normally receives from the mother. Her early deprivation in affection forced her to test each new friend to the limits of his endurance to prove that what she basically believed was not true. What she basically believed was that she, as a person, was unlovable. No ordinary display of love could begin to satisfy such a craving for reassurance. Her seclusive behavior with her lovers was a response not unlike the starved animal that hoards food. She wanted love so desperately that she tried to hide her sweetheart lest someone steal him from her. Her need to be loved was so great that she was unable to receive love, or to return it, in any positive way.

Independence

During the first years of life a child needs to depend on adults for food, comfort, attention, and affection. If these dependency needs are met in a reasonably consistent way the child develops a *basic sense of trust* or confidence in people. After he has developed a sense of trust the child begins to strive for independence and can develop confidence and trust in himself. As he grows in self-awareness, he gains in social awareness and develops feelings of appreciation, concern, and affection for others. His attitudes and patterns of emotional behavior will be influenced largely by these early relationships.

The relationship a child has with his parents determines the concept he has of himself. If he feels accepted, he becomes acceptable to himself, and if he feels rejected he learns to see himself as unworthy and unacceptable. His social development is likewise influenced by the pattern of interaction with his parents. When parents are overprotective the child tends to lack initiative and depends on others to do everything for him. Some parents are overprotective of their children because of their own insecurity and lack of confidence in themselves as parents.

A child needs to feel that his parents have confidence in him and in his ability to do things for himself and by himself. He should feel that his parents want him to grow up and that they encourage him to try new things. He needs to feel that they will let him grow and develop in his own way, but they will be there to help him when he needs help. Sometimes it is difficult to allow a child to satisfy his need for independence because parents get satisfaction from feeling needed and wanted by a dependent child.

The need for independence or freedom is important, not only in childhood, but throughout our lives. Most people place a high value on freedom of speech, freedom of choice, freedom to make one's own decisions, and to defend one's rights.

As you satisfy your needs for independence, you gain self-confidence and feel secure in your ability to control your own behavior and direct your own life.

Control

A child needs to know that his parents are in control of him and that he can rely on their judgment. He should learn to recognize the limits they set for him and know that they will hold him to these limits until he is capable of self-control and good judgment.

Positive patterns of interaction between parents and children result when parents are able to avoid the extremes of rejection and overprotection, and can reach a balance between excessive punishment and lack of control and guidance. Parents who are tolerant of children's mistakes but able to give praise and encouragement for their efforts contribute to the child's security and self-concept in a positive way. Parents who are sensitive to their children's feelings and respect their rights as individuals help their children to learn respect for other people. The child who is overindulged has difficulty in social relationships. If parents cater to all his whims and shower him with material things, he is likely to develop an exaggerated opinion of himself and fail to develop adequate tolerance for frustration. At the other extreme, parents who demand strict obedience and use severe punishments often set standards too high for the child to meet and cause him to have a poor opinion of himself.

Family structures differ with respect to the patterns of authority and the status of each member. In some families the father is the ultimate authority and in others the mother may be in control even when the father is the chief provider. Often authority is shared by both parents equally and the family may be a democratic unit. Regardless of the structural organization of the family the child must learn to respect authority in the home if he is to make a satisfactory social adjustment in later life. Children who accept authority as it is intended, for their protection and guidance, find it easy to accept the authority of teachers, policemen, and employers. They also learn that authority carries responsibility for protection, guidance, and control for the benefit of the child.

Techniques of discipline that parents use to assert their authority over a child can arouse feelings of hostility and resentment to such an extent that they interfere with the child's identification with his parents. The most disruptive effects on the child seem to occur when the parents are inconsistent in their handling of the child. Parents who are quite strict or parents who are quite lax, as long as they are consistent in their approach, have better results than parents who are overly strict one time and lax another. Consistency in parental behavior, even when it is harsh, gives the child a dependable situation in which he can organize himself and adjust. Firm and consistent limits that are enforced with affection and kindness lead to greater acceptance and identification with his parents on the part of the child. Resentment and hostility toward parents is often expressed in aggressive and hostile behavior directed against society.

Achievement

The need to achieve mastery over the environment spurs people on throughout life. When you master a task you have set your sights on, you experience a sense of satisfaction, but you usually set out to master something else. When you are defeated in your attempts to achieve some goal you experience feelings of frustration, but you probably continue to strive for some other achievement. This need for achievement must be satisfied repeatedly if you are to be well-adjusted and mentally healthy. Frequent failure to achieve has the effect of producing emotional disturbance which can lead to serious personality defects and mental disorders.

Why do some people seem so much more highly motivated for achievement than others? This is probably due to a combination of many factors, including family pressures, social class expectations, and general cultural influence. The very young child gets some inner satisfaction from his accomplishments but also is rewarded for achievement, and he soon learns that through his own achievements he is able to help satisfy his needs for security, independence, and control. Thus the need for achievement becomes the means for realizing his potentialities and making them actual accomplishments of the developing self (Figure 5-3).

The need for achievement in any individual is closely related to the standards set by his parents. Children from middle-class families tend to have a stronger need for achievement than do children from upper- or lower-class families, although the range of individual differences within any social class is great. The American culture, in general, places a great deal of emphasis on achieve-

Figure 5-3. The need for achievement motivates these youngsters to learn to play the guitar. (Photo courtesy of Saratoga County Mental Health Clinic.)

ment. Most of you feel the pressure to "get ahead," "better yourself," and continue to set your goals higher and higher. It is wise to set a series of lesser goals on the road to the important goals in order to experience success along the way and to avoid the feeling of failure if your major goal is never reached.

Satisfaction of the need for achievement depends upon setting realistic goals. The person who sets his sights beyond the limits of what he can reasonably expect to accomplish is doomed to failure. The difficulty comes in trying to determine in advance what goals are realistic. It is very important for every individual to have some understanding of his capabilities and limitations in order to be able to set realistic goals. The way you develop awareness of your own potentialities and limitations is by trial-and-error learning and the

Figure 5-4. Scouting offers young people the opportunity to satisfy their needs for recognition as well as achievement. (Photo by Jim Sargent.)

comparisons you make between yourself and other people (Figure 5-4). Understanding individual differences is the subject of the next chapter.

Recognition

Closely related to the need for achievement is the need for recognition. We not only need to achieve or accomplish, but we need to have our accomplishments recognized by other people. In infancy and early childhood we learn to seek approval and avoid disapproval by conforming to the behavior patterns that bring favorable recognition.

When you behave in a way that brings you recognition and approval, you experience a pleasant emotional state of well-being which contributes to your feeling of personal worth. When your behavior brings you unfavorable recognition and disapproval you feel bad so you make some changes if you can. But when you fail to gain recognition at all you find yourself in a state of emotional tension. People in public life would rather have bad publicity than no publicity, just as the 10-year-old would get greater satisfaction from being recognized as the worst boy in school than he would from not being recognized or identified as anyone in particular. This is especially evident in some children who will go to any lengths to be recognized, and if they cannot gain favorable recognition will continue to misbehave and get unfavorable recognition.

The need for recognition is a powerful factor in the motivation of human behavior. Much of what you do, the places you go, the way you dress, and the groups you join are influenced by your needs for recognition and status. You need the admiration and respect of other people in order to develop self-esteem and to establish your own identity. Consequently, the needs for recognition, appreciation, and approval have been designated as *ego needs* or esteem needs (Maslow, 1954).

All the basic emotional needs: security, independence, control, achievement, and recognition, must be satisfied to some extent for self-actualization to be possible. Failure to satisfy these basic needs leads to emotional insecurity, self-doubt, self-depreciation, or the development of neurotic needs which are nearly impossible to satisfy. You cannot realize your potentialities and develop them to the fullest if your behavior is dominated by emotional needs which are largely unmet or unsatisfied. All of us have some unsatisfied emotional needs but so long as these are balanced by enough need satisfactions we can continue to interact with the environment and realize our potentialities.

Satisfaction of emotional needs leads to developing a basic sense of trust in people, acceptance of freedom and responsibility, feelings of self-confidence and personal adequacy, and a sense of identity as a unique and worthwhile person.

SOCIAL MOTIVES

The third order of motivation goes beyond the biological drives that are necessary for survival and the emotional needs necessary for development, and brings us to a consideration of the social motives that are necessary for fulfillment. *Motive*, as it is used here, means the desire for a goal that, through learning, has acquired value for the individual. Social motives are the least urgent but most human aspects of our motivational system.

Fromm (1968) has termed these motives "trans-survival needs" because they are specifically human and they transcend the function of survival. He believes that man's need to express his capabilities as a human in relation to other humans and to the world is a basic part of human nature. "This means: because I have eyes, I have the need to see; because I have ears, I have the need to hear; because I have a mind, I have the need to think; and because I have a heart, I have the need to feel. In short, because I am a man, I am in need of man and of the world," (Fromm, 1968, p. 72). Maslow (1954) has suggested that the higher human motives do not emerge until the more primitive biological and emotional needs have been satisfied. Other theorists attribute the social motives to learning without regard for human nature. Most religions consider man as a spiritual being and encourage the development of higher motives in order that we may transcend the needs of physical survival and experience the divine.

The social motives we consider necessary for fulfillment in life and for self-integration include: (a) the desire for knowledge as a basis of understanding; (b) the need to find meaning and develop appreciation for life; (c) the need for expression which leads to creativity; (d) the need for unity; and (e) the need for humanism.

Knowledge

The desire to satisfy curiosity and gain knowledge is an important motivational force behind human behavior. Even the infrahuman species have an inborn tendency to explore their surroundings. Curiosity is a basic attribute of every normal child. As we grow and develop we continue to seek answers to the questions of what, when, where, why, and how of human existence.

The unique human ability to communicate thoughts and ideas by means of language and other symbol systems has enabled our civilization to make remarkable technological progress. If man had not had the curiosity to pursue the question, "what if?," there would be no wheel, automobile, computer, technical know-how, or knowledge of space. We are curious to explore the universe and expand the boundary of our awareness of the world in which we live. As we gain more knowledge we ask more questions, and develop our capacities for understanding even more. We want to know what has gone before and what will be likely to happen in the future.

The quest for knowledge applies not only to understanding of the world, but also to understanding ourselves and our relationship to the world and to other people (Figure 5-5). We need to know what is necessary to survive and to develop, but beyond this, we want to know what life is all about. We seek knowledge that will enhance our understanding of human nature and the value of human life and human experience.

Continuing education is important as a preparation for contributing to the

Figure 5-5. Communication with others in a learning situation helps to satisfy the need for knowledge and understanding. (Photo by Dave Bellak, San Jose State College.)

progress of humanity. We need to understand history in order to prevent the repetition of past mistakes and failures. The solutions to present social problems depend upon increased knowledge and improved understanding of the under-lying conditions, trends, and forces that have resulted in these problems. But even more important to human progress is the need for accumulated wisdom in guiding the decisions that will determine the course of history in the future.

Meaning

The need to find meaning in our lives is an important part of the process of self-integration. We need to perceive the universe as orderly and comprehensible and to recognize our place in it. We need to question and explore our feelings as well as our thoughts until we fulfill the need for a philosophy of life and a meaningful set of human values we can live by.

People whose lives lack meaning and purpose are usually depressed and often suicidal. Such people need help to realize their own potentialities and to develop appreciation for the opportunities life offers. Some people find it easier to blame parents, childhood experiences, or environmental forces for their unhappy plight rather than to assume responsibility for finding some meaning in their existence.

Individuality is punctuated by two inevitable events—birth and death. In the space of time between these two events we have some freedom of choice and responsibility for choosing the directions our lives will take. In the process of becoming a person we make many decisions about the kind of person we will become. Some philosophies emphasize the will to pleasure, some the will to power, and some the will to meaning. "This will to meaning is the most human phenomenon of all since an animal never worries about the meaning of its existence" (Frankl, 1955, p. 9). To find meaning in life depends upon developing moral and spiritual values. We need to decide for ourselves what purposes we would be willing to die for and what we consider worth living for.

"The qualities of freedom, responsibility, courage, love, and inner integrity are ideal qualities, never perfectly realized by anyone, but they are the psychological goals which give meaning to our movement toward integration" (May, 1953, p. 236). The need to find meaning and strength within ourselves, to value, to choose, and to live in accord with our values is essential to a life of fulfillment and self-integration.

Expression

The need to express our feelings and ideas can serve as powerful motivation. The conversations we have with other people are a means of self-expression, and we also express ourselves through music, art, and literature. People who are denied the freedom and opportunity for expression of their own individuality are generally unhappy and dissatisfied with life.

The urge to be creative is an expression of individuality that can be satisfied in numerous ways, such as having a baby, planting a flower, drawing a picture, writing a poem, building a house, making a dress, or developing a hobby.

Young people today are very insistent on "doing their own thing," which means expressing their individuality and resisting conformity to traditions of the past. Popular forms of music and dancing are a reflection of the need for expression on a feeling level. Many modern art forms also reflect the trend toward greater freedom of expression that characterizes youth today.

Now, more than at any time in history, we see the expression of feelings, thoughts, and ideas influencing the social structure of our institutions. It is not enough that we acquire knowledge and gain understanding of social problems, and that we find meaning and purpose in our lives, but we must also feel committed to the cause of human progress. If we have the courage of our convictions we will find ways to express our ideas and feelings so that they will have a positive influence on society.

We need self-expression to make our influence felt (Figure 5-6). Through successive generations our impact on the values and attitudes of our children leaves our mark in the world to some extent. Our participation in group activities further spreads the influence of our ideas and feelings. This will be discussed further in Chapter 11.

Figure 5-6. Art work is used to encourage expression of feelings and individuality. (Photo courtesy of Skidmore College.)

Unity

The need for unity stems from the need for affiliation or belonging—the need for closeness and mutual experiences of caring and sharing your ultimate concerns with another person or people. Some psychologists are convinced that the basic source of all anxiety is man's feeling of separateness and aloneness in the world, and that desire for interpersonal fusion with another human is the most powerful striving in man. Fromm (1956) defines love as an active power in man which unites him with others while still preserving his own integrity. The capacity to experience love of all the different kinds (brotherly love, mother love, erotic love, self-love, and love of God) represents the ultimate in the fulfillment of self-integration. Unity with our fellow man enables us to experience relatedness to humanity and the spiritual nature of our existence.

The life tasks we undertake and the goals we set for ourselves, which will be the subject of Chapter 7, are influenced by the need for unity and the concerns we have for other people who are important parts of our lives (Figure 5-7).

Figure 5-7. Volunteers working with underpriviledged children in the Project to Excite Potential derive personal satisfaction of their needs for unity and humanism. (Photo courtesy of Skidmore College.)

Humanism

The highest motive man strives to fulfill is the need for humanism or responsibility for his fellow man now and in generations to come. To feel the satisfaction of making some contribution to the progress of humanity is important to a person's self-integration and full participation in life.

The motivational force of humanism is eloquently portrayed in the words of a young black American writing from his prison cell. The following is an excerpt from *Soul on Ice*:[†]

> *After I returned to prison, I took a long look at myself and, for the first time in my life, admitted that I was wrong, that I had gone astray—astray not so much from the white man's law as from being human, civilized—for I could not approve the act of rape. Even though I had some insight into my own motivations, I did not feel justified. My pride as a man dissolved and my whole fragile moral structure seemed to collapse, completely shattered.*
>
> *That is why I started to write. To save myself.*
>
> *I realized that no one could save me but myself. The prison authorities were both uninterested and unable to help me. I had to seek out the truth and unravel the snarled web of my motivations. I had to find out who I am and what I want to be, what type of man I should be, and what I could do to become the best of which I was capable. I understood that what had happened to me had also happened to countless other blacks and it would happen to many, many more.*
>
> *I learned that I had been taking the easy way out, running from problems. I also learned that it is easier to do evil than it is to do good. And I have been terribly impressed by the youth of America, black and white. I am proud of them because they have reaffirmed my faith in humanity. I have come to feel what must be love for the young people of America and I want to be part of the good and greatness that they want for all people. From my prison cell, I have watched America slowly coming awake. It is not fully awake yet, but there is soul in the air and everywhere I see beauty. I have watched the sit-ins, the freedom raids, the Mississippi Blood Summers, demonstrations all over the country, the FSM movement, the teach-ins, and the mounting protest over Lyndon Strangelove's foreign policy—all of this, the thousands of little details, show me it is time to straighten up and fly right. That is why I decided to concentrate on my writings and efforts in this area (Cleaver, 1968, pp. 15–16).*

[†]SOUL ON ICE by Eldridge Cleaver. Copyright © 1968 by Eldridge Cleaver. Used with permission of McGraw-Hill Book Company.

Today's youth, not only in this country, but all over the world is in the throes of a massive rebellion against the social–political–economic system that prevails today. These young people are different from any previous generations of youth in rebellion because they are driven by a higher level of social motives. What we see is not a revolution of downtrodden peasants demanding satisfaction of their survival needs, nor a generation of neurotics crying for gratification of their emotional needs, but we are witnessing a knowledgeable segment of the population expressing the need for faster progress toward humanitarian goals. (Figure 5-8).

MOTIVATIONAL PATTERNS

Psychology seeks to understand why people act, think, and feel as they do. We look for reasons, but we do not expect to reduce all human behavior to a set of

Figure 5-8.   Service with the Volunteer Emergency Corps offers many opportunities to satisfy humanitarian needs. (Photo by Jim Sargent.)

simple cause-and-effect relationships. Most human behavior cannot be traced to a single drive, need, or motive, because it involves some combination of these functioning together as an integrated system. The exact number of motives that direct human behavior is a controversial issue with theories ranging from Murray's elaborate system of 37 needs to Combs and Snygg's one. The latter reduce all human motivation to the basic need for adequacy and state, "Whenever we refer to man's basic need, we mean that great driving, striving force in each of us by which we are continually seeking to make ourselves more adequate to cope with life" (Combs and Snygg, 1959, p. 96). Whether we attribute behavior to one force or to many we must recognize individual differences.

Each individual's motivational pattern is unique to that person. Although we may have the same drives, needs, and motives in common with each other, the relative strength of these forces in determining behavior will vary from one person to another. The social and cultural environment in which we live and our past learning are influential in shaping our characteristic motivational pattern. The pattern is not fixed at any one point in time, but it changes gradually as we gain experience and maturity.

UNCONSCIOUS MOTIVATION

The idea of unconscious motives was first proposed by Sigmund Freud, a man whose theories are still controversial. Freud believed that human behavior could be dramatically influenced by hidden wishes and desires that were completely unknown to the individual, and he developed the technique of free association to bring these unconscious determinants of behavior into conscious awareness. While there is widespread disagreement with Freudian theory among modern psychologists, there is general agreement on the existence of unconscious motivation.

Can you really explain all your thoughts, feelings, and actions on the basis of conscious motives alone? You may be able to offer plausible reasons for what you think, feel, and do, but can you be sure you always recognize your true motives? You must have done something sometime and wondered why you did it. Most people have had the experience of thinking thoughts that were unpleasant, annoying, or stressful and being unable to stop thinking them even though they consciously wished to do so. "Slips of the tongue" or saying something you did not intend to say can be interpreted as unconsciously motivated. How behavior can be influenced by unconscious motivation is illustrated in this case.

Max was sixteen and failing his junior year in high school in spite of above-average intelligence and a past record of above-average grades. His parents were at a loss to understand what was the matter and his teachers could not explain it. He was very attentive in classes, well-liked by his peers, and regarded by teachers as a potentially capable student who could not seem to apply himself. His poor grades were the result of not turning in assignments and failing nearly all examinations.

Max was concerned about his school grades because he knew that he would be unable to go to college if he could not succeed in high school. He offered no excuses for his failures, but seemed honestly puzzled by the fact that he enjoyed school, liked his teachers, found the subject matter interesting, and had no difficulty in keeping up with his classes, but when he was faced with an examination or assignment he could not seem to function. He said that he prepared for exams and usually felt confident but when he tried to answer questions his mind went blank. He considered assignments fair, understood how to do them, spent considerable time on them, but could never seem to complete them to his satisfaction.

Max was not aware of any emotional problems and he had fairly well-defined goals. After his graduation from high school he planned to attend college and then return to work in his father's insurance business. Future prospects for Max looked very good because he was the only son and it was planned that he would take over the business when his father retired. The boy felt fortunate that his father was able to offer him this opportunity and he could see no disadvantages in such a plan. He admired and respected his father and felt confident that the two of them would enjoy working together.

After several interviews it became evident that Max did not really want to follow through on his plans to take over his father's business. He really wanted to be like his father who had suffered some hard knocks and built his business on his own initiative without help from anyone. Max did not feel justified in refusing his father's offer because he had no alternative plan and no other vocational interests of his own. He also felt that it would be a serious disappointment to his father if he "let him down" and he wanted to avoid hurting his father's feelings. Max had been unable to openly admit his conflicting feelings even to himself, but finally he began to realize that he had been unconsciously sabotaging his own plans by failing in school. His lack of success in high school would prevent his going to college and entering his father's business, thus he would be forced by circumstances beyond his control to get out in the world and see what he could do on his own initiative.

Gaining insight into the nature of his unconscious motivation enabled Max to deal with his conflicting feelings more realistically. His grades improved and he was able to develop a satisfactory understanding with his father that left him feeling free to make his own decisions regarding his future.

When you are able to recognize the drives, needs, and motives which are having an influence on your actions at any given time you are in a better position to understand, predict, and control your behavior. If you are not satisfied with yourself and wonder why you behave as you do, try to analyze your motives. If you can discover what need it is that you are trying to satisfy and the present results are not satisfying you may be able to change your behavior in a way that will offer greater satisfaction of your needs. More often you will discover that many things you do are satisfying several needs at once. You may have lunch with a friend because you are hungry, you need companionship, you need to be recognized, you need to get away from the campus, or you may recognize your friend's needs and be motivated by your desire to be an understanding friend.

SUMMARY

Motivation is defined as the push behind behavior that directs action toward certain goals and the relative energy that is put into reaching the goals. The viewpoint taken here is that motivation is a result of biological drives, emotional needs, and social motives functioning as an integrated system.

Biological drive refers to the state of tension and anxiety that is aroused by a lack or deficiency in the body tissues that directs behavior toward satisfaction of the need and return to a state of equilibrium. Biological drives are influenced by learning and experience. Failure to satisfy the hunger drive can result in striking personality changes that affect the entire range of an individual's behavior. Biological satisfaction of the hunger drive can still result in emotional problems if the conditions under which the drive is satisfied are not emotionally satisfying. Psychological problems are often associated with eating behavior.

Rest and sleep are biological drives that are affected by emotional and social learning. The need for a continuous supply of oxygen to the brain is crucial to healthy functioning. Temperature regulation and elimination of bodily wastes are functions of the autonomic nervous system but they are subject to voluntary control and may be a source of conflict leading to personality problems. In lower animals the sex drive is a purely biological process but in man it is a more complex emotional process regulated by learning.

Emotional needs are dependent upon forming satisfying interpersonal relationships. Emotion is a disturbed state of equilibrium resulting from psychological causes and experienced as conscious feeling called affect. Failure to satisfy the basic emotional needs of childhood can result in personality and behavior disorders in later life. Emotional security is the feeling of being loved, accepted, protected, and belonging and it is crucial to healthy emotional development. When a child feels emotionally secure he develops a basic sense of trust in people and begins to strive for independence or trust in himself.

A child needs parental control until he is capable of self-control and good judgment. Satisfaction of the need for control enables a child to learn respect for authority. The need for achievement must be satisfied repeatedly if one is to develop a healthy personality. The need for recognition is essential for development of self-esteem and establishing identity. Self-actualization depends upon satisfaction of all the basic emotional needs.

After the biological drives and emotional needs are satisfied, social motives become more influential in the motivational system. The social motives include knowledge, meaning, expression, unity, and humanism. The need to gain knowledge and satisfy curiosity leads to technological and social progress. The need to find meaning in life is important for self-integration as is the need for expression of feelings and ideas. The need for unity is met by the capacity to love which represents the ultimate in self-integration. Man's highest motive is the need for humanism or responsibility for mankind.

Most behavior stems from multiple motivation rather than a single drive or need. Sometimes our behavior is motivated by needs of which we are not consciously aware and which we are unable to control without gaining a better understanding of them. Recognition of the drives, needs, and motives influencing our actions helps us to understand, predict, and control behavior.

SUGGESTIONS FOR FURTHER READING

Beach, Frank A. (Ed.), *Sex and Behavior*, New York, Wiley, 1965. Survey of contemporary studies of sex role behavior and the changing trends in today's world.

Buhler, Charlotte and Massarik, Fred., *The Course of Human Life*, New York, Springer,

1968. A study of goals concerned with the wholeness and significance of man's experience.

Cofer, C. N. and Appley, M. H., *Motivation: Theory and Research*, New York, Wiley, 1964. A critical and comprehensive coverage of the theoretical and research literature of motivational psychology.

Maslow, Abraham H., *Toward a Psychology of Being*, Princeton, N. J., Van Nostrand, 1962. Human motivation is viewed in terms of the hierarchy of needs leading to self actualization.

May, Rollo, *Psychology and the Human Dilemma*, Princeton, N. J., Van Nostrand, 1967. The importance of providing for personal satisfaction of man's humanitarian motives is considered in relation to today's complex and impersonal world.

Understanding Individual Differences

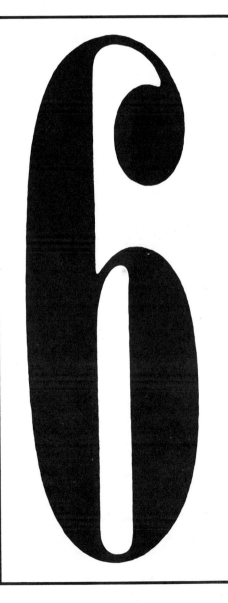

Have you ever wondered what life would be like if every individual felt, thought, and acted exactly like every other person? We have seen how behavior is expressed in the functions of sensation, perception, and motor activity, and how the forces of heredity and environment interact to shape each individual into a unique person. We have identified the basic drives, needs, and motives common to all individuals and have seen how learning serves to increase individual differences as each person grows and develops his own unique personality. Every person has a certain quality of individuality that distinguishes him from everyone else even though he may have many characteristics in common with other people.

Understanding human behavior must include studying the ways in which people differ from each other, the nature and extent of their differences, and the effects of these differences on behavior. As you recognize the multitude of ways in which people may differ, you should bear in mind that not all differences are equally important. Satisfactory human relationships depend upon recognition and acceptance of individual differences and the ability to evaluate which ones are important at any particular time or for any specific purpose. If you were choosing an employee from a group of applicants, for example, differences in color of hair and eyes may not be important but differences in education and experience would be. Many people are inclined to prejudge others on the basis of relatively unimportant differences and to categorize people into groups: blondes are unstable, tall men are overbearing, dark-skinned people are lazy, orientals cannot be trusted, etc. The failure to recognize individual differences among members of a group indicates ignorance and prejudice.

ASSESSMENT OF INDIVIDUALITY

As we look at the people around us we notice individual differences in biological characteristics. People differ in height, weight, appearance, body shape, and proportions. When any one of these physical characteristics is measured, using a standard measuring instrument on a representative sample of the population, a continuous variation is found.

The height of adult males, for example varies by degrees from the shortest to the tallest man. Measurement also reveals that most men are near the middle of the range for height or close to the average. The number of men at each level of height decreases as you move from the average toward the extremes of shortness and tallness. The average height for men is 5 feet 9 inches. In Figure 6-1 you can see that there are more men at 5 feet 9 inches than at any other

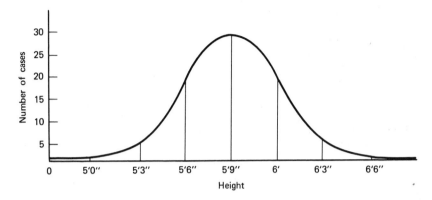

Figure 6-1. Distribution of height of adult males.

height. There are more men 6 feet tall than there are 6 feet 3 inches, and on the other side of the average, more men are 5 feet 6 inches than 5 feet 3 inches. The farther we move from average toward the extremes the fewer men we find at each height.

The Normal Distribution

The measurements shown in Figure 6-1 follow what is called *normal distribution* because it is found whenever most biological traits are measured. When psychological characteristics are measured they usually follow the same pattern of distribution. When the measurements of a characteristic being studied are plotted on a graph they approximate a bell-shaped curve like the one shown in Figure 6-2. Notice that the units of measurement are recorded on the horizontal or base line of the graph and the numbers of individuals who have been measured are indicated on the vertical line, as in Figure 6-1. We can see that the bell-shaped curve is high in the middle and tapers off in each direction toward the extremes. Mathematicians call this bell-shaped curve the *normal curve* because it has been plotted from a normal distribution of measurements.

Figure 6-2 shows the normal curve and the percent of cases we would expect to find in each area of the curve if the distribution is normal. You can see in Figure 6-2 that the average point of the curve is in the middle, and that there are as many people above the average as there are below average. You can also see that there are many more people near the average than at the extremes. When we apply this mathematical model to the example of height we would

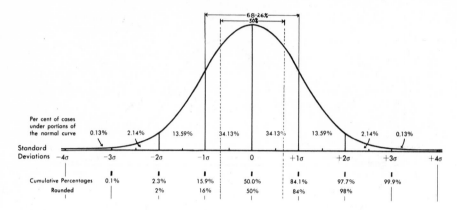

Figure 6-2. The normal curve. (Courtesy of the Psychological Corporation.)

find that 34 percent of adult males are between 5 feet 6 inches and 5 feet 9 inches and another 34 percent are between 5 feet 9 inches and 6 feet 0 inches. The *average range*, then is between 5 feet 6 inches and 6 feet 0 inches because this would include 68 percent or about two-thirds of all adult men. We would expect to find only about 2 percent of all men taller than 6 feet 3 inches and about 2 percent shorter than 5 feet 3 inches.

The normal curve has proven to be one of the most valuable aids to the study of human behavior. It provides us with a means of locating individuals relative to one another. When we use the terms "normal" or "typical" in psychology we are referring to the normal curve or normal distribution. This simply means the way in which human traits are distributed. It is not a curve of rightness, goodness, health, or any other ideal. It is the basis on which we can say that most people are average for most traits. You might think you would like to be at the extreme right of the normal curve for intelligence, like Einstein, or for amount of income or accumulated wealth, like the Rockefellers, but would you also like to be at the extreme for such traits as weight, susceptibility to disease, or selfishness? To be in the average or normal range may not always seem glamorous, but extreme deviation is not necessarily preferable. Any given individual will be located at different points along the normal distribution for different traits. All of us have more or less of every human characteristic.

Principles of Measurement

Measures of individual differences become meaningful only by comparison with other persons. Just as scales have been devised to measure height and weight, and instruments have been perfected to measure heart rate, blood pressure, and temperature, techniques have been developed to measure the psychological characteristics of individuals. A psychological test involves the following essentials of measurement: (*a*) a uniform task, (*b*) performed under comparable conditions, (*c*) yielding scores of time, number, difficulty, or quality, (*d*) which are compared with an appropriate norm group.

Good measuring instruments must be accurate and dependable. We would not use an elastic yardstick to measure height nor would we use a different set of problems to compare the arithmetic ability of one child with another. Comparison or measurement demands that the instrument or test be based on a *uniform task* or the items included be *equal in difficulty*.

Comparison of individuals requires that each person be given an *equal opportunity to perform* or that the task be *performed under comparable conditions*. To give one person more help than another in solving a set of problems would be like measuring the height of some people when standing and others when sitting or kneeling. The conditions under which a test is taken should be alike for everyone. When psychological measurements are involved, this principle is extended to include internal conditions of individuals such as rest, nourishment, health, and freedom from anxiety. Equal opportunity to perform in terms of these internal conditions is not easily accomplished and they can be sources of error in measurement. For example, suppose you report for a college entrance examination at 8 o'clock in the morning after driving all night to get back from an unexpected emergency trip. Your performance on the test might be hindered by fatigue. Or suppose you had applied for employment and were asked to take an intelligence test, and on the day of the test your fiancee became ill and was taken to the hospital. Your anxiety and worry could interfere with your ability to concentrate and your score on the test would be lower than it would be under ordinary circumstances.

The measures used to assess or evaluate performance, such as time scores, error scores, or indicators of quality, should be the same for all persons being compared. *Scoring must be consistent* from one test to another if the scores are to be meaningful.

The group with which an individual is being compared is called the *norm group*. The norm group should be appropriate in terms of age, education, special training, background factors, and other characteristics important to the trait being measured and shared by the individuals being studied. For example, suppose a 10-year-old child can solve 20 of a given set of arithmetic problems correctly. Is this good or poor performance? We really know nothing about his arithmetic ability unless we know how well other children of the same age and level of education do under similar conditions. It would not make sense to compare the 10-year-old with college students or with men in general. The *appropriate norm group* in this instance would consist of a large number of 10-year-olds or a large number of fifth-graders who average 10 years of age. The group with which an individual is being compared is of utmost importance.

Dimensions of Difference

The ways in which people differ are called *dimensions*, because variation occurs from one extreme to the other of any given characteristic. People are not short or tall, weak or strong, smart or dull, capable or incapable, dependent or independent. Everyone is all these things to some degree. Measurement is aimed at determining the degree of height, strength, wisdom, capability, and independence rather than categorizing a person in one extreme or the other. How any one person measures up on these characteristics is best determined by comparing him with others and finding his relative position with reference to an appropriate norm group.

Some of the important psychological dimensions in which individual differences are found include intelligence, aptitudes, special abilities, interests, values, and personality. All of these dimensions are interrelated and function together to make each person a unique individual. We study them separately only to make the complexity of human behavior more understandable.

INTELLIGENCE

The term intelligence is commonly used to mean "brain power" or mental ability. It indicates general mental alertness, problem-solving capacity, and the ability to learn or to profit from one's experiences. Intelligence has been defined as the total "ability of an individual to act purposefully, think rationally, and to deal effectively with his environment" (Wechsler, 1958). Thus, intelligence is seen as an overall kind of general ability that enables a person to solve whatever problems confront him, making use of what he has previously learned and applying it to a new situation.

The Nature of Intelligence

Most people can agree on what is intelligent behavior in specific situations but the concept of intelligence is still an important area of investigation in psychology. Is it a single ability or a complex combination of several different abilities? To better understand intelligence we can break it down into three main types: (*a*) abstract or verbal intelligence; (*b*) practical or concrete intelligence; and (*c*) social intelligence.

Abstract intelligence is the ability to deal with words and symbols. It is used in reading, writing, speaking, mathematics, and any other skill where numbers and symbols must be used. Abstract thinking involves ideas and concepts of varying degrees of generality. Any word that describes a quality apart from a concrete object is abstract. Understanding the meanings of words such as justice, loyalty, kindness, friendship, honesty, and theory requires abstract intelligence. Most of the subject matter studied in school requires abstract intelligence. A high level of abstract intelligence is needed to succeed in professions which require formal education beyond college graduation, such as medicine, law, science, and college teaching.

While abstract reasoning and thinking are important they are not the only factors involved in intelligence. We have to deal with other people and with things as well as with thoughts and ideas.

Practical intelligence is what we usually think of as common sense. It is the ability to deal with things or objects such as tools, materials, and instruments skillfully and in a useful way. People with a high degree of practical or concrete intelligence can usually figure out how to do things like make repairs, assemble an object, or find a better way to do something without having to be told or shown. Driving a car, operating a camera, and cleaning a house all require practical intelligence. Many occupations in engineering, mechanics, health sciences, and business technology require practical, as well as abstract intelligence.

Social intelligence is the ability to get along well with people of all kinds. It means the ability to fit in and to act appropriately in public, at social gatherings, or in small groups. The socially intelligent person knows how to form effective relationships and understands social roles. Social intelligence includes sensitivity to other people's feelings, the ability to predict the outcome of a series of events (see where things are leading), and the use of good judgment in one's behavior. People high in social intelligence are usually well-liked by others and are often chosen as group leaders. Occupations in public relations, sales, personnel management, social service, and youth work demand a large degree of social intelligence.

These three types of intelligence are interrelated, but all individuals are not equally endowed with them. When we speak of general intelligence we mean the general factor of adaptation and the capacity to recognize and cope with all the problems one encounters in adjusting to his environment.

Another way to describe intelligence is in terms of its basic elements of understanding, memory, and association. The ability to understand conversations, directions, or what is read is the first element of intelligence. *Understanding* means to know, to "catch on," to comprehend. The less intelligent a person is, the more detailed and simplified an explanation he requires to understand things that are new or unfamiliar. The more intelligent person grasps ideas quickly and has less difficulty acquiring new concepts.

The second element of intelligence is *memory*. Memory and understanding are dependent on each other. For example, to read this book depends on your capacity to understand. The better you understand the material, the better it will be remembered. The better you remember what you read now, the easier it will be for you to understand what you read later. The physical nature of memory is unknown, but theory suggests it is probably some biochemical change in the neuron cells of the brain. The behavioral function of memory, however, is known; it is to retrieve or recall one's experiences whether they be sensory, symbolic, or motor.

The third, and perhaps most important, element of intelligence is the ability to form *associations*. To understand and to remember isolated bits of experience would not be very helpful unless one could put them all together in some meaningful form of association. Associating facts and ideas is called *reasoning*. In the study of psychology you are learning many facts and acquiring a lot of information about the nervous system, heredity, learning, and other topics. You may understand the important information about each topic and you may remember numerous facts. To master the task of understanding human behavior, however, you must relate all this material together to form a whole picture. The elements of general intelligence then are recalling what we have learned at one time, associating it with what we learn at a later time, and relating it all effectively to our personal lives.

Measuring Intelligence

Attempts to measure intelligence have led to the conclusion that what we are measuring is not a single dimension of individual functioning, but a complex combination of factors.

In one of the early approaches to analyzing intelligence into measurable factors it was concluded that intelligence is a combination of seven *primary mental abilities* (Thurstone, 1938). These primary mental abilities are the following:

Word fluency: ability to use words in speaking and writing with ease.

Verbal meaning: ability to understand ideas that are presented in word form.

Numerical: ability to work with numbers and do simple arithmetic functions.

Memory: ability to retain and revive impressions and to recall and recognize past experiences.

Reasoning: ability to solve complex problems by making use of past experiences.

Space perception: ability to perceive size and spatial relationships correctly.

Perceptual speed: ability to identify stimulus objects quickly. To develop reading skill it is necessary to identify whole words without looking at each letter in the word.

Items have been devised to sample each of the primary mental abilities as a basis for constructing tests of intelligence. Such tests are widely used in the public schools today.

When we look at the primary mental abilities identified above several facts become apparent. First, the elements of understanding, memory, and association are all represented. Second, the kind of intelligence being measured is limited to the abstract or verbal, and does not include practical and social intelligence. Finally, the type of learning that would be necessary for one to do well on tests of this sort is learning of a *symbolic* nature. Since most symbolic learning is achieved through formal classroom instruction, the person who has not attended school or profited from his school experience will not perform well on such tests.

Group tests of intelligence are useful as a measure of the extent to which individuals have benefitted from their educational experiences. When school children do poorly on such tests they can be assigned for remedial instruction or put in special classes where more individual help is given. Thus, we can see the benefit of testing as an aid in assessing school progress which is a necessary achievement in our society.

The unfortunate effects of mass testing of intelligence are the faulty conclusions to which they often lead. When individuals do not perform well on intelligence tests it should *not* be assumed that they lack any intelligence or that they cannot learn or profit from experience. Remember that practical and social intelligence are not measured in these tests and they are very important. There are also other kinds of learning as well as symbolic learning, but these are not measured in most tests. In addition, there are other ways besides formal school instruction in which learning, including symbolic learning, can and does occur. We must keep in mind that low performance on intelligence tests does not mean that an individual is intellectually hopeless. It may mean that our methods of school instruction are just not meeting the challenge of educating all individuals.

Much of the practical knowledge and judgment needed to cope with everyday problems in real-life situations is gained through experience outside the schoolroom. Consider, for example, how you learned to repair a bicycle, prepare a meal, plant a lawn, resist high-pressure salesmen, apply for a job, take care of your car, make friends, and what to do when emergencies occur. All these experiences and many more require intelligent behavior that is not learned in school or measured by intelligence tests given in the classroom under the heading of primary mental abilities.

Recent developments in the area of mental testing have led to a new concept of intellectual abilities. According to this model the structure of human intellect can by analyzed into 120 interrelated factors (Guilford, 1966). This systematic framework is comparable to the chemist's periodic table of the elements. Scientists are still working on developing tests for each of the 120 factors. Such an exhaustive analysis makes it appear that intelligence is extremely complex, but if all factors can be identified and organized into a unified system it may be much more easily understood.

Individually administered tests of intelligence offer many advantages over the group tests that are used by classroom teachers. Individual tests require a high level of skill and training on the part of the examiner, and the time required to test each individual is at least 1 hour and often more. Examiner skill and time involved prevent the routine use of these tests in school classrooms, but they are definitely preferable for assessing the intellectual functioning of individuals. The individual tests include measures of practical and social as well as abstract intelligence. When the tests are administered individually the examiner can observe the attitudes, responses, and methods of performance of each person as an individual. The ways a person responds to individual test situations and how he performs each task are important in the diagnosis of learning and adjustment problems and are valuable in the interpretation of test results (Figure 6-3).

The most widely used individual intelligence tests are the *Stanford-Binet* and the *Wechsler Intelligence Scales*. These tests are available in different forms for different ages so that they provide a measure of individual intelligence in individuals from ages 2 to 70. Table 6-1 lists and describes the 11 subtests of the Wechsler Adult Intelligence Scale (Wechsler, 1958).

Figure 6-3.   Individual intelligence testing with the Stanford-Binet Scale. (New York State Mental Hygiene photo by Julian Belin.)

Notice in Table 6-1 that a number of different verbal and non-verbal or performance skills are included in the measurement of intelligence. One advantage of this type of test is that it does not penalize individuals whose verbal skills are not well-developed due to different cultural or subcultural backgrounds. For example, people from minority groups whose families speak a foreign language rather than English tend to score higher on the tests of performance skill than on tests of verbal skills. In a group test of intelligence the scores for these people would not be an accurate measure of mental ability.

Tests of general intelligence or mental ability are used by schools, industries, hospitals, clinics, and vocational counselors. They are generally employed for the purpose of predicting success in school or on the job, in diagnosing or

Table 6-1. The Sub-tests of the Wechsler Adult Intelligence Scale.
(From: Wechsler, 1958.)

Test	Description
Information	A measure of the subject's fund of general knowledge and ability to assimilate facts and information relative to his environment.
Comprehension	A test of common sense, depends on possession of a certain amount of practical information and a general ability to evaluate past experiences.
Digit Span	A measure of rote memory and span of attention, also an indication of flexibility, mental control, tension, and anxiety.
Arithmetic	Primarily a measure of arithmetic reasoning and facility with numbers, also measures concentration and attention, reveals capacity for sustained effort.
Similarities	Measures capacity for concept formation and for abstract reasoning at the verbal level, will help detect impairment of thought processes or deviant thinking and type of mental approach.
Vocabulary	One of the most stable tests for appraising intellectual capacity, content is often of diagnostic value.
Picture Arrangement	Tests understanding of familiar social situations and reflects ability to anticipate consequences of initial action.
Picture Completion	Measures alertness to environmental details, ability to differentiate essential from nonessential parts in an organized whole, and capacity for perception of reality.
Block Design	A test of visual–motor organization involving abstract capacity and spatial perception; entails a certain amount of manipulative ability, spatial orientation, and capacity to shift; also reveals the tempermental traits of persistence and frustration.
Object Assembly	Involves perception, motor coordination, and practical manipulative ability, related to mechanical comprehension. It is useful for evaluating mode of approach to a set task (trial and error versus planned attack) and reaction to frustration.
Digit Symbol	Measures speed and accuracy of learning new associations; depends on perceptual alertness, immediate memory, and motor speed; also calls for concentration and directed effort; sometimes an indicator of subject's energy and drive.

Figure 6-4.   The psychologist here is administering a nonverbal test of intelligence, the Columbia Mental Maturity Scale, which only requires the child to recognize similarities and differences in pictures. (Photo courtesy of Saratoga County Mental Health Clinic.)

understanding learning and behavior problems, or to help in choosing a career. Figure 6-4 illustrates individual intelligence testing.

The Meaning of I.Q.

Intelligence test scores are reported as I.Q. or *intelligence quotient*. The I.Q. is determined by comparing an individual's score with the distribution of scores in the norm group. Norm groups for intelligence tests are made up of large samples of individuals at each age level. Whenever a large group of people the same age are given a mental test and the scores are converted to I.Q.'s, the results approximate a normal distribution (refer back to Figure 6-2). The average I.Q. for individuals of all ages is 100, and 50 percent of the people at all ages have I.Q.'s between 90 and 109. Table 6-2 shows the normal distribution of I.Q.'s, how they are classified, and the percent of the population included in each classification.

Table 6-2. Classification of Intelligence. (From: Wechsler, 1958.)

Classification	I.Q.	Percent included
Defective	69 and below	2.2
Borderline	70–79	6.7
Dull normal	80–89	16.1
Average	90–109	50.0
Bright normal	110–119	16.1
Superior	120–129	6.7
Very superior	130 and above	2.2

We have already discussed the difficulties and limitations in measuring intelligence, all of which make it clear that the I.Q. is not an absolute and unchanging or easily measured characteristic of an individual. Numerous studies have shown that improved educational opportunities and increased stimulation from the environment can produce significant increases in I.Q.

The *relationship between I.Q. and occupation* has been studied extensively by military psychologists. During World War II over 12 million men and women took the Army General Classification Test (AGCT), a group test of general intelligence. Probably no other test has been administered to such a large segment of the population of this country. On the basis of available data it was possible to determine the average I.Q. for men in various occupations prior to their military service. The results, illustrated in Figure 6-5, show marked differences in average I.Q. for men in the different occupations, but even more remarkable is the wide range of I.Q.'s found within every occupation (Harrell and Harrell, 1945).

Notice in Figure 6-5 that the average I.Q. for farm workers, teamsters, and miners is around 90 and the average for accountants, lawyers, and engineers is around 125, but there were some farm workers with higher I.Q.'s than some accountants. The study indicates that in every occupation there are some individuals well above the average who could succeed in occupations having the highest average I.Q. We know that many of these men lacked the education, opportunity, or motivation to prepare themselves for higher level jobs. There are more opportunities for higher education today but many people do not realize their own potentials.

Functioning at I.Q. Extremes

The I.Q. concept has been used to make many judgments and decisions about individuals and to limit as well as to provide opportunities for them. The range of I.Q. from 70 to 130 has been shown to include about 95 percent of the population (see Table 6-2). Within this broad range of individual differences most persons are able to function intellectually within what we call the normal range or borderline normal. Those at the extremes of the I.Q. distribution are atypical and their intellectual functioning should be expected to be different from most persons. The question, of course, is how and why are they so different? And how can we better understand their capabilities and limitations? At the upper extreme of the I.Q. distribution we have about $2\frac{1}{2}$ percent of the population or approximately $4\frac{1}{2}$ million people who are considered "gifted" because of their superior intellectual ability. At the other extreme we have about $2\frac{1}{2}$ percent or approximately $4\frac{1}{2}$ million people with I.Q.'s below 70 who are considered "retarded" because of their defective intellectual ability.

The Gifted. An outstanding study of 1300 individuals with rated I.Q.'s of 140 or above was started in 1922 and has been continued by followup studies at intervals since that time (Terman et al., 1925, 1947, 1954, 1959). When the study began, 1000 of these individuals were either just ready to start school or had just started, and 300 were entering high school. The data of this study fills volumes of books, but we can summarize the general findings of interest.

Educationally, this group advanced easily through the school program, some skipped one or more grade levels, most earned high achievement in school marks. Eventually, 93 percent of them were graduated from college and about 50 percent earned higher educational degrees. Their rated intellectual promise was matched by their educational achievement.

Socially, this group as children formed friendships easily and seemed to enjoy play activities as much if not more than average children. The gifted group was active in extracurricular activities at the schools they attended and many held positions of elected leadership. Occupationally, more than 70 percent entered the professions when generally only about 10 percent of the total population does so. By age 30 years, their average income was twice as high as the national average.

AGCT SCORES FOR

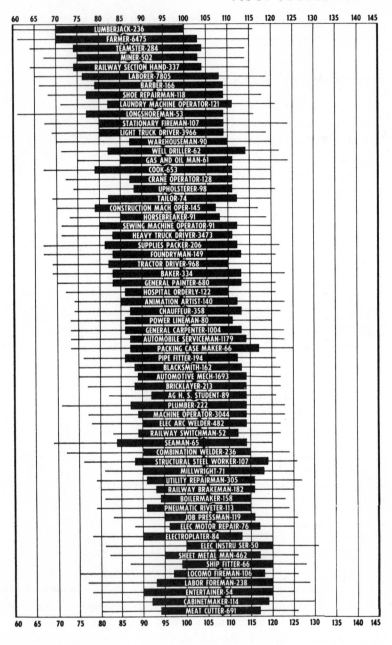

| | | | | | | | | | | | | | | | | | |
|60|65|70|75|80|85|90|95|100|105|110|115|120|125|130|135|140|145|

LUMBERJACK-236
FARMER-6475
TEAMSTER-284
MINER-502
RAILWAY SECTION HAND-337
LABORER-7805
BARBER-166
SHOE REPAIRMAN-118
LAUNDRY MACHINE OPERATOR-121
LONGSHOREMAN-53
STATIONARY FIREMAN-107
LIGHT TRUCK DRIVER-3966
WAREHOUSEMAN-90
WELL DRILLER-62
GAS AND OIL MAN-61
COOK-653
CRANE OPERATOR-128
UPHOLSTERER-98
TAILOR-74
CONSTRUCTION MACH OPER-145
HORSEBREAKER-91
SEWING MACHINE OPERATOR-91
HEAVY TRUCK DRIVER-3473
SUPPLIES PACKER-206
FOUNDRYMAN-149
TRACTOR DRIVER-968
BAKER-334
GENERAL PAINTER-680
HOSPITAL ORDERLY-122
ANIMATION ARTIST-140
CHAUFFEUR-358
POWER LINEMAN-80
GENERAL CARPENTER-1004
AUTOMOBILE SERVICEMAN-1179
PACKING CASE MAKER-66
PIPE FITTER-194
BLACKSMITH-162
AUTOMOTIVE MECH-1693
BRICKLAYER-213
AG H. S. STUDENT-89
PLUMBER-222
MACHINE OPERATOR-3044
ELEC ARC WELDER-482
RAILWAY SWITCHMAN-52
SEAMAN-65
COMBINATION WELDER-236
STRUCTURAL STEEL WORKER-107
MILLWRIGHT-71
UTILITY REPAIRMAN-305
RAILWAY BRAKEMAN-182
BOILERMAKER-158
PNEUMATIC RIVETER-113
JOB PRESSMAN-119
ELEC MOTOR REPAIR-76
ELECTROPLATER-84
ELEC INSTRU SER-50
SHEET METAL MAN-462
SHIP FITTER-66
LOCOMO FIREMAN-106
LABOR FOREMAN-238
ENTERTAINER-54
CABINETMAKER-114
MEAT CUTTER-691

| | | | | | | | | | | | | | | | | | |
|60|65|70|75|80|85|90|95|100|105|110|115|120|125|130|135|140|145|

CIVILIAN OCCUPATIONS

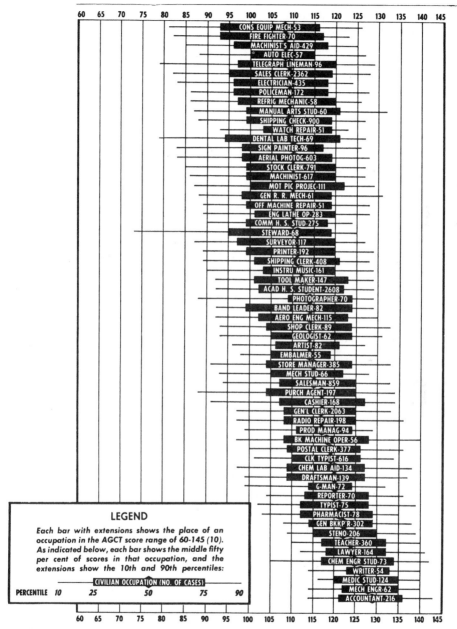

Figure 6-5. AGCT Scores for men by occupation. (Permission granted by Science Research Associates, copyright 1947.)

In their physical and emotional health the intellectually gifted also proved to be fortunately endowed. Their physical health and development was superior compared to other children, puberty was generally reached at an earlier age, and good health was a continuing characteristic of the group. At followup, their marriage rate was as high as the national average and their divorce rate was lower than the rate for the state (California) where they had lived during childhood. Their mental illness and suicide rates were below the national average. They had an average of 2.4 children in their marriages and these children had an average I.Q. of about 127.

This study of gifted individuals served to disprove some of the commonly held notions of gifted intellectual functioning. This group was not puny and sickly physically, socially withdrawn or friendless, emotionally restricted, or intellectually dreamy and unproductive. The group can best be described as active, vigorous, alert, successful, happy, and free of the degree of illness that most persons experience. Not every member of the group could be described in this way, there were individual differences, but as a group the promise identified early in their lives proved accurate and lasting.

Why were these individuals gifted? The data reported for their background and family give us some information. Generally, the parents of this group were above average in intelligence and educational achievement, general health, and income levels. About one-third of the parents were in professional occupations and only 7 percent in unskilled occupations. The parents were in the prime of life at the time their gifted child was born and it was usual that this child was the first-born of the family. From these data we can say that heredity plus environmental factors were involved. The parents of the group were above average in many respects and their life circumstances could provide a supportive and stimulating environment in which the gifted child could grow. Some of the findings for members of the gifted group who were relatively less successful or less well-adjusted than the others are suggestive of this heredity–environment interaction. These relatively less successful gifted individuals came more often from broken homes or families of lower occupational level. This suggests that family security, comfort, and opportunities for stimulating experiences are needed to translate potential to full realization of promise.

The Retarded. This group has been of greater concern to society than has the gifted because they present special problems of functioning effectively in society. Of the $4\frac{1}{2}$ million retarded individuals in the United States today approximately 200,000 are confined to public and private institutions for complete care. Even below I.Q. 70, however, classification is necessary to describe functioning. We must remember that no where along the range of I.Q. scores can we draw a line and find sharp distinctions, so again we must work in ranges.

The standard classification of the mentally retarded, from mild to profound retardation, is shown in Table 6-3, with a description of their characteristics as infants, children, and adults (U.S. President's Panel on Mental Retardation, 1963).

Most cases of mental retardation fall into the categories of mild and moderate retardation, and it has been found that they can profit from special training. Recent advances in training have demonstrated that many state institutions are able to prepare the retarded to function as useful members of society. There is a growing trend in recent years for public schools to offer special classes for both educable and trainable mentally retarded as an alternative to institutional care and supervision.

What can research tell us about the life adjustment of retarded individuals? Let us look at two studies of the same group of mildly retarded persons at different times in their lives. Baller (1936) identified a group of 190 mildly retarded persons who had in common "opportunity room" experiences in their school history. He selected a control group of nonretarded persons who were matched with the retarded for age and sex ratios as a basis for making comparisons. Again, we will summarize the findings of greatest interest.

Baller reported that by average age 21 years, 7 percent of the retarded group had been placed in institutions for care and supervision. At the same time 83 percent of the group were found to be employed and self-supporting at least part of the time. About 60 percent of the retarded girls had married and this percentage was the same for the girls in the normal control group. Only about one-third of the retarded males had married and this percentage was lower than that of the normal males. About 25 percent of the retarded group had juvenile court and 18 percent had police court records, compared to 4 percent and 6 percent, respectively, for the normals.

Charles (1953) reported a followup study, at a later date, locating about 150 of the original 190 retarded subjects in Baller's study. The average age of the surviving members of the retarded group at this time was 40 years. The death rate of the retarded group had been high, especially accidental deaths. The marriage rate and average number of children (2) were below the rates for the general population. Of those who had been employed (about 83 percent of the group), half of them had held their jobs for periods ranging from 3 to 20 years. One of the important findings of Baller and Charles's studies was that some of

Table 6-3. Characteristics of the Retarded by U.S. President's Panel on Mental Retardation (1963)

Type	Characteristics from birth to adulthood			
	Birth through 5 yr	6 through 20 yr	Over 21 yr	
Mild (I.Q. 53–69)	Often not noticed as retarded by casual observer but is slower to walk, feed self, and talk than most children	Can acquire practical skills and useful reading and arithmetic to a third to sixth grade level with special education. Can be guided toward social conformity	Can usually achieve social and vocational skills adequate to self-maintenance; may need occasional guidance and support when under unusual social or economic stress	
Moderate (36–52)	Noticeable delays in motor development, especially in speech, responds to training in various self-help activities	Can learn simple communication, elementary health and safety habits, and simple manual skills; does not progress in functional reading or arithmetic	Can perform simple tasks under sheltered conditions; participates in simple recreation; travels alone in familiar places; usually incapable of self-maintenance	
Severe (20–35)	Marked delay in motor development; little or no communication skill; may respond to training in elementary self-help—for example, self-feeding	Usually walks barring specific disability; has some understanding of speech and some response; can profit from systematic habit training	Can conform to daily routines and repetitive activities; needs continuing direction and supervision in protective environment	
Profound (below 20)	Gross retardation; minimal capacity for functioning in sensorimotor areas; needs nursing care	Obvious delays in all areas of development; shows basic emotional responses; may respond to skillful training in use of legs, hands, and jaws; needs close supervision	May walk, need nursing care, have primitive speech; usually benefits from regular physical activity; incapable of self-maintenance	

the retarded group near I.Q. 50 had done as well or better in adjustment than some near I.Q. 70. Again, success and failure in life adjustment was related to something besides the I.Q. level. The children of the retarded group members ranged in I.Q.'s from 50 to 138 with an average of about 95 or normal!

The findings of these two studies led people to reconsider some commonly held notions about retarded individuals in this 50–69 I.Q. range. They can be useful, responsible citizens supporting themselves and their families. They do not marry in greater proportion than others in the population or produce more, and defective, offspring. Their death rate is higher than the rate for most persons of the same ages and accidents are a common cause of death. The higher accidental death rate, like the arrest records for minor offenses, indicate that poor judgment is one of their major problems.

The studies of Baller and Charles, like other studies, also indicate slower physical development and greater susceptibility to disease among the retarded. Kaplan (1940) found that the average age of death for institutionalized profoundly retarded (I.Q. 0–25) was 19 years. We would assume these early death ages for the retarded in institutions occurred even when good personal and medical care was available. Physical inferiority seems to accompany lower intellectual potential.

What causes retardation? Some is due to low inherited potential in families of low ability. An extra chromosome, in otherwise normal parents, is involved in the severe form of retardation called mongoloidism. Some is due to damage to the brain during the prenatal period by viruses such as the German measles, Rh blood antibodies, and toxic (low blood oxygen) conditions. Metabolic disorders like PKU, deficiencies of hormone secretion from the thyroid gland, and inadequate nutrition account for some retardation. Some retardation is caused by brain damage during birth or from accidents after birth. Finally, some illnesses of childhood accompanied by high fever can cause retardation. The exact percentage of all retardation due to each of these factors is not known. Some retardation probably is a combination of many of these factors as well as factors not presently identified.

APTITUDES AND SPECIAL ABILITIES

The potential capacity to develop some particular ability is called an aptitude. Aptitudes are dormant or undeveloped abilities that will respond to training. For example, when the Army selected a group of men with average intelligence to be trained as auto mechanics the results were not entirely satisfactory. Some of the men took to the training like "ducks to water" and became very skilled. Others in the group had greater difficulty and required a longer time to gain any skill. Some of the men seemed unable to profit from the training and could not qualify for this specialty. The group had been alike in intelligence, but they differed in their aptitude for mechanical work.

Assessment of Aptitudes

The assessment of aptitudes becomes important in situations of *selection* and *personal choice*. Selection occurs whenever there are more candidates for a particular opportunity than there are positions to be filled. When industry or other employers are seeking trainees for expensive programs of skill development, they want to select those persons who will profit from the training and return their investment by a high level of job performance. When training schools and colleges can take only a limited number of students, they try to select those applicants who can benefit from the training and complete the curriculum. Our society does not dictate to persons what they will do with their lives, but permits us freedom of personal choice. "What shall I be?" is a question that all of us have the freedom to decide. Aptitude becomes an important consideration in answering this question about life directions. We generally like best those activities we do well, but because of limited experience we may not be aware of all the things we can do well. Assessment of aptitude helps to identify possible choices for career development that have not even been considered. At the same time aptitude assessment may raise some helpful questions about choices that have already been made without complete knowledge of one's abilities. Many false starts in educational efforts or employment experiences can be eliminated by assessment of aptitudes.

Many tests of aptitude have been developed especially in the mechanical and clerical fields. The principal approach used for development of an aptitude test has been to identify the skills that seem important to a particular task and then find a way to measure these. Aptitude tests may be of the paper and pencil question and answer type or they may be of the performance type. In Figure 6-6 some typical items from aptitude tests are illustrated. A performance-type test item attempts to sample behavior in a situation that involves the same skills as some larger task. For example, fine assembly jobs require speed in recognizing, sorting, and placing small parts. A short timed test that requires the person to select pegs of a given shape or color and place them in a pattern on a pegboard can identify aptitude for fine assembly work.

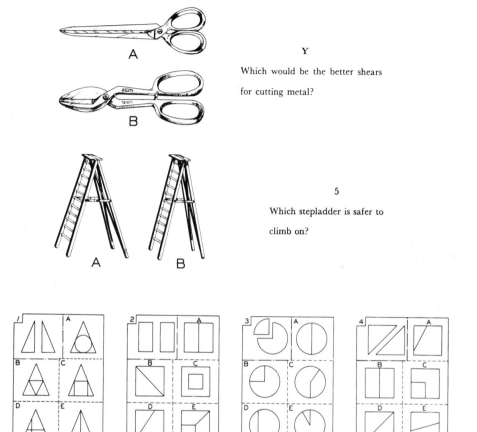

Y

Which would be the better shears
for cutting metal?

5

Which stepladder is safer to
climb on?

Figure 6-6.   Aptitude Test Items. Questions at the top of the page are used to measure mechanical comprehension; the lower items are from a test of spatial perception, related to aptitude for engineering. (Copyright The Psychological Corporation, reproduced by permission.)

During World War II the U.S. Employment Service developed a battery (or series) of tests to measure aptitudes. This battery, called the *General Aptitude Test Battery* (GATB), was based on research with aptitude tests dating back before 1930. The Employment Service had found the development of aptitude tests for each of the thousands of possible jobs that exist an impossible and inefficient task. It was apparent that many jobs required similar aptitudes and the GATB represented those factors of aptitude found to be most common to all jobs. The factors of the GATB and descriptions of the aptitudes they sample are given in Table 6-4.

Standards of performance, or norms, were obtained for the GATB from a large sample of workers in many occupational fields. When an individual

Table 6-4. Factors Measured by the General Aptitude Test Battery (GATB)
(Source: U.S. Department of Labor, 1962)

Factor	Description
G—Intelligence	General learning ability. Capacity to "catch on" or understand instructions and principles, to reason, and make judgments.
V—Verbal	Ability to understand the meaning of words and ideas associated with them and use effectively. Ability to present ideas and information clearly.
N—Numerical	Ability to use numbers and to perform arithmetic operations quickly and accurately.
S—Spatial	Ability to think visually of geometric forms and comprehend pictorial representation of solid objects. Ability to recognize relationships resulting from movements of objects in space.
P—Form Perception	Ability to recognize important details in objects, pictures, or graphs. Ability to make visual comparisons and detect slight differences in shape or shading of figures, widths and lengths of line.
Q—Clerical Perception	Ability to recognize important detail in written or tabular material. Ability to observe differences in copy, to proofread words and numbers, and to avoid perceptual errors in arithmetic computations.
K—Motor Coordination	Ability to coordinate eyes and hands or fingers rapidly and accurately in making precise movements with speed.
F—Finger Dexterity	Ability to move the fingers, and manipulate small objects with the fingers, rapidly or accurately.
M—Manual Dexterity	Ability to move the hands easily and skillfully. Ability to work with the hands in placing and turning motions.

takes the GATB, his factor scores on the tests are referred to patterns of scores for all occupational fields. He is then advised what occupational fields he matches in aptitude most closely. For example, mechanical aptitude as a general trait involves the factors of S, P, and G. Jobs like electrician, plumber, auto mechanic, and television repair all require S, P, and G, but in different amounts and in different combination with some of the other test factors like F, M, and N. Knowing only that one has mechanical aptitude is not very helpful unless one can also know how much and what kind in relation to the demands of particular jobs. The Employment Service does continuous research with the GATB revising the tests and the norm data to meet changes in employment opportunities. The GATB takes about $2\frac{1}{2}$ hours to administer and is available only at State Employment Services offices. School and college counseling services use tests and batteries of aptitude similar to the GATB tests to assist students in problems of education and vocational choice.

Special mention should be made of tests of *scholastic aptitude*. These tests include such instruments as the SCAT (School and College Ability Test), SAT (Scholastic Aptitude Test), and ACT (American College Testing program). You have probably taken one of these tests for admission or program counseling purposes when you started college. These tests are not so much measures of aptitude (potential to learn) as they are measures of achievement (what you have learned). They are most similar to our tests of general intelligence. They measure abstract or verbal intelligence based upon symbolic learning experiences.

If one has done poorly in school he will not score as well on scholastic aptitude tests as persons who have done well in school. Low results on these tests should not be taken to mean one cannot learn in school. A more accurate interpretation would be that one has not learned as much or as well as others, and diagnosis of learning deficiencies and approaches to learning should be made. When schools and colleges, with limited budgets for operation, have more applicants than they can handle, these scholastic aptitude tests are used for *selection*. Those students who score high on these tests are admitted because their scores indicate they have benefitted from past education. This is a reasonable solution to problems of overcrowding in colleges. To the person who is left out, however, it may not seem reasonable and may be very discouraging. Such a person should seek counseling help to determine if his problem is one of ability, application, or actually low aptitude for the kinds of skill required in education. Counseling for educational goals can be obtained at State Employment Service offices as well as at college counseling service offices.

Development of Aptitudes

Aptitudes develop out of hereditary potentials for behavioral functioning. Basic to all aptitudes is some degree of general intelligence. The popular idea that people who cannot "work with their head" can work well with their hands is not accurate. The individual with mechanical aptitude must have some measure of intelligence, especially the kind called practical or applied. The intellectually retarded score low on tests of aptitude just as they do on tests of intelligence.

Considering the factors measured by the GATB found common to most aptitudes we can identify other aspects of behavioral functioning that must be involved. One of these is motor speed made possible by integration of nervous and muscular systems. Another is accuracy of perception which depends on sensory and nervous system interaction as well as experience. Hand and finger dexterity depend on the coordination of sensory processes of vision and kinesthesis with nervous and muscular systems. Hereditary potentials for general intelligence, sensory, nervous, and muscular function account for some of the individual differences of aptitude.

Other individual differences in aptitude cannot be explained by hereditary potentials; for example, why are most men higher in mechanical aptitude than most women? Similarly, why are most women higher in clerical aptitude than most men? These two kinds of aptitude, mechanical and clerical, have some common factors possessed by both men and women. The answer to the questions seems to be that experience provides opportunities and develops preference for some activities in men different from those for women. Most of these experiences result from the masculine–feminine *sex roles* that children in our society learn.

Boys are encouraged in childhood to explore, assemble, and take apart objects of a mechanical nature and girls are not. Encouraged in these activities, boys gain practice that helps them to develop those factors of mind and movement involved in mechanical aptitude. Because such activities for boys are expected and are rewarded by the approval of parents and others, a pattern of preference for these activities develops which causes boys to continue the behavior. On the other hand, girls who have the same potentials as boys to gain mechanical aptitude are discouraged from activities necessary to develop these potentials. Instead, girls are encouraged in less active pursuits like sewing and cooking that train or exercise their potentials in ways different from boys. The approval girls get from parents for engaging in "girllike" activities reinforces their behavior thus developing a preference pattern for the behavior.

Clerical activities are relatively inactive tasks of sorting, classifying, and ordering, not very different from many household duties. This interaction between hereditary potentials and life experience results in the development of different aptitudes.

Special Abilities

Unlike aptitudes, there are some special abilities in humans that develop apart from general intelligence. This does not mean that persons who possess these abilities may not be intelligent, but that these abilities are in addition to the trait intelligence. Put another way, a highly intelligent person can score well on any test of aptitude but not possess any of these abilities. Included among these special abilities are art, music, athletics, and creativity. These special abilities develop primarily from inherited potentials. Training or practice can improve them but not create them. Opportunities of life give the experience to express these abilities and are necessary for their development.

Art. This special ability finds expression in activities such as painting, drawing, sculpture, architecture, interior decorating, costume design, drafting, photography, and crafts. If you were to examine drawings produced by first-grade children you would observe striking individual differences in the absence of any training. If you were to view a display of art work by art school students with several years of training you would again find individual differences. This would be true in spite of the fact that students with limited ability become discouraged and drop out of art schools early. Creative art work depends more upon artistic ability than it does upon training in art. Some of the best-known works of art have been produced by persons who have had little or no training at all in art.

Studies indicate that drawing ability is related to a capacity to appreciate differences between good and bad art as judged by artists (Crannell, 1953). Tests of art appreciation, therefore, are often used to assess artistic ability. Some items from an art appreciation test are illustrated in Figure 6-7. The test from which these items came consists of 90 sets of drawings and the subject is asked to indicate his preference for one in each set. The score is the number of choices the subject makes that agrees with choices made by a group of successful artists (Graves, 1946).

Music. There is no single, overall musical ability, but rather a combination of several factors that are related to success as a musician. These factors include pitch discrimination, sense of time, rhythm, sense of intensity, sense of

Figure 6-7. Test items used to measure art appreciation. The task is to choose which of the drawings is the best. (Copyright The Psychological Corporation, reproduced by permission.)

purity, and memory for tones. An individual may score high in some of these factors but not in others. Success in music seems to depend upon a person being strong in some combination of several of these basic abilities. Music ability can be improved by training that occurs during the elementary school years (Hewson, 1966; Kersey, 1966).

Abstract intelligence is necessary to understand the symbols of music. Motor coordination and finger dexterity are required to play a musical instrument. Pitch discrimination, or the capacity to detect differences of frequency (length) in sound, is essential to musical ability. Yet none of these factors can guarantee musical ability for it is obvious that many persons who possess them lack musical ability. Musical ability is all of these things, plus others, in special combination.

Athletics. Studies of athletic ability reveal a consistent tendency for persons who excel in one type of athletics also to excel in others. This has led to a conclusion that athletic ability is an overall kind of trait (Brogden and Harman, 1948). This is probably due to the fact that those characteristics required for performance in one athletic skill are also required to perform other athletic skills. These characteristics include strength, coordination, speed, flexibility, and endurance. Let us look at these characteristics more closely.

Strength is the capacity of muscles to exert force against resistance. Strength depends upon body structure. More specifically, strength depends upon the development of individual muscle fibers in the body. Athletes must possess strength, but they must also be able to expend it in explosive outbursts of power. Coordination means to make body systems work effectively together. Most important to athletics are probably eye–hand (visual–motor systems) and balance (visual–kinesthetic–equilibrium systems). Speed includes both the speed of movements and response to stimulation (reaction time). Flexibility is the capacity to make specific joints move through their entire range of motion. Shoulder flexibility is important in swimming, in throwing as in baseball or football, and in tennis. Ankle flexibility is needed for running as done in track sports. Dancers must possess flexibility in most body joints. Endurance is resistance to fatigue and quick recovery from fatigue. All of these characteristics are needed for athletic skills. They are closely related to each other and lacking any one in great measure would make possession of the others of little value in athletics. For these reasons, athletic ability is probably an overall special ability.

Creativity. This special ability has become, in recent years, the focus of great interest and concern. Creativity means new, novel, the capacity to envision something new, or original. From a personal standpoint, whatever is produced that is new or original is creative. From the viewpoint of society, however, creativity is originality that is also useful. This social emphasis upon usefulness has limited recognition of creative efforts largely to fields of science or technology. However, creativity can find expression in many ways besides science including the visual, literary, and performing arts and personal–social relationships.

Creativity is the ability to work comfortably with problems that are poorly defined or vague, finding new and original approaches, or trying new applications. Creative thinking is unconventional because it does not follow the ordinary, fixed paths of identifying or solving problems. This quality of novelty is not "bad" it is simply different from approaches and solutions usually produced by most people. Because creativity means newness it can result in change. People find change hard to accept unless they can see immediate benefit or usefulness. The problem for society is that creativity must be allowed to be exercised and its usefulness determined after it occurs. To demand of creative people that they think only in useful terms restricts and destroys the very quality of their ability that may lead to valuable discoveries.

The significant finding of efforts to measure creativity has been that it is not the same as general intelligence and that our intelligence tests (and scholastic aptitude tests) are not measuring it. People who score high on intelligence tests are not necessarily creative, but rather may be exceptionally good at solving problems in already defined ways. Such persons are valuable for performing difficult intellectual tasks, but they are not necessarily pioneers of new ideas or inventors of new approaches.

Tests of creativity use items that call for new answers to old questions and are scored for the degree of differentness from the norm group rather than for agreement or similarity (Barron, 1958). In Figure 6-8 some items for measuring creativity are illustrated. Studies of creativity indicate that everyone possesses some degree of this special ability and that it can be developed by training or practice (Gowan et al., 1967). Industry has used "brain-storming" sessions to stimulate creative thinking in production, sales, and management personnel.

Parents and teachers can encourage creativity in children by rewarding originality as well as conformity in their behavior. Behavior that is associated with creative output includes curiosity, exploration, questioning, unusual answers, independent thinking, imagination, and experimentation (Torrance,

Figure 6-8. The arrangement of colored squares into designs is used as a test of creativity. (New York State Mental Hygiene Photo by Julian Belin.)

1965). Society can encourage creative people by recognizing that their non-conforming thought patterns are not "bad," but a valuable and necessary asset to human progress.

INTERESTS AND VALUES

How dull life would be if everyone had the same interests. Yet social activities and interpersonal relationships would be very difficult if persons did not have interests in common. An interest usually refers to an activity that a person prefers to engage in, would not avoid, and would choose in preference to many other activities. Interests also refer to the kinds of things one appreciates and enjoys. The selection of an occupation and the satisfaction one gets from his work usually depends more on one's interests than abilities. However, interests and abilities are closely related. An individual strongly interested in doing something will work harder at it than if he is not interested. If his effort results in high performance the person will become even more interested. If, in spite of effort, the person fails to perform he tends to lose interest.

Vocational interests, or the patterns of preference related to success in various occupations have been extensively studied. Test inventories have been devised to measure individual interests and relate these patterns to groups of persons successful in various occupational fields. Interest inventories can indicate whether one's interests are more like those of salesmen, bookkeepers, artists, mechanics, or any of a number of different occupations. The interest inventories used most widely by schools and agencies for vocational guidance are the Kuder Preference Record—Vocational and the Strong Vocational Interest Inventory.

Values indicate the relative importance an individual places on goals. Interests are concerned with many specific activities. Values reflect general directions in life. The goal that is most important to a person is the one that has the highest value for him. A goal that is less important has a lower value for the individual.

People behave in accordance with their system of values, the order of preference they give to different goals. Values as well as interests develop in childhood principally through conditioned learning and in response to life experiences. For example, a child raised by parents who value material wealth above everything is likely to learn this same value and be guided by it. Such individuals may be drawn to the world of business or finance where the major goal is economic gain. In contrast, a child whose parents value power, influence, and recognition would seek a goal consistent with these experiences. Such a person might spend everything he owns to win election to high public office. Persons with religious and social values have learned to enjoy sacrifice and helping others. Such individuals would gladly work for little or no pay in fields such as missionary or social service. There are people who value beauty and will give up security and economic gain to enjoy the aesthetic qualities of life in artistic activity.

Values and interests are important not only in vocational choice, but also in the choice of friends and marriage partners. Partners in a marriage may have interests in common but different values and this can lead to difficulties. For example, both partners may enjoy extensive social activities (interest) but for different purposes (values). One does so in order to gain influence and recognition (power) and the other partner does so because he wants to know and help people (social). The need of the one to use others and the need of the partner to serve others may clash. Differences of interest and/or values are very hard to resolve for these preferences are developed early in life and values especially are fairly well-fixed by adolescence.

Much has been said about the effects of college experience on changing the value system of students. Exposure to new ideas and a wider variety of interpersonal relationships which are part of the college experience cause students to test their values by questioning, experimenting, and discovering for themselves. As a person matures a new set of values emerges which are his own rather than those of his parents which were imposed upon him earlier. As society advances and young people are part of the changing society there is always a "generation gap" causing older people to wonder, "what is this younger generation coming to?"

PERSONALITY

The concept of personality has no standard meaning and many definitions. Most definitions attempt to include the whole person; all the abilities, aptitudes, interests, values, emotions, and behavioral characteristics that distinguish one person from all others. We have already considered many of these separate aspects of personality, how they vary among individuals, and the interaction of heredity, environment, and time which produces these differences. Methods for understanding individual differences in personality are many and varied.

The complexity of personality and the wide range of individual differences have given rise to a multitude of tests, self-inventories, techniques, and devices for the assessment of personality. You may be called upon to take personality tests when you apply for a job or when you consult a vocational counselor or if you see a psychotherapist about your personal problems. The personality test or assessment technique is a shortcut to understanding you as an individual and the ways in which you are alike and different from other individuals.

What Personality Tests Measure

Personality tests are designed to measure how a person feels about himself, his world, and other people, and to study the organization of characteristics or traits which influence behavior and adjustment. Each person maintains some consistency through time but he also makes gradual changes. Personality is organized into a pattern or structure which is more than the sum of traits or characteristics; it is the product of their interaction.

The popular use of the term "personality" usually refers to the outer appearance and behavior of an individual as these affect other persons. Psychologists call this the *social stimulus value* of an individual. A person who is popular and well-liked is described as having a "good" personality and has high social stimulus value. Individuals who make poor impressions on others may be said to have a "bad" personality or lacking in personality and have low social stimulus value. Because people use outer appearances to draw conclusions, the social stimulus value of an individual greatly affects the way others treat him and respond to him. Personality cannot, however, be viewed only from the outside for beneath the surface appearance there is an inner structure and functioning.

The internal aspect of personality is organized around the *self-concept*. Persons behave in terms of their idea of self; the person they think they are, should be, or would like to become. The self-concept begins developing in infancy and is the accumulated result of one's experiences and reactions to these experiences. The values of the society in which one lives and the roles one is expected to perform strongly influence the experiences persons have that shape their sense of self. Behavior cannot be understood simply by making a study of the facts of a situation for these are the outer appearance of things. The actions of an individual are guided by what he thinks the facts are and the way they make him feel. For example, Jack is convinced he is inferior to his sister and that both his parents and teachers prefer her to him. It does not matter that this is not true because Jack's behavior is guided by what he thinks and the feelings he has as a result.

The word *ego* means the sense of self or self-concept. The ego is not good or bad, but it may be strong or weak. A strong ego is one that is well-defined, is satisfactory to the self, and adjusts adequately to the demands made on it. When the concept of self is ill-defined or uncertain, the person has trouble answering the question, "Who am I?" When a large difference exists between one's social stimulus value and one's self-concept his behavior may be inconsistent, confusing, or disturbed.

In Chapter 5 we discussed the basic human tendency of persons to strive for the development of their potentials called *self-actualization*. This means that persons need to discover the potential abilities within the self and make these abilities actual. Self-actualization brings the concept of self and the social stimulus value of the self into harmony. The assessment of personality is one means of discovering the potential abilities within the self. Let us look at some of the techniques used to assess personality.

Personality Inventories

Besides the techniques already described to assess intelligence, aptitude, and other aspects of personality, there are methods to assess the social stimulus value and self-concept of personality. A representative test inventory is the *California Psychological Inventory* or CPI (Gough, 1957). This test is a paper and pencil type designed to measure personality from a social-interaction point of view. It consists of over 400 items arranged in 18 scales for traits like dominance, responsibility, tolerance, and self-control. The individual reads items such as "I often doubt my judgment and cannot make decisions easily." He then responds by indicating whether this is true or false. The 18 scales are further grouped into four categories:

Class I.   Measures of poise, ascendancy, and self-assurance
Class II.   Measures of socialization, maturity, and responsibility
Class III. Measures of achievement potential and intellectual efficiency
Class IV.   Measures of intellectual and interest modes

The Class I measures of the CPI give information about the self-concept in terms of feelings of confidence, adequacy, and resourcefulness. The other Class measures give information about the social stimulus value of the individual. The degree of involvement with others as well as the nature of this involvement (mature–immature, responsible–irresponsible) are reflected in the Class II measures. The potential for achievement relative to the capacity for achievement or intellectual efficiency can be assessed from the Class III measures. Both achievement and efficiency may be affected if the feelings about the self are negative, the degree of involvement with others is low, or the nature of involvement with others is immature. The Class IV measures give some idea of the flexibility, sensitivity, and helpfulness of the personality. A person low in these traits might feel good about himself, but the persons he comes in contact with may not.

Another method of understanding personality is to measure the relative importance within the individual of the basic needs which motivate his behavior. Edwards (1954) has developed a technique for measuring needs that is widely used in personality research as well as in personal counseling. He has defined 15 personality variables and described the needs associated with each of them as follows (copyright The Psychological Corporation, reproduced by permission):

1. ACHIEVEMENT: To do one's best, to be successful, to accomplish tasks requiring skill and effort, to be a recognized authority, to accomplish something of great significance, to do a difficult job well, to solve difficult problems and puzzles, to be able to do things better than others, to write a great novel or play.

2. DEFERENCE: To get suggestions from others, to find out what others think, to follow instructions and do what is expected, to praise others, tell others that they have done a good job, to accept the leadership of others, to read about great men, to conform to custom and avoid the unconventional, to let others make decisions.

3. ORDER: To have written work neat and organized, to make plans before starting on a difficult task, to have things organized, to make advance plans when taking a trip, to organize details of work, to have meals organized and a definite time for eating, to have things arranged so that they run smoothly without change.

4. EXHIBITION: To say witty and clever things, to tell amusing jokes and stories, to talk about personal adventures and experiences, to have others notice and comment upon one's appearance, to say things just to see what effect it will have on others, to talk about personal achievements, to be the center of attention.

5. AUTONOMY: To be able to come and go as desired, to say what one thinks, to be independent of others in making decisions, to feel free to do things that are unconventional, to do things without regard for what others may think, to criticize those in positions of authority, to avoid situations where one is expected to conform.

6. AFFILIATION: To be loyal to friends, to participate in friendly groups, to make as many friends as possible, to share things with friends, to do things with friends rather than alone, to form strong attachments, to write letters to friends.

7. INTRACEPTION: To analyze one's motives and feelings, to understand how others feel about problems, to put oneself in another's place, to judge people by why they do things rather than by what they do, to analyze the behavior and motives of others.

8. SUCCORANCE: To have others provide help when in trouble, to seek encouragement from others, to have others be kindly, sympathetic, and understanding about personal problems, to receive a great deal of affection from others, to be helped by others when depressed, to have others feel sorry when one is sick.

9. DOMINANCE: To argue for one's point of view, to be regarded by others as a leader, to be elected or appointed chairman of committees, to persuade and influence others to do what one wants, to supervise and direct the actions of others.

10. ABASEMENT: To accept blame when things do not go right, to feel the need for punishment for wrong doing, to feel better when giving in and avoiding a fight than when having one's own way, to feel timid in the presence of superiors, to feel the need for confession of errors, to feel inferior to others in most respects.

11. NURTURANCE: To help friends when they are in trouble, to assist others less fortunate, to treat others with kindness and sympathy, to be forgiving and generous with others, to show affection toward others, to have others confide in one.

12. CHANGE: To do new and different things, to travel, to meet new people, to try new and different jobs, to experience novelty and change in daily routine, to move and live in different places, to participate in new fads and fashions.

13. ENDURANCE: To complete any job undertaken, to work at a single job before taking on others, to put in long hours of work without distraction, to stick with a problem even though it may seem as if no progress is being made, to avoid interruptions.

14. HETEROSEXUALITY: To go out with members of the opposite sex, to participate in discussions about sex, to read books and plays about sex, to listen to or tell jokes involving sex, to become sexually excited.

15. AGGRESSION: To attack contrary points of view, to criticize others publicly, to make fun of others, to tell others off when disagreeing with them, to get revenge for insults, to blame others when things go wrong, to tell others what one thinks of them, to become angry, to read newspaper accounts of violence.

Numerous other personality inventories ranging from very simple to complex have been devised to help an individual bring out in his own words the contents of his inner world of self. Inventories are based on self-report, so it must be assumed that an individual will respond honestly with whatever accuracy he possesses about himself. The obvious limitations of self-report inventories are that under some circumstances (applying for a job) a person is apt to respond in terms of what he knows is acceptable and desirable rather than what is true about himself, making the use of the test a waste of time. For example, insurance companies want to select sales trainees who will show the personality characteristics they have found to be associated with successful salesmen—self-confidence, extroversion, competitiveness, freedom from neurotic tendencies, and other traits. Several companies are using a personality inventory that asks such questions as these: Are you uncomfortable when meeting new people? Do you avoid social gatherings? Do you frequently suffer headaches? Would you rather be alone than with friends? Obviously the intelligent job applicant would be able to answer these questions satisfactorily even if his answers were not true.

Projective Techniques

Projective devices are not tests in the usual sense because they have no right or wrong answers and the interpretation of results depends upon the professional skills of the psychologist who administers them. The projective methods attempt to reveal the inner content and organization of the individual personality by presenting stimulus materials that are ambiguous or only partially structured, and analyzing the responses. The rationale of projective techniques is that since the stimuli and instructions are the same for all those tested, differences in responses are a reflection of personality differences in the people being tested.

The following general descriptions are intended to provide examples of some of the more widely used projective techniques for understanding individual differences in personality.

Word Association Tests date back to 1879 and the original work on individual differences. They were later popularized by Freud. Their use today is mainly in crime detection in connection with lie detector tests but they are also used in personality research.

The test material consists of a standardized list of words, usually between 50 and 100 in number, several of which lists are widely used. The subject is instructed to respond as quickly as possible with the first word that comes to mind after the examiner gives the stimulus word. Reaction time is measured with a stop watch. Verbatim response to each word is recorded, together with comments, sounds, or gestures made by the subject. The extent to which responses agree with those commonly given by normal individuals yields a measure of the conformity between the subject's thinking and that of the average person. Poorly adjusted individuals have different patterns of associations in common with each other which may have diagnostic significance. Unusual responses are often a source of information about special problems in the personality.

Sentence Completion Tests, originating with Ebbinghaus in 1897, have had wide usage in military research during World War II and in industry and schools in more recent years.

Materials consist of a printed series of 50 to 100 incomplete phrases with instructions being to complete each sentence in writing. The technique allows much latitude in expressing underlying drives, emotions, sentiments, and complexes that the subject is unwilling or unable to admit. In writing his responses the subject may inadvertently reveal these hidden tendencies by completing the phrases with highly personal material.

The test offers a means of understanding personality factors as they influence behavior and group adaptation. Areas of investigation include aspirations, self-evaluation, inner conflicts, reactions to others, family relationships, sexual adjustment, suppressed wishes, neurotic tendencies, hostility, and aggression.

Hermann Rorschach, a Swiss psychiatrist, was the first to develop a technique for using inkblots in the diagnosis of underlying personality structure. Since its introduction in this country in the 1930's the Rorschach technique has been subjected to a vast amount of experimentation including extensive military and civilian research.

A series of 10 inkblots are presented to the subject one at a time with instructions to mention anything the blots remind him of or that they could represent. After all associations have been recorded an inquiry is conducted to obtain elaborations needed for scoring purposes. The various scoring factors are then interpreted as expressions of personality.

This widely used clinical instrument attempts a picture of the total personality structure including such aspects as intellectual potential, characteristics of the thought processes, imagination, creative ability, interests, emotional stability, temperament, and character. It is also a valuable tool in psychiatric diagnosis. Figure 6-9 shows an ink blot of the type used in the Rorschach technique. What does it look like to you?

The *Thematic Apperception Test* or TAT was developed by Henry A. Murray as an instrument for exploring unconscious motivation and deeper regions of personality then could be tapped with more structured tests.

A series of from 10 to 20 pictures are presented with the instructions that the subject regard them as illustrations for stories which he is to make up. He must

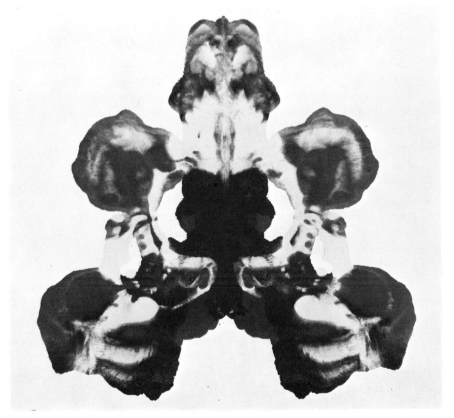

Figure 6-9. Ink blot of the type used as a projective technique. (Photo by Sharon Wright.)

tell each story by identifying the characters and explaining their relationships in the situation, by describing what led up to that situation, and by supplying an outcome.

The stories or picture-descriptions, together with any attendant conversation and behavior, comprise the data subjected to interpretive analysis. The method is intended to reveal the needs and conflicts underlying behavior and the person's characteristic mode of adjustment. The method reveals level of aspiration, motivation, attitudes toward authority figures, and behavior tendencies. It is useful in the prediction of vocational adjustment potential. Several variations of this technique have been developed for use with children, adolescents, and rehabilitation clients. One of the stimulus cards from the TAT is shown in Figure 6-10.

The *human-figure drawing* is a widely used clinical diagnostic tool which has been subjected to numerous reliability studies and has been found useful as an industrial screening device. John N. Buck has devoted nearly 20 years to the study and clinical usage of the freehand drawings of *House, Tree, and Person.*

The present form of this technique is designed to aid the clinician in obtaining information concerning the sensitivity, maturity, flexibility, efficiency, and the degree of integration of a subject's personality, as well as the interaction of that personality with its environment—both specific and general.

The analysis is based on interpretation of functional categories, structural and formal aspects of the drawings, and the apperceptive aspects (subject is encouraged to define, describe, and interpret the objects drawn and their respective environments, and to associate concerning them). The technique affords the opportunity to observe a subject while he is under direct and indirect stress and may thus provide information concerning reactive behavior (Figure 6-11).

As instruments of examination the projective techniques have some advantages over other tests of personality. The subject is generally unaware of the meaning or value of different types of response, so he cannot deliberately create an impression of himself that is falsely favorable or unfavorable. These methods in the hands of skilled psychologists encourage the expression of many facets of personality and give some indication of the interaction of internal factors within the individual.

Other Techniques for Assessment

Personality assessments are often accomplished by using interview techniques

Figure 6-10. One of the stimulus pictures from the TAT used to elicit stories for personality analysis. (Reprinted by permission of the publishers from Henry A. Murray, *Thematic Apperception Test*, Cambridge, Mass., Harvard University Press, copyright 1953 by the President and Fellows of Harvard College.)

Figure 6-11. Self Portraits: these human figure drawings were each made by a different person, representing a wide range of clinical problems. (Photo courtesy of Saratoga County Mental Health Clinic.)

and by observation of behavior in a variety of situations. The use of a one-way mirror to observe behavior in a structured situation has proven useful as the illustration in Figure 6-12 shows. Evaluation of response by observational methods rests on the skill and training of the examiner.

The case history method which involves the collection of all information about the individual's development and functioning in the past is a valuable aid to personality assessment. The case history indicates what the person has done, suggests why he has done so, and offers ideas of what he will probably do in the future.

Figure 6-12.   Observation with a one-way mirror is used to evaluate the interviewing skills and techniques of psychologists during their professional training. (New York State Mental Hygiene Photo by Julian Belin.)

Personality assessment is necessary in situations of counseling such as educational–vocational choice. Many employment opportunities require personality assessment as employers attempt to select candidates most suitable for the job. Aiding persons whose adjustments are unsatisfactory to them and causing them unhappiness often involves personality assessment. In all these situations the goal of assessment is an attempt to understand and to help people discover those aspects of self that will make self-actualization possible.

SUMMARY

Understanding human behavior includes studying the ways in which people differ from each other, the nature and extent of their differences, and the effects of these differences on behavior. In the assessment of human behavior we find psychological characteristics follow a normal distribution represented by the normal curve.

Psychological tests involve the following essentials of measurement: (*a*) A uniform task, (*b*) performed under comparable conditions, (*c*) yielding scores which are (*d*) compared with an appropriate norm group. Some of the important psychological dimensions in which individual differences are found include intelligence, aptitudes, special abilities, interests, values, and personality.

Intelligence can be better understood as falling into three main types: (*a*) abstract or verbal—ability to deal with words and symbols; (*b*) practical or concrete—common sense; (*c*) social—ability to get along well with people. Another way to describe intelligence is in terms of its basic elements of understanding, memory, and association. Intelligence is not a single dimension but a complex combination of several factors, not all of which are known.

I.Q. is a measure of intelligence based on comparison with a large sample of persons one's own age. I.Q. is related to occupation but there is a wide range of I.Q.'s within each occupation. Approximately $2\frac{1}{2}$ percent of the population at the upper extreme of the I.Q. distribution are considered gifted and approximately the same proportion at the lower end of the distribution are considered retarded.

Aptitudes are potential abilities that have not been developed. Aptitude test batteries are helpful in giving an individual an idea of his potential for vocational development. Aptitudes develop from hereditary potential, environmental stimulation, and social learning, and are closely related to general intelligence. Special abilities that are more independent of intelligence include art, music, athletics, and creativity.

Interests refer to the kinds of preferences a person develops and the kinds of things one appreciates and enjoys. Values refer to the relative importance an individual places on goals, and are more general than interests. Both interests and values are important in vocational choice and in selection of friends and marriage partners.

Personality refers to the combination of characteristics that distinguish one person from all others. Personality is organized into a pattern or structure which includes the social stimulus value and the self-concept or ego. Personality assessment is one means of discovering the potential abilities and limitations within the self. Techniques used in assessment include personality inventories or self-report methods, projective techniques, interview, case history, and observational methods. The goal of personality assessment is an attempt to understand and to help people discover those aspects of the self that will make self-actualization possible.

SUGGESTIONS FOR FURTHER READING

Anastasi, Anne, *Psychological Testing* (3rd ed.), New York, Macmillan, 1969. A comprehensive guide to the major psychological tests in use today.

Barron, Frank, *Creative Person and Creative Process*, New York, Holt, Rinehart and Winston, 1969. Creativity is regarded as a process within a person that can be aided by education.

Baumeister, Alfred A. (Ed.), *Mental Retardation*, Chicago, Ill., Aldine, 1967. A sourcebook of contributions from many fields dealing with the diagnosis, special education, and rehabilitation of the mentally retarded.

Kirkpatrick, J. J., Ewen, R. B., Barrett, R. S., and Katzell, R. A., *Testing and Fair Employment*, New York, New York University Press, 1968. Discusses the controversial issues of fairness and validity of personnel tests for different minority groups and suggests how to reduce unfair discrimination in employment.

Madison, Peter, *Personality Development in College*, Reading, Mass., Addison-Wesley, 1969. Theories of personality are illustrated in case studies which are closely related to the student's actual experience.

Mischel, Walter, *Personality and Assessment*, New York, Wiley, 1968. A critique of personality testing and a clear presentation of current developments in social behavior assessment.

Life Tasks

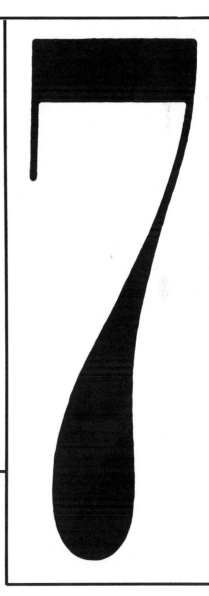

Society provides the means to satisfy basic human needs and opportunities for the growth and development of individual potentials, but society also sets standards and expectations and imposes limits on the behavior of its members. As you develop and change in the direction of psychological maturity you are faced with an increasing complexity of tasks to be mastered as a participant in an organized society. If you are to succeed in your adaptation to the social environment it is important to recognize the life tasks as challenges to be met at each stage of development throughout your life span.

The socialization process demands that a child achieve certain basic motor, language, and social skills which are the developmental tasks of childhood (Chapter 4) in order to be prepared for the challenges ahead. Satisfaction of the basic emotional needs of childhood (Chapter 5) provides him with the security and independence to go ahead on his own to explore his own potentialities and limitations (Chapter 6). The next step is to establish his identity as a unique personality capable of self-awareness, self-evaluation, and self-satisfaction. Establishing identity is a complex process involving acceptance of sex roles, choice of educational and occupational goals, marriage, productivity, and retirement. These factors are all interrelated but we look at them separately in order to understand them better.

MASCULINE AND FEMININE ROLES

Sex roles refer to the stereotyped pattern of beliefs, attitudes, and activities which are defined by the culture as appropriate for one's sex. Sex roles in the Western civilization are based on the conviction that males and females should behave differently. Beliefs about the specific ways the sexes should differ vary from one society to another, and enforcement of the stereotype varies in our society with socioeconomic class.

Sex Stereotypes

From a very early age boys and girls are made aware of their particular sex role by the use of superficial appearances and patterns of approved behavior. They are dressed differently, given different kinds of toys, and encouraged to play differently. Most parents reward behavior that is considered appropriate for the sex of their child and punish or discourage behavior that is considered inappropriate. Traits regarded as desirable for boys are physical aggression, dominance, competence in athletics, achievement of motor skills, competitiveness, and independence. Dependence, passivity, politeness, social poise, and neatness are some of the characteristics considered more appropriate for girls (Tyler, 1951).

Preference for sex-typed activities increases during the preschool years, and by age 5 most children are aware of many sex-appropriate behaviors. Most boys prefer to play with guns and trucks, and be cowboys and Indians, while most girls prefer dolls, dishes, and toy furniture. The stereotyped notion of the male role is usually represented by a robust physique, fearlessness in the face of danger, less sentimental and emotional expression than the female, more practical and logical thought, less evidence of tenderness, and a greater display of potential for leadership and assuming responsibility.

The learning of appropriate sex-role behavior in early childhood has some expected consequences in adulthood. Actually there is no evidence to support the notion that boys are more emotionally stable, less fearful, more courageous, less capable of tenderness, or more inclined than girls to be guided by reason rather than sentiment. However, since boys are expected to be braver, stronger, and less emotional than girls, it is not surprising that the self-concepts of adult men and women are in keeping with this early learning. Studies have shown that in large groups of adults, women describe themselves as less adequate, more negligent, more fearful, and less mature than men (Mussen, Conger, and Kagan, 1963). These adult attitudes about the self are not always realistic for either men or women, but they seem to reflect the sex-role behavior training in early childhood.

The myth of masculine superiority is gradually being dispelled in modern society with the advent of equal educational opportunities for women and the legal protection against discrimination in employment. It is interesting to note that in many respects males are the weaker sex, at least during the first years of life. Slightly more males than females are born, but the infant mortality rate is greater for males. Boys are slower in their growth, as measured by skeletal development, and they have more defects in vision, hearing, and speech than girls. Child guidance clinics and special services in the schools find learning difficulties, behavior problems, and emotional disturbance more prevalent in boys than girls. Delinquency, school dropouts, and educational failures are much more common for boys than girls. Some of the difficulties encountered by males in our society may be due to the greater demands made on the males for achievement, independence, and acceptance of responsibility (Figure 7-1).

Figure 7-1. These children are showing sex-typed interests and sex-appropriate behavior. (Photo by Jim Sargent.)

Sex-Role Identification

The child acquires sex-appropriate behaviors and attitudes for at least three reasons: (*a*) the desire for praise and acceptance by parents and peers which he gets for sex-appropriate behavior; (*b*) the fear of punishment or rejection he might get for inappropriate behavior; (*c*) his need for *identification* with the same sex parent (or parent substitute).

The process of identification begins when the child recognizes the difference between himself and his parents. He sees his parents as having the power to give and withhold love, the power to control the child and other people, and as having mastery over the environment. In other words, he sees his parents as all-powerful and himself as powerless and dependent. If the parents are warm and accepting the child sees their behavior as rewarding and he will want to be like them and act as they do. Thus, the little girl cares for her doll just as mother cares for her and in this way she makes herself more like her mother. Boys choose their father as their model and try to become more like him. Identification with the parent of the same sex is usually stronger for boys than for girls because the father is usually perceived as the more powerful parent.

Parents are not the only models with whom children identify. Older siblings, teachers, group leaders, or any adult whom the child regards as stronger, more competent, and rewarding may serve as a model for the child's identification. This potential in all adults to be seen by children as models for acceptable sex-role behavior often compensates children whose own parents are unsatisfactory models or are absent from the home. Society, through its sex-role-expected behaviors, exerts continuous pressures upon individuals to accomplish appropriate sex-role identification. When the child achieves identification with the same sex parent (or parent substitute), he is rewarded with approval and acceptance and these rewards serve to further strengthen his identification.

Personality Development and Sex Roles

Although the average preschool child identifies primarily with his parents, school-age children begin to find more glamorous models outside the immediate family. New heroes appear in movies, on television, and in books and magazines. The football hero, the pilot, the scientist, the doctor, the nurse, the fireman, the policeman, and the astronaut have dramatic appeal for the child. Children's interests develop in relation to the heroes or models they have chosen for identification. Again social pressure forces boys to choose male models and girls to choose female models.

A child's acceptance by his peer group becomes more dependent on his conformity to traditional sex-role behavior as he grows older. In a study of 200 fourth-grade children Tyler (1955) found that most of the average child's interests are determined by their sex appropriateness; in other words, whether or not the interest fit the social stereotype of male or female activity. For example, athletics, mechanics, and science were seen by children as strictly for boys and rejected by girls; clothes, cooking, gardening, music, and art were seen as acceptable interests for girls. Studies have shown that acceptance of sex appropriate activities during early school years tends to become a permanent part of the child's attitude structure that influences his goals, values, and vocational interests throughout adolescence and adulthood.

Sex-role identification aids the development of personality because it furnishes a basic unifying theme. The ability to perceive the self clearly in the sex role helps to shape the self-concept and establish identity. Similarly, the social stimulus value of the personality, which reflects the responses of others to the individual, is aided by sex-role identification. Because one perceives the self in sex-role terms, functioning in the role is achieved and the expectations of others are positively fulfilled leading to their approval and acceptance.

Social Class Differences

Children from working-class families living in urban industrial areas have been compared with children from upper-middle-class suburban families whose fathers were in executive, business, or professional positions, to see whether social class background made any difference in sex-role behavior (Rabban, 1950). The study revealed that both boys and girls of the lower-class group became aware of sex-role patterns at a younger age than did the middle-class children. Lower-class boys reached a high level of sex identification by 5 years of age, but middle-class boys did not do so until they were 6. Lower-class girls showed definite acceptance of their roles by age 6, but with middle-class girls the acceptance was not so clear-cut even by the age of 8. The findings suggest that social class sex-role standards for boys are more clearly defined than for girls. Middle-class standards are probably more flexible for girls than for boys. To have a 7-year-old girl who is a tomboy is probably more acceptable in middle-class families than to have a 7-year-old boy who is a sissy. Among lower-class families adult male and female roles are also more clearly differentiated than in the middle-class families.

As education level increases, the difference between masculine and feminine roles becomes less clear. For example, consider the occupations of people with less than a high-school education; men work as truck drivers, laborers, salesmen, service station attendants, deliverymen, and factory workers. Women with limited education hold domestic, clerical, and sales jobs or work in factories. Men are hired for work that requires physical strength and endurance and they usually earn more money than women. In many factories it is still customary to pay women less than men for doing the same work. In the skilled and semi-skilled occupations there is some overlap, but for the most part some jobs are considered more appropriate for one sex or the other. Mechanics, repairmen, barbers, tailors, and photographers are usually men; typists, beauticians, receptionists, and nurses are usually women. In business and the professions where a college education is required, sex differences are much less pronounced. Teaching, social work, accounting, law, medicine, and science are not considered as either strictly masculine or feminine occupational roles.

The individual's choice of a career is limited by the sex and social class appropriateness of the vocation. These social class and sex-typed attitudes are established in early childhood and are very resistant to change. It should not be surprising, therefore, to find some individuals from lower social class families who cannot permit themselves to consider certain occupations in spite of educational opportunities in those fields.

EDUCATIONAL AND OCCUPATIONAL GOALS

The level of education we strive for and the kind of work we prepare for determines our social identity which is an important part of our self-concept. The kinds of people with whom we will associate and our position in the community are largely functions of the career we select and the jobs we accept. The work we do serves to satisfy many different needs: need for belonging, need for self-respect and self-esteem, need for self-expression, as well as need to provide for our security and satisfaction of material requirements. Work is more than the means of earning a living; it is an important part of the process of living. Some of the factors that influence vocational choice are: (*a*) socioeconomic factors; (*b*) interests; (*c*) abilities; and (*d*) opportunities.

Socioeconomic Factors

Family background has a strong influence on the goals set by young people. While social class and economic status of the family do not compel or limit a person's choice of goals, the parent's way of life and their expectations for their children do exert considerable influence on vocational choice. Parents who are themselves successful in business or the professions often make their children feel that a vocation with less prestige and social status would be a mark of failure. Parents who have been at a disadvantage because of their own lack of education often pressure their children to set goals that are beyond realistic limits for the child. Many people feel that success is marked by the progress you make up the occupational ladder to positions of higher prestige. For some families security is more important than recognition, and for others the most important factor is the amount of money you can expect to earn. Whatever the social and economic values of the family are, they operate as important considerations in the choice of a career.

In setting realistic goals you must be concerned with the amount of education or training that is required to prepare for employment and the cost of such preparation. Unless you have adequate financial backing it is difficult to get into certain professional schools, particularly in the fields of medicine, dentistry, law, and veterinary science. These fields require a large investment of money for the required education as well as a long period of preparation. The level of specialization in these fields also requires a concentrated effort reducing the possibility that you could do much in the way of self-help through part-time work. Most professions are not so limited, however, and people who are willing to work and make some sacrifices can obtain their desired goals.

There are many routes available to some goals that may not seem readily apparent at the time you are trying to make a choice. Most professions have loan plans available to persons who have demonstrated the ability and interests needed for a particular field. For those who might wish to be teachers, government loans are available under the National Defense Education Act of 1958. The government will retire, at their expense, up to 50 percent of a loan under the NDEA for five years of employment as a teacher. Most communities have night school classes for adults where one can progress toward a college degree or obtain technical–vocational training. Many industries offer educational opportunities for their employees either through on-the-job programs or released time to attend college classes.

In considering vocational choices it seems necessary to take a long-range view as many occupations are changing rapidly. You might take an A.A. degree in Business Technology and after obtaining employment in the field begin a systematic program of part-time study to reach Bachelor degree level preparation. The student who takes an A.A. degree in Law Enforcement may want to work part-time after he joins a police force on a degree program that will permit him to advance toward administrative positions. The young woman who receives her R.N. in the concentrated junior college nursing programs may decide to pursue continued education part-time toward her Bachelor's degree.

The opportunities to advance upward through education which are available today make the socioeconomic limits of the family less binding than ever before.

It is not uncommon today for a person to prepare in one field at the A.A. degree level, work in that field both for the experience and earnings, and at the same time be preparing either to assume a higher position in that field or to change to another field with greater prospects. If you can keep long-range plans in view, while at the same time make good use of present opportunities, your prospects need not be limited for reasons of money.

Interests

Interest in an occupation may be based on factors of prestige, status, or level of earning, but it should also include the kinds of things you like to do. Some individuals like to work with people while others like to work with things or ideas. In choosing an occupation it is important to know what is involved in that work and whether you would enjoy doing what the work requires. It is unfortunate when you find yourself in a job position that offers economic security and status but you cannot enjoy the work.

Teaching is an occupation that has many attractive features. The salary levels are increasing, the work atmosphere seems pleasant, prestige and status factors are improving, and an often-mentioned factor is the long summer vacation. What is not so apparent on the surface is that teaching, at any level, is an exacting intellectual task. Teachers must pursue their own education continually to keep up with new advances and to benefit financially. A teacher progresses on the salary schedule partly for each year of experience, but also partly for the number of additional college credits earned. Attendance at summer educational sessions is what most teachers do with their vacation. Teachers work with people and with ideas and also must be involved with many things in preparing displays, demonstrations, or aiding in student activities. Some teachers who love to teach find the demands of clerical, supervisory, and even janitorial tasks, which are a part of the job, unpleasant and a source of irritation.

Few jobs are ever just what they appear to be from an outside view. You can determine fairly easily what salary, status, and prestige factors are for a given occupation. To find out what you would actually do in the work requires more determined analysis. You have opportunities to get an inside view whenever you use the services of a person in the occupation. Before choosing to be a beauty operator a girl should have a talk with a few beauticians and keep her eyes and ears open when she patronizes a beauty shop. Making people look beautiful can be very satisfying. Working with harsh chemicals and solutions, listening patiently to the complaints, criticisms, and opinions of patrons, and standing on your feet for long periods of time may not be as satisfying.

It is desirable that you know what your interests are before choosing an occupation. Individual differences in interests, ways to assess them, and sources for guidance were discussed in Chapter 6. When assessing your interests, information can also be obtained from guidance sources about the actual requirements of a given job. The things you like to do and the things you are required to do can be consistent. Guidance sources know enough about helping persons to understand themselves and the world of work to make poor choices unnecessary. It may be in some cases that the choice of field is right, but the level within the field, or the typical functions in that aspect of the field are unsuitable. Time spent in self- and work-analysis may be time, effort, and happiness saved (Figure 7-2).

Abilities

Interests are a vital part of job selection and satisfaction, but an equally important consideration is ability. Knowledge of the requirements of a job will include an awareness of the necessary abilities and skills to do the job. When people enter an occupation for which they lack the necessary intellectual, technical, or social skills, they feel inadequate to cope with the work, become discouraged, and may lose confidence in their ability to do anything well.

If you are currently lacking in needed ability for a field it is important to determine why that skill is deficient; for example, you might like to go into engineering at some level but be deficient in mathematics. Is the math ability low because of little interest in numerical work, low aptitude for numerical work, or a poor background in math courses? Your low abilities can be improved with remedial instruction if interest and aptitude are sufficient for improvement. Sometimes low ability is a warning that interest in this kind of activity is low. If you choose a field dependent upon skill with numbers and numerical concepts, you must be sure you have the ability as well as the interest in these tasks.

Sometimes abilities are _latent,_ or not developed, because of little opportunity or awareness that you have this particular capacity. Some people have aptitude to learn languages but do not have an occasion to take languages or otherwise discover their skill. Many jobs as interpreters, translators, foreign sales representatives, and positions in the diplomatic corps go unfilled because there are not enough applicants with language skills. The Peace Corps has proved impossible for some who could not master concentrated language training, but it has opened doors for many others who discovered, for the first time, that they had an aptitude for languages.

Some persons receive little encouragement at home in art. The family may not feel they can afford simple art supplies or encourage an interest in such a "frivolous" activity. Yet, an individual may possess sufficient aptitude to benefit from training and function successfully in jobs such as drafting, design, interior decoration, architecture, or stage production.

Occupational choice requires analysis of abilities relative to job demands. Abilities, however, are not necessarily limited to present skills. Some may be latent and some perhaps can be improved with remedial instruction. It is important to know what you are not able to do, as well as what you are able to do, or able to learn. Abilities and aptitudes, like interests, were discussed in Chapter 6 and some appropriate guidance sources recommended.

Opportunities

It is important to consider, in addition to interests and abilities, what the chances are of finding a need for the kind of work you plan to do. The matter of opportunity plays an important part in realistic career planning. Opportunity is dependent upon factors of time and place. Relying upon "chance" to be the right person at the right place at the right time is not very realistic in our increasingly complex social structure.

The *time* factor involves both current possibilities and future trends. Economic analysts predict marked occupational changes for the future. It is increasingly apparent that job opportunities in the future will develop faster in occupations which require more education and specialized training than in occupations of a semiskilled or unskilled nature. For the years 1960–1970 a 40 percent increase in professional and technical workers has been predicted, no change in the number of jobs for unskilled workers, and a decrease of 18 percent in jobs for farmers and farm workers (Claque, 1962). Viewed in another way, less than half our present labor force is employed in the actual production of consumable goods from raw materials, and the others are employed in distribution of goods (marketing, sales), clerical and financial services, and personal services. The spread of *cybernated* production systems may change the entire complexion of the world of work as we know it today. This development will be explored at greater length in Chapter 12.

Present opportunities may be assessed in a variety of ways. The local office

Figure 7-2. Career preparation in conservation, ornamental horticulture, and practical nursing are among the many specialized programs now available on the high school level for people who do not plan to attend college. (Photo credits: Board of Cooperative Educational Services, Occupational Educational Program of Saratoga–Warren Counties, New York.)

of the State Employment Service lists current demands in technical–vocational jobs and also many professional fields on a state wide and national basis. The U.S. Department of Labor makes available to all interested persons and agencies a constant supply of occupational opportunity information and trends. One such publication from the Bureau of Labor Statistics is the *Occupational Outlook Handbook* which describes current needs and job requirements and forecasts future trends. The *Occupational Outlook Handbook* is available in the occupational library of most schools and colleges. The want ad section of large city news-papers is another means to evaluate current situations in employment. The increase in ads for technical, scientific, and professional workers is a reflection of the higher educational and specialization demands currently operating in employment. Most colleges are now offering placement services to students, arranging time and space to permit interviewers to come to the campus to contact prospective employees. Students should examine the interview lists posted by their school placement offices to develop awareness of the needs and requirements they will have to meet in their chosen field.

Opportunity also involves the factor of *place*. In the United States there are regional differences in the concentration of certain industries. Large metro-politan areas must be considered the most advantageous for opportunity as these represent concentrations of population and resulting demand for services of all kinds. The aerospace industries are concentrated at the present time in the Pacific coast states. The southern states of our country have traditionally been rural agricultural areas. However, the low industrial tax rate of the southern states is very attractive to competitive industries with narrow profit margins and practical necessity may result in a build-up of such industries in the south. The more flexible one can be about place of work the greater the opportunities available to him.

The world of work is vast and diversified. The *Dictionary of Occupational Titles* lists over 40,000 jobs in 600 occupational fields. Published by the U.S. Employment Service, the Dictionary is revised periodically and represents a comprehensive view of demands and opportunities. Anyone willing to learn about himself and the world of work should be able to find the opportunity that best suits his needs, interests, and capabilities.

Personality Factors in Career Choice

Why is it difficult for college students to choose a major and decide on future goals? Most young people today are confused by the abundance of opportunities available to them and their lack of certainty about the future. No one wants to run the risk of spending several years in preparation for a career that may be obsolete 10 years later. Nor do they want to risk preparing for a career that will turn out to be poorly suited to their personalities. The problem revolves around the fact that interests, abilities, opportunities, and personalities are not absolute factors but are relative factors that change with time and experience.

If you could be certain exactly what kind of person you are and what you want to be it would make the problems of career choice much easier. What usually happens is that people make tentative choices based on what information they have at the time and as they grow in experience they modify their plans and goals in accord with new interests and new knowledge acquired along the way. It is important to allow yourself enough room to grow and develop new interests so that you will not feel overly restricted by the choices you have made. You should feel free to take advantage of new opportunities as you see them even after you have made a choice of career goals. Flexibility is a valuable asset in occupational adjustment but it should not be confused with indecisiveness. You can decide on what you want to do or be without making such a firm commitment to these goals that you rule out all other possible alternatives.

There are some facets of your personality that may be fairly well-established by adolescence or may not be clearly established until you have tried yourself out in the world of work. These will also be modified somewhat with advancing maturity. We refer to such aspects of personality as the dependence–independence dimension, security versus risk-taking, and perfectionism versus comprehensiveness. Suppose, for example, your main occupational interest is in auto mechanics. There are numerous possibilities for personality growth and development within this single interest area. You may find that your greatest satisfaction would come from owning your own shop rather than working for someone else. Your personality would influence the directions you take whether it meant working alone in your own garage at home and overhauling engines or building a big business and hiring numerous employees to do the work. Or you may find you prefer to work in a small shop where someone else takes the responsibility and risks and gives you the security of a set salary. Perhaps it will be better to work in a large operation where there is opportunity for advancement to a position of supervisory importance. You also have to decide whether to specialize in one aspect of the work (carburation, ignition, transmission specialist, etc.) or to become a specialist in one particular make of car (race cars, foreign cars, experimental models, trucks and heavy equipment) or to develop a comprehensive knowledge of all phases of auto mechanics (trouble shooter, auto diagnostician). Interest in auto mechanics combined with different personalities can lead to satisfactions as remote as the backyard hotrod repairman and the research and design engineer in General Motors advanced experimental laboratory.

In choosing educational and occupational goals you need to ask yourself many questions: Would I be better satisfied in a big business, a small one, or on my own? Do I find more security in doing one job extremely well or in being able to do many things fairly well? Do I want a job that is precise, orderly, and well-planned or would I prefer the excitement of doing new and different things? Do I want to take responsibility for myself, share responsibility with others, or let someone else take the responsibility? You may not be able to answer these questions in advance but as you gain experience you will find that these personality factors influence the choices you make and the directions your career will take.

MARITAL CHOICE

Marriage, establishment of an independent home, and the rearing of children are important life tasks in any society. The maturation of the capacity to give and to receive affection is often presumed to be evidenced by the selection of a partner and marriage. Most persons hope to make a wise marital choice to accomplish a necessary life task and to achieve personal happiness. Current statistics on divorce, however, almost one in every five marriages, suggest that for many people their hopes do not become reality. Bowman (1954) has emphasized that it is easier to "match than patch" and much can be said for the idea that marriage failure results primarily from faulty choice of a marriage partner. The Hollywood plot of meeting, falling in love, marrying, and living happily ever after is an ideal seldom realized in actual experience. What factors are important and how are marital choices made?

Sociological Factors

Most research in psychology and sociology favors an interpretation of *homogamy*, that is, like marries like (Hollingshead, 1950). Important sociological factors identified have been race, religion, age, socioeconomic level, education, national origins backgrounds, and residential closeness. These factors operate to define for individuals a "field of eligible spouse candidates" (Winch, 1958).

The probabilities of meeting a person are limited by many of these sociological factors to begin with and the nature of these factors is such as to favor a choice of one's "own kind."

There is evidence that departure from similarity with respect to some of these factors is not necessarily a forecast of failure. *Religious differences*, for example, are rarely a major cause of marriage failure, although they are a factor in broken engagements (Monahan and Chancellor, 1955). Wide differences in age and educational level occur, usually with the male being older and better educated, and these differences are to some extent considered desirable in our own culture.

Many persons wonder what is the best *age* to marry. In practice, the 1960 census report indicates the average age of males at first marriage is about 23 years and for females it is 21 years. Some persons believe that marriage even at these ages is too young for the many adjustments required. Age alone, however, is not a good predictor of success or failure. There are some persons whose level of personal and social adjustment is so low that there would never be a "best age" for them to marry. The complex nature of any individual's maturity reflecting his experiences, and his general capacities for personal growth make a single best age of marriage for everyone impossible to determine.

A better predictor of marital success than age seems to be the *length of courtship*. The more time two persons take to know one another and the number of interactions they have in different situations, the greater the probability that each will make a good choice. Goode (1956) reporting a comprehensive study of divorce found nearly 90 percent of marriage failures involved courtship periods of less than 6 months. In the same study it also appeared that longer courtships were related to longer length of marriage even though in all of the cases studied the marriage did end in divorce.

Psychological Factors

Among the psychological variables studied have been interests, attitudes, needs, values, neurotic tendencies, and temperamental factors. The general conclusions of most of the psychological studies have also favored an interpretation that like marries like.

Kelly (1940) reported a study of 300 engaged couples using interviews and an extensive battery of psychological personality factor tests and concluded that similarity between prospective spouses was the rule. In a followup of the same group after 20 years (Kelly, 1955), the findings indicated that the initial similarity in the couples was neither greater or less with the passing years. Of the original 300 couples, 227 were still married and together, 39 marriages had ended in divorce, 12 had been terminated by the death of one partner, and 22 couples had broken their engagements and married someone else. Carman (1955) reports data contrasting a married group to a divorced group in terms of psychological factors as related to stability of marriage. His findings indicate: (*a*) Married persons possess characteristics more typical of their appropriate sex role than do divorced persons; (*b*) difference patterns in personality needs are not particularly important to stability of marriages; and (*c*) individual personality characteristics, especially in men, are more closely related to marital stability than are husband–wife patterns of likeness or difference.

Winch (1958) has proposed a theory of mate selection based on *complementary* needs, i.e., that opposites of psychological need attract. For example, a person low in needs to dominate, achieve, or be independent would be attracted to a person high in these needs. Marital choice, according to this theory, is made to complement the self and to achieve in marriage a balance of need-expression and need-gratification for each partner. The individual, consciously or unconsciously, must be aware of his needs, accept them, and be able to recognize the complementary needs in another individual. This is not an easy task to master. The social sex roles tend to hide many needs from your awareness in yourselves and others. Males, for example, might find it hard to accept or express their needs to be passive and dependent, or to be lacking in the need to achieve. Females might find it difficult to accept or express their needs to be aggressive, dominant, independent, or striving. If the courtship can be long enough and informal enough to permit need-expression, the possibility of discovering your own needs, the needs of the other, and the degree of fit would be increased.

Carman's data, previously described, that indicates divorced persons possess characteristics less typical of their appropriate sex role may reflect failure to find complementary needs in the partner. The social sex roles are familiar to both sexes and are the basis upon which *expectations* are formed as to how an individual is going to feel and behave. It may be that when an individual is not typical of his appropriate sex role, his behavior fails to meet the expectations of the partner and leads to failure in the marriage. The problem is not so much a matter of being atypical in the sex role as it is failure to meet *expectations* based on sex roles. Again, the courtship becomes the important factor. If, for purposes of courtship, individuals play roles which are not really consistent with their personalities, they are setting their partners up for disappointment and themselves for unhappiness. If a female wants to be the decision-maker and the male wants to do the shopping and the cooking, these personality needs should be expressed in courtship so that each can make a choice based on reality factors. Many good, lasting marriages reflect reversals of sex roles in the partners. Where these factors are clear in courtship, disappointed expectations do not occur after the marriage.

How Choices Are Made

We may answer our initial question as to how marital choices are made by saying in terms of most sociological and psychological factors, like appears to marry like. At the time of selection sociological variables may be the most important because they tend to limit the field of prospective choices. After marriage, the psychological variables may become more important as both partners try to adjust to the choice they have made. The extent to which a person fulfills the expectations of his partner may be more important than any one of several psychological characteristics. The courtship is the best opportunity to test the degree of harmony in the personalities. A relationship that cannot stand the strain of an honest courtship will not survive simply as a result of marriage.

In closing, we might take note of a growing trend to match mates by computers. Some people believe that computers have a special knowledge that can reduce the probability of error. There is no magic in a computer that has not been put there by a human. The program instructions by which computers match potential partners are based on the like-attracts-like evidence from sociology and psychology. Examination of the questionnaires to be filled out for computer matches will reveal that the items give emphasis to the sociological variables; age, race, education, religion, size of home town, income levels of family, etc. The few psychological variables employed emphasize fairly broad categories of interests, values, and temperament. What the computer achieves is to bring in touch with each other persons whose life circumstances have not permitted them to explore widely in a "field of eligible spouse candidates." The computer serves effectively to bridge a gap created by physical distance and/or social opportunity. If the questionnaires have been answered accurately the matches made by the computers represent probable choice partners. The computer cannot eliminate the necessity for a realistic courtship period and it cannot guarantee success in marriage. Some people in filling out computer questionnaires answer inaccurately out of some need to impress or some fear that they might "get stuck" with a poor match if they answer correctly. The computer does not know the difference between an honest and a false response. The computer, however, is not planning to marry, it is just processing data. Computers do well what they are designed to do, but the best choice of a marriage partner is done by a person on the basis of feelings, needs, and responses relative to another person.

PRODUCTIVITY

After a person has completed his formal education, established himself in his career, selected a mate, and started raising a family, he is entering the period of his greatest productivity. The years from 30 to 60 offer mature adults the opportunity to realize their maximum potential individually and collectively. These are the years in which we usually make whatever contributions we can to the world in which we live. Productivity does not mean simply achieving a great amount of work. The quality of the work, whether it be the production of a product or the offering of ideas or personal service, must be considered as well as the personal cost of its production. A person who must labor to turn out a product or service of low quality or who because of his labor has no time or energy for anything else is not a productive person in a psychological sense. Productivity then refers to the ability to use one's capacities effectively to function occupationally, socially, and personally. Two important elements in productivity are job satisfaction and the use of leisure time.

Job Satisfaction

Many different factors contribute to your job satisfaction. Some of these are directly related to the job such as wages, hours, fringe benefits, working conditions, and relationships with employers and fellow workers. These are called *morale* factors and have been the subject of much research and study. Poor morale lowers production and quality of production, contributes to accidents and absenteeism, and leads to high personnel turnover, all of which are costly to employee and employer.

Although wages, hours, and working conditions are important to worker satisfaction, other factors are of at least equal importance. A clear understanding of what is expected in the job and how the job is related to other jobs adds to high morale. Workers need to know what their responsibilities are and to whom they are responsible. The relationships between workers and supervisors are also important to morale. People like to have good work recognized and criticisms be constructive. An important feature of supervisory training deals with increasing skill in the area of human relations and developing satisfactory forms of interaction with workers.

A second set of factors contributes to job satisfaction in ways that are outside the control of employers. *Psychological* factors have to do with what the individual can contribute to his own job satisfaction in terms of his attitudes and personal approach to the job. A person who can look at himself realistically seeing his weaknesses as well as his strengths will approach his job with some clear ideas of what he can expect to accomplish. He will recognize his personal needs and set goals that are within his ability to achieve.

Personal satisfaction and success in your work depends upon the feeling of getting ahead both in terms of what you are able to give and what rewards you get. Work offers a means of self-expression and personal growth. The person who approaches his work with self-confidence and ambition for self-improvement will usually find greater satisfaction from his work than one who merely regards his job as a means of earning a living.

A third set of factors related to job satisfaction has to do with personal relationships outside the job. *Social* factors include family pride and friendship needs. Work should offer opportunities to meet people with common interests and similar social standing. A person should feel that his family can be proud of him for what he does and where he works. His family's standing in the community will be determined by his occupational status and it should open the way for social group participation. Professional associations, labor unions, business organizations, service clubs, and many community groups offer social participation on the basis of occupation.

The work one does and the opportunities for advancement determine the income level of the family. The income level of the wage-earner will set the style of living for the family. The home they live in, the neighborhood, the necessities and luxuries they can enjoy, the clothes they wear, the places they can shop, the kinds of transportation they can use, the recreational and cultural opportunities they can participate in—all these and more are determined for the family by the income level of the wage-earner. Everyone who works would be glad to earn more, but it is important to know that for what you do you receive a fair wage relative to what others receive for similar capacities and effort. When a person can feel he is providing as well for his family as his ability allows, he has a sense of pride which enables him to enjoy what he can earn to the fullest measure.

Unfortunately, family members can cause dissatisfaction in a worker that he may not feel in himself by making demands for a higher level of living than his earnings allow. In some cases these demands may be realistic in terms of the abilities the individual possesses but is not using on his present job. Sometimes the family situation is such that the wage-earner feels like that is all he is in the home and he has no motivation to do as well as he can or better. Family members dependent upon one person's efforts need to recognize that the family can be a source of recognition, approval, and reward to a worker just as much as his job. The concern, appreciation, and affection of a family can only be provided by a family. When these factors are present in the home the worker is further motivated to do his best.

When more than one person works to contribute to the home their efforts also need to be recognized. Increasingly, wives are working outside the home to supplement income levels. There is no answer to the question "should wives (mothers) work?" that will fit every situation. The attitudes within the home, the willingness of each family member to make his own contribution to the family life, and awareness of the effort made by those who earn the living provide the answer. In some homes, everyone works who is able to be employed, no one person earns a great deal, but all enjoy a better life because each does what he is able to do. In other homes, only one person works and the family lives above its means in a constantly growing burden of debt, feeling resentment for not having more. In such an atmosphere, it would be easy to feel that nothing one could do would be enough or would even matter.

Use of Leisure Time

Leisure time has, until recent years, been a precious commodity. Perhaps one of the most striking changes occurring in our society is the steady decline of the number of hours in the average work week. Labor unions in their contract negotiations with management are pressing more insistently for a standard 30-hour work week. This trend to the shorter work week is also being pushed by the rapidly growing change in the industrial process from a human production system to a system that produces by cybernated equipment. Leisure, once a rare experience, is becoming a necessity (Figure 7-3).

As we find ourselves confronted with increasing time for leisure we are also being forced to consider what leisure really is. When leisure was rare it seemed pleasurable in almost any way it was used, people defined it in various terms, and called it by many names. One of the most common definitions of leisure perhaps is "spare time." Leisure has been considered something that only

Figure 7-3.   These senior citizens are making use of their leisure time to develop social and recreational skills. (Photo by Gloria L. Hutchins.)

wealthy people could have and for many has represented a kind of ideal of the "good life." Now that leisure is becoming more abundant and available for all to enjoy it is losing its ideal quality. Many people do not seem to know what leisure is and as a result some are even fearful of this change in our society. The ability to use leisure in an effective manner is a challenging new life task that previous generations have not had the opportunity to master. Personal productivity may someday be measured primarily in terms of use of leisure time rather than in terms of work-related activities. For these reasons we need to understand what leisure is as well as what it is not.

One misconception of leisure is that it is the opposite of work or activity, that it is a condition of rest or inactivity. Rest and relaxation are necessary to relieve fatigue and restore energy, but this need can be adequately met through the biological mechanism of sleep. Another misconception is that leisure is the frantic pursuit of entertainment or pleasure. People who subscribe to this view may spend their time away from work vigorously engaged in a series of activities that are neither enjoyable nor refreshing simply because they have to work too hard at them. Another misconception, and perhaps the most frightening, is that leisure is an empty time with nothing at all to do. Leisure is not any of these things—rest, pleasure-seeking, or empty time—although it has some of these aspects.

Pieper (1963) has written an interesting account of the nature of leisure which presents the concept in a psychologically meaningful manner. Leisure, according to Pieper, is a period of time which permits the individual to become one with himself, to reflect, to discover, and to realize the self in relation to all other things in the universe. It is time, but not empty time because it is filled with awareness and expression of self. It is pleasure because it permits one to discover and explore the many aspects of the self which have been neglected or un-developed because of the demands of work or other responsibilities. It is restful, relaxing, and refreshing because it is engagement of the self in activities that one finds enjoyable. Leisure as a condition of being is at right angles, not opposite poles, from the condition of work. Idleness is the opposite of work or activity, but leisure is a state of vitality in which the individual discovers and enriches the self.

If we can think of leisure in this manner we can appreciate that the person who is one with himself will be more capable of being one with other persons. Just as work may serve to achieve *self-actualization*, leisure effectively used can also serve to make the perceived self actual. The difference, of course, is that work by its very nature requires the individual to meet the demands of the job first, satisfying his own personal needs secondarily. Leisure, however, permits the individual to meet the demands of the self first and in satisfying these to be better able to satisfy any other demands. Leisure offers us the chance to think, to wonder, and to develop our creative potential if we can learn to use it effectively. What are the means by which this challenge can be met?

One obvious answer is to see leisure in the positive terms suggested by Pieper. Evidence to support his view can be found in the bored, discontented, and restless condition of those who think of leisure only as inactivity, pleasure-seeking, or empty time. Another means is to take some time to consider the nature of the self. The undeveloped interests, the latent skills, the neglected talents, the lack of knowledge and experience which one finds in the self do not have to be permanent conditions. Another means is to try using available time to enrich the self or to give expression to some heretofore unexpressed aspect of the self. If your efforts bring you a new enthusiasm, a new sense of worth, and a new feeling of refreshment you will know Pieper's meaning of leisure.

Perhaps the most difficult aspect of adopting a positive approach to the concept of leisure involves the attitude most persons have of "self." In a society that consumed the majority of its time in work activities people tended to think of the self as a tool or a means to accomplish work related goals necessary for the well-being of everyone. As a result, leisure had to be "stolen" from the demands of work and people felt guilty and "selfish" for whatever leisure they took. In a society of increasing leisure, however, the self must be employed as a tool to accomplish self-related, not work-related, goals. It is necessary to the well-being of everyone in a society that provides abundant leisure that individuals develop their resources of self and engage them constructively. Whether leisure will prove to be the "good life" as once idealized or the curse of modern man will depend upon how successfully people can adapt to the use of the self to define their goals as well as to accomplish their goals.

RETIREMENT

The final major task of life is the challenge of retirement. Technically, retirement has always meant the end of participation in employment. Socially and psychologically, however, retirement has had different meanings to different persons. For some, it has meant they are in the decline of life. For many, it has meant adjustment to a lower standard of living dependent upon accumulated benefits or social assistance at levels below those enjoyed as a result of earnings. For others, retirement has been welcomed as freedom from work-related responsibilities and an opportunity to explore new aspects of life related to self-interests. Some persons carefully plan their retirement saving both personal and material resources toward a time when they can at last enjoy life in terms of their own values and desires. Others are forced out of employment in work by compulsory retirement practices and they dread this time of life more than any other. Psychologically then, retirement has been seen by some as the beginning and by others as the end of life.

The nature of our society has until only recently done very little to help persons see retirement in a positive manner. We have valued youth, used human energies to their utmost, and been rather callous about getting rid of persons whose contributions seem diminished by the process of aging. Compulsory retirement systems were started initially to make room at "the top" for younger, more vigorous persons. To soften the blow of compulsory retirement practices employers have contributed generously to company retirement benefit plans. Society, too, in an effort to compensate those removed from employment has coined new terms like "senior citizen" to give retired persons some measure of status, voted to increase assistance payments and tax benefits, and encouraged the development of retirement communities removed from the center of activity. Currents of change in our society, however, must cause us to wonder at the harvest to be reaped from such practices.

Partly as a result of the unhappiness created when compulsory retirement systems became common, much research has been focused on the nature of change in individuals as a function of age. The outstanding finding of these researches has been to emphasize that aging is very much an individual matter. Declines of strength, vigor, sensory acuity, reasoning, judgment, social competence, and other skills do not appear to be as great as commonly believed or feared (see Anastasi, 1958 and Tyler, 1965). Much that appeared to be lost by aging seems in fact to be accomplished by oldsters through the use of new approaches to problem tasks and skills. The evidence is convincing that there is much productivity left in many persons age 60–65 and older and some of it is superior in quality to that of younger persons.

In spite of such evidence, the necessity to make room for younger persons in positions of leadership has been a justification for compulsory retirement practices. This perhaps would continue to be true if the economic system were to remain unchanged. The economic system, however, is changing and the nature of the change is to replace many human workers with cybernated equipment. The 30-hour work week and increased leisure are creating, in effect, a disengagement from employment for everyone. Retirement, as the end of participation in employment, once forced upon persons because of age is already being forced upon some persons because they lack the needed skills of a new industrial system. Compulsory retirement at given ages will have to continue, and the age of retirement will have to be younger than the 60–65 range commonly in practice. The reason, however, will be different. The "make room at the top" philosophy is being replaced by the reality of a limited need for human employment in all age ranges. The persons in our society who know the most about constructive use of leisure and making an adaptive adjustment to disengagement from employment are the senior citizens. Forced to retire because of their age, but still possessing much productive capacity, they have gained valuable experience in learning to use leisure effectively. Society will increasingly require the leadership of its senior citizens to serve as models for adjustment in a changing economic system. The removal of senior citizens to communities apart from the rest of society ultimately can only be society's loss.

The problems of retirement and the problems of effective use of leisure are identical. To call it leisure when a person is young and retirement when a person is old is to place an unwarranted low value on our older citizens and to create additional problems for ourselves. We must reconsider our attitudes about the worth of human beings. In an era when survival could only be obtained by human labor, a fair measure of a man's worth was the work he could *do*. As we move toward an era in which survival is assured by scientific technology, a fair measure of a man's worth will be what he *is*. The one certain resource we will all possess in a time called greater leisure or earlier retirement will be the self. Whether this new era will be psychologically a beginning or an end for you personally will depend upon your ability to develop your resource of self.

SUMMARY

Life tasks are the challenges of society that enable us to establish identity and find satisfaction in social living. The life tasks are acceptance of sex roles, choice of educational and occupational goals, marriage, productivity, and retirement, all interrelated parts of the life process.

Sex roles are stereotyped patterns of beliefs, attitudes, and activities that are culturally defined as appropriate for one sex or the other. In our culture greater demands are made on males for achievement, independence, and responsibility. Children learn sex-appropriate role behavior by identification which helps to shape their self-concepts and establish identity. As educational level increases the distinction between male and female occupational roles becomes less clear.

Choice of educational and occupational goals is important because the work we do determines our social identity and provides the means of satisfying psychological as well as material needs. Vocational goals are influenced by socioeconomic factors. It may not be possible to determine in advance which specific career goals will best suit your personality because work experience and personality development are interdependent.

Success in marriage is partly a function of making a wise choice of marriage partner. The selection of a mate is limited by sociological factors which define the field of eligible candidates. Length of courtship is the most significant single factor related to marital success. Psychological factors related to stability of marriage include appropriate sex-role behavior, recognition of personal needs, and ability to fulfill expectations of the marriage partner. Longer courtship tends to produce more realistic expectations and lead to greater chances of success in marriage. The use of computers in mate selection offers some promise but has many limitations.

The period of greatest productivity, from about 30 to 60 years of age, should bring individual satisfaction as a result of maximum realization of potentials. Satisfaction with your work is a product of morale factors associated with the work setting, personal feelings about the work as a means of self-expression and growth, and social relationships outside the job. Self-actualization depends upon meaningful use of leisure time as well as successful career development.

Retirement can be an opportunity or a burden depending upon how well a person has achieved a balance between the satisfaction he finds in work and in leisure. In youth we emphasize work as the source of satisfaction because it requires more of an individual's time and effort, but with increasing maturity a balance is achieved between work and leisure which tends toward greater satisfaction on the side of leisure. In retirement the emphasis is on leisure and reaping the rewards of what has been accomplished both in terms of material gains and self-actualization.

SUGGESTIONS FOR FURTHER READING

Berscheid, Ellen and Walster, Elaine, *Interpersonal Attraction*, Reading, Mass., Addison-Wesley, 1969. Considers the problems of evaluating others for whom a person feels attraction or rejection in individual relationships and in groups.

Blanch, Rubin and Blanch, Gertrude, *Marriage and Personal Development*, New York, Columbia University Press, 1968. Views marriage as a developmental stage in personal growth of the self.

Coleman, James C., *Psychology and Effective Behavior*, Glenview, Ill., Scott-Foresman, 1969. A practical approach to problems of human adjustment, including marriage, work, social process, and personal development.

Cox, Frank, *Youth, Marriage and the Seductive Society*, Dubuque, Iowa, Brown, 1968. Considers four major problem areas confronting youth today: dating patterns, premarital sexual behavior, young marriage, and economic influence on young marriage.

Packard, Vance, *The Sexual Wilderness*, New York, McKay, 1968. Stresses the sensual content of our modern environment as the basis for present day confusion of sex roles, and discusses their widespread influence on society and the individual.

Times of Crisis

A crisis is a critical time or decisive moment, a turning-point in the course of events. Sometimes a crisis occurs as a result of the "coming to a head" of a stress situation that has been building up tension over a long period of time. Other crises occur suddenly and without warning. How an individual or a family responds to a crisis will help determine how serious and damaging the effects of the crisis will be. Everyone in the course of his life will have the experience of facing some crisis. If minor crises are not handled well they may lead to other more serious crises.

A crisis has the effect of disrupting adjustment, temporarily at least, and sometimes for a long time before readjustment is possible. Some crises may leave permanent and damaging effects that may never be remedied. The outcome of a crisis situation depends upon how it is handled by the person who is experiencing it. Developing an awareness of those times in life that are apt to be stressful or difficult, and recognizing the critical elements in each situation, can help us to adjust to crises when they do occur.

FRUSTRATION AND CONFLICT

The most common crises we all experience are times of frustration and conflict. Frustration occurs whenever we are blocked or thwarted in our progress or when we are prevented from reaching our goals. Whenever something we want very much is unattainable or something we want to do is impossible we feel a very negative emotion. Frustration refers to the obstacles or events that get in the way of satisfying our needs and to the negative feelings we experience as a result. In our daily lives we meet frustration repeatedly and we develop characteristic ways of handling it. Most of the daily frustrations we encounter are minor ones which we can ignore, overcome, or learn to live with for a long time: rush-hour traffic, broken dates, late appointments, flat tires, lost pens, unexpected events, and so on. Unfortunately, not all frustrations can be regarded as minor. Some more serious frustrations constitute a real threat to an individual's self-concept and may have disrupting effects.

Sources of Frustration

The frustrating events or obstacles that prevent us from satisfying our needs or solving our problems arise from three main sources: (*a*) external or environmental conditions; (*b*) internal or personal limitations; (*c*) conflicting motives or goals.

Social—physical disagg

Environmental conditions that stand in our way and produce frustration may be a part of the physical environment such as floods, storms, earthquakes, or weather. You try to raise a crop and there is no rainfall. You try to commute to your job in a neighboring town and the road is washed out. More often the external sources of frustration stem from the social environment. You want a job but no work is available. You want to get married but the law prevents you from marrying until you are of age. If you belong to a minority group in a prejudiced community you suffer many social frustrations.

Personal limitations may be real or they may be imagined but in either case they can serve as frustrating obstacles. You may want to participate in sports but lack the size, strength, or skill to make the team. You may want to be an engineer or scientist but lack the mathematical ability needed to succeed in preparing for such a career. Personal frustration and the feelings of inferiority it engenders depend largely on the goals we set for ourselves. If your goals are unrealistic you are setting yourself up for frustration and failure. A goal should be a challenge that you can realistically expect to achieve.

Conflicting motives or goals are the most common sources of frustration. We are continually faced with making choices between two or more alternatives and trying to make a wise decision. Some choices are easy to make and others are very frustrating because they arouse conflicts which are often difficult to resolve.

② Social: Restrictions — laws — minority group

Types of Conflict ③ *Personal: wont souler — bad cook —*

Conflict may involve matters about which we feel positively (attraction and desire to attain) and toward which we wish to approach. Conflict may involve matters about which we feel negatively (rejection and desire to escape) and these we attempt to avoid. Some of our conflicts deal with matters we wish to approach as well as to avoid. Let us look at each of these more closely (see Figure 8-1).

Approach–approach conflict occurs when individuals must decide between two desirable but mutually exclusive goals. For example, a young man may want to join friends for the weekend at the opening of hunting season but it is the same weekend he has planned to take his girlfriend to the club dance. He cannot do both, he would enjoy doing either, and he has to decide. If both positive goals have equally strong appeal indecision may be prolonged and great frustration experienced. This type of conflict, when it is resolved, always results in obtaining some desired goal and for that reason it is less disrupting than other types of conflict.

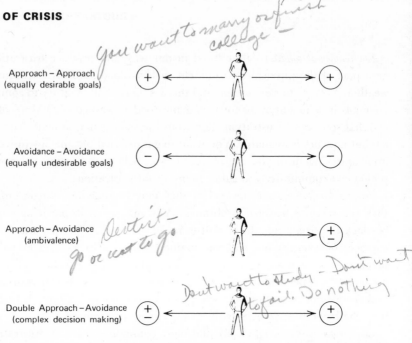

[handwritten: You want to marry or first college —]

Approach – Approach
(equally desirable goals)

Avoidance – Avoidance
(equally undesirable goals)

Approach – Avoidance
(ambivalence)   *[handwritten: Dentist — go or not to go]*

Double Approach – Avoidance
(complex decision making)

[handwritten: Don't want to study — Don't want to fail. Do nothing]

[handwritten, left margin: Goes back to a man named Lewine]

Figure 8-1. Types of conflict.

Avoidance–avoidance conflict is more difficult because the choice is between two undesirable alternatives. An individual must do one or the other but he would like to avoid both. A person suffering the severe pain of a toothache would like to be relieved of it but he wishes also to avoid what he fears the dentist will do to eliminate the toothache. This type of conflict causes a great deal of indecision and frustration because whatever outcome is chosen is not desirable. Resolution of avoidance–avoidance conflict becomes a choice between "the lesser of two evils." Rather than to go toward either choice the individual will, if possible, attempt to escape both. Study or fail is an avoidance–avoidance conflict for some students. They cannot bear the necessary activities involved in study but they also wish to avoid the shame and pain of failure. Rather than experience either of these solutions, some students escape the conflict situation by dropping out of school. Escape or running away from a conflict situation is not necessarily a maladaptive adjustment. If escaping the conflict leads to added problems (loss of self-esteem) or disrupts other behaviors (progress toward a career) then it of course is maladaptive. In the avoidance–avoidance conflict of being shot or hung at dawn, escape is a very adaptive solution.

Approach–avoidance conflict results when we have both positive and negative feelings toward a goal. We are attracted to something but repelled by some aspect of it at the same time. A woman may very much wish to marry a man of a different religious faith, but to do so will cause her to violate the principles of her own faith which means very much to her. A man may want to go to night school to increase his education and improve his opportunity for a better paying job, but he may not want to give up the little free time he has for class attendance and study. The more strongly he is attracted toward the goal the more he is repelled by the negative aspects of it. This type of conflict often results in indecision and inconsistent behavior. This is the most common type of conflict people face since nearly everything has some good and some bad factors associated with it. *contradictory feelings about same situation*

The feeling of wanting and not wanting, or liking and disliking at the same time, is called _ambivalence_. Children often feel very ambivalent toward their parents because they like the love, acceptance, and security the parents give them, but they dislike the discipline, domination, and control their parents have over them. People often feel ambivalent toward their work because they enjoy the rewards but resent the obligations, or they may enjoy what they are doing and feel that they are not being paid enough.

When people are faced with approach–avoidance conflict or ambivalent feelings they sometimes revert to childish dependency and rely on someone else to make the decision for them. Mature people have to learn to pay the price of making an occasional mistake in order to be decisive. Otherwise, they become so overwhelmed by their ambivalence that they are unable to resolve even minor conflicts.

In our society approach–avoidance conflict is expected in behavior related to sex and aggression. In childhood we are taught to control our sexual and aggressive impulses and to place high value on moral standards. When control is too strong we experience frustration and great anxiety (vague, nonspecific fear) when we do attempt to express our sexual or aggressive feelings. When control is lacking we may experience guilt and anxiety because of the violations of moral standards. The best resolution of this conflict must be determined individually in terms of the most satisfying balance between control and expression for one's own personal adjustment.

Double approach–avoidance conflict is the most complex kind of conflict. The individual must choose between two alternatives both of which have positive and negative aspects. A graduating student in police science may have two positions offered to him. One is with the small department in a town where he wants to live but the pay is very low. The other is in a large city with better pay and greater opportunities for advancement, but a faster pace of living than he feels he can enjoy. To resolve conflicts of this type a decision must be made in terms of the positive and negative values of both situations. Seldom do you find a solution to a problem that meets all your needs and has no drawbacks. Usually you must consider several courses of action and weigh the pros and cons of each before you can feel confident that your choice is a wise one.

Dealing with Frustration

Frustration and conflict are impossible to avoid. Learning how to handle them begins at birth and continues throughout life. The indecision and unpleasant emotions generated by these events increase tension and added anxiety in the individual. The tension and anxiety may be disrupting psychologically and also find expression physically in sleeplessness, poor digestion or elimination, and other uncomfortable symptoms. The disturbed emotional state of frustration is called _stress_ and it continues to develop until some satisfactory means to the blocked goal is found. Severe and prolonged stress can lead to serious physical illness (heart disease, ulcers) as well as to emotional and mental illnesses which we will discuss in Chapter 9.

Dealing with frustration in a constructive way depends upon our ability to develop frustration tolerance. As children we have a very low tolerance for frustration. Many children respond to the slightest frustration with violent outbursts of anger. However, it is obvious that adults differ widely in their ability to tolerate frustration. Some people are always upset, angry, frustrated about something, and others seem to take major frustrations in their stride. The difference is related to the fact that different persons interpret or perceive frustration in different ways. Those who can interpret frustration as a problem to be solved will focus their attention on the obstacles to be overcome and will look for new methods to reach the goal. As long as they are working on the problem and the goal is still in sight frustration tolerance can remain fairly high. People who perceive frustration as a personal threat become anxious and defensive and their ability to tolerate frustration is lost.

To illustrate how frustration tolerance works, consider the reactions of two young men who failed the first quiz in their psychology course which was required for graduation. Bob interpreted this failure as a temporary setback and decided that he needed to improve his study habits. Thus, frustration was not too difficult for him to tolerate. Bill interpreted the failure as a sign of inferior mental ability and thus perceived the frustrating event as a personal threat to his future security. Frustration tolerance varies among individuals but it may also vary for a single individual at different times. When you are relatively free from worries you can usually tolerate a frustrating experience better than when you are disturbed by other problems. When you are faced with too many frustrations one small thing may be "the straw that breaks the camel's back."

Through processes of maturation and learning people develop characteristic ways of handling their frustrations and conflicts. Some of these methods, such as childish behavior (temper tantrums, destructiveness) excessive dependence on others, escape or withdrawal, and blaming or fault-finding, become increasingly maladaptive as they become habitual ways of responding. The well-adjusted mature person views frustrations as problem situations rather than disasters and takes a problem-solving approach to them, seeking guidance or additional information as it is needed.

SEPARATION ANXIETY

Whenever you are separated from people you have learned to depend on for emotional security, or when you are cut off from your accepted sources of need satisfaction, you usually experience a heightened level of anxiety and discomfort. This particular stress is called *separation anxiety*. In the normal life span we are continually striving to establish close meaningful personal relationships with others and we are repeatedly faced with anxiety produced by separation from them. There are times in life when we can normally anticipate separation and anxiety and be prepared to cope with it.

Beginning School

The beginning of school marks an important crisis point in the life of a child. It is his first real venture into the world on his own and a step away from his family toward independence. For many children school is the first separation from the family. The child comes to school with attitudes and expectations that will influence his learning and adjustment and will affect his whole future. Parents, both deliberately and unintentionally, prepare a child for school and set the pattern for his behavior. If his parents have encouraged him to perceive school as an exciting place to learn new things and make new friends he will probably look forward to school with enthusiasm. If his parents have emphasized the negative aspects of school, stressing the lack of freedom and control of

Figure 8-2. Many different feelings characterize these children as they board the bus to go home after the first day of school. (Photo by Jim Sargent.)

behavior, he may feel that going to school is a form of punishment. The child's perception of school is colored by the attitudes of his parents (Figure 8-2).

In a recent study psychologists asked a group of mothers to describe how they would prepare their children for school. Here are the responses of two different mothers and the author's interpretation of each response (Hess and Shipman, 1965).

> *First mother:* "First of all, I would remind her that she was going to school to learn, that her teacher would take my place, and that she would be expected to follow instructions. Also that her time was to be spent mostly in the classroom with other children, and that she could consult with her teacher for assistance on any questions or problems that she might have."
>
> *Interpretation:* "In terms of promoting educability, what did this mother do in her response? First, she was informative, presenting the

school situation as comparable to one already familiar to the child; second, she offered reassurance and support to help the child deal with anxiety; third, she described the school situation as one which involves a personal relationship between the child and the teacher; and fourth, she presented the classroom situation as one in which the child was to learn."

Second mother: "Well, John, it's time to go to school now. You must know how to behave. The first day at school you should be a good boy and should do just what the teacher tells you to do."

Interpretation: "In contrast to the first mother, what did this mother do? First, she defined the role of the child as passive and compliant; second, the central issues she presented were those dealing with authority, and the institution, rather than with learning; third, the relationship and roles she portrayed were sketched in terms of status and role expectations, rather than in personal terms; and fourth, her message was general, restricted, and vague, lacking information about how to deal with the problems of school, except by passive compliance."

It is easy to see which of these children will be off to a better start when he arrives at school. A child's attitude toward school is often colored by casual remarks the parents make without realizing their effect on the child. For example, remarks like these: "I'll be glad when school starts so I can have some time for myself." or "He won't be able to act like that when he gets to school!" or "If he thinks I'm strict just wait 'til he starts to school!" can have a damaging effect on a child's perception of school.

The child entering school is faced with many new experiences and frustrations that are not shared with his family. How well he can handle his fears and frustration depends largely upon his self-confidence and emotional maturity. The mother who "hates to see her baby grow up," and has encouraged him to be overly dependent on her, may find that her child cannot cope with the problems of adjustment to school. Unless a child has had some experience in dealing with new and unfamiliar situations he may be at a complete loss without his mother. Children who are too emotionally immature and dependent tend to withdraw and develop feelings of inferiority which further limits their ability to gain self-confidence. The child who withdraws in the classroom misses many learning opportunities and after a while his feeling of emotional inferiority may be matched with real learning deficiencies.

The problems of school adjustment are equally difficult for a child who feels rejected at home. Such children often make excessive demands for attention, and by their "show-off" behavior make themselves obnoxious to others, further contributing to their feelings of rejection. The child who is excluded because his behavior offends others, like the child who withdraws, may soon have real learning deficiencies to add to his problems. Parents who have younger children at home need to make a special effort to help a child master his *separation anxiety*. Anxiety means a very vague, unspecific kind of fear. The anxiety of starting school for some children involves fears relating to the lost place in the family as well as the unknown experiences ahead with the teacher and other children. Many children start school feeling that their mothers are more interested in the younger children and want them out of the way. Children can usually be made to see that school is a reward for their greater maturity rather than a form of punishment if parents can recognize and deal with the child's anxiety.

A separation anxiety which resulted in a severe *school phobia* (fear out of proportion to the danger) is illustrated by the case of Nancy.

> Nancy was 8 years old and in the second grade when school officials requested the help of a mental health consultant to assist their understanding of her behavior. She had repeated first grade and was scheduled to repeat the second. On an individual intelligence test, administered with great difficulty, she attained an I.Q. score of 132. The first two years in school she had to be dragged to the classroom. She bit the teachers and other children and became very adept at petty stealing. She kicked, screamed, and disrupted the classroom. She was assigned to a variety of teachers, but none could establish a relationship with her. During second grade her violence began to diminish and she used every available excuse to go to the nurse's office where she would curl up quietly until time to go home. Nancy was an only child of a marriage between two young persons which ended in divorce when she was a year old. Her father left the community and did not make his required support payments. When Nancy was 3 years old her mother remarried. Nancy was a source of conflict in the new marriage because she was a reminder of the first husband and an added economic burden to the second. Just before Nancy entered school, a baby boy was born into the family. The new baby was the focus of attention of both the mother and Nancy's stepfather

for he was the first child of their love and marriage. Nancy's mother was glad to send her to school because Nancy disliked the baby and could not be trusted alone with him. In this atmosphere of rejection at home, and the competition of the new baby, Nancy was sent off to begin school. Her anxiety about a place in the family and the demands of the classroom situation with other children overwhelmed her. Her first responses were of violent rage and anger, symptoms of her frustrated needs for love and security. By second grade, she had changed her approach from attack to withdrawal seeking refuge in the office of the nurse. She had suffered both emotionally and intellectually. The rejection she felt at home was matched in part by the rejection of her teachers and classmates due to her behavior. The efforts of several agencies proved futile because Nancy's mother refused to acknowledge any problem or cooperate in any way. Finally, through action of the juvenile court Nancy was placed in a foster home of high quality where she was the only child. When last seen Nancy was in fourth grade and beginning to achieve at a level consistent with her ability. Her behavior reflected her new home environment of love, care, and attention.

Emancipation

The problem of achieving freedom from parental control (emancipation) must be solved before a person can reach psychological maturity. This may seem like a simple developmental task of growing up, leaving home, and becoming independent, but it is a critical time and marks a turning point in the lives of young people and their parents. While the law may regard an individual as independent of parents upon reaching legal age, a person does not achieve emotional, intellectual, and economic independence quite so easily.

The period of adolescence marks the beginning of an individual's transition from the role of a dependent child to that of an independent adult. The adolescent typically struggles with the conflict of wanting to be his own boss and making his own decisions, and also wanting the security and freedom from responsibility that goes with dependence. Most parents have conflicting feelings toward their adolescent, too, because they want him to be able to handle his own problems in a mature way and at the same time they want to protect him from making mistakes and being hurt. Parents often behave inconsistently toward an adolescent's struggle for independence because of their confusion as to what society expects of them and because of their own conflicting needs. Parents who have not been able to satisfy their needs for love, acceptance, and importance apart from their children are inclined to foster dependency and cling to their children as a source of gratification for their own needs.

The ease with which a person achieves the goal of independence depends to a large extent on previous parent–child relationships. The child whose parents have been overly dominant and authoritarian tends to become overly dependent and submissive to authority. If his dependence has been rewarded by his parents throughout childhood the habit patterns are so well-established that by adolescence the individual will have difficulty in responding to the demands of society for independent behavior. As he grows older, and the demands for independent behavior increase, his dependent behavior becomes more and more inappropriate. The following actual case is not unusual.

> Mr. C. was referred for psychological help because of extreme anxiety for which his family physician could find no organic cause. This young man of 28 was single, living with his parents, and employed as an electrical engineer. He had worked for the same company for the six years since his graduation from college and he had been promoted to a responsible position. Mr. C. had many friends and was engaged to marry a girl who was well-liked by his family. He had already completed the management training program in preparation for an executive position in a new plant his company was developing in another state, when he began to feel overwhelmed by anxiety. As his marriage and moving to the new location drew nearer he became more anxious and fearful until he was unable to leave his home unless his mother and father were with him. Mr. C. had to postpone his marriage and take a leave of absence from his work for several months before he was able, with the help of a therapist, to handle his anxiety about leaving home. Emancipation was a long and painful process for Mr. C. but he was finally able to accomplish it.

Going to college is often an important turning point in life and it can be a source of separation anxiety. On a more complex level the same factors operate that produced anxiety for the child of 5 or 6 years when he started to school. The beginning college student is faced with the physical separation from parents and a whole new set of expectations and frustrations that cannot be shared with his family. A greater degree of independence and judgment are part of the difference between high school and college. Emancipation is still a crucial problem to most college students even though many of them would deny their dependency on and control by parents.

The rebelliousness and unconventional behavior that is characteristic of many college students is a natural reaction to the newly found freedom from parental domination and restriction. The college years are especially important for emancipation because it is during this time that you establish your own identity as an individual apart from your family. Your choice of vocational goals may be in conflict with your parent's hopes and ambitions but they are an essential part of your emancipation. It is during the college years that most young people achieve intellectual emancipation. That is, you learn to think for yourself and develop attitudes and opinions independent of parental influence.

Establishing oneself as an independent person outside one's parental residence, as in marriage, and becoming economically independent does not assure a person of emancipation from parents. Many marriages are destroyed by the lack of psychological maturity which permits or invites interference by in-laws. Immature people who are still in need of acceptance and approval from parents often have difficulty in adjusting to marriage. The conflict of loyalties between parents and spouse must be resolved if a marriage is to succeed. As adults you belong to a different generation from your parents and you have to develop your own values, attitudes, and standards of conduct. When an individual has developed genuine self-determination and has made a satisfactory adult adjustment his parents can respect him as another adult.

When a person has attained psychological maturity his parents usually accept him even though they may not always understand or agree with him. Similarly, the mature person is able to view his parents realistically: appreciating their strengths, accepting their shortcomings, loving them for what they are as well as for what they are not. The person who reaches maturity in years still finding fault with his parents, making demands upon them to improve by his standards, or loving them out of a sense of obligation is psychologically immature. The mature person finds new satisfaction and meaning in his relationship to his parents on an adult basis rather than as a dependent or demanding child.

In clinical practice we see numerous cases in which marriage has become a near-disaster because one or both partners were unable to achieve emancipation from parents. An example of this was Mrs. B. who came to the clinic following a suicide attempt reportedly because her husband cancelled their plans to go on vacation.

Mrs. B. was 35 years old and had been married to Mr. B. for 17 years. During the entire course of their marriage Mr. and Mrs. B. had spent every vacation and holiday with Mr. B.'s parents. Mrs. B. and their three children had planned to spend the Christmas holidays in their own home on several successive years, but at the last minute Mr. B.'s mother would not feel like coming and the family would have to go to her home. The same was true of summer vacations. Each year the family would plan a vacation together but Mr. B.'s mother always wanted him to spend his vacation helping his father with repairs on their property or taking them to visit some other relatives. Each year Mrs. B. and the children went on their vacation without Mr. B., or they cancelled their plans and stayed home. Mr. B. also felt that he needed his parents approval before making any major expenditure, so Mrs. B. was never able to purchase any furnishings or decorations for her home without their approval. Whenever Mr. and Mrs. B. entertained friends in their home Mr. B.'s parents were always invited because they lived nearby and might be offended if they were left out. In the 17 years of their marriage Mr. B. had never gone with his wife to visit her parents or relatives in the next state, some 500 miles away, although she and the children had been there every few years. On the occasion of her parent's 50th anniversary Mrs. B.'s family planned a reunion with all her brothers and sisters and their families. For a year in advance Mr. B. planned to go with his wife and family to the reunion and from there on a camping trip which the children had planned on and looked forward to for several years. It looked as if everything would work out well at last; Mr. B.'s parents had raised no objection to their going, the car was packed, all last-minute details taken care of, and the family was getting into the car, when Mr. B.'s father drove up. He begged them not to go because his wife was too upset and he was afraid she might have a heart attack if they left town. When Mr. B. came back from talking with his mother he helped the children unpack the car and promised them he would take them on the camping trip later. He hated to face his wife, so he put it off as long as he could, until one of the children went into her room and found she had taken an overdose of sleeping pills. At the hospital Mr. B. said he had no idea why his wife would have done such a thing but he hoped that his mother would not have to hear about it.

Broken Homes *Not a valid statement!*

Broken homes have been blamed for delinquency, crime, failure, and un-happiness by those who seek reasons and excuses. The fact that family members are separated from each other by reason of employment, military duties, illness, death, or divorce does not mean that they are on the road to ruin. Some families can face these crises without damaging effects to the individuals while others are so demoralized by the crisis that they seem to be unable to recover and readjust. If people can keep a problem-solving attitude rather than a fault-finding attitude they are more likely to adjust successfully.

The extent to which children suffer from broken homes depends largely upon the nature of the interpersonal relationships within the family. If a husband and wife are hostile and resentful toward each other, what they say and do may be deeply disturbing to a child. If the atmosphere of the home is filled with anger and conflict rather than love and acceptance there is little, if any, benefit to the child from merely having two parents. In such instances the child may be much better off living with one reasonably adjusted parent. The prolonged exposure of a child to the tension of an unhappy marriage often has more harmful consequences than the effects of a divorce.

In our society children whose parents are divorced are usually awarded to the custody of their mother and are expected to receive financial support from their father. This frequently means that the children have to adjust to a different standard of living since the father often has the added economic burden of supporting two households. When the father is unable or unwilling to meet his obligations the mother is faced with having to find employment or seek assistance from relatives, friends or public welfare agencies. Unless a woman has sufficient education or special job training it is very difficult for her to find employment. Many divorced women marry again because they find themselves unable to cope with the responsibilities and problems of holding a job, maintaining a home, and meeting the demands of their children, as well as filling their own needs for adult affection. It is not uncommon today to see families composed of a husband and wife, his children, her children, and their children. While such families may be able to make a satisfactory adjust-ment, the number of them seen in mental health clinics leads us to believe that more emphasis needs to be put on selection of a mate and prevention of divorce.

Many of the problems that disturb children from broken homes can be remedied if they are recognized early enough and the child is given help in acceptance and understanding. A boy who is closely identified with his father may feel rejected by his mother when she divorces his father. If she criticizes the father and devalues him the boy may take this as a personal rejection and develop feelings of inferiority and inadequacy in relation to women. On the other hand, he might feel defensive of his father and develop feelings of resentment and hostility toward his mother which could color his perception of all women. Sometimes parents who are divorced forget that the children are products of both of them and as such they are very sensitive to their criticisms. Children need to feel that both their parents love them and are worthy of their love even if the parents do not live together. This seems especially true in relation to the parent of the same sex as the child. Since the mother usually keeps custody of all children, a boy has a hard time loving a missing father and feeling his father is worth loving. This may be one reason why delinquency involves boys more than girls. Children often tend to harbor guilt feelings about divorce because they do not understand why their parents have separated and they try to find reasons within themselves. Children need help with the problems of divided loyalty because respect for both parents is important to their self-esteem and later adult adjustment.

Children of broken homes who are being brought up by one parent sometimes have the disadvantage of not having available models of both sexes with whom to identify. Women who are rearing children alone frequently express the concern that their sons will lack masculinity because they do not have a father to pattern themselves after. The fact that one parent is not present in the home on a day-to-day basis does not mean that the parent has ceased to exist for the child. Too often the missing parent is idealized and becomes the model of what the perfect parent should be in the child's mind. This ideal parent may be the source of serious difficulty in a child's future adjustment to a substitute parent or stepparent. This is because the child compares the new parent to his ideal parent image and finds the substitute an imposter with many shortcomings.

One of the ways that has proved helpful in adjusting to broken homes is the development of social clubs or groups for people with common problems. "Parents Without Partners" is a national organization with local clubs in many communities. PWP will help any group organize a club if one is not already established in your community. These clubs sponsor a variety of social activities for families in which one or the other parent is missing, and they provide opportunity to meet new people and develop new interests.

Separation or divorce is a serious crisis for all members of a family but it is seldom a sudden or unexpected event. It is usually the outcome of a series of crises which have not been handled adequately. Generally speaking, most divorces result from the failure of one or both partners in marriage to satisfy their emotional needs and to achieve what they expected from the relationship. While the adjustment to divorce may be difficult, it is frequently preferable to the demoralizing effects of a marriage that is beyond repair.

ILLNESS, DISABILITY, AND TRAGEDY

With all good intentions and best efforts to keep healthy, it would be unrealistic to expect to go through life without facing the crisis of sudden injury or prolonged illness, either directly or indirectly. Except for the relatively small proportion of people who are killed instantly, no one dies healthy. Most of us, at some time in our lives, are involved with disability resulting from illness or injury to ourselves or some members of our family (Figure 8-3).

Effects of Disability

When a person is injured accidentally his family routine is temporarily interrupted while attention is centered on his immediate needs. If he progresses satisfactorily the crisis is minor and the family soon returns to normal. However, if the injury is severe and the person is disabled for a long time the family will have to make many changes and adjustments. His increased need for care and attention causes tension and strain for the rest of the family as well as discomfort for himself. Prolonged or *chronic* illness can also have a disorganizing effect on a family. The financial burden of illness affects every member of the family but the emotional stress may be an even greater burden.

Research has been conducted to study the effects of illness and accidents and to try to find out why some people can adjust to disability so much better than others. *Disability* is used here to mean any personal handicap that is acquired by injury or illness and limits the person's ability to function as well as he could before the injury or illness. When we think of disability we usually think of a physically handicapped person, but we must recognize that a physically handicapped person also has emotional or psychological problems. Some disabilities are obvious to other people and may attract attention or gain sympathy, such as blindness, loss of an arm or leg, cerebral palsy, and paralysis. Other disabilities, however, are hidden from public view, such as heart disease, epilepsy,

Figure 8-3.   How do you think you would feel and act if you were the victim shown here who has just lost all her possessions in a flood disaster? (Photo courtesy of American National Red Cross.)

multiple sclerosis, diabetes, and cancer. No one really expects to become disabled but when it happens the individual and his family must face the crisis and adjust to it.

How does an individual adjust to an acquired handicap and what are the factors affecting his adjustment? This question has been the subject of much research (Wright, 1959 and Lofquist, 1960). People react to illness and disability with a wide range of individual differences. The same illness or injury will produce different degrees of disability in different people depending upon how each person evaluates himself and his situation. The reactions of the handicapped person depend on his perception of his own power and the power of external circumstances. The person who feels that he is responsible for what happens to himself, that success and failure are his own doing, reacts differently from the person who feels he is a victim of circumstances. The latter may accept his disability and resign himself to being dependent upon others, while the more self-assertive person will regain self-confidence and strive toward overcoming the effects of his handicap.

It is important that people learn to adjust to illness early in life. Children who are ill may be encouraged to accept complete dependence on parents and may gain *secondary satisfaction* from their illness such as increased attention and special rewards. Sometimes people learn to use illness as an escape from unpleasant tasks or as an excuse for failures or lack of effort. Careful attention to the rewards and advantages a child is given when he is ill will help to determine his attitude toward himself and his ability to cope with illness. Acceptance and tolerance of the illnesses or handicaps of other persons is another important attitude to be learned in childhood. The child who is fearful, resentful, rejecting, or hostile toward handicapped people will probably have greater difficulty accepting the limitations and disabilities he may have to face in his own life.

Suicide

For many people the pressures of life seem so intolerable and the problems so insurmountable that they seek to escape from a world in which they are unable to find satisfaction, purpose, and meaning. There are approximately 20,000 deaths by suicide in the United States each year, and another 200,000 persons make serious suicide attempts (McGee, 1965). Suicide ranks among the top 10 causes of death in this country. It is the second most frequent cause of death among college students, the third most common cause of death in teenagers, and the fourth-ranked cause of death among males in the age groups 20–45 years (McGee, 1965 and Faigel, 1966).

However, statistics are not telling the whole story and we must consider figures on suicide to be underestimates of the problem. Many accidental deaths, especially those in motor vehicles, are probably concealing some suicides. In cases of severe illness, death hastened by deliberate overdoses of drugs are often presumed natural deaths or attributed to the illness without investigation. Some suicides occur as a consequence of long-term neglect such as occurs in alcoholism and drug addiction and in these instances the self-destructive purposes are often overlooked. There is also at times an effort to conceal a death by suicide on the part of families and friends. Where the individual has been a prominent member of a community or when it is feared that the suicide will detract from the efforts and contributions that the person has made to the community it seems pointless to make public the real cause of death. In some communities and groups a family suicide is a source of shame and humiliation to the survivors and these are sometimes concealed.

Some people wonder why we should concern ourselves with the prevention of suicide—if a person really wants to die should we stop him? Experience has shown that people who are prevented from committing suicide and given a little help at this critical time are very grateful afterward. The humanitarian and religious beliefs of our culture place a high value on human life. We are all concerned with the prevention of accidents, control of disease, and medical advances to increase life expectancy. Should we not then be concerned with a major mental health problem that costs us some of the most productive members of our communities? Furthermore, suicide does not involve a single life, it affects the lives of all those connected with the victim. His family suffers not only sorrow but usually guilt as they blame themselves for not recognizing his distress and preventing this tragedy. Children often suffer from the social stigma attached to the suicide of a parent, and sometimes they become fearful that they may be destined to follow the parent's example.

Suicide is no longer regarded as a sympton of mental disorder, but it is better understood as the outcome of a negative process of social interaction. A person does not decide to end his life for a single reason. The suicidal crisis comes as the final stage in the progressive breakdown of adaptive behavior. The individual who has tried, failed, lost confidence in himself, feels he has no one to depend on, has lost contact with groups, and feels inadequate to cope with the stress situations he faces may turn to suicide as a last resort. The person who feels that life is no longer worth living has arrived at this stage over a period of time usually as a result of failure to establish meaningful relationships with people and groups that could help him in times of crisis.

In a study of 102 children and adolescents under 16 years of age who were hospitalized because of suicidal thoughts and actions, it was found that the majority came from chaotic homes where one or both parents were absent and the children were reacting to stressful situations (Toolan, 1962). Many people find it difficult to believe that children and adolescents can become depressed and suicidal when they feel inadequate to cope with stress. Another study of 100 attempted suicides by children and adolescents under the age of 18 found that family disorganization and delinquency were highly associated with attempted suicide (Tuckman and Cannon, 1962). Jacobs and Teicher (1967) report a study of the life histories of 50 adolescents hospitalized following suicide attempts compared to a matching group of adolescents who had not attempted suicide. The suicide-attempt adolescents were found to have a much higher incidence of broken homes and to have experienced more commonly a loss of love object (by separation or death) than the other adolescent group. The results indicated that suicidal adolescents experience a continuous process of personal and family disorganization with increasing isolation from "significant" other persons. The broken homes, the delinquency and the suicide attempts in these studies of youths are linked in a chain process of distress resulting from a breakdown in meaningful social relationships.

Suicide in college students may appear to be an impulsive reaction to school failure, a broken love affair, or some other crisis, but on further investigation we usually find a series of related events leading up to the person's inability to face one more stress situation. Parental pressures and the drive for achievement beyond one's capability may result in loss of self-esteem and inability to set more realistic goals. For example, at Harvard University the suicide rate is 1.5 per 10,000 students or 50 percent higher than in the general population (Tenby, 1961).

In an extensive study of the reasons for suicide in 103 white males, ages 20–60 years, in New Orleans it was discovered that they had in common considerable difficulty with work, a crucial aspect of the masculine role (Breed, 1963). The investigator interpreted their distress as a result of *downward mobility*. The fathers of these men had higher occupational status than they did and during their lives the suicide victims had suffered experiences of lost status, reduced income, and unemployment. In our society it is particularly important for men to get ahead and try to move upward. The repeated failure to achieve this *upward mobility* in socioeconomic class results in depression, anxiety, and hostility toward the self. These feelings of self-hatred, guilt, and hopelessness can lead to a suicidal crisis.

Suicide is almost entirely a white phenomenon in this country. Farberow and Shneidman (1961) reporting on data of completed suicides in Los Angeles County, California, during 1957 found 95 percent of completed suicides were white and 3 percent were black. Vitols (1967) reports that suicide among blacks in the south is only about one-fourth the rate among southern whites. The reasons for lower suicide rates among blacks seem to be related to their generally lower status in our society. They are already at the bottom of the social class structure and have no material things to lose. Since they have been in the lower classes for generations there is no unfavorable comparison between themselves and their fathers. Finally, their hopelessness about their situation has been accepted and they do not see any benefit from striving to improve when opportunity is denied them. Unlike their white neighbors they do not believe they can or should move upward and they accept their situation, rather than become depressed and suicidal about it. It is interesting that in communities where blacks have more equal educational and occupational opportunities and incentives their suicide rates are more nearly comparable to whites (Vitols, 1967).

The person who is in constant pain or believes he has an incurable illness, may turn to suicide as an escape from suffering or to end the burden and expense of illness on his family. The likelihood of suicide in terminal cancer patients has been found to be related to such factors as low tolerance for pain, overdependence, excessive demands for attention and reassurance, and prior suicide threats and attempts.

The Suicide Prevention Center in Los Angeles was established in 1958 to treat individuals who have attempted suicide and to study the problems related to suicide and its prevention. The center is supported by the National Institute of Mental Health and it has produced a great deal of research on the subject of suicide. Farberow and Shneidman (1961), codirectors of the center, have designated the suicide attempt as "the cry for help." They have found that almost no one commits suicide without letting others know how he is feeling. Most suicidal people are not fully determined to die. Even when they decide to take their own lives they usually welcome anyone who offers to save them. When suicide prevention services are available, people who are in a suicidal crisis do make use of them to good advantage.

The Suicide Prevention Center in Los Angeles has found, on the basis of extensive research, that several widely held popular beliefs about suicide have no basis in fact. It is important to correct these erroneous beliefs because they can have serious consequences. Better understanding of the facts concerning suicide may help to save lives by making us able to recognize the danger when it exists and calling in expert help. The list of *mistaken notions* includes the following (Farberow and Shneidman, 1961, pp. 13–14).[†]

1. *People who talk about suicide won't commit suicide.* Studies have shown that at least 75 percent of people who had committed suicide had previously attempted or threatened or both. Suicide threats and attempts should be taken seriously.

2. *Suicide happens without any warning.* Studies reveal that the suicidal person gives many clues and warnings to indicate his intentions. Alertness to these clues will help prevent suicidal behavior.

[†]From *The Cry For Help* by N. L. Farberow and E. S. Shneidman. Copyright 1961 by the McGraw-Hill Book Company, Inc. Used with permission of McGraw-Hill Book Company.

3. *Improvement following a suicidal crisis means that the suicide risk is over.* Investigations have shown that almost half the persons who were in a suicidal crisis but later committed suicide, did so within 90 days after the first crisis when they seemed to be on the way to recovery. This is a critical period and the suicidal person should be watched closely.

4. *Suicide and depression are the same.* Depression is the one best single indicator of potential suicide risk. However, not all suicidal persons show signs of depression and not everyone who is depressed is suicidal.

5. *All suicidal persons are insane.* A study of over 700 genuine suicide notes indicate that feelings are intense and disturbed, but reasoning, judgment, and logic appear sound. The perspective of a suicidal person is distorted perhaps but they are not insane.

6. *The tendency to suicide is inherited.* There is no clear evidence to demonstrate suicide is inherited. It does not run in families but is an individual matter that can be prevented.

7. *Suicide is the "curse of the poor" or the "disease of the rich."* Studies indicate that suicide occurs proportionately at all levels of the social class structure.

NATURAL DEATH

Death is the inevitable outcome of the life process. It follows naturally the sequence of development from birth, through maturation and aging. It comes to everyone as an individual and touches us many times in life upon the event of the death of others. It is a time of crisis because it represents an extreme and final form of separation. It is a crisis too because it is typically unpredictable; an exception, of course, are deaths resulting from execution. The elements of death as a crisis include altered relationships, interrupted plans and goals, and helplessness to change the inevitable. There is much evidence to suggest that the crisis of death is intensified and made more difficult by the nature of cultural, social, and personal attitudes toward it resulting in maladaptive rather than adaptive adjustments.

Fulton (1965) has compiled articles from the professional literature and written an analysis of the current status of research and understanding of death in our society. This work provides us with a perspective to view the elements of the crisis of death and we will draw generously from its contents.

Death and Society

Like other concepts death, attitudes toward it, and acceptable behavioral responses of survivors reflect the society and place in which one lives as well as the time during which one lives. Fulton and Geis (1962) report evidence that indicates in the modern, industrial character of American society people view death differently than was true at an earlier time. The accent today is upon youth, health, and material possessions (including the physical self) and in this framework death is seen as a personal insult depriving one of "life, liberty, and the pursuit of happiness." There is a shift away from traditional approaches to handling death which emphasized religious beliefs and values, and found explanations in divine purpose and moral judgment to a kind of new sophisticated view that death is the result of bad judgment, bad luck, or personal neglect. This change in explanatory causes takes the event of death out of the realm of the divine and places responsibility squarely upon the deceased or the survivors. This shift has important consequences, as we will see in terms of individual responses to the loss of loved ones.

A change is also evidenced by an increasing tendency to less ceremony, less religious overtones, and less delay in funeral customs. This too has its consequences for the adjustment of survivors. There also seems to be an increase in criticism, fault-finding, and assignment of blame to persons involved in the care and arrangements for the deceased such as medical personnel and undertakers (Fulton, 1963). In terms of these changes Fulton reports some interesting data that reflect regional differences within our society at the same period of time. These data indicate that people in the midwestern states of Illinois, Indiana, Michigan, Ohio, and Wisconsin have more traditional views and observe more traditional practices than do people in the Pacific coast states of Washington, Oregon, and California. These findings lend support to the idea that population centers on the frontier of the country in areas of concentration of industrial technological occupations are developing new concepts of death at variance with traditional views.

Attitudes toward Death

Attitudes about one's personal death seem to vary considerably in terms of age, conditions of physical and mental health, and degree of religious belief and involvement. Fulton (1965) summarizes many reports by indicating that how and where one dies is probably a greater source of fear and concern than is the fact of dying. In this respect then we must appreciate that what is a satisfactory form and place for death will depend upon many personal factors. In general, however, death at home among family and friends and with dignity would probably represent a majority opinion. We must question therefore the increasing tendency to uproot our aged population from their homes, family, and life friendships and locate them in relatively isolated communities for the aged. Another practice increasingly common is death in hospital settings (Fulton reports 53 percent of deaths in 1963 occurred in hospitals). The restricted visitation and "clinical" atmosphere of the hospital setting may bring an impersonal and formal element to death that violates the needs of the deceased as well as the survivors. Finally, in Fulton's terms, "a dignified death proclaims the significance of all men" (1965, p. 186), this should cause us to consider the practice of capital punishment in our society in reference to the effect it has upon our own attitudes and fears about death.

Reactions to Grief

The outstanding contribution to our understanding of behavioral responses to loss by death is by Erich Lindemann (1944). Lindemann has described the *syndrome* (or collected symptoms) of mourning and the accuracy of his account has been verified many times since his report appeared. These symptoms include the following: (*a*) Unpleasant physical sensations; difficulty with breathing, eating and digestion, low energy level, and a general sense of emptiness. (*b*) A preoccupation with the image of the deceased. (*c*) Feelings of guilt. *Guilt* is self-blame and may arise when a person feels he did do a forbidden thing, wishes he had done it even though he did not, or neglects to do something that might have altered the outcome of a situation. (*d*) A loss of warmth toward others; being irritable, angry, and finding fault or blaming. (*e*) Disrupted behavior patterns, either immediate or delayed.

Lindemann indicates that these symptoms of loss are alleviated by behavior he terms the *grief work*. The grief work includes emotional emancipation (or freedom) from dependence upon the deceased, readjustment to an environment in which the deceased is missing, and the formation of new and satisfying relationships.

Lindemann found that persons who showed the most severe behavioral maladjustments to their loss were persons who resisted the discomfort of the grief symptoms and did not, or could not, do the grief work. The grief work can be assisted by professional mental health help in instances where family, friends, or clergy are not able to aid the individual. The most difficult aspect of the grief work is the emotional emancipation from the deceased. As discussed in the crisis of independence, this must involve dealing with the faults as well as the virtues of the deceased. Family, friends, and others are valuable sources of comfort in terms of the loss, but custom dictates that only kind things be mentioned or remembered. No one is all good or bad and our interactions with them are not all pleasant or unpleasant. When a person dies before we can develop a mature emotional relationship to him, the grief work is difficult and professional help may be required to achieve an adaptive adjustment to the loss.

Another aspect of grief reaction noted by Lindmann and reported by others is the *anniversary reaction* (Hilgard and Newman, 1959). This reaction may take the form of developing symptoms similar to the illness that took the loved one on the anniversary of his death, or great anxiety about one's own death when one reaches the age when the loved one died. The fact that it is the anniversary of the death may not be recognized by the individual showing the symptoms of the reaction. The anniversary reaction seems to reflect an incomplete process of the grief work. It may also reflect a delayed reaction to the death which is aroused unconsciously by the event of the anniversary.

Delayed reactions to death may occur many years after the actual loss. In these instances the death of some other person may set off a very severe grief response quite out of proportion to the relationship that existed between the individual and the deceased. Lindemann found that circumstances of a recent death precipitated for some people all the mourning symptoms in relation to a more significant person who had died many years before, but for which mourning had been delayed. The grief experienced by the American people upon the death of President Kennedy may be understood in part by the fact that he variously represented to many the memory of a son, brother, or husband.

Finally, Lindemann calls to our attention *anticipatory grief reactions*. In these instances, great anxiety for the life of a loved one is generated by reason of their poor health or involvement in dangerous circumstances (servicemen stationed in combat zones). The concern for their life is overwhelming and in anticipation of their loss the individual experiences mourning symptoms and even begins the grief work. The difficulty arises, however, when the loved one recovers from the severe illness or returns unharmed from war. If the emotional emancipation has been achieved a new adjustment is required to reform the attachment and permit continued interaction. This may account for some of those occasions when the recovery of a person or his return to the family seems to cause more upset and disturbance than it does joy or pleasure.

The grief reactions we have been describing are normal in response to death. We should also note that they may occur in varying degrees in response to separations caused by factors other than death. People who have gone through the experience of a broken love affair may have had many of these grief symptoms before forming a new and satisfying attachment. In homes broken by divorce, the children and parents may experience mourning for the broken family circle. In such cases adaptive adjustment will be aided by recognizing the symptoms of loss and the need for some measure of grief work.

Mourning and Mental Health

Volkart and Michael (1957) have analyzed some of the elements involved in mourning as these relate to good mental health. They note how central is the family in our social and personal experience. The centrality of the family to our life results in intense emotional attachments and a belief that family members are unique and irreplaceable persons. As our society grows more complex this ultra importance of the family seems destined to increase because of the security such close relationships offer us in an otherwise impersonal world. At the same time, however, that we need and value family members our feelings about them are *ambivalent.* Family members, especially parents, are sources of love, security, and gratification but they are also sources of frustration, punishment, and loss.

These ambivalent feelings become intensified upon the death of a family member and must be dealt with in the grief work relating to emotional emancipation. The sudden loss of a parent may arouse great anger in the child who feels abandoned, deserted, or deprived of the love and gratification that the parent provided. This anger is a source of frustration in that the child is helpless to change the circumstances. It will also be a source of guilt for expression of anger about the deceased may be punished as disrespect. If our society continues to move toward a concept of death in which the event is seen as the fault of the deceased, then a feeling of anger about this "deliberate" leaving the family must find some socially acceptable means of expression.

Fear and resulting guilt may be aroused by death of a family member for yet another reason. Because the interaction of family members is close, there will be times when they frustrate or punish each other. On these occasions, one might wish a family member dead. These wishes are forbidden thoughts and upon the event of that person's death may be recalled. The guilt of having wished the death at any time and the fear that one caused it or may be blamed for it if anyone finds out can be intense. The release of these forbidden wishes and recognition that they are natural consequences of close relationships will diminish the fear and guilt they cause and aid the grief work.

Many people experience grief as a response to loss and a feeling that the world is empty and meaningless as a result. In this respect our traditional funeral practices have had some helpful aspects. The attendance of many at a funeral is recognition from others that a loss has occurred. Similarly, gifts of flowers, food, and other help to families in mourning are acts of love on the part of others at a time when it may seem that the only source of love has gone. The trend to short, unceremonious funeral customs may deprive many persons who are dependent upon close family ties an opportunity to experience expressions of love from concerned others.

However society moves in its concept of death and forms of handling death, it is apparent that there will be an effect upon surviving persons. The concept of death will shape attitudes about one's own death as well as deaths of others. The forms of handling death must provide a means to achieve the work of grief. The grief experienced will be proportional in some measure to the intensity of the relationship to the deceased. These human needs must be met, and if not provided with adaptive forms of adjustment, they may take maladaptive forms. During 1967 the national press reported the following incident:

> A young man in his twenties fell to his death from an airplane while presumably on a parachute jump activity. Observers who saw the tragedy reported that the young man cut his chute ropes and made no other move except to hold his hands in a "prayerful" posture during his fatal fall. He had a few weeks earlier lost his wife after less than 2 years of marriage when she died in a parachute accident due to a faulty chute. He had urged his wife to take up parachuting because it was his own hobby. He made his jump at the same approximate height and over the same area in which she died. He had made extensive arrangements for his own funeral immediately after the funeral of his wife.

In terms of our discussion, the elements of loss, guilt, and inadequate grief work are apparent in this account. We may also ask, with some foreknowledge of the answer, could this death have been prevented?

SUMMARY

Crisis is defined as a critical time or decisive moment which has the effect of disrupting adjustment. Our most common crises are times of frustration when we are blocked or thwarted in the satisfaction of our needs. Frustration may be caused by a barrier in our environment, a deficiency in our selves, or a conflict we have to resolve. Conflict may involve choosing between two desirable goals (having your cake or eating it), choosing between two undesirable alternatives (the lesser of two evils), or it may involve ambivalence (being attracted and repelled at the same time). Frustration produces stress which can lead to serious physical and emotional illnesses. We cannot always avoid stress but we can learn to handle frustration and conflict in ways that will enhance rather than damage our lives.

The experience of separation or being cut off from the established relationships we have learned to depend on for satisfaction of our needs is a source of intense anxiety. The beginning of school is a normal crisis point in the life of a child because it marks the first large step in his separation from the family. Separation anxiety is a common experience for children starting school, but understanding parents can prevent this crisis from becoming a disaster.

Emancipation is the process of achieving separation from parental control and developing emotional, intellectual, and economic independence. Psychological maturity depends upon emancipation from parents. The mature person finds new satisfaction in his relationship to parents on an adult basis rather than as a dependent or subservient person.

Broken homes and family disorganization resulting from separation or divorce are serious crises for all family members. Some families can face these crises without damage to the individuals while others never seem to recover and readjust. Many of the problems that disturb children from broken homes can be remedied if they are recognized and dealt with early enough.

Almost everyone at some time in life is faced with the stress of illness, disability, or tragedy involving self or some member of the family. The fact that some people are better able to adjust to illness and disability than other people is related to the way a person evaluates himself and his situation. Children who learn to accept and tolerate handicaps in other people find it easier to accept the limitations and disabilities they may have to face later in their own lives. Our characteristic reactions to tragedy and stress are learned patterns of behavior that become a part of our personality and are very difficult to change.

Suicide is the ultimate tragedy that costs this country 20,000 lives a year and creates untold suffering for thousands more. Inability to cope with the stress of life leads to suicide attempts for nearly a quarter million people annually. Where suicide prevention services are available it has been found that people in crisis situations make good use of them.

Death is the inevitable outcome of the life process and a crisis none can escape. Attitudes toward death are a reflection of the society and the times in which we live. Reactions to grief and mourning the loss of a loved one are important functions related to good mental health.

SUGGESTIONS FOR FURTHER READING

Bakan, David, *Disease, Pain and Sacrifice: Toward a Psychology of Suffering*, Chicago, Ill., University of Chicago Press, 1968. Disease and illness are analyzed from the viewpoint of biology, psychology, and philosophy in a thought provoking way.

Carlozzi, Carl G., *Death and Contemporary Man*, Grand Rapids, Mich., Eerdmans, 1968. Discussion of the crisis of terminal illness and its psychological effects.

Kliman, Gilbert W., *Psychological Emergencies of Childhood*, New York, Grune and Stratton, 1968. Studies of children who have suffered severe trauma are presented with some suggestions of how to help children cope with these crises.

Malikin, David and Rusalem, Herbert (Eds.), *The Vocational Rehabilitation of the Disabled*, New York, New York University Press, 1969. An overview of this rapidly growing field with contributions from several different professions.

Moriaty, David M. (Ed.), *The Loss of Loved Ones*, Springfield, Ill., Thomas, 1967. A non-technical presentation of contemporary research concerning the effects of death in the family on personality development.

Shneidman, Edwin S. (Ed.), *Essays in Self-Destruction*, New York, Science House, 1967. Deals with suicide and other forms of self-destructive behavior from the viewpoints of literature, philosophy, sociology, medicine, law, and psychology.

Emotional and Mental Illness

What happens when you are no longer able to cope with stress or cannot face another crisis? How common is mental and emotional illness? Can mental illness be inherited? How are mentally ill people different from normal people? What can be done to prevent mental illness? Where can you find help for people with emotional problems?

There was a time when mystery completely surrounded emotional and mental ills. People reacted both with shame and fear to persons so afflicted and believed there was no hope for improvement or change. Today, though many of the causes are still not completely known, great progress has been made both in early recognition of these conditions and in their treatment. The door of the mental hospital now swings in both directions—many enter sick and in need of care and many leave well and ready to resume their lives.

To term these conditions illnesses is probably more helpful to our thinking about them than calling them diseases. Disease seems to mean to many persons an actual physical process and also implies that it can be "caught by others". Illness more often seems to mean "not well" without the implications that it involves a specific physical process or that someone else might get the same if they come too near it. As we will see, some emotional and mental conditions are accompanied by a change in the physical processes, but just as many seem to have their causes outside the body in the complexities of social living and in relationships with other persons. No emotional or mental illness is "catching" in the sense that term is usually used.

Television has done a lot to make people familiar with the behavior and terminology of abnormal responses, but it has not provided a systematic way of thinking about these so that it is possible to make distinctions between them. We hear words like "guilt complex," "neurosis," "schizophrenic," "nervous breakdown," and tend to think of them all as being much alike. If we approach the subject with some system or frame of reference we can develop an appreciation for the differences in these illnesses and an increased awareness of their relation to normal functioning.

A FRAME OF REFERENCE

The system to be used here views emotional and mental illnesses as different from normal behavior in *degree* not in *kind*. This means that abnormal responses are like normal responses in that the same kinds of behavior are utilized—language, feelings, thoughts, and actions. However, the degree to which these behaviors are utilized differs from normal responses in intensity, duration, and distance from reality or shared meanings with others. Using normal, or what most persons do, as a midpoint on a line that extends continuously, emotionally and mentally ill persons would be represented at points further and further away but still on the same line. All of us have felt sad at some time; an emotionally ill person probably feels what is better described as gloom, and the mentally ill person probably feels what is better described as despair. All of these persons can *feel* but the intensity of the feeling, among other things, is different by degrees.

If we could devise an accurate measure of the exact extent of emotional and mental illness and health we would probably find that people would fall into a normal distribution just as they do on dimensions of any individual characteristic (refer to Chapter 6 for explanation of the concept of normal distribution). Try to visualize a distribution extending from severe mental illness to exceptionally good mental health. You would find the majority of people in the middle (average range) and fewer people toward the extremes. This theoretical distribution is illustrated in Figure 9-1.

Normal means what most people do or what is typical. Reality is shared meanings with other persons. We need another guideline, however, to answer the question of just how far along this line of behavioral reactions a feeling, idea, or act is no longer normal and becomes an expression of emotional or mental

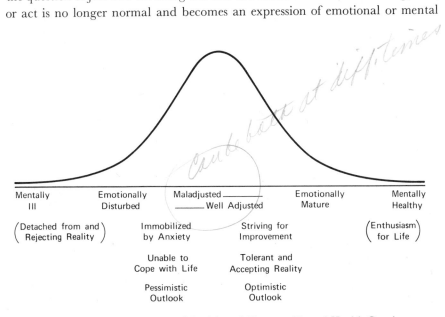

Mentally Ill	Emotionally Disturbed	Maladjusted _____ _____ Well Adjusted	Emotionally Mature	Mentally Healthy
(Detached from and Rejecting Reality)	Immobilized by Anxiety	Striving for Improvement		(Enthusiasm for Life)
	Unable to Cope with Life	Tolerant and Accepting Reality		
	Pessimistic Outlook	Optimistic Outlook		

Figure 9-1. Conceptual Model of the Mental Illness to Mental Health Continuum.

illness. There are several guides we could use: when a person says he is not normal; when other people say he is not normal; when he says he doesn't want to be normal. All of these have been used at some time, but many more problems than answers are raised by using them. A more efficient guide and the one proposed here is that of *social functioning*: when a person can no longer perform the usual and expected tasks of social living, even when he wants to, he is to some degree emotionally or mentally ill.

The usual and expected tasks of social living include self-care, ability to make decisions, fulfilling responsibilities, and communicating effectively with others. An important emphasis in this guideline is in the words "can no longer perform" which imply he could at one time and hence would exclude mentally retarded individuals who might never be mature enough intellectually to perform any of the tasks of social living. A second, but equally important, emphasis in this guideline is in the words, "even if he wanted to." Emotional and mental illnesses are not matters of will; wanting to be well from them is not enough to ensure it. Another group that must be excluded from this guideline, of course, is people with handicaps of body so severe that they cannot perform, for themselves, the tasks of social living. Emotionally and mentally ill persons then differ from normal persons in degree of behavior, not kind, and they can no longer perform, even if they wanted to, the usual and expected tasks of social living.

What Is Normal?

What is normal is an abstract concept, very general rather than specific, and subject to varying interpretations and definitions. Normality is also a very relative concept depending upon place, time, and person.

The *places* which alter the concept of normality include the culture, society, region, community, and, in large cities, even the neighborhood. We live in the western culture sharing with other countries of North America and Europe similarities of language, technology, custom, ideals, goals, and methods to achieve goals that alter our behavior in certain characteristic ways. The American society is somewhat unique in the western culture partly because it is newer in historical terms, and partly because of the variety of persons (and their reasons) who settled this country and continue to be attracted to it.

Within our society we can identify some regional differences of behavior from east to west and north to south which seem to reflect patterns of settlement and reasons for settlement. Some communities and neighborhoods within the community may have characteristic behavior patterns. We are familiar with the expected differences of behavior implied in the terms "uptown" and "slum." A college campus as a small part of a community permits and expects somewhat different behavior patterns than would be true anywhere else in the community. What is normal then depends in part upon where you are.

Normality differs in *time*. In the second half of the twentieth century the behaviors of persons all over the world that are included in the range of normal are greater in number and variety than was true in any previous historical time. The higher level of technology, increased levels of education, and improved means of communication characteristic of this century have altered conceptions of what is normal.

One of the most common distinctions about normality made in terms of time involves the developmental periods of childhood, adolescence, and adulthood. Peoples in most places consider many behaviors of early life normal, but the same behaviors later in life abnormal. Childhood is a time of immaturity and immature behavior is expected, such as lack of self-control, poor judgment, and difficulty in meeting responsibilities. This same behavior in adults is usually considered abnormal.

Normality also differs by *person*. The individual is subject to variations within himself, at different times, and in different places. In these terms, we can all be said to be emotionally upset and to display different behaviors at different times in our lives. Some event, or crisis, may trigger our emotions and we laugh, cry, or become angry out of proportion to the situation. Our memory at times may not serve us well, being inaccurate or even "blank." We may find decisions hard to make or communication and effective relationships with other persons hard to maintain.

Sadness, worry, fear, and uncertainty are experiences common to everyone at some time. These are all examples of a change in degree of normal responding. These changes, however, are usually of short duration and *situational*, i.e., in response to changing circumstances. Some situations of life are very stressful and a normal response would be fear, worry, or uncertainty. Consider, for example, situations involving catastrophes of nature (earthquake, flood), political change (war), or economic reversals (depression). People will differ in terms of the stresses they experience depending upon their life circumstances. They will differ too in the way they respond to these stresses. The times of crisis described in Chapter 8 are common forms of situational stress. Normality for the individual must be considered in terms of what he experiences and his behavioral capacities for responding to these experiences.

What is normal, then, is relative to time, place, and person. Behavioral change must be expected as the circumstances of life undergo change. The important point to remember is that people change (for better or worse) as they continue in constant interaction with the environment. We do not stay at the same point on the illness-to-health continuum very long before something happens that enables us to move toward better mental health or it fails to help and we become more disturbed.

Prevalence of Disorders

How common are emotional and mental illnesses? Statistics show that over half the hospital beds in our nation are occupied by mental patients, and that 1 in every 10 Americans is hospitalized for mental illness at some time during his lifetime. In 1960, a report to the Congress from the *Joint Commission on Mental Illness and Health* estimated that 17.5 million persons in this country were in need of treatment for problems of mental health. It was further estimated that 1.8 million persons actually were in treatment: 1 million of these in hospitals, 380,000 in clinics, and 420,000 seeing psychologists or psychiatrists in their private offices. Industry counts in the hundreds of thousands the lost man-hours of employees with these conditions. The public pays over a billion dollars a year to provide hospitals for the treatment of mental illness. More important, but unknown in actual amounts, is the personal suffering and lost potentials of people who are emotionally or mentally disturbed.

When the Joint Commission made its report to Congress in 1960 the picture was not a bright one. At that time most of the mentally ill were treated in large impersonal institutions isolated from community life. There were 279 state mental hospitals in the United States and three-fourths of them were opened prior to the First World War (1917). A startling finding was that 45 percent of the patients in these institutions had been there 10 years or more. In 1963, President Kennedy proposed a "bold new approach" to mental illness, stressing the need for prevention and increased use of community facilities rather than state care in institutions. When Congress passed the "Community Mental Health Centers Act," in 1964, the prevalence of mental and emotional illness was so great that it was estimated that a clinic was needed for every 50,000 population. Since then the growth of community mental health centers has ushered in a new era in the treatment and prevention of mental illness. The National Institute of Mental Health (1967) has announced that 500 centers will be operational in 1970 and 2000 will be opened by 1975.

With greater emphasis on prevention we should soon see a marked reduction in the prevalence of emotional and mental illness.

Hereditary Contributions

One in every four adults is involved, either directly or indirectly through some member of his family, with emotional and mental illness. One question that always arises in the minds of relatives is, "What are the chances of having this happen to me?"

The fear that these conditions might be inherited is not uncommon in the general public. None of the conditions described in this chapter could ever be inherited directly because they reflect the time and circumstances of an individual's life. What may be inherited is a *predisposition* or tendency to react in certain ways or to be subject to certain stresses. The inheritance of certain genes from the parents may cause some persons to have characteristics of the nervous system that make them unusually sensitive or responsive to any form of stress in the life situation. Or, the inheritance of certain genes may affect the biochemical characteristics of an individual, making him vulnerable to drugs or alcohol or altering his nervous system processes to some degree of instability.

Kallman (1959) has reported on studies of persons related in various ways and their tendency to develop similar behavioral disorders. Kallman's data are based on hospitalized persons and give the percentage tendency of other family members to have a similar disorder. It is apparent from Kallman's data that with increasing degrees of close relationship there is an increase in the tendency to have similar behavioral conditions. The figures reported by Kallman are higher for relatives of any kind than for unrelated persons in the general population.

Among persons with schizophrenia, a severe mental disorder, Kallman's figures for the same condition in close relatives are as follows: identical twins raised together 91.1 percent, identical twins separated 5 or more years 77.6 percent, fraternal twins 14.7 percent, brothers and sisters 14.2 percent, half brothers and sisters 7.1 percent, husbands and wives 1.8 percent, and persons in the general population less than 1 percent. Obviously, identical twins who have an identical heredity develop similar behavioral disorders to a much greater degree than do persons related in other ways. This remains true even when the identical twins are reared apart although with different environments for the individuals the figures are somewhat lower.

Kallman's findings do not, however, exclude a primarily environmental causation of these illnesses. Persons closely related by blood tend to be raised in similar environments. Identical twins are more likely to be treated alike than fraternal twins and twins of either kind share a common experience relative to time or age. The difference reported between identical twins reared together and separated gives some suggestion of the influence of differing environments. If only hereditary factors were involved the findings for all identical twins should be alike.

What Kallman's study, and others like it, may be demonstrating is that heredity determines the general nature of the responsiveness of the individual and his tolerance for stress. Whenever the environmental circumstances exceed the stress tolerance, personality breakdown results. Since the biological response capacities of identical twins should be identical, such individuals should have a greater similarity in stress tolerance. Genetic studies are provocative, but as yet not conclusive evidence, for interpretations of causality in behavioral disorders.

Having defined a frame of reference which views mental illness on a continuum from extreme illness to extreme health, let us take a closer look at some of the departures of differeing degrees of behavioral functioning called emotional and mental disorders. The American Psychiatric Association (1968) has adopted a uniform classification of mental disorders developed by the World Health Organization and this classification will be followed here. Table 9-1 outlines the classification giving examples of each disorder.

EMOTIONAL DISTURBANCE

Psychological conditions or states of maladjustment are certainly normal at times for all people. The life tasks discussed in Chapter 7 require a great deal of stress tolerance and striving for readjustment on the part of everyone. Without some anxiety or dissatisfaction there would be no push for change, growth, and improvement. A mentally healthy, well adjusted person is not immune to worries and problems, but he can handle the usual daily tensions and crises of living which may involve moments of fear, anger, anxiety, distrust, and depression. A person is emotionally disturbed when he is frequently and intensely worried, and tends to exaggerate these same thoughts and feelings of fear, anger, anxiety, distrust, and depression. There is no sharp line of distinction between normality and disturbance but one shades into the other very gradually.

Transient Situational Disturbances

Emotional disturbances in varying degree of severity may occur in individuals without any apparent underlying mental disorders when the individual has an acute reaction to overwhelming environmental stress. If the person has good capacity to adapt, his symptoms will usually recede as the stress diminishes or he gets help in coping with the stress. If the symptoms persist after the stress is removed or if the person cannot find additional resources to help him adjust to the stress he may become more seriously disturbed. Disturbances of this kind are called adjustment reactions and are classified according to developmental stage. Some examples follow.

Adjustment reaction of infancy: A baby's grief reaction associated with separation from its mother, manifested by crying spells, loss of appetite, and severe social withdrawal.

Adjustment reaction of childhood: Bed-wetting and attention-getting behavior associated with the birth of a new baby in the family.

Adjustment reaction of adolescence: Moodiness, temper outbursts, irritability, and depression associated with school failure.

Adjustment reaction of adult life: Resentment, fear, and depression associated with an unwanted pregnancy shown in hostile behavior and suicidal gestures.

Adjustment reaction of later life: Feelings of rejection associated with forced retirement and manifested by social withdrawal.

These reactions are usually temporary and are associated with some real event or set of circumstances. When the symptoms persist and the feelings become internalized and resistant to change these normal reactions can develop into behavior disorders.

Psychosomatic Illnesses

Those illnesses or symptoms of physical disorders that are caused by emotional factors are called psychosomatic or psychophysiological. We refer to those bodily functions that are under control of the autonomic nervous system (Chapter 2). The physiological changes that are involved are those that normally accompany certain emotional states (Chapter 5), but in these disorders the changes are more intense and sustained. Often the individual is not consciously aware of his emotional state. You will recall that the temporary physical changes related to acute emotional states such as fear and anger are changes in muscle tension, glandular secretion, blood circulation,

Nov. 2, 1970 Be able to have working knowledge of these disorders

Table 9-1. Classification of Mental Disorders[a]

General classification	Distinguishing features	Functional impairment	Typical examples
Conditions without manifest psychiatric disorder	Normal individuals with severe enough problems to need help	Social maladjustment which could develop into a mental disorder	Marital maladjustment; occupational stress; delinquent behavior
Transient situational disturbances	Acute reaction to overwhelming environmental stress	Temporary disturbance of normal functioning associated with some crisis in life	Grief reaction to separation; depressive reaction to failure; suicidal reaction to unwanted pregnancy; fear reaction to military combat; withdrawal reaction to retirement
Psychophysiologic disorders and special symptoms	Physical symptoms caused by emotional factors, involving an organ system and the autonomic system	Physical discomfort without awareness of emotional state	Muscle cramps; tension headaches; bronchial asthma; peptic ulcer; hypertension; bedwetting; tics; stuttering
Personality disorders and certain other non-psychotic mental disorders	Lifelong patterns of maladaptive behavior	Interpersonal relationships are difficult to establish, social maladjustment severe and disabling	Antisocial personality; inadequate personality; sexual deviations; alcoholism; drug dependence

[a]Adapted from American Psychiatric Association (1968).

Table 9-1. *Continued*

General classification	Distinguishing features	Functional impairment	Typical examples
Neuroses	Anxiety pronounced; awareness of one's handicapping symptoms	Excessive dependence on defense mechanisms. Inability to deal with anxiety effectively may be severely disabling	Anxiety neurosis; phobic neurosis; obsessive-compulsive; depressive neurosis; hypochondriacal neurosis
Psychoses Functional	Distortion of reality; hallucinations or delusions; profound alterations of mood, inappropriate responses	Severe impairment of mental functioning, cannot meet ordinary demands of life.	Schizophrenia; manic depressive psychosis; involutional melancholia; paranoid states; psychotic reactions
Psychoses Organic	Deterioration of central nervous system functions plus above	Severe impairment of mental and physical functions, cannot care for self	Senile dementia; alcoholic psychoses; syphilis of the nervous system; psychosis with drug or poison intoxication
Organic brain syndrome (without psychosis)	Mental condition resulting from impairment of brain tissue	Impairment of memory, orientation, intellectual functions, and judgement	Epilepsy; brain tumor

respiration, and blood sugar. The autonomic nervous system begins immediately to restore homeostasis. Prolonged emotional tension with overstimulation of the autonomic nervous system and alterations in blood supply can produce tissue changes and may result in structural damage and organic disease. Examples include peptic ulcer, colitis, hypertension, bronchial asthma, impotence, rheumatoid arthritis, and atopic eczema.

Many of the physical illnesses we have are caused in part by emotional distress and others are seriously aggravated by it. It is well-known that over half the patients who visit doctors with physical complaints have emotional problems that are partly or wholly responsible. Interestingly enough, most people get angry if the doctor suggests that the problem may be psychological. They think he means they are making it up or faking illness for some conscious reason, but what he means is that emotional or nervous tension is producing the pain. The pain suffered from a psychosomatic illness is just as great as the pain and discomfort caused by a purely physical injury since the two can never be completely separated. Even such problems as hay fever, laryngitis, and common colds respond well to psychotherapy.

Personality Disorders

When maladaptive patterns of behavior become so deeply ingrained that they interfere with a person's ability to maintain satisfactory interpersonal relationships, the individual is considered to have a personality disorder. The personality disorder becomes a characteristic way of life that offers a means of coping with stress which may not be very healthy but can be very difficult to change. Unlike the situational reactions, the personality disorders develop slowly as lifelong patterns of maladaptive behavior. Excessive dependence on limited defense mechanisms with loss of flexibility impairs personality growth. Such people cope with stress-producing situations by relying on old habit patterns rather than developing new capabilities.

Antisocial personality is a disorder in which the individual is repeatedly in conflict with society. He has failed in the life task of character development which was discussed in Chapter 7. The distinguishing features of the antisocial personality are the complete lack of conscience, inability to experience remorse, inability to delay immediate satisfaction of needs, no long-range plans or goals, no affectional ties, no respect for authority, and impulsive, irresponsible behavior. Such a person is not mentally retarded; he has average or superior intelligence, and he knows the difference between right and wrong behavior in terms of what is legal or socially acceptable. However, his knowledge of moral and ethical values has no influence on his own actions. He is self-centered in his dealings with other people and is often able to assume many different attitudes in order to deceive and take advantage of anyone, including his own family.

Danny was a curly-haired, dimple-faced cherub of 13 when he was committed to a mental hospital, under the law which provides for observation and treatment of psychopathic delinquents. His history was typical of the child with a serious defect of character who has failed to learn by experience and has persisted in behavior which constitutes a threat to society.

Danny's most recent offense, when hospitalized, was breaking into an automobile dealer's showroom and driving a new car through the plate glass window, speeding through town and finally crashing into a police car. He showed no remorse for his acts and seemed to enjoy the attention he had attracted. Danny had been on probation most of his life and had been in juvenile detention facilities on numerous occasions. Records from the school and court were full of reports of truancy, malicious mischief, defiance of authority, and property damage. He was proud of his escapades and made no attempt to deny or make excuses for his antisocial behavior. On one occasion he led an armed robbery attempt on a grocery store, using his father's gun, and accidentally shot one of the two boys who were with him. Another time he set fire to a church, causing serious damage. Each time he was involved in a major offense his parents attempted to protect him by paying for the damages and promising to give him more strict supervision. It became increasingly clear that his parents were unable to control him since he did not respond to either punishment or rewards.

In the hospital, Danny was a model patient and won the sympathy of nearly everyone with whom he came in contact. Within a few days he had convinced the librarian that he was a misunderstood intellectual and only needed some encouragement to become an outstanding scholar. In all her 30 years at the hospital, the little white-haired lady had never seen such an enthusiastic reader. She went out of her way to help Danny find books, and she even arranged to tutor the boy on her own time after working hours. On the third day of the tutoring sessions Danny's tolerance for hospital life came to an abrupt end. On that day he greeted the friendly librarian with a blow on the head, leaving her unconscious, took the money and keys from her purse, and left the hospital in her car. He was picked up several hours later by the police.

Danny rendered all efforts at treatment futile. His behavior required a degree of control and supervision that could not be furnished in the treatment setting of the hospital. He represented a threat to patients whose emotional or mental illnesses made them easy victims of his antisocial personality. After three months of observation in the hospital Danny was transferred to a correctional institution that had a program of behavior modification based on conditioned learning techniques.

Inadequate personality is a behavior pattern characterized by ineffectual responses to emotional, social, intellectual, and physical demands. Such a person is neither physically nor mentally deficient, but he shows poor judgment, social instability, and lack of physical and emotional stamina.

Schizoid personality is characterized by shyness, oversensitivity, seclusiveness, daydreaming, and inability to express hostility and ordinary aggressive feelings. Such a person avoids close or competitive relationships and reacts to stress or conflict by withdrawal and apparent detachment. He is recognized as a "loner" or "eccentric" because he often defends himself against anxiety by retreat into books, philosophy, religion, or unusual interests.

Personality disorders take many forms, often resembling neurosis or psychosis, but are less severe and disabling because the person is able to function fairly well in areas other than interpersonal relationships. Sexual deviations, alcoholism, and drug dependence are symptoms of emotional disturbance and are regarded as personality disorders because they interfere with personal and social functioning. Personality disorders may lead to more serious emotional and mental disorders.

THE NEUROSES

Anxiety is the chief characteristic of the neuroses. It may be felt and expressed directly, or it may be controlled unconsciously and ineffectively by the defense mechanisms. Whenever the defenses against anxiety break down or produce symptoms of inability to cope with stress and conflict the person experiences distress and seeks relief of the symptoms. The distress is aggravated by the person's awareness of his own disturbed functioning.

Neurotic behavior differs from normal behavior not in kind, but in degree of discomfort that is experienced by the individual and the extent to which his personal and social functioning is restricted. Neuroses are severe enough to require professional help and they can usually be treated successfully if help is given early enough.

We will look at some representative neuroses to get a general idea of these conditions, but it should be observed that they often overlap and the distinctions by name are really most valuable to focus thinking about the behavior involved. A given person might have one of these conditions or might show the symptoms of several. There are some psychologists who believe that all the neuroses are just variations of the first one to be described, anxiety, and that anxiety is the emotional illness of our times reflecting the complexities, uncertainties, and stresses of our modern life.

Anxiety Neurosis

Anxiety is a nonspecific, generalized sense of fear, doom, or impending disaster. The anxious person may perspire profusely, have sudden chills, a rapid heart beat and pulse, or feel the need to get more air and hence breathe more deeply and rapidly. The person may shrug involuntarily as if trying to shake something off. These physical responses are coupled with a mental attitude of danger or foreboding, yet the reason is not clear—he feels the danger but he does not know what the danger is.

This condition should be distinguished from the way the words "anxiety" and "anxious" are often used in popular speech. A student who says, "I am anxious about an examination," more correctly is fearful. He knows what it is that is threatening, it is the examination and possible failure and all that it may imply. Neurotic anxiety is not fear because in fear the source of the danger is known. In anxiety the exact nature of the danger and its consequences are not known and as a result are more frightening. Similarly, someone might say to a person leaving on an auto trip, "I am anxious for you, so drive carefully." What they really mean is they are concerned because of the danger of traffic conditions and probably justifiably so.

Anxiety states can be very incapacitating, interfering with normal processes of thought like memory, problem-solving, concentration, and decision-making. Socially, anxiety can limit functioning by lowering morale, sapping enthusiasm, and creating a tendency to withdraw from others. The physical symptoms described above can be unpleasant, embarrassing, and alarming in themselves. Because the exact nature of the danger is unknown to the individual, expert professional help should be obtained. Anxiety may begin in a rather limited way—perhaps when on the job, or just when at home on weekends—but it tends to become more general as it persists and soon begins to invade all of the individual's waking hours. In this neurosis, as in the others to be described, early help-seeking is important to limiting the extent of the problem.

Anna was a 38-year-old housewife who was referred to a therapist because of nervousness for which her family doctor could find no physical basis. She complained of heart palpitations, difficult breathing, jittery feelings, jumpiness, and lack of sleep. She paced the floor wringing her hands and was unable to relax at any time. Her appetite was poor and she frequently suffered indigestion. She cried easily and often and felt guilty because she could not exercise better control of herself. She felt certain that something dreadful was about to happen but she did not know what it would be. She hated to answer the phone for fear of hearing bad news and she was reluctant to leave her house. Her husband said she had always been somewhat anxious and tense but had rapidly become worse. Each time the family faced some crisis her symptoms became more pronounced and she became more incapacitated and unable to cope with the stresses of everyday living. When her son was drafted into the Army she suffered a complete breakdown and had to be hospitalized for a brief period. Her physician referred her for psychological help. Her symptoms gradually improved with treatment directed to the underlying causes of her anxiety. She recovered from her anxiety and has been employed for several years as a receptionist in a busy office.

Obsessive–Compulsive Neuroses

We think of obsession as a characteristic of thought processes and compulsion as a characteristic of actions. Some neurotics are only obsessed, some show compulsion, and often the two symptoms tend to go together. An *obsession* is a fixed pattern of thought. It is preoccupation for long periods of time and in great intensity as contrasted to the occasional preoccupations of normal persons when working, for example, on a knotty problem. Obsessions also tend to be morbid, rather than pleasant kinds of thoughts. However, it is on the basis of the duration, intensity, and narrowness of the thought content that we should make the distinction of an abnormal process.

Physical symptoms of sleep loss, appetite loss, and consequent weight and energy loss may develop as the continued involvement in an obsession distracts the individual from the usual self-care activities. Social functioning becomes impaired as the obsession grows stronger and more demanding of the individual's attention. Work tasks may be neglected or poorly performed because of the individual's inability to concentrate. Social contacts may be missed or avoided because they compete for attention and energy with the obsession. Decision-making may be faulty or withheld because not enough thought energy is free for problematic thinking or analysis.

> Peggy was a 29-year-old secretary who was obsessed with death. She first became interested in death about age 7 years when her younger brother died. She said that she crawled into the casket with him and had to be removed forcibly. Her father died when she was 15, leaving her very emotionally disturbed. There were no other deaths in her family, but after her father died she began attending funerals frequently. She always read the obituary notices in the newspapers, and she spent a great deal of time visiting cemeteries and reading the inscriptions on tombstones. She took a night class in college and wrote a term paper on funeral customs. She bought all the books she could find on death, embalming, and mortuaries. She was so obsessed with death that she avoided social contacts and did not make any close friends. Her work began to show neglect, and her co-workers became concerned because of her lack of interest in anything but death, funerals, and cemeteries. Finally, her employer convinced her to seek professional help.

Compulsions are actions that are repeated over and over and are generally associated with some degree of thought obsession. A commonly cited compulsion is the need to wash the hands or other parts of the body repeatedly because of an obsession with germs or other forms of contamination. Another compulsion might involve constant checking and rechecking of details in work or study assignments because of thoughts of error, uncertainty, or inferior performance. Compulsions may, like obsessions, lead to physical symptoms of sleep loss, weight loss, and neglected personal care. If the compulsion involves washing, or other aspects of physical care, physical symptoms may be caused, such as extreme rawness of the flesh from use of harsh cleansers. Social functioning again may be severely impaired as the time and energy needed for the compulsion consumes more and more of the individual's life.

Wanda was an immaculate housekeeper, but after two years of marriage her husband complained that he could not stand to live with her any longer. She spent the entire day and evening cleaning and arranging the house. When her husband used an ash tray she would immediately wash it and replace it in the exact spot where it had been. When he sat in a chair she would anxiously wait for him to get up so that she could rearrange it and vacuum around it. She had a definite routine for cleaning the house and if anything disturbed the routine she would have to start over again from the beginning. She did not like to have company come because she was never ready for them and could not put the cleaning equipment away. She would often run the vacuum cleaner when guests were in the room, or get up and dust the tables in the midst of a conversation. She was never able to go anywhere on time because of her compulsive need to dust everything in the house before she left. Wanda did not have any insight into her condition and was quite hurt that her husband thought something was wrong. She could see no need for treatment and refused to join her husband in marriage counseling.

Phobic Neurosis

A *phobia* is an intense, exaggerated fear out of proportion to the actual danger. The object is known, although the reason why that object is so intensely feared may not be known. The phobic person can say it is crowds, certain animals, heights, water, or other things that he reacts to so intensely, but usually why or how the phobia got started is not known to him. The phobic person is usually able to function if he feels safely away from the feared object, but sometimes, depending on the object, this staying a safe distance can be very incapacitating. Cases have been recorded of people who lost jobs because of continuous tardiness due to their having gone miles out of their way to avoid the object of their phobia. Phobias tend to generalize so that what begins as fear of one object becomes fear of that class of objects, for example, fear of dogs may become fear of all animals. The potential for limiting social functioning is extensive in phobias. Sometimes phobias can be traced back to some intense, fear-producing incident in childhood that has been repressed or forgotten. When the phobic patient is able to recall the original fear-producing incident the fear is lessened and the phobia is relieved. Such was the case with Jack, a college student, who suffered from a morbid fear of being in closed spaces. The term for this is *claustrophobia.*

Jack was able to attend college but he was unable to remain in a classroom unless he could sit near the door, and even then he was uncomfortable when the door was closed. He could not sleep in a room with the door closed and he complained of dreams in which he was tied up and unable to move. He could not stand to be in a crowded room or theater and he would not ride a bus, train, or airplane. He was afraid to ride in the back seat of a car, and he went to any lengths to avoid riding in an elevator. It was difficult for Jack to buy clothing because as soon as he walked into a store he felt he had to get outdoors. He could not study in the library or eat in the cafeteria because the feeling of being closed in caused him to panic. Jack had experienced this fear of closed places since childhood, but he had no idea when it began or how it had started. After extensive psychotherapy he was finally able to recall an incident that happened when he was 4 years old. Jack had followed his older brother and some other boys when they broke into a vacant house. When the boys saw Jack they were angry at him for following them. The older boys locked Jack in the attic of the house where there were no windows or doors and left him there for several hours. They finally returned and released him but they threatened to lock him up and leave him there forever if he told anyone about what had happened. He was so frightened that he put the episode out of his mind, but he became more and more fearful of being contained in closed places as he grew older. After he remembered the incident and talked about it several times he was able to relieve his fears and in a short time he overcame his phobia.

Hysterical Neurosis, Conversion-Type

This form of neurosis is characterized by physical symptoms as well as impaired social functioning. In this condition the person unconsciously converts or transforms anxiety into a physical ailment. Paralysis is a common feature. One who must give his first speech in front of the class may know a trembling of the legs and difficulty in walking to the front of the room. The neurotic with a conversion reaction is a matter of degrees different—he just cannot walk to face the threatening task. Cases have been recorded of soldiers on the battlefield experiencing such stress of danger and threat to their lives that they could not move their arm to lift their gun or hold it to sight on target. One who has ambitions for a great career in singing may appear for audition and find he has no voice. These physical symptoms tend to persist long after the immediate threat is passed and for this reason are considered neurotic. Actual physical loss can become a secondary problem for limbs that are not exercised may show atrophy of muscles, a stomach that is favored by limited diet because of neurotic vomiting may become aggravated and ulcerous. In time, conversion reactions may create realistic physical illness or impairment and their psychological origins may go undetected.

These representative types of the neuroses serve to illustrate for us several characteristics of emotional disturbances as contrasted to normal behavior. First, they last longer than ordinary concern, preoccupation, or fear. Second, they generalize or spread to include other objects or events and consume more and more of the individual's life. Third, although not initiated by a physical condition in the body the personal neglect which they cause often is harmful to the body and these accompanying body reactions may become major health problems, too. Finally, they get worse as time goes by and the likelihood of improvement without expert professional care becomes increasingly doubtful.

We do not know exactly how many persons in the population at any given moment have neuroses. It should be apparent, however, that a neurotic person might be able to maintain himself with his neurosis for a long time before others would become aware of it or before it became intolerably uncomfortable. In a sheltered life situation, where the stresses could be kept at a minimum, a neurotic could get along. But getting along would come at the price of full participation in life.

THE PSYCHOSES

The psychoses are the most severe degrees of departure from normal functioning. People are considered psychotic when their mental functioning becomes sufficiently impaired to interfere grossly with their capacity to meet the ordinary demands of life. The major difference between psychosis and neurosis is the loss of contact with reality. The psychoses are characterized by disturbances of thinking, mood, and behavior. While the neurotic is aware of his symptoms and disturbed by his mental condition, the psychotic is so severely disturbed that his capacity for mental grasp of his situation is lost.

Thought disturbances associated with psychoses are profound. Relationships easily understood by normally functioning persons are misinterpreted by psychotics or perhaps not comprehended at all. Typical of these confused relationships are difficulties in understanding concepts of "right" and "wrong" or the moral principles usually shared by people in the same society. The psychotic suffers frequently from disorientation in time, place, or person. This means the psychotic may not be able to say with accuracy the time or day, the location, or even who he is, because the ordinary guidelines of thought available to normal persons to orient themselves in these respects are disturbed in their functioning. The psychotic may appear feeble-minded when it comes to simple mental tasks, not because his faculties are lost, but because they are impaired by the illness process. False beliefs or *delusions* about who he is or where he is or what is happening may be part of the psychotic's thought impairment. False sensory experiences or *hallucinations*, such as seeing things that are not there, hearing voices not there, or smelling poisonous gases that do not exist, may also be a part of the psychotic process. Hallucinations occur when the mind generates sensory experiences out of itself rather than receiving sensory impulses from an environmental stimulus. Another way to view these thought disturbances is to say that reality contact is lost; many of those meanings which we share with others that enable us to understand ideas of time, morality, or physical events are no longer functioning for the psychotic.

Expressions of emotion by the psychotic often demonstrate a difference in intensity from normal emotional functioning. Psychotic emotions can be very flat, as if not feeling at all, or they can be very extreme. Anger may be expressed as rage, pleasure by loud shouting and wild gestures, sorrow by moans and strange postures. It was these atypical expressions of emotions that led people in earlier times to call the mentally ill "lunatic, crazy, or insane" (without a sense of proportion). Such terms, while describing perhaps the emotional reactions, are unfortunate because they focus upon the unusual features of the disturbance and overlook the fact that while extreme, these are still human emotions. A mentally ill person has not *lost* his mind and he is not *out* of his mind, but he is disturbed in the mind that he has.

Social functioning is severely impaired by the pyschoses. Self-care may be so neglected that supervision in a hospital setting may be necessary to protect the patient's life. Decision-making is impaired and judgment may be so faulty that the patient may be destructive of his person or property. The psychotic individual finds it difficult or impossible to fulfill responsibilities because his disturbed mental functioning and loss of reality contact make the concept of responsibility hard to understand. Communications with others become impaired for the psychotic because he is working with faulty interpretations of situations and a loss of shared meanings which are basic to communication.

The *functional* psychoses are not caused by known physical agents and do not show known physical changes in the brain or nervous system. It is generally believed, at this time, that the functional psychoses, like the neuroses, have their origins in the circumstances and relationships of social living. Some physical changes in the blood, urine, cells of body tissue, and antibody concentration of psychotic persons have been reported, but as yet no definite, cause-and-effect relationships have been demonstrated. Some of these reported physical changes in the body may be the result of the general altered body condition in emotional and mental illnesses as the physiological system attempts to resist greater and greater psychological stress.

Functional psychoses include many types of disorders having in common those characteristic disturbances of thinking, mood, and behavior described above. Schizophrenia, in which the mental status is attributable primarily to a thought disorder, is distinguished from the major affective illnesses which are dominated by a mood disorder. The paranoid states are different because of their limited distortion of reality and absence of other psychotic symptoms.

Schizophrenia

The broad category of functional disorders called schizophrenia includes many types and a variety of symptom features. Schizophrenia is especially marked, however, by disorganization of the sense of self. The term "split personality" is descriptive of schizophrenia in the sense that personality is chaotic and lacking integration, but not in the sense that two or more personalities are functioning in one individual. The schizophrenic's disorganized sense of self is accompanied by severe reality distortions and these serve to further impair efforts to reorganize the self.

Schizophrenic symptoms include confusion, perplexity, emotional turmoil without ability to express appropriate emotional responses, ideas of reference (feeling that a sign on the wall or picture in a magazine has a meaning that refers only to the patient), delusions, hallucinations, and bizarre (very unusual) thoughts. The distinctive feature of the illness is a separation within the individual of his thoughts and his feelings. The two simply do not go together; morbid thought content may be accompanied by emotions that would normally indicate pleasure, and rational thoughts may arouse agitated and inappropriate emotional responses. Sometimes both processes are erratic, but not in the same way, giving an impression of complete behavioral disorganization.

For some schizophrenics there is a gradual withdrawal from reality that reflects a lifetime of perpetual daydreams. Their problems seem too great to face; as children they were seclusive, oversensitive, and introspective. They avoided friends, kept to themselves, and gradually lost interest in external affairs. Their lives show lack of ambition and interest in sustained work. Their indifference toward reality extends to bodily needs and they neglect personal appearance, forget to eat or sleep, and become preoccupied with their own daydreams.

A schizophrenic might believe he is a plant, an animal, or an inanimate object and his behavior would reflect his belief in strange postures, actions, or expressed thought. Verbal communication may be difficult with a schizophrenic and progress in treatment is often delayed until it can be determined just what idea of self the patient has that is guiding his functioning. Hospitalization is often necessary to remove the schizophrenic from the responsibilities of social living that he cannot fulfill and to provide the opportunity for observation and study of his condition.

Bill was 23 years old when he was admitted to the hospital for observation because of his peculiar behavior and inability to get along with people. His mother described him as a shy, withdrawn boy who never made friends and spent most of his time reading. He completed high school with good grades and went to college for one year, but decided to study at home rather than return to school the following year. He lived with his mother and held several jobs for very short periods of time until two months before he came to the hospital. In those two months Bill had spent the daytime hours in his room with the door locked, coming out only at night. He became sullen, irritable, and talked very little. He refused to talk to his mother and would not eat with her. He ate only bread and peanut butter which he kept in his room. At the request of his mother, his aunt and uncle tried to talk him into seeking some professional help but at that time he became very excited—shouting, throwing things, and threatening suicide. His mother called the police who came and took him to the hospital. He resisted going with the officers, and all the way to the hospital he chanted "I'm a Buddhist monkey Hiawatha on strike and it can't hurt me because I'm dead already."

On admission he was cheerful, smiling without apparent reason, and acting as if the whole thing was a joke. He shook hands with the police officers, thanked them for the ride, and assured them that everything would be well taken care of. In a few days his mood changed and he became quiet and withdrawn. He seemed preoccupied with his own thoughts and would frequently talk to an empty chair, making up his own words. Later he became more talkative with others and would lecture other patients on philosophy. His conversation, however, was made up of word combinations without meaning. He became more preoccupied and incoherent in his speech and more careless about his personal habits.

Bill was under observation and treatment of various kinds for two years before he began to show signs of improvement. He finally recovered sufficiently to leave the hospital and was accepted for vocational rehabilitation.

Major Affective Disorders

This group of psychoses is characterized by a single disorder of mood, either extreme elation or depression, that dominates the life of the patient and is responsible for whatever loss of contact he has with the environment. The onset of the mood does not seem to be directly related to a particular stress situation or crisis experience, so it differs in this respect from a depressive neurosis or psychotic depressive reaction. These disorders are marked by severe mood swings to the extremes with a tendency to recover and then repeat the occurrence. We are all accustomed to some ups and downs in our mood states and emotional responses. We feel good, very good, low, very low, and could probably chart for any month these ups and downs.

Mania is characterized by great emotional excitement and a mood state not unlike intoxication. Nothing seems impossible to the manic person, reality is badly distorted and judgment is especially affected. In a state of mania an individual might attempt impossible feats of strength or endurance, or might commit his resources and property to contracts beyond his ability to meet such obligations. The faulty judgment and inflated mood state of the manic individual may lead to excessive risk of his life. Self-care may be completely neglected.

Depression is a mood state quite opposite from mania. The depressed person does not care if he eats, or sleeps, or lives, because he feels so low. The depression of mind may involve the total body so extensively as to affect digestion, elimination, and other vital functioning. The depressed person is a high suicide risk because he finds his low mood state so intolerable that death seems a welcome respite. Close supervision may be required to protect the depressed person from self-destruction or from failure of body functioning.

Manic-depression is a combination of the symptoms of mania and depression in the same person. The individual fluctuates in his illness between these high and low mood states. How long each phase might last, how long an interval between phases, and the particular elements that would trigger a change would vary according to differences in the life history of the individual.

Sam was a veteran of World War II who had suffered a mental breakdown during combat. He had been treated in a military hospital and given a medical discharge. After the war Sam had several brief periods of hospitalization in Veterans Hospitals, each time being able to recover and return to the community. He was diagnosed a manic-depressive psychotic because of his extreme mood swings from elation to depression which recurred regularly at intervals of about two years.

At one time when Sam was discharged from the V.A. Hospital his case was followed by a Mental Hygiene Clinic in the community where he lived. He was seen frequently but not regularly for two years before he returned to the hospital. During this time Sam was at first enthusiastic and eager to make a good adjustment. He obtained a job selling home improvements for a contractor and also obtained the franchise to sell a new type of awning. He bought a new car and took on a third job as a car salesman. He began attending an artist's workshop and produced a volume of abstract paintings which he attempted to sell on street corners. He joined numerous organizations, attended meetings, and became a lecturer on mental illness. As he gained momentum he took on more and more activities until he was unable to sleep nights because of his excessive interests, involvements, and plans. He developed an idea for turning Alcatraz Island into a rehabilitation center for mental patients and wrote the President of the United States asking for approval of his plan. He ran up many debts for the printing of flyers and brochures advertising the Alcatraz project, and he interviewed numerous psychologists, psychiatrists, and civic leaders to enlist their support for the venture. He became so excited and elated about his ideas that he neglected to go to work and to pay his bills. When he was finally picked up by the police for creating a disturbance in the city park he resisted arrest, became quite violent, and had to be returned to the hospital in restraints.

Hospital treatment enabled Sam to calm down and regain normal functioning within a few weeks. Sam was an ideal patient for several months and then he began showing signs of depression and apathy. His mood could be controlled by medication while he was in the hospital, but when he was discharged to return to the community he would not follow through with regular visits to the clinic and his episodes of mania were repeated.

Some patients experience only manic episodes, others have only depressive episodes, and still others alternate between manic and depressive extremes. The stage of acute illness can usually be prevented if the patient has enough awareness to recognize the symptoms coming on and seek appropriate help. Between episodes of acute psychosis these people are able to function reasonably well although they tend to be moody and usually show signs of an affective personality disorder.

Paranoid States

The principal symptom of this functional psychosis is an extensive, well-developed delusional (false beliefs) system. The paranoid person may have *grandiose* ideas (that he is a famous person) or ideas of *persecution* (that others have organized for the purpose of hurting him). Mental and social functioning may be maintained at a high level in a paranoid person until circumstances occur which bring the delusional system into expression.

Many of the more sensational kinds of mentally ill behavior reported in news media appear to involve paranoia. A person who barricades himself in a building and begins shooting at passers-by is a very alarming and dangerous person to others. What is generally not reported is that the person is suffering a paranoid psychosis and *believes* that others are deliberately attempting to hurt him. Seen from this view, his behavior is still alarming and dangerous, but it is not deliberate malice. As far as the paranoid person is concerned, he is justifiably shooting at others in his own defense. When the paranoid delusions are of grandeur, rather than persecution, the individual's behavior may arouse scorn rather than fear in other persons. If he believes he is the savior of mankind, he will act in ways consistent with this belief. When others reject his efforts to "save" them he may interpret this as their failure to appreciate his importance and behave in an even more extreme manner. He may decide to prove who he is by killing himself so that he can return to life before them.

If we can know the nature of the delusional system the behavior of the paranoid individual becomes understandable, even though it is inappropriate and not normal. It is especially in the loss of contact with reality and loss of shared meanings with others, that the paranoid disturbance is revealed. Because the paranoid illness is focused around a delusional system, the rest of behavioral functioning may be quite adequate. Unless situational factors irritate the delusional system the paranoid individual may live an essentially normal life with little evidence of his illness. Of the functional psychoses, paranoia is most likely to go undetected, and tends to be very resistant to treatment because it involves fundamental systems of belief elaborated and reinforced by lifelong learning experience.

To illustrate the thought processes in paranoia, the following is a recorded interview with a patient who had been hospitalized in a mental hospital for approximately 6 years at the time the interview took place.

George was 30 years old, single, in good physical health, above average in intelligence, and had been a student at the University for 3 years prior to his mental breakdown and subsequent hospitalization. George had a well-systematized delusional system with delusions of grandeur and delusions of persecution. He thought he was a nuclear physicist (grandeur) who was being held prisoner in the institution because of the special knowledge he had (persecution). The interview reported here was the first time I had talked to George alone in my office so he was not well acquainted with me. At subsequent interviews during and following therapy his delusional system remained intact.

I began the interview with, "Hello, George, how are you today?"

"Just the same as I've been for years, no change comes about rapidly," he said, leaning back in his chair and looking around the room.

"How long have you been in this hospital?" I asked.

"Six years, three months, five days, four hours, and twenty-two minutes," said George, looking at his watch.

"Are you expecting to go home soon?"

"No," said George hesitatingly, "I suppose I'll be here the rest of my life."

"Do you like it here?" I wondered.

"Not particularly, but I make the best of it," looking around he added, "Is this room bugged?"

"No", I answered, "do you want to leave?"

"Look, who's crazy, you or me?" he questioned.

"Why do you ask that," I queried.

"Well, I know you think I'm crazy and I think you are, but there are more people crazy like you than crazy like me so you have me locked up, but there will come a day!" he said threateningly.

"A day?"

"Yes", emphatically spoken, "a day when you will look back and *know* that I was right."

"When will that be, George?"

"Who can say?" he relaxed again, "Maybe another fifty thousand years will see some progress."

"Progress along what lines?"

"Thinking, just human thinking. Did you ever try it?," he laughed, "Well don't! I have, and look where it got me."

"What were you thinking about?"

"I was trying to figure it out for years and years, and it finally *came* to me, and I worked it out mathematically. *I* have the answer," he said, rather proudly.

"Answer to what?" I asked, puzzled.

"To the question! What do you think?" he sounded annoyed.

"What question, George?" I asked calmly.

George jumped to his feet. "There, you see! You don't even know the question!" he began to pace back and forth across the room angrily directing a rapid fire of questions toward me without waiting for answers, "What have you *done* all your life? Have you never *thought*? What *are* you? Where did you *come* from? Where are you *going*? What is the *purpose*? Have you never thought about *why*?"

Without waiting for my reply, he suddenly slumped in the chair, held his head in his hands and began again, "It's just as well because once you have the knowledge you are lost to this life and you only wait for the end to come. No one knows, or practically no one. I know, but very few others, even here, know. I think one patient on (ward) 12 knows, but he can't tell—can't talk at all, he just sits and waits. I showed him the equation, but he wasn't impressed. He knows already, I think."

"What is the equation?" I asked.

"If I told you," said George, sounding very hopeless, "you wouldn't understand it. No one does but me."

"Will you show it to me?" I asked.

"Yes!" he said, very emphatically, "Give me some paper and a pencil."

I handed him some plain paper and a pencil, and then sat back and watched as he worked. For the next 25 minutes neither of us spoke a word as George worked intently drawing an elaborate diagram of lines, figures, planes, numbers, letters, and symbols resembling formulas which covered one entire sheet of paper.

"There—that's it!" he suddenly exclaimed. "There is the answer to the whole thing—its *complete!*"

I studied the paper for a few minutes before I asked, "What does it mean?"

George sounded crushed. "Can't you *understand?*" he pleaded, "Can't *you* understand?" he paused, then he went on, "Even the physicists who could understand it won't because they are afraid, and so they think I'm crazy." He sounded resigned.

"May I keep this to study it a little more?" I asked, feeling very sorry for him.

"No! I should say not!" he shouted, jumping up and grabbing the paper from my hands, "This will go with me to death and humanity is saved." He tore the paper into tiny bits, put a few pieces in each of his pockets, and threw the rest in the wastebasket.

"Shall we go now, George?" I ventured.

"Thank you," he said politely extending his hand, "I will speak with you again."

We shook hands and returned to the ward.

Organic Psychoses

The psychoses, like the psychoneuroses, are not limited to involvement of mental functioning, but may also include involvement of the physical body. Some psychoses are caused by known physical agents which affect the entire body of the individual. We distinguish between those psychoses which result from a physical agent and show actual change in physical processes and those which do not.

The psychoses caused by physical agents are called *organic* psychoses. Included among these would be mental impairment and/or deterioration due to excessive use of alcohol, advanced syphilitic infection, extreme malnutrition, habitual use of drugs such as heroin, inhalation of fumes such as carbon monoxide or other gases, and disturbances in chemical or metabolic body processes. Organic psychoses may also develop from injuries to the head, illnesses such as brain tumor, and changes in the brain as a result of aging processes (senile psychosis).

The organic psychoses develop slowly over time. Early identification of the threatening physical agent and early initiation of treatment may forestall their full damaging effect. If not forestalled, tissue damage to the brain may occur and the resulting loss of behavioral functioning will be permanent and irreversible. Because many of the physical agents of organic psychoses are known and their course and effect relatively predictable, neglect to obtain early treatment in these conditions is especially unfortunate.

TREATMENT AND PREVENTION

During the past twenty years, tremendous advances have been made in the treatment of mental illness but progress in prevention is only beginning. New methods of psychotherapy and new drugs along with changing public attitudes toward mental illness are contributing to a brighter outlook for the mentally ill and their families. The trend is away from the large state hospital of the past toward community mental health centers and treatment in general hospitals near where people live. We hope that the old-style, overcrowded, understaffed institution will soon be a thing of the past and in its place will be modern, well-equipped, well-staffed units in general hospitals. Experience has shown that the average length of stay in a hospital for an acute mental disturbance can be reduced from about 3 months to about 10 days when the patient is treated in a modern general hospital instead of a public institution. It has also been demonstrated that many patients who were formerly confined to mental institutions for years can be treated more successfully in outpatient clinics, halfway houses, day treatment centers, and other rehabilitation programs in the community (Figures 9-2 and 9-3).

The complexities of behavioral impairment in the neuroses and psychoses do not lend themselves to simple comments about how to treat them. More importantly, these disturbances are serious, often severe, and require expert professional help. They should not be handled in a do-it-yourself treatment approach. The beginning student of human behavior needs to be aware that appeals to common sense, appeals to reason or responsibility, and appeals to "pull yourself together" are not likely to be effective in helping these conditions. The best you could do for someone with serious mental problems would be to

Figure 9-2. Mental patients committed to public institutions where conditions such as these are common do not have an optimistic future. (New York State Mental Hygiene Photo by Julian Belin.)

Figure 9-3. The modern mental hospital offers an atmosphere much more conducive to recovery than the old style institutions but it still has many of the same limitations. (New York State Mental Hygiene Photo by Julian Belin.)

encourage early help-seeking and to have some concrete suggestions about the kind of help available and how to obtain it. If professional help is obtained early enough it is usually possible to prevent the development of a severely disabling, chronic mental illness which would require long-term hospital care.

How can mental illness be treated? The methods can be grouped into three main types although they are often used in combination. They are milieu therapy, somatotherapy, and psychotherapy.

Milieu Therapy

The oldest and most common method of treating mental and emotional illness is by changing the environment or removing the disturbed individual from his stress-producing situation to a more therapeutic environment called *milieu*. By removing a person from those conditions which have caused or aggravated his symptoms he has a better opportunity to regain his control and get back in touch with reality through creative activity and therapy of different kinds.

In such places as hospital units, rehabilitation centers, day treatment programs, special classes, preschool nurseries for disturbed children, and specialized group living facilities for alcoholics or drug addicts, the environment is structured to produce a therapeutic effect on the individuals. Through contact with trained helpers patients learn how to get along with others and to understand and control their own feelings and attitudes. Milieu therapy includes occupational, educational, and recreational therapy aimed at helping people deal more effectively with the stress and tensions they encounter in their relationships with people at home, in school, on the job, and in the community (Figure 9-4).

Somatotherapy

Working with the nervous system and physiological foundations of behavior (described in Chapter 2) is called *somatotherapy*, and includes such procedures as brain surgery, chemical and electrical shock therapy, and the use of drugs.

Figure 9-4. Occupational therapy offers patients the opportunity and encouragement to develop their individual potentials. (New York State Mental Hygiene Photo by Julian Belin.)

Somatotherapy of any kind is employed only by licensed physicians (M.D. degree) with special training in the treatment of mental and emotional disorders, usually psychiatrists or neurologists. Psychiatrists also use techniques of psychotherapy in conjunction with somatotherapy.

Chemotherapy, which means the therapeutic use of drugs, is rapidly becoming the most widely used somatotherapy for mental and emotional illness. Pills cannot solve problems, and drugs cannot cure mental illness, but they can make mental and emotional disorders easier to treat by calming anxiety and counteracting depression. Certain drugs relieve the symptoms of mental illness by acting on the central nervous system through the blood chemistry (refer to Chapter 2). Exactly how these drugs affect the brain is not completely understood, but in theory, they appear to produce chemical changes in the brain which alter the processing and interpretation of sensory information.

Psychotherapy

Psychological approaches to the treatment and prevention of mental illness are called *psychotherapy*. There are many varieties of psychotherapy being practiced today, but they are all directed toward the goal of helping people achieve a more satisfying and successful life adjustment through talking with a qualified therapist.

The training and preparation of psychologists was discussed in Chapter 1. We should note here that only those psychologists who specialize in clinical or counseling areas offer psychotherapy services to the public. The possession of a doctoral degree (Ph.D.) from an approved graduate school and/or licensing by a state examining committee are evidence of competency to practice psychotherapy. Psychotherapists are usually licensed clinical psychologists or psychiatrists, although other professionally trained persons including psychiatric social workers and psychiatric nurses often offer psychotherapy under psychiatric supervision.

Typically, psychotherapy involves the development of a confidential relationship between patient and therapist, exploration of the life history, increasing awareness of the patient's feelings and responses to them, and the understanding of his problems. Psychotherapy deals in content with feelings, thoughts, and actions. The therapist offers the patient a genuine interest, unconditional acceptance, belief in his worth as a person, and professional skill in clarifying his feelings and thoughts. In an atmosphere of objectivity, free of judgment and punishment, a patient is encouraged to explore and reorganize his attitudes and feelings so that he can change his behavior and personality in the direction of better mental health.

Psychoanalysis is a specialized technique in which an individual patient is seen by the analyst for several hours a week over a period of two or more years. Unconscious motivation is explored and repressed conflicts brought into consciousness. Such intensive psychotherapy is neither necessary nor practical for most people because of the time and money it costs. There are only about 1200 qualified psychoanalysts in this country and most of their patients are advanced students who are preparing to become psychotherapists. Psychoanalysis was originated by Freud and has been very influential in the development of newer, briefer methods of psychotherapy.

Group psychotherapy has become a widely used method of treatment and prevention of more serious emotional problems. A therapist may work with a small group (usually 6 to 10 persons) who talk about their problems and get help from each other as well as the therapist. A specific form of group therapy is family therapy in which all members of a family are seen as a group including the one who has been identified as the patient. Family group therapy views individual behavior as a product of the interaction that takes place within a family, and it attempts to assist the family members to better understand and help each other resolve psychological problems.

Psychodrama is a specialized technique of group therapy in which patients are encouraged to "act out" their problems with the help of others. Sometimes the patients are asked to exchange roles and act as if they were the other persons with whom they are engaged in problem situations. Thus, patients can observe how they appear to others and can often see themselves more objectively.

Play therapy is a technique for helping children communicate their feelings through the use of toys. A child may not be able to explain to the therapist that he is behaving badly because he is so angry at his father, but in the play room he can allow the father doll to fall off the roof of the doll house and be run over by a truck. Children project their feelings and attitudes in their play and through fantasy. A skilled therapist can help a disturbed child to recognize and handle his feelings more effectively even though the child may be unable to talk about them.

Behavior therapies based on learning theory and conditioning techniques (discussed in Chapter 4) have found increasing application and effectiveness in recent years. Assuming that behavior disorders are the result of past learning, the therapy is essentially a process of relearning. Conditioning and reinforcement techniques are used to modify undesirable behavior and to establish new habit patterns and more effective responses. Reinforcement therapy programs have shown remarkably good results in a number of large mental institutions where individual insight therapy is impractical because of staff limitations (Liberman, 1968).

The modification of behavior using scientific procedures has been effective in treating learning disabilities, speech problems and stuttering, sex problems, severely disturbed behavior in mentally ill children, and in developing more appropriate behavior in mentally retarded children (Figure 9-5). Application of behavioral techniques to adult problems has opened an expanding area of new possibilities that will undoubtedly continue to grow as research continues.

Psychotherapy is dependent upon communication between patient and therapist and for this reason an effective patient–therapist relationship is essential to progress. Early help-seeking is not a sign of weakness, but a valuable resource in the psychotherapeutic process. If help-seeking is delayed the impairment of communicative and relationship skills by the illness process lengthens and complicates the therapeutic effort.

WHERE TO FIND HELP

Rapid changes are occurring in the prevention and treatment of mental problems everywhere. One of the most important developments we see is the change in public attitude which makes prevention and treatment more readily available to everyone.

Community Mental Health Centers

One of the newest developments in the treatment of emotional and mental illness is the community-centered mental health programs financed jointly by state and local government funds. New York was the first state to enact community mental health services legislation (1954) followed by California (1957). These programs provide treatment services for emotional and mental illness at a cost consistent with the patient's ability to pay (sliding fee) and are located within the community and within easy access of population centers. The usual services offered by community mental health programs include outpatient service, inpatient service, rehabilitation, education-information, and consultation (Figure 9-6).

Outpatient service is a treatment program where patients come to the center

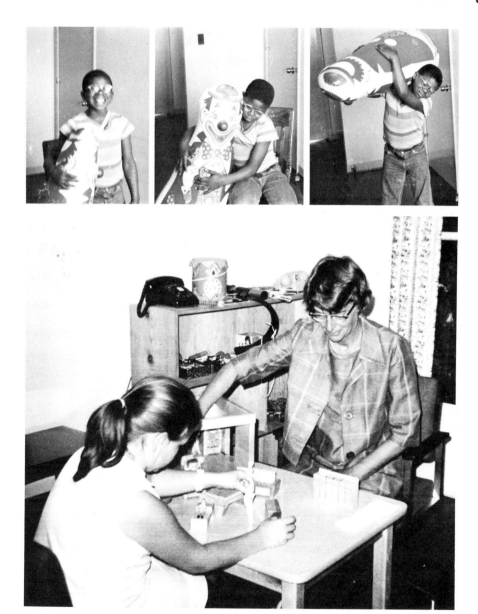

Figure 9-5. Play therapy allows acting out of feelings as this boy is doing with the inflated plastic clown, and also encourages the projection of feelings through play with the doll house and family dolls as the girl is doing. (Courtesy of Saratoga County Mental Health Clinic.)

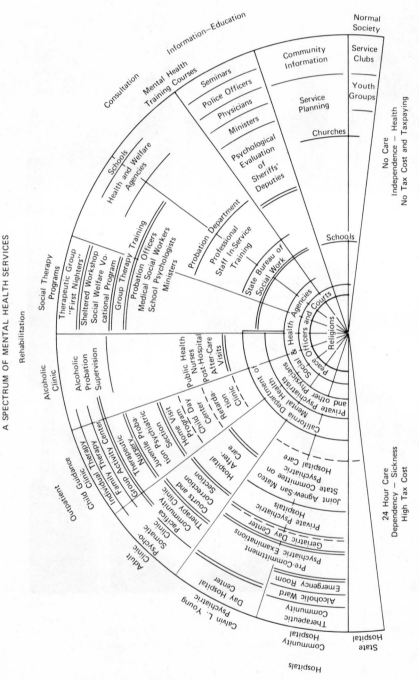

Figure 9-6. A spectrum of mental health services. This diagram shows the progression of prevention, care and treatment from normal community living to total dependency in a hospital. The farther to the left of the spectrum you must go the more difficult and costly the treatment becomes. (Reprinted by permission of the Mental Health Services Division, Department of Public Health and Welfare, County of San Mateo, California.)

on a weekly or biweekly basis or some arranged schedule, receive treatment, and then continue with their daily life affairs. The patients do not reside in the center. Outpatient programs include individual and group psychotherapy procedures, or perhaps for a given individual a combination of both approaches. Outpatient services are a preferred procedure when possible because the patient stays at his own home and continues with his work or school rather than being removed to a hospital setting.

Inpatient service is one where the patient resides in the treatment center usually on a short-term basis of a week to a month. Inpatient service is sometimes necessary to give the patient some relief from the demands of daily living and permit closer supervision or opportunity for observation. The inpatient service is offered within the community at or near a local general hospital and is provided on a voluntary basis. Because inpatient services are of short duration, located in the community, and voluntary, they do not seem to be as disrupting to the individual's life as often occurs with confinement in a mental hospital. Varieties of inpatient service are the day-care and night-care services. In a day-care program the patients remain 6 to 8 hours in the treatment center participating in the therapeutic programs and then go to their own homes for the evening. Night-care patients would be on the job or at school during the day and come to the treatment center afterward to participate in individual and/or group psychotherapy, stay overnight in the treatment center and then return to work or school the next day.

Rehabilitation programs are designed to assist those who have been ill to become readjusted and reintegrated into the community. Halfway houses are rehabilitative in purpose. They provide an intermediate living situation between the mental hospital and the individual's own home where the former patient can gradually become accustomed to meeting daily demands. The halfway house provides support and encouragement in the readjustive process rather than treatment.

Education-information services are designed, as the name implies, to provide as wide a dissemination of information about emotional and mental illnesses as can be accomplished. Mental health professionals (psychologists, psychiatrists, and social workers) engaged in education-information services may meet with P.T.A.'s, church or neighborhood groups, civic organizations, or groups of non-mental health specialists such as teachers, lawyers, police and clergymen. Techniques of education-information may include lectures, films, discussions, and in-service training seminars. The purpose of education-information programs are primarily early identification of potential mental health problems, increased awareness of treatment resources, and effective utilization of treatment resources.

Consultation services attempt to gain maximum utilization of the available mental health professionals by making them available to groups of non-mental health professionals who work with people with potential mental health problems. The consultant attempts to help such persons as teachers, nurses, and industrial supervisors, to work more effectively with the mental health problems that confront them in the course of their own professional functioning. Everyone cannot be a mental health specialist, yet we cannot avoid mental health problems in many fields of work with people. Consultation attempts to bridge this gap and give people who work with people the benefit of the limited mental health professional manpower resources. The community-centered mental health programs are predicated on the belief that emotional and mental illnesses arise principally out of the complexities of social living. These programs attempt to meet mental health problems as soon as they happen and where they happen, in the community, instead of dealing with them in a remote mental hospital after they happen.

Information Sources

Information about community mental health services programs in your area can be obtained from the administrative offices of city, county, or state government or public health departments. Local chapters of psychological associations and medical societies are an excellent source for lists of certified psychotherapists in your area. The local chapter of the *National Association of Mental Health* can provide information about public and private treatment resources. Current directories of local community services are made available by many local chapters of the Mental Health Association. The local United Fund agency can provide details of programs supported by their contributions including Adult and Child Guidance Clinics, Screening and Counseling services, Suicide Prevention centers, Family Service Association, and residential (live-in) facilities for groups with special problems (unwed mothers, alcoholics, drug addicts, delinquent-neglected youths). If you live in a remote area of your state the local county librarian can assist you in locating the nearest treatment resources.

Initial Contact

A telephone call is enough to initiate an intake or evaluation interview in most treatment centers. During this first interview the problem is discussed, the services of the agency or therapist are described and matters of fee can be determined. The evaluation interview may be extended to two or three sessions before any treatment procedures are suggested. Diagnostic procedures such as psychological tests or a physical examination may be suggested to help clarify the problem presented. If the problem presented does not fall within the competencies or resources of the therapist or agency, appropriate referral suggestions will be made.

The first step toward solution of any problem begins with the recognition that a problem exists. This is as true of problems of an emotional or mental health nature as it is of all problems. Early help-seeking is especially desirable when the problem involves the emotions or the mind. Competent specialized help is available and the suggested sources of information are a means of ready contact. From the time of the initial contact every effort that follows is potentially therapeutic.

SUMMARY

A frame of reference is presented that views mental illness as different from normal behavior in degree but not in kind. Mental illness is evident when the degree of deviation from the normal is so great that the person can no longer perform the usual and expected tasks of social living. These tasks include self-care, ability to make decisions, fulfilling responsibilities, and effective communication with others. Normality is defined as a relative concept depending upon time, place, and person.

The prevalence of emotional and mental disorders is so great that over half the hospital beds in the country are occupied by mental patients. One in ten adults now living will be hospitalized at some time for emotional or mental disturbance. One in four adults is involved, either directly or indirectly, with emotional and mental illness. Studies of hereditary factors are provocative but not conclusive evidence for interpretations of causality.

A certain amount of emotional distress is normal. There is no sharp distinction between normality and disturbance, but one shades into the other very gradually. Reactions to overwhelming stress are to be expected. The physical effects of emotional tension may be damaging if prolonged. Persistent patterns of maladaptive behavior that interfere with personal relationships become personality disorders. Examples of personality disorders are: antisocial personality, inadequate personality, and schizoid personality. Sexual deviations, alcoholism, and drug dependence are included with the personality disorders.

Anxiety is the chief characteristic of the neuroses. Examples of common neuroses given are: anxiety neurosis, obsessive–compulsive neurosis, phobic neurosis, and hysterical neurosis, conversion-type. Neuroses are different from normal behavior patterns in the degree of discomfort the person experiences because of his awareness of impaired functioning.

Psychoses are disturbances of thinking, mood, and behavior to such a severe degree that contact with reality is lost. Psychosis may be functional or organic or a combination of both. The functional psychoses include schizophrenia (attributed to thought disorders), major affective disorder (dominated by mood disorder), and paranoid states (limited distortion of reality). Organic psychoses develop slowly over time and are associated with physical damage or deterioration of the brain making the disturbance more permanent.

Treatment of mental and emotional illness is of three main types: milieu therapy, somatotherapy, and psychotherapy. Psychotherapy may be individual or in groups and includes specialized techniques such as psychoanalysis and play therapy.

Social progress has brought about the development of community mental health centers making it possible for anyone to obtain help fairly easily. Services in community centers include outpatient, inpatient, rehabilitation, education-information, and consultation services. Information is readily available and initial contact is as close as your telephone.

SUGGESTIONS FOR FURTHER READING

Bettelheim, Bruno, *The Empty Fortress*, New York, Macmillan, 1967. A non-technical description of the problems and treatment of mentally ill children with interesting case studies.

Green, Hanna, *I Never Promised You a Rose Garden*, New York, Holt, Rinehart and Winston, 1964. A novel about an adolescent girl, her illness, and treatment in a mental hospital. An especially good description of life in a mental institution.

Milton, O. and Wahler, R. G. (Eds.), *Behavior Disorders: Perspectives and Trends*, (2nd ed.), Philadelphia, Lippincott, 1969. A collection of 24 articles giving an overview of current thinking and research findings, stressing the psychosocial approach to understanding abnormal behavior.

Myers, J. K., Bean, L. L. and Pepper, M. P., *A Decade Later: A Follow-up of Social Class and Mental Illness*, New York, Wiley, 1968. A study of long range results and adjustment of former patients in the community shows how treatment and recovery are related to the person's social class and position.

Stern, Edith M., *Mental Illness: A Guide For the Family*, (5th ed.), New York, Harper and Row, 1968. Common sense advice to help the family understand and find appropriate help for mental illness, including information about insurance and other ways to finance care.

Mental Health

Mental health is more than the absence of mental illness: it includes a zest for life, an enthusiasm that makes it possible to engage your capacities to the fullest and to find satisfaction and enjoyment in living. At the other end of the mental illness-to-mental health continuum is an ideal set of conditions which people strive toward but few ever attain completely. Mental health, like illness, varies by degrees with some of us relatively more healthy than others. Within each person there are varying degrees of mental health at different times.

For many years science has tried to understand and prevent mental illness, but only in recent years has there been much emphasis on improving mental health in those who were not mentally ill. In terms of the conservation of human resources and the potential happiness to be experienced in living, developing and maintaining mental health is much preferred to treatment and rehabilitation from illness. Human potential is humanity's greatest resource —how can we be sure this potential is not wasted?

DEVELOPING MENTAL HEALTH

Mental health is everybody's business. We are not only responsible for ourselves but we have an obligation to our fellow man since none of us can function as a completely independent being. By recognizing our dependence on each other we can work together toward mutually satisfying goals. Mental health begins in the home, develops in the schools, and depends on the community. Let us see how each of these forces work together for the benefit of society and the individual.

Mental Health Begins at Home

The human infant is helplessly dependent upon parents for the satisfaction of basic needs. We can easily recognize the child's physical needs for food, sleep, warmth, fresh air, and comfort. The basic emotional needs are equally important but sometimes not so easily recognized. To grow into a mentally healthy adult a child must have both physical and emotional needs met by his family.

The home should provide, in addition to physical and economic security, satisfaction of a child's needs for love, acceptance, belonging, independence, and control (see Chapter 5). The home must also provide socialization and education, it must answer his questions and give him guidance and direction. Every child needs to have a set of moral standards to live by. His home should give him a belief in the human values of honesty, kindness, generosity, courage, and justice. He must learn from his family the difference between right and wrong, good and bad, and how to make these value judgments for himself. He needs to have faith in a power greater than the individual.

Conditions in the home that are conducive to good mental health are love and affection, concern for the children, acceptance of roles, compatibility, and consistency in handling children. Unfortunately, not all children come from such mentally healthy homes and they look to society for some means to overcome deficiences in their early background.

Mental Health and the Schools

Children come to school bringing with them the whole range of hopes, fears, joys, sorrows, enthusiasm, unmet needs, and problems. While the primary purpose of schools is to educate, the school serves a unique function in the development of good mental health. School is the place where children learn to live by living. The problems a child encounters in school and the way he learns to handle them will help to determine his adult attitudes and behavior patterns.

What is the mental health responsibility of the schools?

Equal Opportunity. To provide each child with an equal opportunity to learn and to develop his potential capabilities requires the recognition of individual differences. Modern education stresses cooperative efforts in the classroom and at the same time encourages children to work independently. This means that the child is permitted to work at his own speed while striving to develop new skills and he is accepted as part of the group working toward group goals. In this way the child shares in the success or failure of his group rather than having to stand or fall on his own merits.

Peer-Group Activities. School offers the unique opportunity for children to enjoy equal status in a group. The behavior of his peers provides a standard by which a child can evaluate his own abilities, attitudes, and limitations. In peer-group activities the child is able to compare himself with children his same age and to learn acceptance and respect for others who are different. Peer-group activities also help children to develop leadership potential and a spirit of cooperation or teamwork.

Level of Aspiration. Much of what we do as children, and as adults, is directed toward achieving success or reward and avoiding punishment or failure. The feelings of success and failure depend upon the goals and expectations of the individual. This expected goal is called the level of aspiration and the actual goal reached is called level of achievement. When the level of achievement reaches the level of aspiration the person feels success and when achievement falls short of aspiration he feels failure. For example, the student who aspires to be an outstanding scholar and who hopes and works for A grades may feel he has failed miserably if he earns a grade of C, while another student whose level of aspiration is lower may feel very successful if he earns C grades.

The school should be able to help students set realistic goals so that their levels of aspiration will not be too high or too low. If the level of aspiration is too high the student will soon become discouraged by his repeated failures. If the level of aspiration is too low the goals are too easy to attain and the student loses interest in achievement. Parents frequently make the mistake of setting unrealistically high goals for their children and criticizing them when they fail to achieve their expectations. The school must help a child recognize his abilities and limitations and set goals that are realistic for himself.

Emotional Help. Schools have another mental health responsibility, that of early detection of emotional problems in children and referral to appropriate sources for help. We do not expect our schools to treat all emotional problems but we do expect them to recognize problem behavior and make recommendations for early treatment before the problems become deeply ingrained and resistant to change.

Community Mental Health Responsibility

Some communities take a more active role in mental health than others but the trend in recent years is toward greater involvement of the community in providing for the needs of its people. Most of us would agree that there are some responsibilities that cannot be avoided, others that are desirable, and still others that are idealistic. We feel that good mental health depends in part upon community acceptance of responsibility for providing the following:

1. Protective custody for children who are neglected or abused.
2. Foster homes for children who cannot adjust in their own homes and need help.
3. Professional help for families who recognize problems and want help (including marriage counseling, child guidance, family counseling).
4. Treatment resources with emphasis on prevention.
5. Education for people of all ages to aid in understanding and acceptance of self and others.

6. Recreational facilities and opportunities for socialization and group participation.
7. Sufficient economic opportunities to provide for independence and self-esteem.

The ways any given community goes about providing these services will vary from time to time, and we can never be sure the people in a community will take advantage of the services that are available. But in spite of these factors it is an informed citizenry, able to recognize and deal with problems on a community level, that is best able to assure us of a mentally healthy environment.

WHAT IS GOOD MENTAL HEALTH?

The characteristics of good mental health can be described in term of feelings: about self, about others, about the demands of life. The elements of good mental health are self-acceptance and self-fulfillment, both of which are harder to achieve than to define. Keeping in mind that "perfect" mental health is only an ideal and that progress in the direction of our ideals is in itself satisfying, let us see what is meant by the description of mentally healthy people.

How It Feels to Be Mentally Healthy

Feeling Comfortable about Yourself. Mentally healthy people neither underestimate nor overestimate their capabilities and they can accept their own limitations. They have a sense of independence and self-respect. They feel confident that they will be able to deal with problems as they arise. They can laugh at themselves and can take disappointments in their stride. They are aware of their own emotions—their fears, anger, love, jealousy, guilt— but they are not overwhelmed by them. They have a problem-solving attitude and can depend on their own judgment, initiative, and resourcefulness. They have personal values, ideals, principles, aims, and a philosophy of life. They gain satisfaction from the simple pleasures of everyday living.

Feeling Good about Other People. Mentally healthy people have self-confidence but they also have confidence in other people. They are able to give and accept love and affection, and they form close personal relationships that are lasting and mutually satisfying. They treat other people as they would like to be treated. They trust others and are trustworthy. They accept other people and respect their differences. They try to help people but do not expect them to be perfect. They can function as members of a group and enjoy their associations with others. They feel a sense of responsibility for their fellow men.

Feeling Able to Meet the Demands of Life. Mentally healthy people do something about their problems as they occur. They shape the environment when it is possible and they adjust to it when it is necessary. They are capable of conforming to social norms but they are free to choose whether to conform or not. They accept responsibility and are sensitive and responsive to the needs of others. They do not regret the past, they plan ahead, and they do not fear the future. They set realistic goals and strive to make use of their capabilities. They are able to think for themselves and make independent decisions as well as to participate in group decisions and to abide by the majority opinion. They gain satisfaction from putting their best effort into whatever they do.

How do people acquire these characteristics? The answer is that they learn them. They learn them as a result of the experiences they have and the responses they make to these experiences. Basic to the characteristics of mentally healthy persons is a core of attitudes and feelings about the self.

Self-Acceptance

Complete acceptance of the self is probably one of the most difficult attitudes we attempt to attain. Some people are able to achieve self-acceptance through their own efforts, some need professional help, and others never do achieve it to any appreciable degree. Self-acceptance can be understood as a process which involves self-awareness, self-understanding, and self-realization. A self-accepting person must have some awareness and understanding of what he is and why, and he must be satisfied with himself not only for what he is, but for what he is becoming.

Good mental health requires a basic understanding and appreciation of the fundamental needs which underlie and motivate our behavior. We have in common with other human beings needs for love, affection, security, recognition, independence, achievement, and mastery. There are many ways of defining and classifying human psychological needs, but all of them may be summarized as a basic need to become more adequate in our efforts to cope with the demands of reality.

Behavior arises out of unsatisfied needs and for this reason it is always purposeful and directed. We are not robots responding to unknown forces or circumstances. We are attempting to satisfy a need, overcome an obstacle, or make progress toward a goal in whatever we do. Reality considerations may require that we delay some satisfactions until a later time, find another route to our goal, or even redefine our goals, but even at these times we retain control of our directions and our fate.

We must be satisfied to do the best we can with the capabilities we have at any given time and try to improve these capabilities as we go along. We must also learn to accept our limitations and not be defeated by them. Every person has some skills and characteristics deserving of respect. We can become so involved with ideas of what we should *be* that we fail to appreciate what we *are*.

Your relationships with other people are often a reflection of your relationship with yourself. One who can see only the defects in himself usually sees only defects in others. One who makes harsh or unreasonable demands upon himself usually is critical and dissatisfied with the performance of others. You become sensitive to the feelings of others to the degree you are sensitive to your own feelings. You find common cause with others to the degree that you recognize that you have needs, strengths, and limitations just as they do. Love, compassion, and responsibility for others can develop only from acceptance of the self. Cooperation and mutually satisfying relationships with others indicate an identification of the self with humanity and a desire to achieve common purpose with one's fellow man.

Self-Fulfillment

Self-fulfillment is essentially an experience of mastery, of having coped effectively with the demands and challenges of life. The life tasks and the times of crisis described in Chapters 7 and 8 represent the most common demands and challenges that we experience. Failure to achieve self-fulfillment results most often from a lack of awareness or an unwillingness to accept the self. The goals you set for yourself in life reflect your self-awareness and self-acceptance. Your goals and your progress toward them become the measure by which you judge your success and experience either a sense of fulfillment or failure.

People who know and accept themselves set goals that are within their capabilities to achieve. When their progress toward their goals is interrupted, they can use a problem-solving attitude because they have an objective attitude about themselves. They do not waste their time or their personal resources in self-doubt, fault-finding, or excuse-making. They can handle the unexpected circumstances of life because they know what they are, where they are going, and are confident that their goals are within the range of their capacities. Self-aware and self-accepting persons can make compromises with necessity and not feel they have been defeated or personally devalued.

Self-fulfillment cannot be achieved at the expense of other people or by excluding others. Developing good interpersonal relationship skills are among the life tasks to be mastered and they are also vital to the realization of one's goals. Total independence from others and complete self-sufficiency are unrealistic, and consequently unhealthy, goals. We need other people throughout our lives and they in turn need us. The nature of your dependency upon others changes as you grow from the helplessness of infancy to the adequacy of adulthood, but you never reach a point where you can do without others entirely. The self-fulfilled person recognizes his need for others and in exercising it appropriately for affection, companionship, recognition, and cooperative endeavor he finds enjoyment for himself and contributes to the happiness of others. Effective relationships with others provide you with the encouragement and assistance you require to meet your own goals. Others also serve us as guides to make progress toward our own self-fulfillment. How do other people feel? How do they handle their problems? How often do they need help and where do they find it? The answers to these questions may save us unnecessary doubt and loss of morale. For these reasons we turn next to a national study of mental health.

WHAT IS NORMAL?

In 1955 the Congress passed the Mental Health Study Act which provided, among other things, for the establishment of a *Joint Commission on Mental Illness and Health* as a nonprofit organization. One of the purposes of the Joint Commission is to investigate problems related to mental *health* and to report to the Congress findings and recommendations for action programs. To accomplish its purposes, and with financial support from private groups, the Joint Commission has drawn upon the talent of research and treatment specialists to identify and investigate problem areas. One of the studies sponsored by the Joint Commission is *Americans View Their Mental Health* (Gurin, Veroff, and Feld, 1960). This study was conducted by investigators at the University of Michigan Survey Research Center.

The investigators, using interview and questionnaire techniques selected 2460 persons to participate in the study. The persons were selected to be representative of the general population in respect to age, sex, education, income, occupation, and place of residence. All persons included in the study were at least 21 years of age and resided at home. Not included were persons who were patients in hospitals, prisoners confined in jails, or persons otherwise removed from society. The investigators attempted to get a cross section of the presumably *normal and stable* population. The interviews and questionnaires were administered at the homes of the persons selected for the study. The report of this investigation provides us with valuable information about the kinds of mental health problems most persons experience and tells us something about what they do about them. The report is too comprehensive to be summarized completely here, but we will examine portions of the information provided by the study.

Happiness, Unhappiness, and Worry

One question studied was the degree of happiness or unhappiness people experience and the relationship between happiness and worrying. About nine-tenths of the 2460 persons studied reported that they were "happy" or "pretty happy" most of the time. Some happy as well as unhappy people never worry. Most people worry to some extent and unhappy people seem to worry more.

What kinds of things make people happy or unhappy and cause them to worry? The responses of the group studied are reported in Table 10-1 in terms of the first two mentioned reasons given. (In Table 10-1, as in some tables to follow, the total percentage is greater than 100 because more than one response per person is counted.) One of the striking findings in Table 10-1 is that the sources of happiness, unhappiness, and worry are not necessarily the same. Economic factors are a greater source of worry to people than they are of either happiness or unhappiness. Other people (marriage partner, children, and friends) are an important source of happiness. To a lesser degree other people are more often a source of worry than they are a source of unhappiness. This finding supports the impression of most mental health workers that the satisfactions we gain from others and our concerns for them outweigh the pain they may sometimes cause us. Problems of the community, the nation, or the world represent a much smaller proportion of worries and unhappiness than might generally be believed.

It appears that it is the circumstances and persons closely associated with one's life experience that are the sources of happiness, unhappiness, or worry.

Table 10-1. First Two Mentioned Reasons for Happiness, Unhappiness, or Worries[a]

Reasons	Sources of happiness, %	Sources of unhappiness, %	Sources of worries, %
Economic and material	29	27	41
Children	29	7	15
Marriage	17	5	2
Other interpersonal sources	16	3	7
Job	14	11	9
Own health	9	7	10
Family's health	8	5	18
Independence; absence of burdens or restrictions	8	0	0
Personal characteristics (and problems)	2	13	5
Community, national, and world problems	0	13	11
Miscellaneous	12	4	5
Not happy, unhappy, or worried about anything	5	18	10
Not determined	2	2	0
Number of persons	2460	2460	2460

[a]Adapted from *Americans View Their Mental Health* by Gerald Gurin, Joseph Veroff, and Sheila Feld, copyright 1960 by Basic Books, Inc., Publishers, New York.

Problems such as war, the bomb, or the population explosion do not seem to be personally and directly experienced. These findings do not seem to be just a result of the time when the study was done. Annual reports of the *Gallup Poll Organization* in the years since 1960 tend to confirm these general findings.

The investigators provide additional data relating to Table 10-1 that indicates younger and better educated persons are happier, but worry more than do older or less educated persons. This findings suggests that worry, at least for some people, may be a sign of more active involvement in life. For young, well-educated persons, worry may not only indicate involvement but also indicate an active attempt to do problem-solving.

Older persons in the study (55 years or more) report more unhappiness as a group but a much smaller tendency to worry. The unhappiness of older people may be related to their health, their disengagement from employment, and their lower standard of living. That older people worry less, in spite of greater felt unhappiness suggests a kind of acceptance of defeat. When one feels hopeless about change in his situation worry is unnecessary.

If mental health is defined simply as the presence of happiness and the absence of worry, very few people in this study would qualify as mentally healthy. If mental health is defined only as happiness then younger, well-educated persons would be considered most mentally healthy. However, if mental health is defined only as the absence of worry then persons over age 55 would be considered most mentally healthy. Obviously, mental health must be something besides just the presence of happiness or the absence of worry. Part of this something else is the way people handle their problems.

How do people deal with their worries and unhappiness? The responses of the group studied are reported in Table 10-2 in terms of the percentage who use a particular approach. The investigators have identified some of the approaches as "passive" and others as "coping." We have already defined coping as taking an active, problem-solving approach to crisis situations and making attempts to master them. In Table 10-2 it appears that people take more of a coping approach to worries than they do to unhappiness. This

Table 10-2. Ways of Handling Worries and Unhappiness[a]

Methods	Worries, %	Unhappiness, %
Passive methods	34	23
Denial—forgot it	(18)	(15)
Did nothing	(10)	(7)
Lived with continued tension	(6)	(1)
Coping methods	44	31
Tried something	(14)	(6)
Informal help seeking (family, friends)	(26)	(20)
Formal help seeking	(2)	(2)
Formal–informal help-seeking combined	(2)	(3)
Prayer	16	33
Other	2	5
Never worried or unhappy	2	4
Not determined	2	4
Number of persons	2460	2460

[a]Adapted from *Americans View Their Mental Health* by Gerald Gurin, Joseph Veroff, and Sheila Feld, copyright 1960 by Basic Books, Inc., Publishers, New York.

further supports our earlier interpretation that worry reflects a feeling that something can be done to change a situation. People try to cope with worries because they believe these things may be subject to change. In contrast, unhappiness is experienced as something that cannot be changed and probably must be endured.

The investigators provide additional data that indicate the variables of sex, age, and education are related to the handling of worries and unhappiness in different ways. In respect to age, the younger the person of either sex the more he attempts to cope with worries and unhappiness by seeking help from family and friends. However, women and older persons as groups tend more than any others to use prayer as a means of handling worries and unhappiness. Educational differences appear important in the handling of worries. The more educated the person the more likely he will take an active, coping approach to the things that worry him. There is no consistent relationship, however, between education and the handling of unhappiness.

Attitudes toward Self

We have already indicated that a significant aspect of mental health is based upon attitudes about the self. The investigators for the Joint Commission report some interesting information about self-attitudes and adjustment.

The persons studied were asked to describe how they felt they differed from other people and their responses were rated by the investigators in terms of how positive they seemed about the perception of self and their felt shortcomings. The results indicated that persons with a negative or ambivalent self-perception see their shortcomings most clearly in terms of personality factors. However, people with positive self-perceptions see their shortcomings more in terms of factors external to the self. Of the personality shortcomings, deficiencies in social and adjustment skills are the most frequently mentioned. Of the external sources of shortcomings, education is clearly the greatest felt deficiency. The more positive the self-perception, the more likely the individual does not mention any shortcomings at all.

Additional data indicates that men tend to emphasize external shortcomings more, especially educational. Women tend more to emphasize personality factors, especially adjustment skills. Older persons (55 years or more) have generally more positive self-perceptions than do younger persons.

This last finding may not be so much a result of age as it is a generation difference in educational level. Older persons have less education because education was not as common when they were younger. Younger people who tend to have higher educational levels also tend to have more negative self-perceptions. It is the educational variable that is more closely related to negative self-perception than it is the age variable. Why should this be so? We have already noted that lack of education is the most often expressed shortcoming. Why then should people of higher educational levels view themselves more negatively? The investigator's interpretation emphasizes that education, because it leads to greater self-awareness, results perhaps in more realistic self-criticism and as a consequence to a more negative self-perception than is true of people who are less aware. The investigators conclude that "groups more positively adjusted in terms of one component (self-awareness) are less adjusted in terms of the other component (self-evaluation)" (Gurin et al., 1960, p. 83).

This relationship between awareness and evaluation of self or other aspects of experience is repeated many times in the study. The greater the awareness and sensitivity of the individual, the greater are the expectations for the self and others, and the greater the possibilities for being satisfied or distressed. These characteristics of sensitivity and awareness are found most often in women as a group and highly educated persons of either sex. Such persons appear to have greater potentials for both satisfaction and dissatisfaction than do other persons.

Mental health cannot be judged simply in terms of a positive or negative self-perception. The relationship of self-perception to other characteristics of the individual must be considered. A positive self-perception may be reflecting only a lack of awareness and general insensitivity. A negative self-perception may be reflecting greater awareness and sensitivity.

Sources of Stress

What kinds of experiences push people to their individual breaking points? To get at this question the investigators for the Joint Commission asked the 2460 persons in their study, "have you ever felt you were going to have a nervous breakdown?" In reply, 464 persons or about 1 in 5 said "yes." Nervous breakdown means different things to different people but in this study it seemed to mean to most people any one of a variety of severe emotional or mental distrubances. The sources of this degree of felt stress in the individuals studied are reported in Table 10-3 in terms of the first-mentioned reason only.

External sources of stress represent the largest category reported in Table

Table 10-3. Sources of Stress (First-Mentioned Reasons Only)[a]

Reasons	Percentage
External	39
Death or illness of loved one; other separation	(16)
Work-related tension	(14)
Financial or other circumstances	(9)
Own physical illness or disability	18
Personality problems; general tensions	18
Interpersonal difficulties	16
Menopause	4
Not determined	5
Number of persons	464

[a]Adapted from *Americans View Their Mental Health* by Gerald Gurin, Joseph Veroff, and Sheila Feld, copyright 1960 by Basic Books, Inc., Publishers, New York.

10-3. However, if we examine these external sources we find that most of them are concerned with other people. In fact, if we combine just those categories which clearly indicate feelings about the self or other persons we find they represent 68 percent of the total responses.

What did these people do about the stress they experienced? The investigators report that about half of them (228 persons) sought help. The most common source of help used (88 percent) was the nonpsychiatric physician. The others who did not seek help (236 persons) indicated they did not think these sources of stress were relevant for professional help. This finding is really quite interesting because the sources of stress reported in Table 10-3 are of the kind psychologists, psychiatrists, and social workers believe to be most common in people and are prepared for and expect to treat.

It appears that the initial definitions people give to their experiences, relevant–not relevant, and psychological–not psychological, determine if they will seek help and what kind of help they will seek. Those who felt near a "nervous breakdown" and considered it relevant for help sought the aid of a physician for their "nervous" condition. This importance of definition or naming of one's experiences was seen earlier in terms of behavior related to the handling of "worries" and "unhappiness." Perhaps this failure to seek help for extreme felt distress was caused in part by the very disruptive experience of the stress condition. If so, we might expect people who have problems, although not as extremely felt as stress, to behave differently in handling them. The investigators provide information about such persons.

Personal Problems and Help-Seeking

In response to the question "have you had personal problems that could have used professional help?," 565 persons or about 1 in 4 said "yes." These people represent a group who have had some problems they would consider relevant for help. However, only 345 of these people actually sought help and 220 of them did not. What were the differences between those who did and those who did not seek help?

One possibility is that the kinds of problems they had were different. In Table 10-4 are reported the problem areas identified by these persons. The nature of the problems experienced does not seem to be particularly different for the two groups. Those who did not seek help report more marital problems and fewer problems with children but otherwise the groups do not appear to differ greatly. Something other than the nature of the problem is involved. Why then did some of these people not seek help?

The reasons reported by those who did not seek help are given as: desire to help self, lack of information, and feelings of shame. These are considered by mental health professionals to be the usual barriers to help-seeking. Many people believe that help-seeking is a sign of weakness in the self. However,

Table 10-4. Problem Areas Identified by Those Who Did and Did Not Seek Help[a]

Problem areas	Percentages	
	Did go for help	Did not go for help
Spouse; marriage	42	52
Child; relationship with child	12	4
Other family relationships—parents, in-laws	5	6
Other relationship problems—unspecified	4	4
Job or school problems; vocational choice	6	4
Non-job adjustment problems in self	18	14
Situational problems involving others (death or illness of a loved one)	6	6
Nonpsychological situational problems	8	6
Nothing specific; a lot of little things	2	3
Not determined	1	3
Number of persons	345	220

[a]Adapted from *Americans View Their Mental Health* by Gerald Gurin, Joseph Veroff, and Sheila Feld, copyright 1960 by Basic Books, Inc., Publishers, New York.

as noted in Chapter 9, mental health professionals see help-seeking as a sign of strength and a valuable resource in effective treatment. It is interesting that expense is a fairly minor consideration. When people think of going for help, even though they do not, cost appears to be one of the least of their concerns.

Additional data by the investigators reveal other characteristics of the non-help-seeker. The males in this group report less awareness of the need for help when they had a problem and relied more upon time to take care of the problem. Females more often reported lack of information about how to get help and greater feelings of shame about seeking help. Older persons preferred the self-help approach more than younger persons. The lower the educational level, the more likely the person was to give a "don't know" or an ill-defined reason for not seeking help.

Conclusions

The data reported here, as previously indicated, are a small portion of the larger study entitled *Americans View Their Mental Health*. What conclusions can we draw from these data to aid our understanding of mental health? The first seems to be that any definition of what is mental health must include a variety of variables. Mental health is happiness but it is also to some extent unhappiness and worry. The perception of the self is an important feature of mental health, but more than just its nature (positive or negative), the meaning of this self-percept to the individual must be considered. The degree of awareness of problems a person has and the methods of handling, or not handling, problems also contribute to mental health.

Another important conclusion is that younger, better educated persons have a greater awareness of themselves and events around them. As a result, such persons have a greater potential for both satisfaction and distress in the life experience. They are more likely to feel enough involvement in life to want to change their experiences. They believe they can change their experiences and they often use worry in a problem-solving way or actively seek help to do so.

Finally, personal definitions of experiences play an important part in how people handle their experiences. Unhappiness as an experience seems to be defined in a more defeating way and as a more permanent condition than do either worries or problems. The importance of these personal definitions are reflected in the data that sources of stress and problems are not very different, but the methods used to handle them are different. If an experience is initially defined as nonpsychological or nonrelevant for professional help, then help-seeking is not likely to occur.

The sources of problems, worries, and unhappiness reported in this investigation for the Joint Commission are not new or unusual from the viewpoint of psychology. We have already considered in Chapters 7, 8, and 9 many of these causes of distress, examined their origins, and noted resources for help-seekers. The report does, however, give us documented evidence of how common these sources of distress are in the presumably normal, stable, cross section of the population contacted in the study. The report should help to sharpen your own awareness of similar experiences in your lives and increase your effectiveness in handling these experiences in an adaptive manner.

RELIGION AND MENTAL HEALTH

The topic of religion seems especially appropriate in a discussion of mental health attitudes and behavior. The positive as well as the negative contributions of religion to behavior are reflected most clearly in the mental health of individuals. To say that religion may make a negative contribution to behavior is not to say that religion is bad, but rather to emphasize that its potential for a positive contribution is not always realized.

Some people think that science and religion are antagonistic and that psychology, the science of behavior, is particularly in conflict with religion. This idea seems to reflect a misunderstanding of the nature of science, of which psychology is only one, and the nature of religion. Some people would try to make a religion of psychology, interpreting everything from a psychological point of view. Others would try to make a science of religion reducing it to simple statements of absolute truth and generating laws and proofs of its reality. Still others would make science and religion completely separate. The view taken here is that religion is a vital part of the behavior of most persons and demands consideration if behavior is to be understood, but it does not lend itself easily to scientific study.

Religion and Science

Religion and science are not necessarily antagonistic and in conflict, but the basis of belief in each is quite different. Religion is based upon *faith*, a feeling and an attitude of belief in the absence of conclusive proof. People have many occasions in life to test their faith, but even at these times do not expect conclusive proof of their beliefs to be given. Situations that test faith demonstrate only that one does believe, they do not prove that these beliefs are true.

The outstanding quality of faith is the capacity to believe in spite of the lack of any proof. Religious teachings do employ factual accounts of events and persons to convey their message, but it is not the accounting of facts that conveys a religious meaning, it is faith. Those persons who would attempt to make a science of religion do so by trying to accumulate facts to substitute for faith. It should not be surprising that many religious leaders do not appreciate these efforts. The objective, unemotional, noninvolved, factual approach to religion is the exact opposite of what most religions want in their members. Faith, as the basis of belief, demands a subjective, emotional, totally involved person willing to commit himself without any guarantees of proof.

Science, including psychology, is based upon *evidence* that has been obtained in a systematic way and that can be verified, repeated, and understood in relation to other evidence similarly obtained. The usual way science obtains its evidence is the experimental method. In Chapter 1 we discussed some of the problems of the experimental method when it is used in psychology. Subject matter that does not lend itself to study by the experimental method is not accepted by science as a demonstrated fact. Many topics in psychology, for example, ESP experiences, cannot at the present time be demonstrated in a reliable, scientific manner. People who use psychology like a religion to interpret everything, ignoring the demands of science for demonstrated evidence, do themselves and psychology a disservice.

Do these differences in the basis of belief between religion and science mean that they should be separate? Informed persons from both religion and science think not. In 1956, religious and scientific leaders joined together to form the Academy of Religion and Mental Health to explore issues and questions and to share information of importance to both religion and science. Facts that are consistent with faith strengthen religious belief. Similarly, facts that are consistent with scientific principles strengthen science. Sometimes the same facts strengthen both religion and science. One such fact reported in the 1960 proceedings of the *Academy of Religion and Mental Health* is that religion does make a positive contribution in the lives of many persons. What is the contribution of religion to people's lives, and why is it helpful to some and not to others are appropriate questions of study for psychology.

Religion and the Individual

Religion, expressed through the social agency of the church, has provided for the physical needs of many who would be destitute without such assistance. Without the church such charitable work would probably be accomplished by other means, but the church has given leadership and inspiration to such efforts. The church has also been vigorous in promoting *literacy*, the ability to read and write. The reasons for church efforts to raise levels of literacy are related to the spreading of faith, but the results have extended beyond the religious aspects of life to create improved social and economic opportunities. Religious teachings have influenced moral and ethical codes of conduct and as a consequence have affected legislation and principles of justice.

Religion primarily affects the individual, however, in the development and maintenance of faith. Religious faith sustains many people in times of personal or social crisis. Carroll (1964) has emphasized the many positive contributions of religion to the development of emotional security including: (*a*) religious membership provides a sense of belonging and a feeling of worth in being; (*b*) religion offers a Supreme Being to depend upon when all others may fail or forsake the individual; (*c*) most religions provide, through faith, a promise of the eternal preservation of at least the spiritual aspect of self; (*d*) religion does provide answers to ultimate questions of cause and purpose such as "Who am I?" "What is my worth?" and "What is the meaning of life?" These features of religious involvement; acceptance, hope, and understanding cannot be easily dismissed in value to the personality for they are the themes expressed by many persons as the ingredients of a healthy, happy self. Carroll notes, however, that when religion attempts to base its case or make its appeal on fear and threat of punishment that these needs for emotional security are frustrated and many turn away from such religious teachings.

Blocher (1966) notes the contribution of religion to both the self-concept and the social aspect of personality. In relation to the self-concept, religion offers some "anchor points" as the individual seeks to establish his self-identity, his uniqueness and value apart from all others. At the same time, religion, through the organized church, provides a ready *reference group* for the individual providing him with role models to imitate in his own development as well as building constructive attitudes, values, and aspirations to live by.

These self and social values, however, are not always of a positive nature. McKinney (1958) indicates that the close identification of some young people with religious groups sets them apart from their age-mates by reason of strict religious practices, making their adjustment to other persons very difficult. McKinney also notes that strict adherence to some religious teachings develops attitudes of prejudice, intolerance, and inflexibility of thought just as other religious teachings develop habits of honesty, generosity, and cooperativeness.

If religious teaching is to be valuable it seems it should emphasize not only acceptance of self, but acceptance of others and their shortcomings and foster a desire to be of help rather than to judge.

Schneiders (1967) reports that religion is not a guarantee of mental health; ministers, priests, nuns, and rabbis have mental disorders as frequently as do persons in the general population. This finding may be related to the observations of others that when religion is used only as a means to control behavior, rather than as a means to express ideals, it can be more harmful than it is helpful. Schneiders also notes that religion can be the source of much guilt, shame, and self-rejection for failure to live up to ideals that are not realistic in terms of human capacities. In this same manner, persons who are, or try to be, religious and who also experience mental distress may feel added frustration and anguish because they suffer in spite of their religious beliefs.

The positive and negative contributions of religion to the individual seem well-summarized by Thorpe (1960). In terms of the positive values, religion fosters mental health when it provides: (a) aid to the individual in understanding and achieving moral goals appropriate to his stage of development; (b) counseling for better social relationships and the establishment of inner security and self-acceptance; (c) opportunities for participation and experience in a social environment; (d) strength in marriage and responsibility for family living; and (e) aid in developing maturity and sound ethical values for healthy living and growth (Thorpe, 1960, p. 511).

The negative contributions of religion to mental health occur when emphasis is given to: (a) in-group attitudes that exclude and criticize persons of differing beliefs; (b) threats of lost self-esteem and guilt for sin; (c) the life "hereafter" as a substitute for enjoyment in the present life; (d) the use of religion to escape reality and responsibility, such as denying a serious problem as "God's Will" and leaving all responsibility for change to a Supreme Being (Thorpe, 1960, p. 506).

Thorpe also reports that the most common conflicts relating to religion seen in various forms of mental illness include: concern over "unpardonable sins" (usually sins of the flesh), too strict adherence to dogmatic religious beliefs, confusions of self with the deity (delusions of being God), preoccupation with impending events such as the end of the world, and extreme forms of social withdrawal. It seems apparent from these accounts that religious attitudes have the potential to expand the self in terms of feelings and behavior toward the self and others, but also have the potential to narrow and restrict functioning.

Change in Religious Attitudes

From a psychological view, religious attitudes probably begin in childhood in the relationship of the child to the parents. The child sees the parents as all-powerful and the source of many good things (nourishment, affection) as well as bad (punishment, loss of affection). Later, when the child is exposed to formal religious instruction, these early attitudes toward the parents are generalized in thought to include an external all-powerful, ever-present Supreme Being.

There is evidence to indicate that the nature of religious attitudes change during the developmental periods of childhood, adolescence, and young adulthood. These changes are partly a consequence of the increasing mental maturity of the individual which causes him to seek reasons and explanations for many beliefs, not only religious, that have previously been accepted without question on the basis of parental authority. The changes in religious attitudes are also partly a consequence of the increasing experience of the individual with other persons and with new situations.

Growth in mental processes and experience increase the individual's awareness and sensitivity to differences, inconsistencies, and conflicts of his own beliefs relative to the beliefs of others. These challenges to his beliefs cause the individual to consider his beliefs more carefully, to test their worth, and to adjust them in accordance with whatever additional information he discovers through learning or other experiences. Some beliefs will be strengthened as a result of growth processes, some will probably be abandoned, and most will be tempered and become more flexible. We would expect changes in attitudes and beliefs of all kinds to occur more commonly to persons who continue in education during the developmental years. Two studies, one concerned with adolescents and the other with college students, offer us insight into the nature of change in religious attitudes as a result of increased physical and mental growth.

Kuhlen and Arnold (1944) report a study of 547 boys and girls in the age groups 12, 15, and 18 years. These age groups correspond approximately to the developmental periods of preadolescence, adolescence, and postadolescence. At the time of the study the youths were in grades 6, 9, and 12. The young people studied belonged to Catholic, Protestant, or Jewish faiths and a few indicated no church affiliation.

Comparison of the responses of the individuals in each age group to 52 statements of religious belief revealed some important age group differences. Many rather specific beliefs held by 12-year-olds are believed by fewer 15-

year-olds and fewer yet of the 18-year-olds. An example of some of these changes is given in Table 10-5. It is apparent from Table 10-5 that the very literal beliefs expressed in the statements are accepted less with increases in age level.

Another finding of this study was that the percentage drop with age of individuals who said they "believed" a statement was not necessarily followed by an increase in the percentage who said they "did not believe." For some statements, as age increased so did the tendency to indicate "wonder about" the statement rather than just "do not believe" it. An example of some of these changes is given in Table 10-6. The investigators interpret this finding to mean that changes of religious attitudes during adolescence show a trend to increased wondering or uncertainty not just a change to disbelief. This suggests that older adolescents are testing their beliefs and have not necessarily shaped a final conviction about them. The direction of change is away from specificity to a more general type of belief. The investigators report additional data that suggest the direction of change also includes greater tolerance for the beliefs of others with increases in age level.

Adolescence then is not necessarily a time of increased religious disbelief, but it does appear to be a time of increased wondering about religious beliefs. A final question of interest studied concerned the kinds of problems experienced

Table 10-5. Percentage of 12-, 15-, and 18-Year-Olds Who Believe
Specific Religious Statements[a]

Statement	Age groups, %		
	12	15	18
God is someone who watches you to see that you behave yourself, and who punishes you if you are not good	70	49	33
Hell is a place where you are punished for your sins on earth	70	49	35
People who go to church are better than people who do not go to church	46	26	15
Every word in the *Bible* is true	79	51	34
It is sinful to doubt the *Bible*	62	42	27

[a]Adapted from Kuhlen and Arnold (1944).

Table 10-6. Percentage of 12-, 15-, and 18-Year-Olds Who Believe, Disbelieve, or Wonder about Specific Religious Statements[a]

Statement	Believe, %			Disbelieve, %			Wonder, %		
	12	15	18	12	15	18	12	15	18
There is a heaven	82	78	74	4	5	5	13	16	20
Only good people go to heaven	72	45	33	15	27	32	13	27	34
Only our soul lives after death	72	63	61	9	11	6	18	25	31
Good people say prayers regularly	78	57	47	9	29	26	13	13	27
Every word in the Bible is true	79	51	34	6	16	23	15	31	43

[a]Adapted from Kuhlen and Arnold (1944).

with religion as a result of change in age. Again, the findings indicate that there are not necessarily more problems with religion with increased age, but the nature of problems experienced does change. In Table 10-7 the findings related to problems with religion in the different age groups are summarized.

Failure to attend church is given as a problem by the same proportion of each group and difficulty in getting help with religious problems shows the same pattern. These problems then do not appear to become greater or less with changes in age. The objection of parents to the young person's membership in a church appears to become less of a problem with age as does being teased about religious feelings. Four problems appear to become greater with increases in age and these represent for the older adolescent significant areas of conflict and concern. These problems include: conflict between science and religion, the nature of heaven and hell, disliking church services, and wondering what becomes of people when they die. If we consider these problem areas more closely it seems apparent that they represent fundamental questions that individuals attempting to shape a philosophy of life would be concerned about.

Kuhlen and Arnold suggest that one very practical application of the findings of their study would be the implications for religious education

Table 10-7. Percentage of 12-, 15-, and 18-Year-Olds Who Report
Problems of a Religious Nature[a]

Problem areas	Age groups, %		
	12	15	18
Failing to go to church	67	67	67
Getting help on religious problems	53	54	56
Parent's objection to church membership	23	14	11
Being teased about my religious feelings	26	22	18
Conflicts of science and religion	42	50	57
Heaven and hell	53	53	66
Disliking church service	33	47	60
Wondering what becomes of people when they die	67	56	80

[a]Adapted from Kuhlen and Arnold (1944).

procedures. For example, more attention might be given in discussion programs to the topics that youth appear to wonder about more as they get older. Similarly, some of the beliefs that appear to be discarded with increases in age might be reconsidered in terms of their presentation at earlier ages. These specific beliefs that do not appear to hold up well with increased maturity of mind and experience may be the cause of some individuals turning completely away from all religious beliefs as a result of disillusionment. A different presentation of these specific beliefs might strengthen their value in the later years. We would also add here that Kuhlen and Arnold's study has implications for the counseling programs of religious groups. Getting help with religious problems was a concern of over half the youths in each age group. Is this because religious counseling services are in short supply; is it perhaps that the needs of youth in this area are not recognized; or is it that youth do not know how to use the religious counseling services that are available?

Allport (1950) reports data about the religious attitudes of college men and women. His findings indicate that religion is very much a part of the values of college students, but also represents for them some important problem areas and conflicts. In association with others, Allport studied the responses of approximately 500 students at Harvard and Radcliffe to a questionnaire dealing with religious attitudes and beliefs. We can summarize the findings as follows.

About 7 out of 10 of the college students in the study think of themselves as religious or potentially so and believe that religion in some form is an essential part of their lives. The women students in the study were somewhat more inclined to positive religious attitudes than the men (82 percent to 68 percent). However, the important finding is the high degree of involvement in persons usually thought of as detached from religious interest. While the majority of the students did indicate a belief in *God*, only about one-fourth of them were willing to endorse the orthodox views of the Catholic or Protestant churches. This finding does indicate a more independent, less traditional type, of religious attitude in college students.

In terms of religious practices, the majority of the students attended church services only once a month or even less, but at the same time engaged often in prayer or experienced feelings of devotion and reverence in an individual manner. The evidence indicates a turning away from organized religious participation as well as a decreased level of belief in formal religious doctrine during the college years. While college students turn away from organized religion they maintain a personal religious attitude and engage in religious practices. Allport gives additional data that indicates that college students are dissatisfied with organized religious activities, rather than anything else, and certainly could not be said to be antireligious in attitude. The implications of this study for religious leaders raises the question of the procedures employed in organized religious services. It seems apparent that these practices are lacking in meaningfulness at least for some intelligent, well-educated persons.

One other finding of the Allport study is of interest. In response to a question concerning the conflict of science and religion 53 percent of the students felt there was no problem and another 17 percent felt there was a conflict but it could be resolved. This finding, in contrast to the Kuhlen and Arnold data (see Table 10-7) suggests that increased maturity and educational level place this issue in better perspective.

Religion and Adjustment

How religion affects adjustment is a rather complex question to study. The difficulty encountered concerns how to evaluate the intensity and depth of the religious sentiment and then relate this to some fairly direct adjustment measures. One approach to the subject is reported in the study of *Americans View Their Mental Health* (Gurin et al., 1960) previously described. The investigators used frequency of church attendance as their measure of religious involvement. Church attendance, while not proof of religious conviction, is certainly related to it and has the advantage of being relatively easy to measure. The investigators compared approximately 1600 adults of Protestant faiths and 500 adults of the Catholic faith in terms of the frequency of their church attendance and several adjustment measures.

Low church attendance (a few times a month or less), especially for professed Catholics, is associated with somewhat greater reported unhappiness, tendency to worry, and more negative self-perceptions. The investigators call this finding greater "felt distress" but are not sure if it is a result of the low church attendance or the cause of it (Gurin et al., 1960, p. 240). High church attendance (once a week or more) is associated with greater reported happiness and fewer worries especially for Protestant church members.

The relationship of church attendance to marital satisfaction is stronger than it is to general adjustment measures of happiness or extent of worries. The greater the church attendance for both Protestant and Catholic members, the greater the reported happiness in marriage. The lowest marital happiness scores are given by Protestants who never attend church and Catholics who attend only a few times a year. Among Catholics, high church attendance is also associated with fewer feelings of inadequacy in the marriage relationship, but there appears to be no similar association of these variables for Protestants.

In terms of the parental role, Catholics generally feel more adequate as parents than do Protestants and this finding increases with increased church attendance. Interestingly, it is Protestants who attend church most frequently who report the greatest feelings of inadequacy as parents. This finding probably reflects fundamental doctrinal differences in Protestant and Catholic faiths. It may be that Catholicism is more specific about the parental role and functions making it easier for its members to meet these role expectations and feel adequate. Protestants, perhaps, must interpret the parental role on a more individual basis and feel less certain and inadequate about their performance. The number and kinds of problems with children is not related to church attendance or membership.

In terms of the occupational role functioning, men who attend church most frequently report greater job satisfaction. Protestant men report generally greater job satisfaction than do Catholic men, but the highest job satisfaction is reported by Catholic men who attend church most frequently. In terms of job-related problems, Protestant men report more problems than do Catholics. This may reflect the greater emphasis of the Protestant faith upon the work role and consequently a greater involvement in the job by the Protestant men (Gurin et al., 1960, pp. 244–245).

These findings do give rather concrete evidence that religious involvement, measured only by frequency of church attendance, does make some positive contributions to adjustment. The relationships between church attendance and experiences in the marital, parental, and occupational roles are greater than the relationships to general measures of happiness. The differences between persons who attend church and persons who do not are greater than the differences between persons of different religious faith. There seems to be no question that persons who have religious convictions of some kind, and act upon them in terms of church attendance, do find strength and satisfaction in important areas of personal and social functioning.

SUMMARY

Mental health includes much more than the mere freedom from mental illness: it includes development of human potential. We are not only responsible for our own mental health but we have some obligation to our fellow men upon whom we are dependent.

Mental health depends upon satisfaction of basic physical and emotional needs, usually provided by the family or home. Mental health responsibility of the schools includes providing equal opportunities for children to develop their potentials, offering peer group activities that aid a child's growth, helping children to establish a realistic level of aspiration, and early recognition of emotional problems. There are some responsibilities that can only be assumed by the community to assure a mentally healthy environment.

The characteristics of good mental health include feeling comfortable about yourself, feeling good about other people, and feeling able to meet the demands of life. Self-acceptance depends on awareness of motives and understanding what you are and why, and is crucial to good mental health. Self-fulfillment comes from the feeling of progress toward goals that are realistic.

What is normal is based on a study of the mental health of a representative sample of the "normal and stable" population in this country. Most people report that they have some degree of happiness but they worry. Worry and unhappiness are not the same and are handled differently by people of different ages, sexes, and educational levels.

About 20 percent of the normal group indicated that at some time they had felt that they might be facing a nervous breakdown. About 25 percent admitted having had personal problems that could have used professional help but only about 60 percent of those who admitted a need for help actually sought help.

Religion has the potential to help or to hinder the development of good mental health. Religion differs from science in its dependence on faith rather than evidence. Religious teachings have an important influence on human behavior and religious faith often makes a positive contribution to emotional security, the self-concept, and social values. Attitudes toward religion change with age in the direction of greater tolerance, generality, and doubt during adolescence as the individual struggles to develop his own philosophy of life. Religious involvement in later life tends to be associated with good adjustment. The differences between church attenders and nonattenders was found to be greater than the differences between members of different faiths.

SUGGESTIONS FOR FURTHER READING

Berger, Peter L., *The Sacred Canopy: Elements of a Sociological Theory of Religion*, New York, Doubleday, 1967. An organization of scattered observations concerning religion in man's life into a modern theoretical framework.

Mowrer, O. Hobart (Ed.), *Morality and Mental Health*, Chicago, Rand McNally, 1967. A collection of 75 articles by professionals in several different fields who explore mental health and illness in terms of personal morality and individual values.

Soddy, Kenneth and Ahrenfeldt, Robert, *Mental Health and Contemporary Thought*, Philadelphia, Lippincott, 1967. Considers the mental health aspects of such contemporary social problems as urbanization and population explosion.

Sutherland, R. I. and Smith, B. K. (Eds.), *Understanding Mental Health*, Princeton, N. J., Van Nostrand, 1965. A collection of original essays by professionals and laymen on some significant recent developments in mental health.

Torrance, E. P. and Strom, R. D. (Eds.), *Mental Health and Achievement*, New York, Wiley, 1965. A collection of papers by leaders of new and exciting programs for improving the influences of home, school, and community on mental health.

The Individual and His Groups

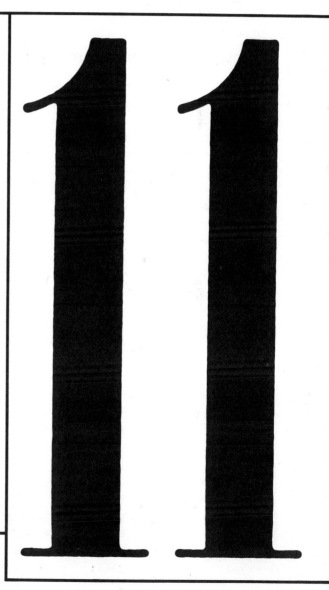

Individual behavior cannot be fully understood or explained without reference to the groups to which an individual belongs. Most human behavior involves interaction between two or more persons, and most of the relationships we have with others are formed as members of groups. Some group memberships are temporary and others endure throughout life. In this chapter, we will examine some of the groups common to our experience, the process of groups, and how they influence human behavior.

HOW WE ATTAIN GROUP MEMBERSHIP

Individuals become members of groups in at least five different ways: by birth, by force, by invitation, by mutual consent, and by choice.

Birth automatically provides the human newborn with membership in several groups. He is born into a certain family group which has membership in some social and economic class. His family will also belong to a racial or religious group whose membership is extended to include the child. Many people resent their membership in groups they were born into and they may rebel against the family, the group, and the larger society.

The sex group to which we belong is already determined at birth and without our consent. Some people have difficulty in accepting their sex roles, and a few have even gone so far as to try to change their sex. The problems involved in learning sex-appropriate behavior are discussed in greater detail in Chapter 7.

Groups we join by *force* are usually age groups. From the age of 6 until about 16 we are required by law to attend school. As we advance in age society forces us out of the child group and into the adult group. The period of transition between childhood and adulthood is full of conflict and confusion because the adolescent is neither child nor adult but his behavior often resembles both. In our society most young men during late adolescence are forced to join a group of military recruits and become members of the armed forces. Some, of course, join by choice, but even those who do not choose military service are forced to participate in this group. After serving on military duty, men return to civilian life as members of still another group—veterans. There are advantages to being a veteran and there are many organized groups whose membership is limited to those who are veterans. Sometimes undesirable group memberships are forced upon people as a result of unfortunate circumstances and events. For example, the unemployed, the blind, the crippled, the disabled, and the institutionalized are groups whose memberships are largely involuntary.

Groups whose members are acquired by *invitation* usually offer some status or prestige. They must have some social or cultural value that makes membership desirable. Exclusive social clubs, such as fraternities, sororities, country clubs, and lodges restrict their membership to people with certain specified qualifications who are personally acceptable to the group. To many people, expecially children and adolescents, the invitation to join is more important than actually joining the exclusive social club. Youngsters who are not invited to join social clubs feel left out and rejected by their peers. The child's identity and his concept of himself and his worth may be more seriously damaged by lack of invitations to join clubs than by the actual lack of membership. Members of minority groups are often the targets of discrimination by these closed groups. We will discuss these problems later in this chapter in connection with prejudice and stereotypes.

Most organized groups obtain members by *mutual consent*. That is, they are open to anyone who wants to join and is willing to accept the purposes and goals of the group. They are usually seeking members who will take an active part in the activities of the group and who share some interests in common with the other members. Not everyone places the same value on group memberships, but for all of us they are an important part of our identity. If you describe yourself or anyone you know, you may be surprised to find how many group memberships you will use to identify the individual.

As soon as we are able to make decisions for ourselves we begin to acquire group memberships by *choice*. Children are usually anxious to join groups of their peers in the neighborhood and at school. Adults join many groups by simply choosing to belong. We join the ranks of a particular group of workers in a vocation, business, or profession according to our needs and desires. We join a community simply by moving into the area. Some of our group memberships overlap and some conflict with each other. The extent to which individuals participate in the groups to which they belong depends upon many factors, some of which will be discussed in this chapter.

CHARACTERISTICS OF GROUPS

Groups can be classified into two broad categories as unstructured and structured. *Unstructured* groups include age groups, sex groups, nationality groups, social classes, political parties, and occupations. Unstructured groups are really descriptive categories of people on the basis of some characteristics they have in common. Relationships between members of unstructured groups are indirect, impersonal, or abstract. We may share the attitudes, ideals, and values of a large unstructured group but we do not meet with our fellow members face-to-face as we do in our smaller, structured groups or organizations. It is these smaller, more personal, structured groups with which we are concerned here.

Formal Structure

Most human organizations have a rather definite structure and are relatively permanent even though the members come and go. Groups are usually organized around some purpose and with some fairly well-defined goals. The goals may change from time to time as the membership changes, but if the group no longer serves a purpose, it will usually become disorganized and eventually cease to exist as a group.

Members of a group are expected to share the objectives of the group and to behave in a way that is fitting and appropriate to the group. These group expectations are enforced by various rewards and punishments, such as being elected to office or being excluded from the group. People conform to the *group norms* or expected behavior in the group because of their needs for group approval and acceptance. They may also conform because they feel that the majority opinions and decisions are likely to be more correct and more valuable than their own. People who cannot or will not conform to group pressures usually withdraw from the group.

Formal organizations usually have elected officers whose duties are defined in a set of bylaws agreed upon by the members when the group is organized. These may be in the form of a written constitution, as in lodges and other dues-paying organizations, or they may be an unwritten code of behavior verbally passed on to new members, as in a bridge club or neighborhood gang. Rights and duties of the members are usually specified by the group when it is organized and accepted by members from then on. Meetings of a group usually follow parliamentary procedure or substitute some ritual of their own which has meaning for the group's members.

Power Structure

The location of power and the direction of influence between members and leaders are important characteristics of groups. The formal structure of a group may be very different from its psychological structure. In some groups a small minority of the members may have more power and influence on the group than its elected leaders or the majority of members. For example, a parent–teacher association in a rural school is frequently dominated by a small group of parents who enjoy high status because of superior educational and occupational achievements. These few parents, may speak out freely to influence the other less well-educated parents, who are content to follow rather than lead, even though the more influential ones may decline nominations to hold office in the organization.

Power to make decisions and conduct the business of large formal organizations is often delegated to the officers and a board of directors elected by the membership to act in their behalf. In these groups the members who do the work of the organization function in small subgroups or committees.

When the bulk of power and authority for a group is concentrated in the leader or leaders the power structure of the group is called *authoritarian.* Some groups function best with authoritarian power structures because the members do not want to assume responsibility for solving problems and making decisions. They are content to accept the authority of leaders and delegate responsibility to them.

Groups in which the power, authority, and responsibility are divided among members of the group have what is called a *democratic* power structure. In democratic groups the leader does not dominate the group, but merely encourages communication and freedom of participation for all members. Individual differences in personality make it easier for some people to participate in democratic groups while others are better suited for participation in authoritarian groups.

Interdependence of Members

Another basic characteristic of a group is the interdependence of its members. Different members of a group assume different functions and roles, all of which are necessary for the successful functioning of the group. People assume different roles in a group because of their age, sex, social or economic status, special talent, or general organizational ability. They may also adopt different roles because of personality characteristics. Some people like to be leaders, others prefer to be followers, some want active participation, and others merely want to identify with the group but remain relatively inactive.

Group members have been classified on the basis of their behavior in groups as: task-oriented, interaction-oriented, and self-oriented (Bass and Dunteman, 1963). *Task-oriented* individuals are those who get satisfaction from completing assigned tasks and accomplishing their goals. These people have little or no interest in socializing, but they see the group as a means of getting some work done. *Interaction-oriented* individuals gain satisfaction from being with others and talking things over together. They would prefer working with a group to working alone. *Self-oriented* people prefer to work alone and are more concerned with the satisfaction of their own needs than the needs of the group or the demands of the task at hand. Some of the ways in which people in each of these categories describe themselves are shown in Table 11-1.

The research on group behavior carried out by Bass and Dunteman (1963) indicates that the performance of a group is determined, at least in part, by the personality and orientation of the group members. A group that is dominated by self-oriented or interaction-oriented members will usually have difficulty in getting things accomplished or moving toward the group goals. A group that is dominated by task-oriented members may face internal conflict and lose the support of other members, or it may even be blocked by their resistance and refusal to cooperate unless their own needs are met. If groups are to serve their purposes and achieve their goals, they must find some ways to function that will encourage cooperation from all the different individuals who make up their memberships.

HOW GROUPS OPERATE

The study of methods by which groups are able to become more effective through the development of each member's potential is called *group dynamics.* Psychologists who specialize in group dynamics are attempting to find newer and better ways for groups to operate so that each member will be able to contribute to the best of his ability. We have to *learn* how to interact in groups without sacrificing our individuality if we are to receive the maximum benefit from organized group activity. What are some of the principles of group dynamics that we may apply to improve the effectiveness of our group activities?

Atmosphere or Emotional Climate

Most of us have had the experience at one time or another of walking into a group gathering where the psychological or emotional climate of the group was warm, friendly, accepting, and we were immediately made to feel welcome and glad to be there. We have also experienced the discomfort of walking into

Table 11-1. Self-Description of Task-Oriented, Interaction-Oriented, and Self-Oriented Group Members[a]

Variable	Task-oriented	Interaction-oriented	Self-oriented
Behavior and mood tendencies	Calm and controlled	Dependent on others	Tense and excitable
Feelings toward self	Self-sufficient Resourceful Independent	Confident Dependent	Insecure Fears Failure
Feelings toward others	Aggressive Not sociable	Sociable Tends toward emotional warmth	Jealous of others Tends to be suspicious Competitive
Unmet needs	Endurance Achievement	Affiliation Help from others (dependence)	Aggression Autonomy

[a]Adapted from Bass and Dunteman (1963).

a group in which the air seemed filled with anger, hostility, and resentment, and we wish we had not arrived. We have seen other groups in which the group atmosphere was characterized by indecision, apathy, and lack of enthusiasm. Behavior of the individual members in a group usually reflects their interpretation of the atmosphere or emotional climate of the group. How does the atmosphere of a group get to be good or bad, and what can be done to improve it? The two related factors that determine group atmosphere are *morale and group cohesiveness.*

When the *morale* of a group is high, it means that the members are optimistically working together toward group goals which they have accepted, and they are convinced that their combined efforts will produce worthwhile results. When morale is low, members are reluctant to participate, they lack enthusiasm, are easily discouraged, and are not willing to put forth the effort to work together. A group with poor morale is easily disorganized.

Group cohesiveness refers to the mutual attraction the members of a group have for each other and the extent to which they feel identified with the group and have confidence in the group. Groups with a high level of cohesiveness are usually task-oriented and tend to generate good morale, but this is not always true. Groups which are exclusive, in the sense that membership is difficult to obtain, usually have a higher level of cohesiveness than open groups whose members are not selected. However, the open groups may have very high morale if the members find satisfaction as a result of their combined efforts. High morale usually results in greater cohesiveness of the group, and together they produce a favorable atmosphere or climate within the group.

Several factors have been found to be significantly related to creating a favorable group atmosphere, including such simple things as arranging the physical environment for the comfort of group members. For example, when group members are seated around a table or around the room so that they can all see each other, they are more likely to participate in group discussion than when they are seated in rows facing the group leader. Size of the group is also important in creating an atmosphere conducive to maximum participation. If a group is too large, division into subgroups will usually increase the group's effectiveness. When groups are meeting for the first few times and when new members are brought into a group, the use of name tags often helps put people at ease. New members of a group are usually at least uncomfortable, if not actually threatened, by the experience of being introduced to so many people in a short time that they are unable to remember anyone's name.

Leadership

Groups cannot function effectively without leaders. Even a small leaderless group will find that before one meeting has ended someone will emerge from the group to assume the leadership role. Many groups do function very effectively without formal leaders, but in those groups the various functions of leadership are shared by the individual members of the group. Such a pattern of *distributed leadership*, especially useful in small groups, tends to give each member more confidence in himself and in his fellow members. Task-oriented groups tend to accomplish more when there are not too many changes in leadership; however, some groups achieve their goals very well by having the leadership change from one person to another as the task at hand or the situation changes.

The leader's function in a group is important. Whether he is a formal leader or an informal one who emerges from the group, it is his responsibility to encourage and direct communication within the group, and to insure participation by all. The leader also serves as a representative of the group in its contacts outside the group. The leader, more than any other single member, exerts influence on the group atmosphere. The democratic approach and the leader's attitude which favors sharing power and authority are essential to the kind of group atmosphere in which members are free to communicate. The role of the leader will, of course, vary with the kind of activity in which the group is engaged (Figure 11-1).

Goal Formulation

Organized groups must have some purpose for existing, that is, some reason why people meet together as a group. We get together with other people to accomplish some purpose that we feel cannot be accomplished as well or as easily alone, on the assumption that "two heads are better than one." Individuals who join a group are generally aware of and in agreement with the purpose of the group, which is usually stated or implied in rather general terms.

Some of the purposes for which groups are organized include education, socialization, recreation, economic security, community improvement, social change, and to promote or influence ideals, attitudes, and beliefs. To accomplish the purpose of the group, or to make progress in that direction, the group members must accept some mutually agreeable goals. The extent to which all

Figure 11-1.   Student protest groups such as this one may be organized to serve a general purpose or to accomplish a specific goal. What determines the effectiveness of this group? (Photo by Tom Lynch.)

members accept the group goals as worthy of their best efforts will determine, in a large part, how effective the group will be in accomplishing its goal.

When a group is formulating its goals, the members should bear in mind that the success or failure of the group effort will be determined in part by how realistic and attainable its goals are. If the goals are so high that they are unrealistic, the group is doomed to failure just as an individual is when he sets his level of aspiration too far beyond his reach. Many groups find they are most effective when they formulate a number of short-term goals and some long-range goals. When this is done the members are able to see the results of their efforts as they go along and they are encouraged by the successes.

Once the group goals are formulated there must be some consensus or meeting of the minds as to how the goals can be reached. The members must agree on some activities or methods by which to approach their goals. Although democratic action is based on conforming to the majority rule, small groups are much more effective if they avoid bringing issues to a vote, but instead, continue the discussion until a compromise is reached with which all the members are in agreement.

Group Processes in Action

The following example of effective group organization will serve to illustrate the principles of group dynamics we have been discussing. Among the problems that came to the attention of the Mental Health Association in a rapidly growing community was the lack of any nursery school or day-care center that could handle mentally ill children. These children between the ages of 3 and 7 were not eligible for or acceptable by an organized group in the community serving the needs of children in this age group. The Director of the Mental Health Association was able to obtain the temporary use of a residence that had been purchased by the county in anticipation of a freeway. The Association found among its members a qualified person who was willing to undertake the operation of a day-care center on a trial basis. A local service club of business and professional women agreed to provide operating funds for the first year, and three other women's clubs offered to provide volunteer help to take care of the children. The County Health Department was willing to provide professional consultation on a temporary basis, and therapists in the community were eager to refer mentally ill children. Thus, the project began on a limited basis, and within a short time the Children's Center became an established and valued service in the community.

The four women's clubs continued to volunteer time and money but the Mental Health Association was unable to continue sponsoring the Center after it had become established. Some organization was necessary if the Center was to continue beyond being a demonstration project. The Mental Health Association appealed to the Junior Chamber of Commerce for help.

The J.C.'s responded by calling together a group of people consisting of the president and the service chairman of each of the four women's clubs, three members of the Mental Health Association's Board of Directors, the Director of the Center, and four members of their own group who indicated an interest in the project. The situation was structured so that a favorable atmosphere developed at the first meeting of the group. One member of the J.C.'s assumed temporary leadership and the other J.C.'s assisted as hosts since the meeting was held in their offices. Each new arrival was greeted at the door, welcomed, and introduced to every other person present. When all 15 of the invited individuals had arrived and were comfortably seated around a conference table, the leader asked each one to identify himself (or herself) and to acquaint the group with his interests and activities related to the Children's Center. The discussion which followed brought out the fact that many people within the community were willing and able to work on fund-raising projects and soliciting contributions for the Children's Center, but their combined donations were not sufficient for continued operation of the Center. Everyone agreed that by working together this group could accomplish more than had been done to the present time. The first meeting ended with a decision to organize the group as a private nonprofit corporation as a means of assuring financial support for the Children's Center. The group decided to meet once a month with the next meeting scheduled for formal organization.

The group elected officers, adopted a set of bylaws and became legally incorporated as the Foundation to Aid Mentally Ill Children within 3 months. The purpose of the organization as stated in the bylaws was "to develop various self-sustaining, fund-raising drives and collect moneys for the benefit of the Zonta Children's Center."

The group set as its immediate goal raising enough money to operate the Center for the current year on its present budget. They set the long-range goal of establishing a building fund and accumulating enough money to build a permanent center within 3 to 5 years. To accomplish these goals the members met regularly, discussed numerous fund-raising ideas, and agreed upon three major fund-raising events for the first year. The first project the group sponsored, a premiere theater party, was a great success, with the organization realizing a net gain of over 2000 dollars. The group decided to continue this project as an annual event. The next event, a preview of new cars combined with a fashion show and dance, was not so successful and was not repeated. The third project was another success and so the group continued. By having a common purpose, working together to set and achieve both short-term and long-term goals, interested citizens were able to accomplish as a group a necessary service to the community.

Process Awareness and Evaluation

When individuals begin working together as a group they get to know each other and they become sensitive to each other's feelings. They learn to recognize how individual needs influence the group and they become aware of the process of interaction that is taking place within the group. An effective group must not only develop awareness but it must develop the ability to evaluate its activities and goals honestly and objectively. A group must learn from its failures as well as its successes. For example, in the case of the Foundation to Aid Mentally Ill Children, the group had to ask itself and find answers to many questions related to the failure of its second fund-raising event. Did the members fail to work hard enough selling tickets? Was the event poorly advertised? Was the timing bad? Did it conflict with some more popular event in the community? Was the location a poor choice? Was this an activity that is generally unpopular in this community? Under what conditions might it have been a success? Should it be tried again?

Communication

The essence of group problem-solving is communication. The best way for people to learn how to work together cooperatively is by talking to each other. We make ourselves understood not only by talking but also by listening. When we express an idea or opinion or ask a question we want a response or some *feedback* to let us know that our message has been received. In group activity adequate feedback is especially important. When we put our best efforts into some cooperative activity we need to know the results in order to correct errors and improve effectiveness. We need to know that what we are doing ties in with what other members of the group are doing and that we are not working at cross purposes with them. When communication breaks down group members tend to feel isolated or rejected and the group's morale suffers.

Most organized groups do not allow free-for-all discussion between members when the group is meeting. The leader governs who may talk and when, and frequently group communication is regulated by some prescribed set of rules. Many organized groups, both large and small, elect to be governed by *Robert's Rules of Order* which is based on parliamentary law and the practice of Congress. Thus channels of communication within groups are usually regulated in certain specified ways. The pattern of open and closed communication channels within a group is called its *communication pattern*. The extent to which the communication pattern is free or limited and the nature of the pattern are very influential in determining the morale and effectiveness of a group. Some of the most common communication patterns are illustrated in Figure 11-2.

In the traditional classroom situation a discussion is conducted by the teacher who is the recognized group leader. The leader is free to communicate with any of the students who may in turn communicate with him. The students are not free to communicate with each other except through the leader. This communication pattern is called the *wheel or star pattern*, and it is used by many formally structured groups.

In military organizations communication is conducted through a chain of command. In the *chain pattern* each individual may communicate with his immediate superior who may, in turn, communicate with his immediate superior, but no one may communicate with a person higher up the chain. All official communications must be handled through the official channels.

In each diagram communication is
limited to those channels indicated by
arrows

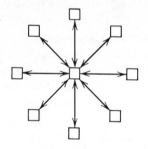

A. Wheel or Star Pattern

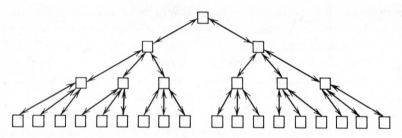

B. Chain of Command

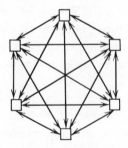

C. Open Pattern

Figure 11-2. Communication patterns in groups.

Many businesses are organized on the chain pattern with authoritarian leadership.

Small groups where everyone is free to communicate with everyone else have an *open pattern*. Studies have found that an open pattern of communication results in increased group cohesiveness and better morale than with any other pattern. The open pattern is not practical in a group larger than about 15 unless it can be divided into subgroups. Problem-solving groups are more effective when all channels of communication are open and flexible. In a democratic group with distributed leadership most of the problem-solving is accomplished by means of task-oriented subgroups or committees with open patterns of communication. Business and industry are finding this a useful technique in solving labor–management problems.

Communication within groups and between individuals does not always mean spoken or written communication. There is some truth in the old adage "actions speak louder than words." *Nonverbal communication* is often more effective than language in getting a message across in a group. Attitudes and especially prejudices are most frequently communicated on a nonverbal level. When we participate in group activities we should try to recognize the nonverbal communication that is taking place so that we can control our own responses to it. The ability to look beyond what people are saying and respond to the feelings and attitudes they are trying to communicate is called *empathy*. Empathy is very important in social group situations. We need to learn how to put ourselves in another person's place, or to know how he really feels in order to communicate with him more effectively. Acceptance and rejection, approval and disapproval, encouragement and discouragement are often communicated by nonverbal means rather than with words.

HOW GROUPS SERVE THE INDIVIDUAL

Groups can serve several functions for the individual which help to make life more interesting and more satisfying. There are many things we can do in groups that would be difficult, if not impossible, to do as single individuals. Many of our personal needs are met by the groups with which we identify ourselves. Let us consider some of the ways in which groups serve the individual.

Problem-Solving

Some problems which are common to a number of people may be solved more easily when we pool our efforts than when we try to solve them alone. In solving a complex problem an individual would have to work out each aspect of it by himself one at a time, but in a group different people can work on different parts of the problem at the same time, arriving at the solution sooner. In group problem-solving, errors made by one person will be seen and corrected by another, making for greater efficiency than when one person works alone. When creative thinking is called for in problem-solving, the ideas produced by a group of people will be more productive than the ideas of a single individual. By observation and participation in group problem-solving processes, we learn to improve our own problem-solving ability and our ability to discuss and debate issues (Figure 11-3).

Socialization

Participation in groups offers the opportunity to meet new people and make new friends. Through their associations in groups children become socialized and learn what is expected of them by the society in which they live. To know what is expected and what one must do to be accepted helps a child feel self-confident and secure. The process of socialization through group participation helps us establish our identity as we become closely associated with the purposes and goals of the groups to which we belong. Successful group functioning enables us to gain appreciation for individual differences and cooperation with our fellow man. It helps us gain a larger perspective on the problems of humanity and sharpens our awareness of our interdependence on one another. In groups we are able to actualize our potential contribution to social progress.

Need Satisfaction

The enthusiasm and willingness with which an individual participates in any group is directly related to how well the group satisfies the needs of that individual. Emotional needs most frequently met by group membership are recognition, acceptance, support, status, and prestige. We need to know that other people feel the same way we do about issues and that our opinions and attitudes are recognized, accepted, and valued by our fellow group members.

Groups are often helpful in meeting our needs for creative expression and achievement. We may be unable to do anything very outstanding by ourselves but we are proud to claim membership in a group whose accomplishments are known and recognized as outstanding. Although we may not have the talent for individual creative expression, participation with others to produce a creative product gives us a feeling of satisfaction and fulfillment.

Figure 11-3. Men of all ages find satisfaction in working together on a project to raise money for a community youth center. (Photo by Jim Sargent.)

To assist understanding and effective use of the principles of group structures and processes discussed in this section they are presented in summary form in Table 11-2.

PROBLEMS IN GROUP LIVING

Recognizing that we cannot exist as individuals in isolation, we must, as humans, acknowledge our interdependence on one another and learn to live together as members of many overlapping and conflicting groups.

The primary unit of social organization is the family, which assumes respon-

Table 11-2. A Frame of Reference for the Study of Groups

Classification	Characteristics	Functions
1. Unstructured	Descriptive Categorized Stereotyped	Convey cultural heritage Influence attitudes Uphold ideals and values
2. Structured	Purposive Goal-directed	Set behavioral standards Assure social progress
A. Informal	Loosely organized Flexible, open	
B. Formal	Controlled structures Interdependence of members	
1. Leadership		Influence group atmosphere Direct communication Insure participation
a. Authoritarian b. Democratic c. Distributive		
2. Membership		Problem-solving Socialization Need satisfaction
a. Task-oriented b. Interaction-oriented c. Self-oriented		

sibility for the care and protection of its members. However, families are not able to meet all the needs of their members without the help and cooperation of others outside the family group. For this reason, families establish themselves in larger groups or units with shared responsibility for meeting the needs of the larger group. Social group living enables us to solve our common problems more effectively and systematically. While social living brings us many benefits it also creates some problems because the needs of everyone are not the same. Some of the major social problems for which we must continually seek better solutions have been identified in the areas of community organization, law enforcement, prejudice, and stereotypes.

Community Organization

Communities are organized to serve the interests and needs of all people living in a specified area. As members of a community, we are expected to assume a share of the responsibility for support and direction of community activities, and we expect to share in the benefits provided by such organization. What are the benefits and responsibilities of the community?

Needs of the individual for which a family can expect help from the community include health, education, and welfare or general well-being. The community provides public health services for the protection of the population. Sanitation, for example, is necessary to prevent the spread of disease and assure a healthy environment in which to live. Control of communicable diseases and the prevention of epidemics, as well as regulation of occupational health and safety measures in industries are usually handled by public health services. Hospitals and clinics are important facilities in any community.

Public education is commonly accepted as a community responsibility. Most communities provide education through high school and some vocational and technological training beyond high school. There is a growing trend in our country toward the establishment of community colleges. The community college offers two years of college work at a lower cost to the student and special classes for adult educational needs. In addition these colleges often provide public recreation and cultural enrichment for the whole community. Communities also encourage the establishment of private schools and colleges to meet the need for specialists in various fields.

The general well-being of all members of the population is a community responsibility. The protection of individuals and their property are duties delegated to police and fire services. The assurance of legal rights are met by systems of law and court procedures. Public transportation, the maintenance of streets, and traffic supervision are necessary services as a community grows in population. The regulation of trade and commerce must be assumed by the community to assure that the needs of people are met and that standards of fairness, health, and safety are supplied by tradesmen. Communities actively promote and encourage the establishment of new businesses and industries to provide employment opportunities for community members.

When the needs of the community for employment are not met or when some group members cannot provide for themselves, some form of public financial assistance is necessary. The term "welfare" has become a negative word in our society because many associate it with a handout or giveaway. Originally, welfare was meant to imply that meeting the needs of all group members for food, shelter, and clothing was in the common interest of everyone. A community is strong to the extent that all its members are provided for and can participate in common causes. Therefore the idea of welfare is not undesirable, but the ways in which it is managed can be very defeating to its purposes.

Communities also provide opportunities for recreation, social, and cultural activities. Parks, art galleries, music and dramatic centers, museums, special displays and exhibits in public buildings add interest, pleasure, and beauty to the lives of community members. If the only recreational, social, and cultural experiences available to us were the ones we could buy, most of us would live a dreary life. The works of great artists, musicians, and collections of historical and cultural significance for all the subcultures within a community can be enjoyed by everyone because of community action (Figure 11-4).

As citizens of a community we must prepare to assume our share of its responsibility. Adults are expected to pay taxes in order to finance community services, and we are expected to elect representatives to govern us and manage our finances. The most important responsibility of mature citizenship is to elect representatives and officials with whom we feel we can communicate. We do this through participation in groups of people who organize for purposes of political action and social improvement. When conditions in a community are in need of improvement the best way to get something done about it is often through pressure groups that draw public attention to the matter and involve large numbers of people in public action and communication with their elected representatives. The solution of community problems requires public awareness and organized group action.

Figure 11-4. Participation in group meetings can be the most effective means of solving community problems. (Photo by Dave Bellak, San Jose State College.)

Law Enforcement

Problems of illegal behavior have always been with us. In any organized community there are always some people who refuse to abide by the law and whose behavior constitutes a menace to society or a threat to the person and property of others. Crime and delinquency pose problems, not only for law enforcement agencies, but for all members of an organized society.

Psychologists and other social scientists are interested in finding ways to help prevent crime and delinquency. Numerous studies have been done to try to identify the factors that are associated with and contribute to a high rate of delinquency. For many years people believed that delinquency was the natural result of poor environmental conditions, overpopulated areas, slum housing, broken homes, and lower socioeconomic class membership, and that until these conditions were improved there could be no hope of change. Recent studies have brought to light some new information which suggests that this attitude represents an oversimplification and failure to recognize the real source of the problems.

The first large-scale study of delinquency was conducted in Chicago during and immediately following World War I. Shaw and his associates studied the case records of 5,480 delinquent boys between the ages of 11 and 17 years (Shaw, Zorbaugh, McKay, and Cottrell, 1929). They found that the city could be divided into a number of zones or delinquency areas, represented by concentric circles spaced at 1 mile intervals, radiating out from the central or downtown district. The rate of delinquency was highest in the central district, an area in the process of transition from residential to business and industry (commonly called a depressed or slum area), and decreased from zone to zone moving from the city center to the suburbs. Delinquency rate was defined, for this study, as the ratio of the number of male delinquents appearing in the Chicago Juvenile Court from 1917–1923 to the total population in 1920. During the years covered by this study many people migrated to the city from European countries and there were large numbers of blacks and Mexicans added to the population there. In spite of the increase in population the delinquency rate remained the same. The results of this study have been interpreted as meaning that the social and economic setting rather than the nature of the people concerned should be considered the cause or source of the delinquency.

Low socioeconomic status, as defined by family income, father's occupation, level of education, and residential area, has been found to be related to a high rate of delinquency in a number of studies that followed the Chicago survey. It has also been shown that the majority of boys in State Training Schools for Delinquents come from lower-class backgrounds (Nye, Short, and Olson, 1958). Statistics such as these tend to be somewhat misleading because they imply that delinquent behavior is not characteristic of middle- and upper-class youth. In this issue, the statistics do not tell the whole story.

Delinquency is defined as illegal behavior on the part of a person less than legal age, usually 18 or 21. Police files and court records provide the statistics on which most studies of delinquency are based. Once a juvenile has acquired an official record of having been involved in illegal behavior the chances of his repeated delinquency are quite high. There is little doubt that a police record is a handicap in finding employment and gaining social acceptability. Most law enforcement officials are reluctant to impose the stigma of a juvenile record on a youthful first-offender if there is any reasonable alternative. For example, if a boy's parents offer to make restitution for the damages and agree to seek the help of a professional counselor, the authorities will usually handle the case unofficially and the incident will not be made a public record. Of course, the cases handled in this way are usually those who come from upper- and middle-class families. Thus, the statistics based on public records may give us a distorted picture of the total amount of delinquency.

Preferential handling of girls who are involved in illegal behavior also gives us a misleading statistic. Girls are given a warning and released to their mothers far more frequently than boys. Our society expects boys to assume greater responsibility than girls and we also tend to perceive females as more innocent and less aggressive than males. If we look only at the statistics we would be convinced that only boys, especially boys from lower social class homes and minority groups, are delinquent. Unofficial handling by the authorities and preferential arrest procedures hide more than they reveal.

We know that not all delinquents come from the lower social and economic class, and we also know that not all members of the lower classes become delinquent. We do not know the real extent of the relationship between delinquency and social class status. Some studies have attempted to determine the extent of illegal behavior in youth by the survey method in which questionnaires are filled out without asking for names or identifying individuals. Studies such as this support the idea that statistics on delinquency do not tell the whole story.

A study by Nye, Short, and Olson (1958) based on the replies of 3,158 high school students indicates that delinquent behavior is no more common among youths in the lower social class than it is among youths in the middle and upper social classes. The students used in this study were in the ninth through the twelfth grades in three small cities. They were given a check list and asked to indicate the frequency with which they had committed various kinds of illegal behavior. Information was also obtained about the family class status. The results showed no relationship between socioeconomic status and admitted delinquency.

Another recent survey using the anonymous questionnaire method with 683 city high-school students found no relationship between social class and amount of admitted delinquency, but the kind of illegal behavior was related to social class. Offenses involving use of alcohol were more common among upper-middle-class youths, while more serious crimes were admitted by those in the lower-middle and lower classes (Pine, 1965). Other studies point out the difference in expected and accepted behavior of the middle-class family as contrasted with the lower-class family. Pine (1965) and Kvaraceus (1966) report findings that delinquency in all social classes is related to what level of aspiration the juvenile has more than to his class background. For example, lower-class youths who are planning to go to college and thus raise their class level are not inclined to be as delinquent as those who do not expect to go to college. Likewise, middle-class adolescents who expect to enter the labor market without higher education are more prone to delinquency than those who are planning on college.

Studies such as these just cited lead us to wonder whether one of the most important factors in delinquency prevention may be the need of an adolescent to have something in the future to look forward to, work for, and plan. The increased availability of public higher education may help remedy this need to some extent, but the real problem seems to be the need for some personal help and guidance to inspire the adolescent to make realistic plans for his own future. If the family does not provide this inspiration it must come from the schools or from other adults in the community.

Guidance clinics and counseling services, as well as counselors in private practice, work with large numbers of juvenile delinquents each year. They find that helping youths to recognize their feelings and talk about them leads to less impulsive acting-out behavior. Youth groups with organized recreational activities and understanding adult leadership provide the alternatives to delinquency for many adolescents. One of the problems in delinquency prevention or treatment programs is that boys in the age of rebellion against society are inclined to refuse the help of an adult counselor. All adults are seen as the "enemy" and breaking through this is difficult.

An interesting experiment in the treatment of juvenile delinquents was conducted at Harvard University under the name of Streetcorner Research Project (Schwitzgebel and Schwitzgebel, 1961). Juvenile delinquents were paid to talk into a tape recorder about anything that came to their minds. During the first few sessions the talk was boastful, aggressive, and hostile, but after a few hours of this the delinquents seemed to run down and become much more subdued. As they continued their moods changed and they began to show some signs of understanding the reasons for their delinquent behavior. After completion of the "treatment" delinquents had a much lower frequency of arrests than a comparable group who did not have the experience of talking themselves out.

The Streetcorner Research Project lends support to the theory that when hostility is expressed verbally there is less likelihood that it will result in acting-out behavior directed against society. Other studies of delinquency also report beneficial results from encouraging delinquents to talk out their anger and frustrations rather than acting them out.

Another method of involving delinquents in treatment was called "Experimenter–Subject Psychotherapy" to get away from the "Doctor–Patient" relationship which is so offensive to many delinquents (Slack, 1960). In this study boys were paid to come to the center to talk to an experimenter who explained that he was trying to learn as much as he could about delinquency. The hourly pay was enough incentive to bring the boys in at first but after a few hourly sessions they began to realize that they really wanted to come in to talk about themselves more than they wanted the money. More innovations of this kind are needed to reach youths from lower social classes with a treatment approach to their problems.

Problems of law enforcement are greater, of course, than just juvenile delinquency. The many forms of adult crime are beyond the scope of this text, but there is no question that illegal and antisocial behavior are major problems in group living. Law enforcement is everyone's business. Only those laws are enacted in our society that in the opinion of the group are necessary to the health, well-being, and protection of the group members. Laws are not sacred; they may be changed as circumstances or attitudes in the community change. Responsible citizens should take the initiative to review laws in their community to eliminate those no longer necessary and strengthen those not serving their purposes. Citizens also need to give greater thought to what kinds of behavior actually can be controlled by passing laws. One source of contempt for law is the existence of laws that cannot be enforced. Prohibition had to be repealed because it could not be enforced and efforts to enforce it made law officers look ridiculous. Laws relating to marijuana, LSD, and abortion cause similar trouble today. We need to examine those areas of behavior that can be controlled by law and fall within the realm of the public good and separate them from behavior which more properly belongs to the private conscience.

Law enforcement has become a matter of serious concern in all parts of the country in recent years. The daily newspapers are full of stories of mob violence and police brutality. How can this be, and what should be done to remedy the situation?

We are living in a time of marked social changes. Many of our traditional social groupings, attitudes, and customs are under attack and are being changed. New groups are being organized to challenge the authority of "the establishment" and to demand change. The relationship between a community and its police force has become an extremely significant factor in the delay or promotion of social progress. In many places the public image of a policeman is not that of a public servant whose duty is to protect the life and property of individuals. In fact, there is probably only a small minority of people who can honestly say they regard the man in blue as their friend and protector.

One reason for the policeman's poor image in the eyes of the public is that there has been no set standard of education or training required for the occupation. Many cities still hire policemen on the basis of physical fitness, consider an eighth grade education sufficient, and make no effort to assess intelligence. In Baltimore, for example, as recently as 1966 over 21%of the police force had never gone to school beyond the eighth grade (Shearer, 1968).

In the last two decades there has been an attempt to elevate the status of law enforcement to a profession. A few four-year colleges now offer a degree in law enforcement, and there is a growing trend in community colleges to offer a two-year curriculum leading to an associate degree in law enforcement. In 1968 the government made available $6\frac{1}{2}$ million dollars in federal funds to finance college education for policemen. This money is administered by the Law Enforcement Assistance Administration in the Justice Department. While this may not solve all the current problems in relation to the police, it does seem like a step in the right direction (Figure 11-5).

Prejudice and Stereotypes

Among the most serious problems in group living, because of their far-reaching consequences, are the problems brought about because of prejudice and the tendency to categorize people into stereotypes. In spite of the laws in our country which guarantee freedom and equality for all, we have been unable to prevent discrimination against members of minority groups based on prejudice. We have found that prejudice cannot be eliminated by legislation but there is some hope that the situation can be improved by education. Laws can change discriminatory behavior, however, and in time can prevent the attitudes of prejudice from dominating the social, educational, and economic opportunities in this country.

Prejudice is a learned attitude of dislike, disregard, or hostility toward a minority group. Prejudice is usually learned from contact with others who have the prejudice and whose opinions are valued. *Stereotypes* are set ideas or erroneous beliefs about the characteristics of certain groups. The prejudices

Figure 11-5.   Continuing education for police officers is of ultimate benefit to society. (Photo courtesy of San Jose Police Department, San Jose, Calif.)

and stereotypes a child learns from his family tend to become a permanent part of his personality and are very resistant to change.

Radke, Trager, and Davis (1949) investigated the racial and religious attitudes of 250 children in kindergarten and the first two grades. They found that group awareness and social prejudices are fairly well developed by at least 5 years of age and that they are direct reflections of family and neighborhood values. The results of this and other studies indicate that social attitudes do not develop as a result of personal contact with the minority group and, in fact, they are often more strongly prejudiced when there has been no contact. Opportunity for direct contact with minority groups often has the effect of reducing the prejudice.

During World War II the Armed Forces assigned some black and white servicemen to the same fighting units for the first time, having previously segregated them into units either all white or all black. The attitudes toward blacks were measured before and after they had served in mixed units, and in almost all cases the white soldiers were less prejudiced after their experience with the blacks than they had been before (Rose, 1946). It was not until after World War II that integration became a reality in the Armed Services of this country.

There are several reasons why prejudice is so difficult to change. First it gives people who are prejudiced a feeling of superiority or higher status than the group they look down upon and consider inferior. Even the poorest, most inadequate, unimportant white person in the south feels superior to black people. Secondly, prejudice provides an outlet for feelings of frustration and aggression. The person who suffers business failure or setbacks may find it easy to blame his trouble on the Jews whom he feels are unscrupulous, shrewd, and unfair competitors. Third, selective perception tends to confirm prejudice. We are inclined to see those aspects of a situation that uphold and support our beliefs and to overlook those incidents that would deny the truth or accuracy of our attitudes. The person who regards Mexicans as inferior, lazy, dirty, and undeserving will observe them living in rundown neighborhoods, driving dirty cars, and looking slovenly. Whenever he meets an ambitious, well-dressed, successful Mexican he will regard him as an exception to the ordinary. We see those things that confirm our beliefs and attempt to ignore or dismiss everything that is inconsistent.

Much has been written about the damaging effects of prejudice on its victims. Prejudice is also damaging to the person who is prejudiced. As noted above, prejudice narrows perception, and limits what we can learn from our experience. We cannot learn from things we will not see, listen to, or entertain in thought. Prejudice is a continuous insult to logic and reasoning. To consider every talented, able, kind, intelligent member of a racial or religious minority simply an exception to the ordinary is to end up with more exceptions than there are ordinaries and from reason and logic we know this cannot be so. The prejudiced person lives with fear of retaliation to the extent that he deprives others of their opportunities. The possibility that circumstances might be changed at some time, and the hated minority become the majority, generates fear that one may someday be treated in the same ugly way. Finally, prejudice cuts one off from others and limits the opportunities for mutually satisfying experiences.

The unfortunate effects of prejudice are that it results in discrimination, segregation, and conflict between groups. The Fair Employment Practices Act makes it illegal for employers to discriminate against anyone on the basis of race, religion, political views, or sex, but we know that the law does not completely stop discrimination. In 1954 the Supreme Court ruled that segregation in education was a violation of constitutional rights, but we have not yet solved the problems of integrating schools in all parts of the country. Discrimination and segregation continue to arouse hostility which results in violent outbursts of social conflict. The effects of race riots are damaging not only to the lives and property of the people directly involved, but they are damaging to the American image of democracy in the eyes of the rest of the world.

Group stereotypes appear to be a universal phenomena in all cultures of the world. In an extensive study of cultural subgroups in different parts of the world, Campbell (1967) found that stereotypes reflect both the characteristics of the group being described and the character of the group doing the describing. For example, the observed violence of the black people is often a reflection of the violent character of the white people who have done the oppressing and have actually done violence to the black people, but the common interpretation is that the violence is a characteristic of black people. Some of the negative stereotypes we see are formed on the basis of behavior of individuals who have tried to evade the prejudice of another group. That is, black people who cannot be trusted are often persons who have found that they have to play a game in order to get what they want. They have found that white persons cannot be trusted and they are forced to behave in a similar way.

Stereotypes begin with the perception of some *real* difference between groups such as a particular custom, detail of physical appearance, or item of material culture, to which are added, by the perceiver, those traits which are rejected, punished, or despised by his own group. Thus, without denying that there are group differences and that group stereotypes do contain some real characteristics, we should be aware of the errors, misperceptions, and projection that are contained in a group stereotype.

In educating people to properly analyze stereotypes we should help them recognize the enormous individual differences within groups and the amount of overlap between groups. The more contact a person has with members of a minority group the more inclined he is to evaluate them in terms of their individual characteristics rather than in terms of the group stereotype. The casual acceptance of minority group members and treatment of them as individuals by television and other public information media can have a positive effect in correcting the erroneous stereotypes people hold.

What is so bad about stereotypes is not so much the falsity of the descriptive content as it is the causal misperceptions that accompany them. There is an irrational tendency to perceive racial rather than environmental causes for the group differences. For example, if we perceive blacks as inferior and inadequate, and we segregate them into inferior schools and housing, and we provide them with inadequate vocational training, they will become inferior and inadequate citizens just as any other group would under similar circumstances. The irrationality occurs when we assume that the racial differences are the cause of the inferiority rather than the result of the treatment experienced. The scientific study of behavior leaves no doubt that individual differences are greater than any group differences and there is no justification for discrimination against any group by another. What group differences do exist seem more clearly related to treatments experienced than to innate human differences.

Social Action Groups

Progress toward solutions to problems in group living requires interested, informed, and active participants in social action groups. For the most part, social action groups are a phenomenon of youth seeking repudiation of the past, improvement of present conditions, and optimism toward the future. Youth, in the educational process of developing future leaders, sharpens its awareness of the political, economic, and social inequities of the society and becomes committed to the cause of bettering humanity. As higher education becomes more readily available to larger numbers of youth, the organized efforts of youthful idealists becomes an even more powerful force in shaping the future of our society.

Youth movements or social action groups in this country have moved from concern with specific issues of the draft, free speech, and slum clearance, to include the larger issues of peace, civil rights, and economic injustices, and they are heading toward even greater involvement with the moral and ethical values of humanity in a rapidly changing technological society.

SUMMARY

The understanding of individuals must include recognition of the important group memberships, both temporary and enduring, that influence human behavior. Individuals attain group membership by birth, by force, by invitation, by mutual consent, and by choice.

At birth, the newborn joins groups to which his family belongs: national, racial, religious, and social-economic class. Involuntary memberships are imposed on individuals by age and circumstances beyond their control. Invitational memberships usually offer some status and prestige. Groups we join by mutual consent are an important part of our identity. Some group memberships are available by choice.

Unstructured groups are really descriptive categories of people based on common characteristics, with whom we may share attitudes, ideals, and values. Structured groups are dependent upon purposes and goals shared by their members.

When the power, authority, and responsibility for a group rests with its leaders the group has an authoritarian power structure, and when they are divided among members it has a democratic power structure. Behavior of group members depends upon whether they are task-oriented, interaction-oriented, or self-oriented.

Group dynamics is the study of how groups operate to insure the greatest benefit to the members. The emotional climate of a group is determined by its morale and group cohesiveness. Successful group functioning depends upon mutual agreement and acceptance of the purpose, goals, and activities of members, as well as awareness and evaluation of its processes. Both verbal and nonverbal communication are important aspects of group functioning.

Groups serve the individual by helping him solve problems, by providing opportunities for socialization, and by meeting his needs for acceptance, recognition, and achievement.

The organization of society into units and groups provides certain benefits through shared responsibility but it also creates problems in group living. Individual needs for which a family must rely on community organization include a healthy environment, educational opportunities, cultural enrichment, financial security, and protection of rights.

Regulation and control of individual behavior in the interests of the larger groups of society poses many serious problems. Studies of juvenile delinquency, based on statistics, indicate that illegal behavior of youth is associated with lower socioeconomic status, minority group membership, and sex. However, preferential treatment of individual cases tends to distort the statistics. Numerous psychological studies of illegal behavior in youth support the theory that it is just as common in higher socioeconomic classes but the treatment by society is different. It is suggested that the universal need of adolescents to have an optimistic view of future opportunities for self-actualization is a crucial factor.

Illegal and antisocial behavior cannot be controlled by passing laws that cannot be enforced. The role of a police force in relation to the community it serves is a significant factor in the delay or advance of social progress. Some steps have been taken in the direction of improved law enforcement through education, but this is only a beginning.

Law enforcement has failed to prevent discrimination based on prejudice and stereotypes. Prejudice is very resistant to change because it contributes to a false sense of superiority, it provides an outlet for frustration and aggression, and it is confirmed by selective perception. Discrimination and segregation based on prejudice arouse hostility and lead to social conflict which is damaging to all members of a society. Public education through mass media holds some promise for changing the nature of group stereotypes. Science has shown that individual differences are greater than any group differences and that group differences are the result rather than the cause of inferiority.

Whatever progress is made toward solutions of problems in group living will be dependent upon the energy, enthusiasm, and resourcefulness of each succeeding generation of youth. Social movements provide the inspiration and determination to see growth and change directed into constructive channels.

SUGGESTIONS FOR FURTHER READING

Grier, Wm. H. and Cobbs, Price M., *Black Rage*, New York, Basic Books, 1968. A psychological interpretation of the relationship between blacks and whites in this country, by two doctors who speak from personal experience and with professional expertise.

Katz, Joseph and Associates, *No Time for Youth*, San Francisco, Calif., Jossey-Bass, 1968. A critique of modern education based on several studies of college student attitudes and behavior including current youth movements.

Newfield, Jack, *A Prophetic Minority*, New York, New American Library, 1966. Analysis of radical youth movements of the 1960's and their potential as a powerful force in bringing about social change.

Sherif, C. W. and Sherif, M., *Attitude, Ego-involvement and Change*, New York, Wiley, 1967. A symposium on social attitudes, their development, measurement, analysis, stability, and likelihood of change.

Sherif, Muzafer, *Social Interaction: Processes and Products*, Chicago, Ill., Aldine, 1967. A collection of research contributions and observations by one of the most influential social psychologists of our time.

Psychology for a Changing World

The times in which we live have been designated the Age of Anxiety, the Era of Great Doubt, and the Age of Uncertainty. Anxiety is at a high level now because of the generalized insecurity people feel with regard to the future. So much has happened so rapidly to change the nature of the world that it is difficult to predict with confidence the direction our progress is taking. Our highly sophisticated technology could be leading us toward mass aristocracy or toward a mechanized society in which man is subservient to his machines or toward total destruction by nuclear war. We do not know what the future holds, but the one thing we can count on with absolute certainty is *change*.

The emphasis throughout this book has been on the process of continuous interaction between individuals and their environment. Over his life span each individual continues to change and during our life span the world around us also changes. Each has its impact on the other. If man is to succeed in realizing his human potentialities he must structure the environment in such a way as to satisfy his needs for self-preservation, actualization, and integration. Thus, interaction is a reality and change is inevitable in both individuals and the environment. Psychology, to be effective in understanding and predicting behavior, must be sensitive to change and its consequences. Psychologists must investigate the forces and directions of change.

In this concluding chapter the final questions to concern us are these: What are the directions in which the world is changing? What do these changes mean to individuals? How can we prepare to master the challenges of a rapidly changing world?

POPULATION AND THE MEGALOPOLIS

Among the more immediate problems that demand our attention are population growth and the unregulated development of our urban centers. The population growth is in part a consequence of the improved health and longevity achieved by applied science. Because more persons are surviving and establishing families of their own, more children are born, and the population increase grows larger. The population explosion is a world-wide phenomenon and this makes the problem *more* rather than less urgent. The demands of greater numbers for resources and opportunities strain our modern technological society to provide equally for all. The demands of even greater numbers of persons in less developed nations of the world simply are not met.

The Population Explosion

The United Nations, in 1966, estimated the world population at slightly less than $3\frac{1}{2}$ billion persons. The population of the United States was about 200 million. Nearly 2 billion persons lived in Asia with Red China having about 750 million and India about 475 million. The United Nations projection of world population at the end of the century is 7 billion persons or double the number in 1966. The most immediate problem of world population growth is decreasing food supply.

Approaches to the problems of population growth here and around the world have been quite varied. One has been research and development of more effective, inexpensive, and psychologically acceptable means of contraception. Educational programs on family planning and birth control are equally as important as development of a satisfactory contraceptive, for unless birth control measures are used correctly their benefit is lost.

Another attack on the problem of population is research and experimentation on soils, crops, fertilizers, planting and harvest procedures, and weather modification and control. The purpose of these programs is to increase yield and to ensure efficient utilization of available agricultural lands. Again, educational programs to teach the new methods of agriculture to farmers in this country and in underdeveloped countries of the world are a vital part of their eventual benefit. The Peace Corps is helping to meet this educational need and the results are encouraging.

A third area of attack is upon the development of new sources of food supply especially from sea vegetation and previously unused mineral resources. In developing new food sources special effort is being given to make them look like, taste like, and feel like already familiar foods. Processed sea algae or a high protein paste without coloration and flavoring might be difficult for many persons to accept even when they are starving.

Urban Sprawl

In 1900 about 40 percent of our population lived in cities, by 1960 about 70 percent of the population lived in cities, and the projection to the end of this century is about 90 percent of the population will live in urban areas. This population shift to the cities has been due in part to the change in our economy from an agricultural to an industrial society. It has also been due to the growth of our population and the demands of increasing numbers for services and opportunities. The shift has not been even, however, in all areas of the country. Some enormous urban centers are developing with large concentrations of people in a relatively small land space. The *megalopolis* is one term that has been used to describe these super metropolitan areas which have sprawled out from a large central city and engulfed the smaller cities around them.

In 1960, the Bureau of the Census reported there were 22 metropolitan areas in the United States with populations over 1 million persons. In Table 12-1 are reported the 10 largest metropolitan areas in the United States in 1966 to the nearest half million of persons. Each of the urban areas in Table 12-1 is a megalopolis and another 10 are taking shape.

The advantages of living in a megalopolis are principally economic, nearness to job opportunities and a wider range of potential employments. Population concentration stimulates the development of many business and service enterprises to supply the needs and preferences of large numbers of people. Health, education, safety, and general welfare services are also of greater number and variety in population centers. Often-mentioned bonus features of urban living are the greater cultural opportunities, visual, dramatic, movement, and musical arts as well as sporting events.

The disadvantages of living in the megalopolis are equally as varied as the advantages. Housing is crowded and "blight" occurs rapidly as the megalopolis

Table 12-1. Ten Largest Metropolitan Areas in
the United States in 1966[a]

	Population (nearest half-million)
New York	$11\frac{1}{2}$
Los Angeles	$6\frac{1}{2}$
Chicago	$6\frac{1}{2}$
Philadelphia	$4\frac{1}{2}$
Detroit	4
Boston	3
San Francisco–Oakland	3
Washington, D.C.	$2\frac{1}{2}$
Pittsburgh	$2\frac{1}{2}$
St. Louis	$2\frac{1}{2}$

[a]Source: U.S. Bureau of the Census, 1966.

sprawls from a downtown center into residential areas creating slum and ghetto living areas in its wake. Air pollution from industrial wastes and traffic exhausts in large metropolitan areas has created a new source of respiratory illness and disease. The traffiic congestion, the noise, and the accelerated pace of life add to the irritations and tensions individuals feel as they see more and more people crowded together in the megalopolis.

Although the economic opportunities are greater in the megalopolis, the extremes of poverty and wealth that live side by side in relatively small physical area are greater too. Crime in our cities is but one consequence of the extreme economic differences that exist among persons there.

The attack upon the problems of the megalopolis is focused principally around programs of urban renewal and regulated development. These in turn depend for their success upon immediate and imaginative planning. Some suggested plans include: restricting entrance of vehicles to central cities and employing skyways or monorails as the only means of travel, preserving land cleared of slum housing for parks, malls, and recreational areas within the cities rather than permitting industrial development; public and private housing efforts to coordinate development of new residential areas of quality construction to accommodate persons displaced by urban renewal; and research to design and develop atmospheric domes for urban air and climate control.

Psychological Implications

Population growth makes individuality harder to achieve and to recognize. Throughout this book we have stressed the importance of the self-concept. Who am I? What is my worth? What difference does my being make? The answers to these questions reflect one's sense of adequacy and purpose or one's loss of the sense of personal identity. Nourishing individuality, respecting its dignity, and helping it to find meaning becomes more difficult and requires more determined effort as the population increases. Large numbers of persons tend to become anonymous members of groups who are more easily handled in numerical and general terms than on an individual and personal basis.

Concentration of the population in the megalopolis adds to the problems of personal identity and makes effective organization for community action more difficult. The town council, the school district, and the neighborhood unit become large and less personal in the wake of urban sprawl. New methods must be devised to insure individuals the opportunity to satisfy their needs and realize their potentials.

The population explosion and urban development are trends that necessitate changes in the basic pattern of human life. The social problems we face today are different and more urgent than they were in previous generations, and they require greater flexibility in finding solutions. With the increasing numbers of people inhabiting the earth we have increasing needs at all levels—biological, emotional, and social. We must restructure our society to accommodate the increasing demands for food, shelter, protection, security, independence, achievement, recognition, knowledge, expression, and faith. We look to science and technology for help in developing resources to meet the needs of our rapidly expanding world population. (Refer to Chapter 5 for detailed description of needs).

THE PRODUCTIVE PROCESS

Technological advances have been the principal stimulus to social change throughout history. Consider the impact on society of the following: wheel, printing press, steam engine, telephone, electric light, radio, automobile, airplane, sound motion pictures, and television. Each of these inventions has influenced individual behavior, attitudes, and values, and each has altered society in ways both positive and negative. One of the most recent additions to the list of great technical achievements is the digital computer. The computer has initiated an entirely new productive process called *cybernation*. What is the nature of this new technology, its present and potential applications, and its important psychological implications?

Mechanization, automation, and cybernation are sometimes used as if they meant the same thing. They do not, however, and there are important psychological differences between them. Each of these terms describes a different relationship between the human worker, a machine, and the work task. They also depict an evolution in the productive process from very simple to very complex technology.

Mechanization

Mechanization is the use of a machine to *assist* the human worker. The worker and the machine are essentially partners in the work task. The machine helps the worker to do the task but the worker must be actively involved, and, in many cases, furnish the power to run the machine. The treadle sewing machine is an example. The operator had to guide the machine by eye–hand movements and power it by leg movements. The typewriter is another mechanized device. The finger touch and speed on the typewriter powers the machine to print, while the pressure of the fingers can alter the lightness, darkness, and evenness of the print. The lawn mower pushed by human strength is a mechanized device which is a great improvement over the use of a scythe. The hand crank ditto machine is another familiar example of a mechanical device.

Automation

Automation refers to devices that can be set to perform a given task by a human operator so that the machine will follow a sequence of operations to complete the task. Automated devices are powered by nonhuman sources of energy, especially electric energy. If the automated device is improperly adjusted it will repeat errors over and over or just not work at all until correction is made by the human worker. Automated devices serve to *relieve* the human worker of much of the actual work. Automated devices have freed the human worker from many tasks that are tedious, dirty, hard, or dangerous. Automated devices require human workers to set them in motion and supervise or guide their functioning, but the greatest share of the work is done by the machine. Power tools and conveyor belts in industries and mines, balers and milking machines on the farm, addressographs and comptometers in offices, and mixers, washing machines, and garbage disposals in the home are a few examples of automated devices.

Cybernation

Cybernation is a process in which machines are attached to computers. The computer starts, stops, supervises, and corrects the functioning of the machines and virtually *eliminates* the need for the human worker at all. Cybernation is the last phase in an industrial revolution that began with assisting the human worker, then relieving the human worker, and will end by eliminating the human worker. How this is possible requires some understanding of what a computer is and what it can do.

Computers are probably best described as information-processing devices. Tasks such as counting, ordering, classifying, comparing, relating, evaluating, transforming, and retrieving are included in information processing. The computer employs extensive use of the *feedback principle* to accomplish these processing tasks. The feedback principle is a method of regulating a system by returning to it periodically the results of its own performance permitting it to monitor and correct itself. In a simple fashion the feedback principle is utilized in heat thermostats and automatic elevators. Feedback in a computer is more complex and extremely rapid permitting a variety of self-guiding functions.

Many changes have occurred in computer technology since the first commercial computer, UNIVAC, was produced in 1950. These changes have so improved computer efficiency that a problem that required 1 hour to be processed by a computer in 1950 could be done in 1965 in half a second (McCarthy, 1966).

Input devices have developed from punch cards, to typewriters, to magnetic tapes, to magnetic cores, and now include stylus devices that can interpret sketches and drawings. Processing units have been speeded from thousands a second, to millions a second, and now can perform billions of operations a second. New methods of computer utilization include interrupt systems that permit users to share time on expensive equipment. Storage units have been improved to hold trillions of information bits and speed access to previously processed information.

It is the speed, accuracy, flexibility, and storage features of computers that make them an effective substitute for the human worker. All that the human mind can know can be programmed into a computer. Automatic retrieval from storage enables the computer to utilize, as needed, any information previously processed and stored.

The feedback mechanisms in a computer serve not only to aid in the processing of information but also in the regulation of computer functioning giving signals of circuits that are faulty or other mechanical difficulties and in some instances making automatic repairs.

From 1950 to 1967 the number of computers in use grew from one to 40,000 and it is estimated that about 80,000 will be in use by the 1970's. Improvements in design and functions as well as increased production will continue to greatly reduce the cost of computerized equipment. For many purposes ownership of a computer is not necessary and rental of terminals to a large central computer at a rate comparable to utilities costs will probably be more common. Perhaps the best way to realize the impact of computer technology is to consider some of its current and future applications.

APPLICATIONS OF COMPUTER TECHNOLOGY

Contemporary applied science is rapidly developing new ways in which machines can be used to perform many functions that were previously carried out only by the human nervous system. The mechanization of functions that are too fast, too dangerous, too complicated and time-consuming for man, or that are unworthy of human effort when machines can do them, has created the new technology. We have only begun to see the possibilities but we can look forward to increasing applications in the future.

Science

Computer applications in science are of both a theoretical and practical applied nature. Theoretically, computers are a valuable aid because they can manipulate calculations from many variables simultaneously comparing and relating information among them. Computers doing calculations on biochemical factors needed to "decode" cellular processes are saving years of research time in the search for a cancer cure. The information contained in scientific publications and reports can be processed by the computer and made available by topic area to individual scholars giving them ready access to the most recent work in their field.

The man-in-space program, the moon photographs, and scientific sampling explorations would not have been possible without the computer to process information and direct the complex equipment involved. The Telstar communication satellite was accomplished by the application of computer technology. Computers are being used to receive and analyze signals from thousands of ocean buoys and balloons that relay data about wind and water temperature, speed and direction of wind and currents, barometric pressure, and ocean depth. These data are a valuable aid in navigation and increased accuracy in weather projections.

Computers are being used in hospitals to monitor patient progress recording oxygen consumption, breathing rate, blood pressure, pulse rate, and signaling change in these functions requiring immediate attention. A computerized blood analysis machine is in use that performs 12 chemical tests on a single blood sample every 2 minutes. The same tests previously required a medical technologist working 4 to 6 hours to analyze a single blood sample. The computer has also reduced the costs of these tests to the patient from 76 to 18 dollars.

The Veterans Administration has stored a mass of diagnostic heart information in a computer in Washington, D.C., where any of 10 hospitals linked with it can transmit an electrocardiogram of a patient over telephone lines. Not only does the computer make a quicker diagnosis, but it can read greater detail than the human eye can see. In cases of thickening of the walls of the ventricle, for example, doctors can make a correct diagnosis 24 percent of the time and the machine scores accurately in 94 percent. Doctors can detect evidence of damage from old heart attacks in 7 of 10 cases and the V.A. computer has never missed yet. This is but one example of the practical applications of computers in science.

New Aids For the Handicapped

Applied scientific and technical knowledge has made some advances to assist those who have no hope of restored function. Because of genetic defect, illness or injury, blindness, deafness and loss of limbs handicap approximately 10 million persons in our population.

For the blind new devices are principally early warning "sensor" mechanisms which utilize high-frequency sound waves to locate and signal objects present in the immediate environment. These devices work on principles similar to sonar detection systems. The signals from the sensing device differ in pitch and intensity depending upon the distance, density, and other characteristics of the object. The blind can be taught to distinguish these sound patterns or effectively to "see with the ears." The sensitivity of the sensor devices and the difference in sound patterns created is sufficiently varied to be able to distinguish grass from concrete. The greater freedom of movement permitted by such devices in contrast to use of a cane as a probe or a seeing-eye guide dog will increase the number and kind of activities that the blind may enjoy. Other devices to aid the blind are designed to improve their access to information presently available only in printed form. One such device is a high-speed computer Brailler. The Brailler is used by typing questions into it and the information retrieved from the computer memory storage is typed back in braille. Another computer device utilizes photoelectric cells to scan printed materials, finds in memory storage a magnetic taped sound for the letters scanned and in a very approximate voice pattern "reads aloud" what has been scanned. This device is likely for many years to be quite expensive. A smaller, less expensive scanner about the size of a flashlight is in development that would employ photoelectric cells for the scanning and activate tiny braille letter patterns achieving a means of fingertip reading. The greater educational, occupational, social, and cultural opportunities that such devices would provide for the blind seem fairly obvious. Not so obvious, and even more important, would be the psychological benefits of greater confidence, feeling of adequacy, and capacity for participation provided by these mechanical aids.

Changes in mechanized aids for the deaf are occurring in two directions. One is greater miniaturization of hearing devices and the other is increased sound sensitivity. A procedural change that seems promising to yield many benefits is earlier identification of children with hearing losses and earlier use of the improved hearing devices. Infants under 1 year of age with hearing deficiencies are now being fitted with mechanical aids. This procedure has important psychological benefits. The hearing-deficient child who has no awareness of sound usually will do some babbling but after this stage his sound production ceases. Thus, speech impairment is often added to hearing impairment. Delayed identification of hearing deficiences creates another problem of a psychological nature. Children of 5 or 10 years who have grown accustomed to a soundless world do not always welcome the world of sound made possible by hearing aids. They find sound a confusing, frightening, unpleasant experience and they may resist participation in such a world. Where at all possible, if the hearing deficit can be aided mechanically, the earlier the aid is fitted the less the added problems with speech and the development of psychological resistance. Infants with hearing aids have been observed to act distressed when these aids are temporarily removed. However imperfect their awareness of sound is, the hearing deficient child who can detect sound at all and be responsive to it is more likely to benefit from special education and training programs.

For many years the individual unfortunate enough to lose his hands, arms, or legs, or like the thalidomide babies be born without limbs, had only the hope of a hook or a stump to use as a substitute. Now in development are artificial limbs nearly equal to those provided by nature. These limbs are powered by amplification of electrical impulses generated within the remaining body muscles called *myoelectricity*. The patient learns to extend and contract the remaining muscle groups to guide the functioning of the artificial limb. Tiny motors in the artificial limbs are powered by the myoelectricity generated in the remaining muscles and greatly amplified by battery power packs worn under the clothing. The limbs themselves are jointed with intricate mechanical parts covered by a flesh appearing plastic. The range of motion and dexterity of these artificial limbs is comparable to real limbs. Thus artificial hands now in use can accomplish fine coordinated tasks such as mending and assembly of model airplanes. Reaching, grasping, pulling, holding, and turning, of small, delicate objects are easily accomplished. The direction of further improvement is the addition of sensors to the mechanical limbs that will provide accurate information in the form of electrical feedback impulses about the weight, texture, temperature, and resistance of objects just as the cutaneous senses do for natural limbs (see Chapter 2). The ultimate goal in research on artificial limbs is the development of a transistorized brain implant for the frontal lobe motor areas that can guide an artificial limb in intricate motor tasks comfortably and with a minimum of energy expenditure.

Industry

The uses for computers in industry are almost unlimited. In petroleum and chemical industries computer systems actually control the routine operations of plants. There is essentially no limit to the complexity of information a computer can handle, so industrial engineers can now devise processes so intricate that it would be difficult, if not impossible, to control them with human workers.

The use of computers will undoubtedly have a profound effect on the future of our economy and society. It is already evident that production can be increased and costs decreased with the replacement of workers by machines. It is understandable that many people feel that their economic security is threatened by industrial cybernation. Even at our present state of development, it is estimated that 2 percent of our population working productively could produce all of the food, clothing, housing, and material needs for the entire population. Some of the applications of computer technology in industry are almost unbelievable.

American Electric Power System uses computers to control the operation of generating units in 15 plants spread across six states. The computer in Canton, Ohio, automatically regulates the power supply by registering the demand from each area, weighing the cost and efficiency of each unit, cost of transmitting power, and making the decision as to where the needed power would come from at any given time to meet the increased demand in any area.

A steel corporation has a computer-controlled rolling mill programmed to turn out 83 grades of steel in 47 different sizes with considerably improved quality and efficiency. The computer cut scrappage $1\frac{1}{2}$ percent, which was enough to pay for the 3 million dollar computer in two years.

At the management level, computers are being used to assemble information on market trends, production schedules, availability of raw materials, transportation costs, and to analyze this information into alternatives for decision making about increased or decreased production. Computers found early use in industry to handle payroll and accounting tasks, charge accounts, and billing. Airline reservations are arranged in seconds by means of computer-controlled information processing. The aerospace industry uses computers to do much of the production work formerly done by diemakers, template makers, and draftsmen.

The United States Post Office in Detroit has the world's first operational mail address reader. The electrooptical scanner can glance over a printed or typewritten envelope, lock on to the state and city, and deposit the letter in the proper bin. The machine can sort 27,000 letters in an hour compared with 1,200 for the human clerk.

An automated traffic control system was installed in Toronto in 1964, with sensors in the streets to measure the number of cars and a computer to regulate traffiic lights and thus control the flow of traffiic. Within 4 months the system was able to speed rush-hour traffic by 38 percent and reduce accidents significantly.

Government

Computers in government now serve a variety of functions. Government record-keeping is of enormous proportions and computers have been invaluable in such agencies as the Social Security Administration, Internal Revenue Service, and Bureau of the Census for registration, recording, and accounting functions. The Department of Defense uses computers for routine accounting and inventory services, but also for strategic planning in the deployment of men and equipment for the national security. Computers are used in "war games" exercises to project outcomes based on estimates of weaponry and manpower strength of potentially hostile activities of other countries.

Computers are used to speed the process of tabulating election results at all levels of government. Economic planning in government is aided by computers. Up-to-date information of the dollar balance in international trade, level of the gold reserves, stock market changes, and rate of expenditures for legislated services are available for continuous analysis and decision making on credit, wage, or purchasing controls.

Law enforcement is finding computers an efficient aid in crime detection and control. Central computer data files on all persons known to the police for minor or major infractions are reducing investigation procedures from 10 days to 3 minutes to get a detailed report on a suspect. In one eastern city computers are used to keep a record of all crimes committed and to identify areas of high crime risk enabling the police department to concentrate patrols in these areas to reduce the risk.

In Frankfurt, West Germany, computers not only regulate traffic, but by means of photoelectric equipment take pictures of traffic violations indicating time and place and vehicle number and mail the offender a printed citation and fine notice.

Education

The greatest advantage to society offered by the computer is probably in the field of education. We do not think it is fantastic to envision the day when teaching machines will be as common in homes as the television set, and when programmed learning will be as readily accessible as the paperback book on the newsstand. Educational technology promises to revolutionize the methods of teaching and the process of learning.

With the talking typewriter, 4-year-olds have been taught to write complete sentences in 4 months. Six-year-olds have edited their own newspaper, with stories, riddles, and poetry. Children are most receptive to learning between the ages of $2\frac{1}{2}$ and 5 years, and should be taught to read then, according to Professor O. K. Moore, Sociologist at the University of Pittsburgh, who developed the talking typewriter. Moore predicts that by 1975 there will be complete systems of automated instruction available. The machinery is already developed and awaits only the programming.

The computer in education is an excellent tool to handle presentation of factual details, and permits individual computer instruction on fundamental skills of reading, writing, and figuring. In the classroom of the near future students may spend part of their day with their personal computer tutor that has in its memory storage a complete record of their progress in learning. The student at his computer will practice his deficient skills until they are mastered and undertake new learnings as he is ready. The rest of the classroom day may be spent in personal and social growth interacting with other children and the teacher, learning to reason about and apply the factual information provided by the computer, and to expand on his special abilities in art, music, or creative talent.

An interesting new educational aid has been produced by the Aero-jet Corporation for the teaching of medical students specializing in anesthesiology. This device controlled by a computer is a plastic skinned dummy that looks like a man and is called "Sim One." The computerized dummy has a heartbeat, eyes that open and close, pupils that contract and dilate, and it can cough and even vomit. The students practice giving various anesthetics to the dummy and the instructor monitors the student performance and the reactions of the dummy on a control panel. The instructor can regulate the dummy to have "crisis reactions" and give the students an opportunity to practice emergency procedures. The inventors hope to expand the range of reactions of the dummy to include bleeding, perspiring, salivating, and turning color from lack of oxygen. Although not yet available in production models for national use, "Sim One" is a promising new educational aid to improve training opportunities without risk to human life. Such aids would be valuable for medical students in all specialties, nurses, dentists, and even first-aid instruction in the schools. Practical applications of computers in education also include the maintenance of records, test scoring, grade reporting, and class registration in colleges.

Entertainment and Recreation

The computer can be used for amusement in both indirect and direct ways. Indirectly the computer is used to report outcomes of athletic games, racing results, and to keep detailed records of athletic participation in baseball, basketball, football, and other sports. The computer may also be used to analyze ground and weather conditions and make recommendations for satisfactory ski, golf, or camping areas. Another indirect application is a computerized motion-picture theater where tickets are sold, change is made, house lights are dimmed, and the film projected on the screen entirely by computer.

Among direct applications are experimental devices that would provide, for example, a living or recreation room golf course. By projecting a famous golf course on a screen the home golfer would tee off in a tent enclosure toward the screen. A computer would record the impact of the ball, project its probable speed and direction and the image on the screen would show where on the course the ball landed. The home golfer could select weather condition to add variety and could "play" some of the famous courses around the world. Computers in conjunction with television could store on tape performances of a wide variety in the arts and make these available on a library lending system to anyone who might have the desire to view them at home.

A recent computer application in entertainment was developed by Woroner Productions of Miami, Florida called, "The All Time Heavyweight Tournament and Championship." Sports writers were contacted to nominate the all-time great boxers and the final selection included 16 names of fighters living and dead. Then, all available statistical information on these fighters was collected including physical measurements, number of fights, number of knockouts, number of times in the ring, etc. Tens of thousands of information bits about the fighters and their performances served as input to the computer. The fighters were matched in the initial bouts by drawings. The computer then provided an extensive blow-by-blow account of the probable outcome of matching these individuals in a bout. By the use of sound effects and a noted sportscaster reading the computer blow-by-blow, round-by-round, outcome of the fights were broadcast on the radio over a period of weeks. Many people listening to these fights believed they were hearing a real bout. Jack Dempsey won the tournament and interest was renewed as arguments in sports columns continued, but the decision was based on the best estimate of a computer processing all available information and projecting an outcome. The potentials in this kind of presentation are unlimited.

Not only all time "dream" sporting contests could be computerized but also other events of a social, political, and military nature could be reviewed in terms of probable outcome. People like to know, "what could have happened if," and the computer is an efficient source of a probable answer.

The applications of computers presented here are certainly not the only ones in current or potential use. Changes and new applications of computer technology are occurring so rapidly these examples will soon be out-of-date. However, they do serve to introduce you to the world of cybernation, the computer-machine age. The importance of the changes this new technology brings to our world has significant implications for psychology.

PSYCHOLOGICAL IMPLICATIONS OF ADVANCING TECHNOLOGY

Computer technology will aid medical science to preserve and extend life. At the same time, by eliminating the traditional forms of work, the question of how people will make their lives meaningful will become more urgent. Applied science cannot insure the opportunities which make life a meaningful experience. These opportunities depend upon purposive planning of present generations.

The greatest challenge of the new technology is to provide opportunities for all humanity to actualize potentialities. The opportunities that will be required must go beyond consideration of education and employment to include physical space in which to live, unpolluted air and water resources, and opportunities for close, intimate contacts of affection and common purpose shared with others. Beyond the survival needs people want to know what life is all about.

Fromm (1968) defines freedom as being alive beyond survival, that is, being rather than having, as the basis for the human qualities of love, tenderness, compassion, interest, responsibility, and identity. To become fully human man needs to find meaning beyond utilitarian work.

The future depends upon how present generations handle the transition now occurring in our industrial productive system. The economy and efficiency of computer technology is a reality and we are moving toward a new society that demands some changes in definitions, values, attitudes, and feelings.

The Meaning of Work

The most immediate psychological consequence of cybernation is the change it is creating and will create upon work as we know it. Work is an important aspect of personal identity, being the means by which many find the opportunity to realize their talents and make a contribution to society. Work is also the means by which the purchasing power is distributed in our society. As indicated in Chapter 7, the work we do determines our style of life and the degree to which we can participate in society.

The nature of work has been changing for several generations. Since the beginning of the century there has been a steady decrease in jobs relating to agriculture and the creation of products from the raw materials of nature and a steady increase in jobs relating to the sale and distribution of finished goods and personal services. There are few jobs, however, that could not be done by computers as our few examples of the applications of computers illustrate. What jobs do remain when cybernation becomes commonplace will be at high levels of technical skill and authority for decision-making. We are already in a period of transition as evidenced by many signs: high unemployment simultaneous with increasing productivity, shorter hours of work for equal pay, longer periods of educational preparation for jobs that could be done with less education, and greater incentives for early retirement.

Some proposals to slow the transition to a cybernated economy include: a lower standard work week at equal pay, massive programs of public works to create employment, retraining programs to develop skills for the new computer technology, and the exportation of workers in many occupations to assist people in underdeveloped countries. Eventually, in spite of the success of these short-term solutions, it seems we must come to grips with either the problem of redefining work or we must find a new way to distribute the purchasing power. Work has traditionally meant toil, labor, sweat, but there is little of that kind of work left in our society. We could redefine work to include many tasks such as going to school, raising a family, developing one's talents, offering companionship and other valuable human activities—and pay people to do these things. A redefinition of work seems preferable, in terms of its effect upon the self-esteem of individuals, rather than to create artificial jobs that are obviously meant to occupy them but not really to employ them in meaningful activity. More than a few people today are engaged in meaningless jobs in which they put in their time and collect pay but feel empty and unproductive as persons.

Proposals for new methods to distribute purchasing power are generally expressed in terms of a guaranteed annual wage. a negative income tax or subsidies of one kind or another. There are many political as well as social and psychological implications in these plans to redistribute purchasing power and solutions will not come easily. An answer must be found to the question of how may the worth of a human being be judged and rewarded if not in terms of the work he does.

Another human problem posed by cybernation is the use of increased leisure made possible or necessary by the computer technology. Some aspects of this problem have already been discussed in Chapter 7. The solutions found to the redistribution of income will have important effects upon people's feelings about and use of increased leisure. The disengagement of people from work with no means to maintain themselves will hardly be welcome, but if they can be economically secure, their approaches to leisure time may be personally satisfying and rewarding. A greater role in government at all levels is one potential area of human activity as an avocation. Policy-making, planning, and supervision of civic affairs is one task that hopefully computers will not do.

Developing a New Philosophy of Life

The rapid changes and increasing complexity of the world brought about by our advances in science and technology have not contributed to feelings of greater security in our society. The lack of certainty in the future is a threat to security and a source of anxiety for many people. Exploration of outer space, development of intercontinental missiles, launching multiple satellites, and inventing newer, more powerful weapons of destruction are the activities going on around us. It is no wonder that we feel uncertain and anxious about the future. Dr. Albert Schweitzer has written in his "Declaration of Conscience" that we now have the power to make this planet unfit for human habitation as well as to bring about actual disintegration of the world of matter. This was about 15 years ago and we have continued to concentrate our efforts on improving the efficiency with which the end of the world can be achieved.

Our individualistic philosophy of the past that places high value on individual competition, stresses faith in individual reason, and recognizes the worth and dignity of the human individual on the basis of material wealth appears to be somewhat obsolete in today's world. We are slowly making the transition from our individualistic philosophy to one of concern and responsibility among individuals and nations. If we are to put the results of creative intelligence into the service of mankind to improve life rather than to destroy it we must develop a new philosophy of life that will enable mankind to view the future with hope rather than fear.

As the time approaches when man has complete mastery over the environment and a minimum of human effort is required to direct the machinery that will do all the work necessary to provide satisfaction of the physical and economic needs of mankind, we face some serious questions. What will we do with our time? What will be the purpose of education? How will we satisfy our emotional needs? What goals will we have to direct our behavior? How will we value individuality and give it meaning? What controls will be needed to insure freedom, equality, justice?

As soon as we have achieved the goal of producing enough material wealth to satisfy the needs of the world population, and when we have solved the problem of distribution so that every living human can be assured of a decent standard of living, perhaps our energies can be redirected toward the development of human resources. If all work including planning and organizing could be handled by machines we would still have problems that machines could not solve. In the areas of interpersonal relationships, responsibility, judgment, and dealing with crises, the machine cannot replace human functions.

Much has been written about the potential dangers of a computerized society, particularly in terms of the invasion of privacy and the loss of individual rights and personal freedom. These are serious considerations that cannot be disregarded, but we should keep in mind the fact that the dangers arise from the way computers are used and not from the machines themselves. The computer remains under human control and the ways it will be used will always be subject to human control and regulation.

The maintenance of personal privacy may be a real challenge in the cybernated world ahead. There have already been proposals of a national "data bank" containing school, military, medical, financial, legal, credit, employment, and tax records for every citizen. The means to collect extensive information about individuals are presently available and the means to store, file, and categorize this information are also available. Such files could be the source of great abuses and loss of personal freedom. It is important to the integrity of individuals that the purposes of such information gathering and its uses be clearly indicated and controlled. If we feel that it is important to prevent human lives from becoming the subject of public files, it is up to us to foresee the dangers and actively enforce controls. Some tentative proposals have been made in Congress for legislation to govern the collection and use of personal data. You cannot avoid being affected by these and other problems that arise as a result of advancing technology.

The future of society depends upon the development of a new philosophy of life that is in keeping with the advances in science and technology that are reshaping the world with alarming speed. The determined efforts of an informed population can direct technology toward the improvement of humanity without robbing man of his individuality, but a passive, apathetic, or fatalistic philosophy can lead to the dehumanized, mechanized society described in fiction in Huxley's *Brave New World* and Orwell's *1984*.

Education for the Future

Our educational system is facing a new set of human needs and values as well as a new technology. Traditionally, education has been concerned with the development of intellectual functions which we now realize can be handled much more efficiently by computers. In the processing of information the computer is clearly superior to the human brain. What, then, should be the goal of education if not to stimulate the higher mental processes, impart knowledge, and develop skill in solving intellectual problems?

Perhaps schools will turn more to the goals of developing those dimensions of humanness that cannot be built into or taken over by machines. We can concentrate on developing uniquely human capabilities to the fullest, rather than preparing for a life that is productive and useful. Education will need to help people develop greater sensitivity and appreciation for beauty, creativity, feelings and emotions, and the cultures and traditions of other human societies. Developing skills in human relations and acquiring good taste and judgment will be given greater emphasis since these are important in decision-making, communication, and learning how to resist influence.

The shift in emphasis from production of goods to provision of services means that schools are already beginning to educate for new qualities. We need people who are qualified for human services. The field of recreation is rapidly expanding as the need increases for people trained to help others toward creative use of leisure time. Opportunities for service in health, education, welfare, recreation, and entertainment are developing in all parts of the world as the routine and drudgery of work is being taken over by machine technology.

Education for the future will be geared to the highest level of man's needs—not merely for survival, but for self-actualization and integration with humanity. It will encourage the capacity for shared feelings of love, tenderness, joy, sorrow, hopes, and fears, which help to confirm our membership in the human race. Education will help to develop cultural life in our communities bringing music, dance, painting, sculpture, and drama to all people, encouraging them to become participants rather than spectators in the expression of what Fromm (1968) has termed *transsurvival needs* (Figure 12-1).

Figure 12-1.   The current trend in higher education is exemplified in this project which emphasizes cultural growth for students who are not turned on by the ordinary academic curriculum. (Photo courtesy of Skidmore College.)

NEW DEVELOPMENTS AND TRENDS

We face many problems in accepting the reality of change and the uncertainty of the future, but without change there could be no progress and society would be dead. The source of greatest anxiety, it seems, is not the fact that times are changing, but that the changes in science and technology are occurring more rapidly than we can assimilate. However, we can see evidence of new developments and trends in social progress that offer encouragement and promise for a brighter tomorrow. Among the more optimistic developments of our time are the revolt of youth, changing concepts in mental health, human relations in industry, systems analysis, and a renewal of humanism.

The Revolt of Youth

Pick up any newspaper or magazine, or turn on a radio or TV news broadcast, you are almost certain to be reminded of the growing dissatisfaction of youth and their demands to have a voice in shaping the future. While we may not approve of their tactics or even agree with them on the issues, we are heartened by their commitment to the cause of an improved society and the fact that they have the courage of their convictions.

The largest antiwar demonstrations in history occurred in 1965 when over 20,000 youth protestors converged on the nation's capital, in a movement sponsored by a student organization. This new generation of activists has already risked their lives to register voters in the south and has brought to public awareness the problems of racism, poverty, war, and the failure of scientific technology to recognize human needs (Figure 12-2).

We are already beginning to see their influence in the major colleges and universities where revolutionary experiments in student determined education are being held. In "New Schools" and "Free Universities," both on and off campuses, students are demanding and getting the kind of education they feel is needed to prepare them for the push-button world of tomorrow, with greater emphasis on building a truly human society.

We view the revolt of youth as realistic and in keeping with our changing society. Since they can no longer uphold the value of achievement in an occupation that has been central to the American way of life, youth today is finding new values which may be called ethical humanism. One aspect of the new value system is the concern with individual expression and self-development and a second concern is for the social condition of others. Youth today is humanitarian. It has compassion and sympathy for the suffering of humanity and it is outraged

Figure 12-2.   Signs of the times! College campuses across the country bear testimony to the involvement of youth in the crucial issues of humanity. (Photo courtesy of Skidmore College.)

at the institutions which deprive individuals or groups of their human dignity. The most optimistic note sounded by the new generation of intellectuals is their willingness and ability to actively pursue their goals rather than to passively withdraw from society because it failed to come up to their expectations.

Changing Concepts in Mental Health

An encouraging trend in our changing society is the change in our concept of mental health. We no longer think of mental health as the absence of mental illness. In our times the World Health Organization defines health as "a state of complete physical, mental, and social well being, not merely the absence of disease and infirmity." Thus, mental health has become a broader concept more like public welfare than individual "adjustment."

The issues in mental health today include nutrition, housing, opportunity to work, family organization, intellectual development, socialization, racial integration, and world peace. Social psychology is turning its attention to such problems as the relationship between poverty and behavior, the psychological effects of malnutrition and inadequate housing, and community organization for advancing human development. Clinical psychology is turning to community psychology as professionals from many different fields join together to devise new ways to promote mental health and social well-being in our communities.

Psychology today is making a significant contribution to on-going research on problems related to war and peace. For example, the psychological aspects of international decision-making is being studied in depth. In 1966 an appeal was made by the International Union of Psychological Science requesting psychologists everywhere to direct their energies toward world peace; various actions were suggested, including emphasis of the generally accepted conclusions that there are no unchangeable human characteristics making war unavoidable or cooperation impossible.

Recognizing that a favorable environment is necessary for the inborn potentialities of individuals to be actualized, we cannot overlook the importance of diminishing the threat of war and solving the population problems of the world. While psychology is concerned with human behavior, it must also be concerned with conditions and forces outside the control of an individual that influence and limit his behavior.

Human Relations in Industry

In this modern age of rapid technological advances where automated machinery is eliminating the need for unskilled and semiskilled workers and creating a demand for more highly skilled specialists, people in industry are becoming more acutely aware of the importance of human relations. To help executives gain a better understanding of the needs of employees as human beings and to help employees find satisfaction in their work, industries are developing more and better techniques for training people in human relations.

Human relations training is the practical application of scientific knowledge about human behavior to the handling of specific problems that arise in industry as a result of people working together in groups. Human relations training is concerned with developing leadership ability, understanding group dynamics, increasing sensitivity to feelings and attitudes, motivating people to work cooperatively, and improving communication between workers and management. The human relations training laboratory is a relatively new development in the application of social science to industry. Several such laboratories have been established throughout the country where the executives from different companies in different cities come to live and work together for a specified length of time in a sort of "experimental community" (Blake and Mouton, 1955). In this setting the executives are able to examine their own behavior and attitudes and to learn how they affect other people. Through participation in training groups they develop sensitivity and skills in solving human relations problems that they can apply when they return to their own organizations. The training of new managers, supervisors, and foremen within an industry can then be geared to the need for better understanding and communication.

Management has found that it is good business to consider the needs of individuals in industry. Production depends upon the worker and his attitude toward his work. People cannot be forced to work efficiently; they must be motivated or encouraged to want to improve. Rewards are effective in motivating people for work, whereas punishment arouses resistance and negative attitudes. Labor leaders, as well as employers, are beginning to realize that worker satisfaction depends upon other factors in the work situation besides just financial rewards and economic security.

Modern industries are beginning to recognize the importance of the individual and to encourage social grouping among employees. Foremen and supervisors are being trained to recognize and help employees handle problems in interpersonal relationships. They are also trained to encourage communication of attitudes, feelings and problems so that management can know how the workers feel and workers can know that management considers their feelings and problems important. There is a growing trend toward the establishment of recreational programs and social group activities after work for the employees of large companies. Many corporations have developed plans for profit sharing by employees and many encourage their employees to buy stock in the company or offer stock as a bonus. These plans serve as rewards to employees not only financially, but they offer recognition and the opportunity to identify with the company ownership.

Some companies are providing extensive counseling services to their employees. Common among these services are counseling for personal and marital problems, rehabilitation services for alcoholics, and financial and credit counsel. Some companies now arrange travel tours by air or sea for employees and their families at reduced rates to give them wider vacation opportunities than they could enjoy as individuals. Another recent development is the encouragement of cultural activities among employees by company matching plans on tickets for the opera, symphony, or other events. Under these plans, when an employee buys one ticket the company gives him another. The result of these efforts is to make employees feel their employers recognize their human worth and needs, and value these as much as their productivity. While some might feel they would rather see this interest in a higher paycheck, there is some value in exposing people to cultural events that they might not otherwise experience.

Systems Analysis

Advances in technology are not limited to computers and mechanical devices. One of the new social technologies that is becoming widely used in business, industries, schools, and institutions is known as "systems engineering." What this means is making a psychological analysis of a complex organization to find out how it functions, both formally and informally, and understanding its stated and implied goals.

Systems analysis has been applied to educational systems by analyzing the activities and goals of the students, teachers, administrators, parents, and school board members and then giving them feedback of information obtained at all levels. The usual result is temporary disruption of functioning with rapid reintegration of the system at a level of functioning that will better meet the needs of all the different people involved. By encouraging this kind of openness and flexibility social institutions including hospitals, health departments, welfare agencies, law enforcement, and other public service organizations are finding it possible to better satisfy the human needs of people within the organization as well as those served by the system.

Humanism

Progress in science and technology is changing our style of life and raising new questions about the value and meaning of human life. One of the most encouraging developments occurring throughout Europe and America is a strong trend toward the deeper values of the humanistic tradition directing attention to human needs and the human condition. Fromm expresses the humanistic philosophy in the following statement: "Man's development requires his capacity to transcend the narrow prison of his ego, his greed, his selfishness,

Figure 12-3. Part of the new generation of leaders emerging from our colleges, these graduates are wearing on their backs the peace symbol—a tribute to humanism. (Photo by Dave Bellak, San Jose State College.)

his separation from his fellow man, and hence, his basic loneliness. This transcendence is the condition for being open and related to the world, vulnerable, and yet with an experience of identity and integrity; of man's capacity to enjoy all that is alive . . . in brief, to *be* rather than to *have* and to *use* are the consequences of the step to overcome greed and egomania (Fromm, 1968, pp. 141–142).

Exploration of the moon and instrument probes of the distant planets give support to the view that life as we know it is confined to our planet Earth. This confirmation of the uniqueness of human life renews the challenge to us to help each individual find in life a satisfying and rewarding personal experience. Humanism finds expression in efforts to bring peace to the world, eliminate poverty and suffering, and insure to all persons dignity and fulfillment of their human potentials. Of great endeavors it has been said, "One man can make the difference and every man should *try*."

SUMMARY

The times in which we live are characterized by uncertainty with regard to the future. We do not know whether we are headed for mass aristocracy, mechanized dehumanized society, or nuclear war, but one thing we can count on with certainty is change. The interaction of individuals and the environment is a reality and change is inevitable in both.

The population explosion and the growth of urban centers are important current trends that make individual needs difficult to satisfy. Science and technology must develop resources to meet the needs of an increasing population.

Technological advances have stimulated social change throughout history. The current stage in technology brought about by the computer is called cybernation. The process of production has evolved from simple to complex through the stages of mechanization to assist the worker, automation to relieve the worker, and cybernation to eliminate the worker. The computer is a complex information processing device that is capable of input, storage, and retrieval of information, and employs feedback principle to detect errors and make automatic corrections.

Computer technology is growing rapidly with new applications developing continuously. Applications in science are both theoretical and applied, speeding the research process and making possible the exploration of space, accurate weather forecasts and improving medical care. New aids for the blind, deaf, and crippled have been developed as a result of computer technology.

The uses for computers in industry are almost unlimited and will undoubtedly have profound effects on the future of our economy and our society. Government uses of computers are widespread and growing rapidly.

The greatest advantage to society offered by the computer is probably in education where it promises to revolutionize the methods of teaching and process of learning. New uses are being found for computers in entertainment and recreation.

There are some important psychological implications of our advancing technology—it can help to preserve and extend life and it can eliminate the traditional forms of work, but it cannot insure the opportunities which make life a meaningful experience. Life in the future depends upon how present generations handle the transition now occurring in our industrial productive system.

The most immediate consequence of cybernation is the change in work as we now know it. We will need a redefinition of work or a new method of distributing purchasing power. We will also need a new philosophy of life in keeping with the reality of changes that are being made. We are moving from a highly individualistic philosophy to one of concern and responsibility among individuals and nations. We should turn our attention to the development of human resources and the advancement of humanity.

Education for the future will have the goal of developing those human qualities that cannot be built into a machine. The emphasis will shift from production of goods to the provision of services and development of cultural life. To be "cultured" in future society will mean understanding many aspects of different cultures as well as one's own culture.

New developments and trends that give an optimistic look to the future are: the revolt of youth and its demands for more humanitarian values, changing concepts in mental health which are broadened to include factors in the environment which affect individuals, human relations in industry and systems analysis which emphasize human needs, and the growing interest in humanism as a philosophy of life.

SUGGESTIONS FOR FURTHER READING

Frank, Jerome D., *Sanity and Survival: Psychological Aspects of War and Peace*, New York, Random House, 1968. Applies the findings of psychology and other behavioral sciences to the issues of deterrence and control of nuclear weapons.

Fromm, Erich, *The Revolution of Hope*, New York, Harper and Row, 1968. An appeal to action based on the conviction that we are at the crossroads and must choose between a completely mechanized society or a social revolution.

Kenniston, Kenneth, *Young Radicals*, New York, Harcourt, Brace and World, 1968. Psychological study of a selected group of student activist leaders, giving insight into the current rebellion of youth.

Theobald, Robert (Ed.), *The Guaranteed Income*, New York, Doubleday, 1966. A collection of essays by prominent social scientists who are concerned with problems brought about by the technical revolution.

Wall Street Journal Staff, *Here Comes Tomorrow*, Princeton, N.J., Dow Jones Books, 1967. A preview of what to expect with cybernation in the years ahead.

Glossary

Absolute Threshold The minimum amount of stimulus energy that is required·to activate a sense organ sufficiently for an awareness of sensation to occur.

Abstract Intelligence Mental ability to deal with words and symbols, concepts and ideas.

Adjustment The continuous process of interaction between an individual and his environment which includes other people.

Affect The subjective feelings of love, fear, anger, etc. that constitute one aspect of emotional behavior.

Ambivalence The simultaneous experience of positive and negative feelings toward the same person, object, or idea.

Anxiety A nonspecific, generalized sense of fear of impending disaster in which the source of the fear is not known.

Attention Span The length of time an individual is able to focus attention on a particular object or event.

Audible Spectrum The range of frequencies of tones that can be heard by the human ear (about 16,000 to 20,000 vibrations per second).

Authoritarian Leadership A pattern of group structure in which the leader has complete authority to make decisions for the group and to enforce his will.

Automation Use of machines that will follow a sequence of operations independent of human energy thus relieving the worker from many of the actual tasks involved in his work.

Autonomic Nervous System That part of the nervous system which controls bodily functions not subject to voluntary control, such as glands and internal organs.

Behavior All activities of an organism including observable actions, conscious processes, and involuntary processes which are not directly observable.

Behavior Therapy The application of learning theory and conditioning techniques to behavior problems for the purpose of modifying new habit patterns and more effective responses.

Body Image How a person values, thinks, and feels about his physical being—an important part of one's self-concept.

Cerebellum That part of the brain that contains the centers for control of body balance and coordination of bodily movements.

Cerebrum The largest and most highly developed part of the brain, it is divided into two halves called hemispheres.

Chance Factors Important but unknown factors that operate as causes to produce certain effects.

Chromosomes Tiny threadlike bodies in the nucleus of cells which are the mechanism of heredity.

Classical Conditioning Learning based on an association between a natural stimulus and a new or substitute stimulus that will elicit the same response.

Closure Process of filling in the gaps in perception.

Communication Pattern The pattern of open and closed channels of communication within a group.

Compensation Making up for feelings of inadequacy in one area by developing superior competency in some other area.

Compulsion The need to repeat some action over and over even though it serves no useful purpose.

Conditioning Learning process in which behavior is modified by forming new associations between stimuli and responses (see classical conditioning and operant conditioning).

Conflict The simultaneous arousal of incompatible needs, drives, or motives.

Connectors Refers to the nervous system which serves to connect the receptors (sense organs) and effectors (muscles and glands).

Conscience The standards, values, and ideals by which a person judges right from wrong and feels obligated to think, feel, and act in accordance with them.

Contour The outline of a figure that separates it from the ground.

Contralateral Dominance Principle of organization by which sensory and motor functions of each side of the body are processed by the cerebral hemisphere on the opposite side of the body.

Conversion Reaction Anxiety is converted into a physical ailment that impairs social functioning.

Corpus Callosum Large nerve tract that connects the two cerebral hemispheres and enables them to work together.

Cortex The outer layer of the cerebrum, where the most complex functions of the higher mental processes are regulated.

Creativity The ability to envision something new, novel, or original.

Crisis A critical time or decisive moment, a turning point in the course of events.

Cultural Heritage Attitudes, beliefs, customs, and traditions that are handed down from each generation to the next.

Cybernation The operation of machines by computers instead of human workers.

Delinquency Illegal behavior of a person less than legal age (usually 18 or 21).

Delusion An idea or belief that has no basis in actual fact.

Dependent Variable The factor in an experiment that changes as a result of changes in the independent variable. *Example:* If we study the effects of drugs on learning ability, the measure of learning ability would be the dependent variable.

Dimensions Characteristics of people in which individuals are found to vary from one extreme to the other.

Disability Any personal handicap that is acquired by injury or illness and limits a person's ability to function as well as he could before the illness or injury.

Drive   The state of tension and activity that is aroused by tissue needs and directed toward regaining homeostasis.

Effectors   The muscles and glands, which constitute that part of the organic system which carries out the response of the organism.

Ego   An individual's experience of himself.

Ego Defenses   The mechanisms a person uses to protect and enhance his self concept in the presence of frustration and anxiety.

Ego Needs (esteem needs)   The needs for recognition, appreciation, and approval.

Emancipation   The process of achieving freedom from parental control and independence.

Embryo   The human organism from the second to eighth week after conception.

Emotion   Complex state of an organism involving bodily changes and subjective feelings called affect.

Empathy   The ability to look beyond what people are saying and to respond to the feelings and attitudes they are trying to communicate.

Endocrine Gland   Ductless gland which pours its secretion directly into the bloodstream. (See Hormone.)

Extinction   The disappearance of a conditioned response in the absence of reinforcement.

Extrasensory Perception (ESP)   Awareness of ideas or objects without the use of any of the known sense organs.

Feedback   Knowledge of results.

Fetus   The unborn human from the eighth week after conception until birth.

Figure–Ground   The tendency to perceive visual stimuli in terms of forms and background.

Fraternal Twins   Twins developed from two separately fertilized eggs, thus having different hereditary potentials.

Frustration   Negative feelings a person experiences as a result of obstacles or events that prevent him from satisfying his needs.

Functional Psychosis   Mental illness for which no known physical causes exist and which does not result in damage to the brain or nervous system.

Genes   The carriers of hereditary factors, located within the chromosomes.

Genetics   Study of the hereditary process and inherited characteristics.

Group Cohesiveness   Mutual attraction the members of a group have for each other and the extent to which they feel identified with the group and have confidence in it.

Group Dynamics   The study of how groups operate to become effective and insure the greatest benefit to their members.

Group Norms   Expected behavior that is considered normal, appropriate, and acceptable by a particular group of people.

Hallucination   Sensory experience that occurs in the absence of any physical stimulus.

Hallucinogens   Chemical substances (drugs) which are capable of producing symptoms in normal persons resembling those of psychotic or mentally ill patients.

Homeostasis   The overall process of maintaining the chemical balance of equilibrium in the body tissue.

Hormone Chemical substance secreted by an endocrine gland and carried by the bloodstream to other organs where it stimulates activity.

Humanism Feeling of compassion and responsibility for one's fellow man now and in generations to come.

Hypothalamus Reward center of the brain, also functions as control center for emotions and biological drives.

Hypothesis A statement or proposition which is subjected to experimental testing in order to support or deny its truthfulness.

Identical Twins Twins which develop from a single fertilized egg, thus having exactly the same hereditary potentials.

Identification The process of developing the self by association with other people and taking on their characteristics.

Illusion Common distortion of experience based on misinterpretation of the actual stimuli.

Independent Variable The factor in an experiment that is deliberately manipulated by the experimenter to produce changes in the dependent variable. (See Dependent Variable.)

Intelligence General mental ability including alertness, problem-solving capacity, and the ability to learn and profit from experience.

I.Q. (Intelligence Quotient) A measure of general intelligence based on comparison with a large sample of persons in the same age group.

Interests The set of preferences a person develops and the kinds of things he appreciates, enjoys, and does not avoid.

Kinesthesis The sense of bodily movement, receptors for which are in the muscles and joints.

Learning The process by which behavior is changed as a result of experience.

Learning Set A readiness to attempt learning in a certain way based on past experience.

Limen (absolute threshold) The minimum amount of stimulus energy that is required to activate a sense organ sufficiently for an awareness of sensation to occur.

Maturation The normal process of growth and development that occurs as a result of hereditary potentials rather than learning.

Mechanization Use of a machine to assist the human worker and to make his work easier.

Megalopolis Super metropolitan area that has spread out from a large central city and engulfed the smaller cities around it.

Milieu Therapy Use of an institutional setting as a therapeutic community so that all aspects of the patient's environment will exert a positive influence on his mental condition.

Morale General attitude of group members toward their group and its goals.

Motive The desire for a goal that, through learning, has acquired value for the individual.

Motivation The relative energy that directs behavior toward certain goals.

Nerve Bundle of neurons bound together as in a cable.

Neuron Individual nerve cell.

Nonverbal Cues   Gestures, expressions, and postures used to communicate an idea or feeling without words.

Normal Distribution   A distribution of scores that when plotted on a graph will follow the lines of a bell-shaped curve having known mathematical probabilities.

Norm Group   The group of subjects with which an individual's performance on a test is being compared.

Obsession   Preoccupation with a fixed pattern of thought over a long period of time.

Operant Conditioning   An association between a response and the stimulus events that follow it.

Organic Psychosis   Severe mental illness caused by physical damage to the central nervous system.

Perception   The process of organizing and interpreting the evidence of the senses in order to become aware of the environment.

Perceptual Constancy   The tendency to perceive familiar objects as we know them regardless of the conditions under which they may appear distorted.

Personality   The combination of behavioral characteristics, abilities, aptitudes, interests, and values that distinguishes an individual from all others.

Phenylketonuria (called PKU)   A metabolic disorder that results in mental retardation.

Phobia   Unreasonable fear, out of proportion to the actual danger involved.

Practical Intelligence   Common sense mental ability or practical judgment in dealing with concrete problems.

Predisposition   Tendency to react in certain ways or to be subject to certain stresses.

Prejudice   A learned attitude of dislike, disregard, or hostility toward a minority group.

Projection   The process of attributing to others those qualities which a person cannot accept or tolerate in himself.

Psychoanalysis   A specialized technique of psychotherapy dealing primarily with uncovering unconscious material.

Psychodrama   A group psychotherapy technique in which patients "act out" their problems with the help of others and in the presence of the therapist.

Psychopharmacology   The scientific discipline that is concerned with the relationship between drugs and behavior.

Psychosis   Severe mental illness in which the person loses contact with reality.

Psychosomatic   Disturbance of bodily function caused by emotional factors leading to physical illness.

Psychotherapy   The process of bringing about changes in personality and behavior by verbal communication between patient and therapist.

Rationalization   The process of substituting socially acceptable reasons for the real reasons.

Reasoning   Associating facts and ideas, solving complex problems by making use of past experience.

Receptors   The input system that picks up stimulus energy from the environment and converts it to neural energy, located in sense organs.

Reflex Pattern   The simplest form of nervous system organization.

Regression   Reverting to earlier, less mature forms of behavior in response to frustration and conflict.

Repression   The process by which painful and anxiety producing ideas and experiences are forgotten or blocked from conscious awareness.

Response   Any activity of an organism, including the action of nerves, muscles, glands.

Schizoid Personality   Characterized by shyness, oversensitivity, seclusiveness, daydreaming, and inability to express hostility and ordinary aggressive feelings.

Schizophrenia   A broad category of functional psychoses marked by disorganization of the sense of self.

Self-Actualization   The process of developing potential ability into actual ability.

Self-Concept   An individual's ideas about himself, what he really is, and how he compares with other people.

Sensation   The stimulation and arousal of a sense organ.

Sensory Adaptation   Change in the threshold of sensory responsiveness as a result of continuous stimulation.

Separation Anxiety   Anxiety produced by the separation of an individual from the person or persons he has learned to depend upon for his emotional security.

Sex Role   The pattern of beliefs, attitudes, and activities which are defined by the culture as appropriate for one's sex.

Social Intelligence   Mental ability applied to the problems of interpersonal relationships, understanding social roles, and ability to predict outcomes of social behavior and interaction.

Social Learning   The development of complex relationships with other persons and the capacity to function in expected roles.

Somatotherapy   Treatment of mental illness by physiological means, including brain surgery, shock therapy, and the use of drugs.

Stereotype   A preconceived set of ideas about the members of a group based on incomplete or erroneous information.

Stimulus   An object, event, energy, or energy change that produces a response (may be internal or external).

Stress   A state of tension and anxiety produced by severe or prolonged frustration.

Stroboscopic Effect   The illusion of movement that is perceived when a series of still pictures are seen in rapid succession.

Subliminal   Stimulation below the absolute threshold (limen) of awareness.

Superego   That part of the personality that exerts control over impulses, also known as conscience.

Systems Analysis (systems engineering)   Psychological analysis of a complex organization to find out how it functions, both formally and informally, and understanding its stated and implied goals.

Unconscious Motives   Hidden wishes and desires that influence an individual's behavior without his awareness of them.

Unity   Feeling of closeness, of being united with others, and sharing mutual concerns and experiences.

Upward Mobility   Improvement of socioeconomic status.

Variable Anything that can change and take on different values.

Vertigo Dizziness and disorientation resulting from contradictory sensory information.

Visible Spectrum The range of light waves to which receptor cells in the eye are capable of responding.

Withdrawal Mechanism for escaping anxiety and frustration by refusing to face it.

Zygote Cell formed by the union of male and female germ cell.

Bibliography

Academy of Religion and Mental Health, *Religion in the Developing Personality*, New York, New York University Press, 1960.

Allport, Gordon W., *The Individual and His Religion*, New York, Macmillan, 1950.

Allport, G. W., Vernon, P. E., and Lindzey, G., *A Study of Values* (3rd ed.), Boston, Houghton Mifflin, 1960.

American Psychological Association, *Directory*, Washington, D.C. 1968.

Amoore, J. E., Johnston, J. W., and Rubin, M., "The stereochemical theory of odor", *Scientific American*, **210**, 42–49 (1964).

Anastasi, Anne, *Differential Psychology* (3rd ed.), New York, Macmillan, 1958.

APA Committee on Nomenclature and Statistics, *Diagnostic and Statistical Manual of Mental Disorders*, Washington, D.C., American Psychiatric Association, 1968.

Baller, W. R., "A study of the present social status of a group of adults who, when they were in the elementary schools, were classified mentally deficient," *Genetic Psychological Monographs*, **18**, 165–244 (1936).

Barron, Frank, *Creative Person and Creative Process*, New York, Holt, Rinehart and Winston, 1969.

Bass, B. M., and Dunteman, G., "Behavior in groups as a function of self-interaction and task orientation," *Journal of Abnormal and Social Psychology*, **66**, 419–428 (1963).

Bernstein, B., "Social class and linguistic development: a theory of social learning," *British Journal of Sociology*, **9**, 159–174 (1958).

Blake, R. R., and Mouton, J. S., *Theory and Practice of Human Relations Training*, Austin, Texas, Hogg Foundation for Mental Hygiene, University of Texas, 1955.

Blaustein, A. I. and Woock, R. R., (Eds.), *Man Against Poverty: World War III*, New York, Random House, 1968.

Blocher, Donald H., *Developmental Counseling*, New York, Ronald Press, 1966.

Bowman, Henry A., *Marriage for Moderns* (4th ed.), New York, McGraw Hill, 1954.

Breed, Warren, "Occupational mobility and suicide among white males," *American Sociological Review*, **28**, 179–188 (1963).

Brogden, H. D. and Harman, H. H., "An analysis of factors in physical proficiency," *American Psychologist*, **3**, 310 (1948).

Calder, Nigel, (Ed.), *Unless Peace Comes*, New York, Viking Press, 1968.

Campbell, Donald T., "Stereotypes and the perception of group differences," *American Psychologist*, **22**, 817–829 (1967).

Carman, Philip M., "The relationship of individual and husband–wife patterns of

425

personality characteristics to marital stability," unpublished Ph.D. dissertation, University of Washington, 1955.

Carroll, Herbert A., *Mental Hygiene: The Dynamics of Adjustment* (4th ed.), Englewood Cliffs, N.J., Prentice Hall, 1964.

Charles, D. C., "Ability and accomplishment of persons earlier judged mentally deficient," *Genetic Psychological Monographs*, **47**, 3–71 (1953).

Clague, Evan, "Demographic trends and their significance," in Simpson, H. S., (Ed.), *The Changing American Population*, New York, Institute of Life Insurance, 1962.

Clarke, R. E., Hoffman, A. C., Hudson, B. B., Mead, L. C., Searle, L. V., and Wagoner, K. S., *Effects of Sleep Loss on a Complex Task*, Washington, D.C., U.S. Department of Commerce, 1946.

Cleaver, Eldridge, *Soul on Ice*, New York, McGraw-Hill, 1968.

Coombs, A. W. and Snygg, D., *Individual Behavior*, New York, Harper and Row, 1959.

Coombs, Philip H., "The global revolution," *Saturday Review*, August 19, 1967, pp. 49–50.

Crannell, C. W., "The validity of certain measures of art appreciation in relation to a drawing task," *Journal of Psychology*, **35**, 131–142 (1953).

Crick, F. H. C., "On the genetic code," *Science*, **139**, 461–464 (1963).

Dement, W., "An essay on dreams: the role of physiology in understanding their nature," in Barron, F., et al., (Eds.), *New Directions in Psychology II*, New York, Holt, Rinehart and Winston, 1965, pp. 135–257.

Edwards, Allen L., *Manual-Edwards Personal Preference Schedule*, New York, The Psychological Corporation, 1954.

Erikson, Erik, *Identity, Youth and Crisis*, New York, Norton, 1968.

Faigel, Harris C., "Suicide among young persons," *Clinical Pediatrics*, **5**, 187–190 (1966).

Farberow, Norman L., and Shneidman, Edwin S., *The Cry for Help*, New York, McGraw-Hill, 1961.

Fisher, C., "Psychoanalytic implications of recent research on sleep and dreaming," *Journal of the American Psychoanalytic Association*, **13**, 197–303 (1965).

Ford, D. N., and Urban, H. B., *Systems of Psychotherapy*, New York, Wiley, 1963.

Frankl, Viktor, *Man's Search for Meaning*, New York, Knopf, 1955.

Fromm, Erich, *The Art of Loving*, New York, Harper and Row, 1956.

Fromm, Erich, *The Revolution of Hope*, New York, Harper and Row, 1968.

Fulton, Robert, *The Sacred and the Secular: Attitudes of the American Public Toward Death*, Milwaukee, Wis. Bulfin, 1963.

Fulton, Robert, *Death and Identity*, New York, Wiley, 1965.

Fulton, Robert, and Geis, Gilbert, "Death and social values," *Indian Journal of Social Research*, **3**, 7–14 (1962).

Funkenstein, D. H., "The physiology of fear and anger," *Scientific American*, **196**, May, 1955, pp. 74–80.

Galanter, E., "Contemporary psychophysics," in Brown, R., et al., *New Directions in Psychology I*, New York, Holt, Rinehart and Winston, 1962, pp. 89–156.

Gesell, A., et al., *The First Five Years of Life*, New York, Harper and Brothers, 1940.

Gesell, A., and Thompson, H., "Learning and growth in identical twin infants: an experimental study by the method of co-twin control," *Genetic Psychological Monographs*, **6**, 1–124 (1929).

Goldfarb, W., "Effects of early institutional care on adolescent personality," *Journal of Experimental Education*, **12**, 106–129 (1943).

Goldfarb, W., "Effects of psychological deprivation in infancy and subsequent stimulation," *American Journal of Psychiatry*, **102**, 18–33. (1945).

Goode, W. J., *After Divorce*, Chicago, Ill., Free Press of Glencoe, 1956.

Gough, Harrison G., *Manual for the California Psychological Inventory*, Palo Alto, Calif., Consulting Psychologists Press, 1957.

Gowan, J. C., Demos, G. D., and Torrance, E. P., *Creativity: Its Educational Implications*, New York, Wiley, 1967.

Graves, Maitland, *Design Judgment Test*, New York, The Psychological Corporation, 1946.

Guetzkow, H. S. and Bowman, P. H., *Men and Hunger*, Elgin, Ill., Brethren Publishing Co., 1946.

Guilford, J. P., and Hoepfner, R., *Structure of Intellect Factors and their Tests*, Report No. 36, Los Angeles, Calif., University of Southern Calif., 1966.

Gurin, G., Veroff, J., and Feld, S., *Americans View Their Mental Health*, New York, Basic Books, 1960.

Harrell, T. W., and Harrell, M. S., "Army general classification test scores for civilian occupations," *Educational and Psychological Measurement*, **5**, 229–239 (1945).

Harrington, Michael, *The Other America*, New York, Macmillan, 1963.

Havighurst, R. J., *Human Development and Education*, New York, Longmans Green, 1953.

Hayden, Tom, *Rebellion in Newark*, New York, Vintage Books, 1967.

Heidbreder, E., Bensley, M., and Ivy, M., "The attainment of concepts: IV. regularities and levels," *Journal of Psychology*, **25**, 299–329 (1948).

Heron, W., "Cognitive and physiological effects of perceptual isolation," in Solomon, P., et al. (Eds.), *Sensory Deprivation*, Cambridge, Mass., Harvard University Press, 1961.

Hess, R. D., and Shipman, Virginia, "Early blocks to children's learning," *Children*, **12**, 189–194 (1965).

Hewson, Alfred, "Music reading in the classroom," *Journal of Research in Music Education*, **14**, 289–302 (1966).

Hilgard, J., and Newman, M. F., "Anniversaries in mental illness," *Psychiatry*, **22**, 113–121 (1959).

Hollingshead, August B., "Cultural factors in the selection of marriage mates," *American Sociological Review*, **15**, 619–627 (1950).

Jacob, P. E., *Changing Values in College*, New York, Harper, 1957.

Jacobs, Jerry, and Teicher, Joseph D., "Broken homes and social isolation in attempted suicides of adolescents," *International Journal of Social Psychiatry*, **13**, 139–149 (1967).

Jarvick, M. E., "Drugs used in the treatment of psychiatric disorders," in Goodman, E. S., and Geltman, A. (Eds.), *The Pharmacological Basis of Therapeutics* (3rd ed.), New York, Macmillan, 1965.

Jersild, Arthur T., *Child Psychology* (5th ed.), Englewood Cliffs, N.J., Prentice-Hall, 1960.

Joint Commission on Mental Illness and Health, *Action for Mental Health*, New York, Wiley, 1962.

Kallman, F. J., "The genetics of mental illness," in Arieti, S. (Ed.), *American Handbook of Psychiatry*, New York, Basic Books, 1959, pp. 175–234.

Kaplan, O., "Life expectancy of low grade mental defectives," *Psychological Record*, **3**, 295–306 (1940).

Kelly, E. L., "Psychological factors in assortative mating," *Psychological Bulletin*, **37**, 473–474 (1940).

Kelly, E. L., "The consistency of the adult personality," *American Psychologist*, **10**, 659–681 (1955).

Kersey, Robert E., "Effects of an exploratory program in instrumental music on the aural perception of instrumental timbre," *Journal of Research in Music Education*, **14**, 303–308 (1966).

Kety, S., "Critique of chemical studies," *Science*, **129**, 1528–1532, 1590–1596 (1959).

Kinsey, A. C., Pomeroy, W. B., and Martin, C. E., *Sexual Behavior in the Human Male*, Philadelphia, Pa., Saunders, 1948.

Kinsey, A. C., Pomeroy, W. B., Martin, E. E., and Gebhard, P. H., *Sexual Behavior in the Human Female*, Philadelphia, Pa., Saunders, 1953.

Kuhlen, R. G., and Arnold, M., "Age differences in religious beliefs and problems during adolescence," *Journal of Genetic Psychology*, **65**, 291–300 (1944).

Kvaraceus, W. C., *Anxious Youth: Dynamics of Delinquency*, Columbus, Ohio, Charles E. Merrill, 1966.

Liberman, Robert, "A view of behavior modification projects in California," *Behavior Research and Therapy*, **6**, 331–341 (1968).

Lindemann, Erich, "Symptomatology and management of acute grief," *American Journal of Psychiatry*, **101**, 141–148 (1944).

Lindsley, D. B., "Emotion," in Stevens, S. S. (Ed.), *Handbook of Experimental Psychology*, New York, Wiley, 1951.

Lofquist, Lloyd H. (Ed.), *Psychological Research and Rehabilitation*, Washington, D.C., American Psychological Association, 1960.

Macdonald, Dwight, *Our Invisible Poor*, New York, Sidney Hillman Foundation, 1963.

Maslow, Abraham H., *Toward a Psychology of Being* (2nd ed.), Princeton, N.J., Van Nostrand, 1968.

Masters, W. H., and Johnson, V. E., *Human Sexual Response*, Boston, Mass., Little, Brown and Co., 1966.

May, Rollo, *Man's Search for Himself*, New York, Norton, 1953.

McCarthy, J., "Information" in *Information-A Scientific American Book*, San Francisco, Calif., W. H. Freeman, 1966.

McGee, Richard K., "The suicide prevention center as a model for community mental health programs," *Community Mental Health Journal*, **1**, 162–172 (1965).

McKinney, F., *Counseling for Personal Adjustment in Schools and Colleges*, Boston, Mass., Houghton Mifflin, 1958.

Michael, Donald N., *Cybernation: The Silent Conquest*, New York, Fund for the Republic, 1962.

Miller, A. B. (Ed.), *Physicians Desk Reference* (22nd ed.), Oradell, N.J., Medical Economics, Inc., 1968.

Minsky, Marvin L., *Computation*, Englewood Cliffs, N.J., Prentice-Hall, 1967.

Monahan, T. P., and Chancellor, L. E., "Religious preference and interreligious mixtures in marriages and divorces in Iowa," *American Journal of Sociology*, **61**, 233–239 (1955).

Montagu, Ashley, "Chromosomes and crime," *Psychology Today*, No. 5, 43–49 (1968).

Mueller, C. G., *Sensory Psychology*, Englewood Cliffs, N.J., Prentice-Hall, 1965.

Mumford, Lewis, *The Myth of the Machine*, New York, Harcourt, Brace and World, 1966.

Mussen, P. H., Conger, J. J., and Kagan, J., *Child Development and Personality* (3rd ed.), New York, Harper & Row, 1969.

Myrdal, Gunnar, *Challenge to Affluence*, New York, Pantheon Books, 1963.

National Institute of Mental Health, *LSD*, Washington, D. C., U.S. Government Printing Office, 1968.

National Institute of Mental Health, *Marijuana*, Washington, D.C., U.S. Government Printing Office, 1968.

National Institute of Mental Health, "Mental health news briefs," *Mental Health Digest*, August, 1967.

National Institute of Mental Health, *Narcotics*, Washington, D.C., U.S. Government Printing Office, 1968.

National Institute of Mental Health, *The Up and Down Drugs*, Washington, D.C., U.S. Government Printing Office, 1968.

Nye, F. I., Short, J. F., and Olson, V. J., "Socioeconomic status and delinquent behavior," *American Journal of Sociology*, **63**, 381–389 (1958).

Olds, James, "Pleasure centers in the brain," *Scientific American*, October, 1956.

Olds, M. E., and Olds, James, "Approach-avoidance analysis of rat diencephalon," *Journal of Comparative Neurology*, **120**, 259–297 (1963).

Ottinger, D. R., and Simmons, J. E., "Behavior of human neonates and prenatal maternal anxiety," *Psychological Reports*, **14**, 391–394 (1964).

Pavlov, I., *Conditioned Reflexes*, London, Oxford University Press, 1927.

Pavlov, I., "Experimental psychology and psychopathology of animals," paper delivered to the International Medical Congress, Madrid, Spain, 1903.

Pavlov, I., *Lectures on Conditioned Reflexes*, New York, International Universities Press, 1928.

Pieper, J., *Leisure The Basis of Culture*, New York, Random House, 1963.

Pine, G. J., "Social class, social mobility and delinquent behavior," *Personnel and Guidance Journal*, **43**, 770–774 (1965).

Provence, S., and Lipton, R. C., *Infants in Institutions*, New York, International Universities Press, 1963.

Rabban, M., "Sex role identification in young children in two diverse social groups," *Genetic Psychological Monographs*, **42**, 81–158 (1950).

Radke, M., Trager, H. G., and Davis, H., "Social perceptions and attitudes of children," *Genetic Psychological Monographs*, **40**, 327–447 (1949).

Rhine, J. B., and Brier, Robert, *Parapsychology Today*, New York, Citadel, 1968.

Rose, A. M., "Army policies toward negro soldiers," *Annals of the American Academy of Political and Social Science*, **244**, 90–94 (1946).

Ruch, T. C., and Patton, H. D. (Eds.), *Physiology and Biophysics*, Philadelphia, Pa., Saunders, 1965.

Schneiders, A. A. *Counseling the Adolescent,* San Francisco, Calif., Chandler Publishing Co., 1967.

Schwitzgebel, R., and Schwitzgebel, R., "Reduction of adolescent crime by a research method," *Journal of Sociological Therapy,* **7,** 212–215 (1961).

Shaw, C. R., Zorbaugh, F. M., McKay, H. D., and Cottrell, L. S., *Delinquency Areas,* Chicago, Ill., University of Chicago Press, 1929.

Shearer, Lloyd, "Intelligence report," *Parade Magazine,* Nov. 10, 1968, p. 4.

Schifferes, J. J., *Essentials of Healthier Living,* New York, Wiley, 1960.

Skinner, B. F., *The Behavior of Organisms,* New York, Appleton, Century, Crofts, 1938.

Slack, C. W., "Experimenter-subject psychotherapy: a new method of introducing intensive office treatment for unreachable cases," *Mental Hygiene,* **44,** 238–256 (1960).

Sperry, R. W., "The great cerebral commissure," *Scientific American,* Jan. 1964, **210,** 42–52.

Spitz, R. A., "Hospitalism: An inquiry into the genetics of psychiatric conditions in early childhood," *Psychoanalytic Study of the Child,* Vol. 1., New York, International University Press, 1945.

Spitz, R. A., "The role of ecological factors in emotional development in infancy," *Child Development,* **20,** 145–156 (1949).

Staff Report, "The challenege of automation," *Newsweek,* Jan. 25, 1965, pp. 73–80.

Stock, Robert W., "Will the baby be normal?", *New York Times Magazine,* March 23, 1969, pp. 25 ff.

Stone, L. J., and Church, J., *Childhood and Adolescence A Psychology of the Growing Person,* New York, Random House, 1957.

Temby, W. D., "Suicide," in Blain, G. B., and McArthur, C. C. (Eds.), *Emotional Problems of the Student,* New York, Appleton, Century, Crofts, 1961, pp. 133–152.

Terman, L. M., "The discovery and encouragement of exceptional talent," *American Psychologist,* **9,** 221–230 (1954).

Terman, L. M., et al., *Genetic Studies of Genius: Vol. I, Mental and Physical Traits of a Thousand Gifted Children,* Stanford, Calif., Stanford University Press, 1925.

Terman, L. M., and Merrill, M. A., *Revised Stanford Binet Intelligence Scale* (3rd ed.), Boston, Mass., Houghton Mifflin, 1960.

Terman, L. M., and Oden, M., *The Gifted Child Grows Up,* Stanford, Calif., Stanford University Press, 1947.

Terman, L. M., and Oden, M., *The Gifted Group at Mid-Life,* Stanford, Calif., Stanford University Press, 1959.

Thorpe, Louis P., *The Psychology of Mental Health* (2nd ed.), New York, Ronald Press, 1960.

Thurstone, L. L., "Primary mental abilities," *Psychometric Monographs,* No. 1, 1938.

Toolan, James M., "Suicide and suicide attempts in children and adolescents," *American Journal of Psychiatry,* **118,** 719–724 (1962).

Torrance, E. P., *Rewarding Creative Behavior: Experiments in Classroom Creativity,* Englewood Cliffs, N.J., Prentice-Hall, 1965.

Tuckman, Jacob, and Cannon, Helen E., "Attempted suicide in adolescents," *American Journal of Psychiatry,* **119,** 228–232 (1962).

Tune, G. S., 'Sleep and wakefulness in normal human adults," *British Medical Journal,* **2,** 269–271 (1968).

Tyler, Leona E., "The development of vocational interests. I. The organization of likes and dislikes in 10 year old children," *Journal of Genetic Psychology*, **86**, 33–44 (1955).

Tyler, Leona E., "The relationship of interests to abilities and reputation among first grade children," *Educational Psychological Measurement*, **11**, 255–264 (1951).

Tyler, Leona E., *Psychology of Human Differences* (3rd ed.), New York, Appleton, Century, Crofts, 1965.

U.S. Department of Labor, *Guide to the Use of the General Aptitude Test Battery, Section III: Development*, 1962.

U.S. President's Panel on Mental Retardation, *Mental Retardation Chart Book: A National Plan for a National Problem*, Washington, D.C., U.S. Dept. of Health, Education and Welfare, 1963.

Vitols, M. M. "Differing negro, white mental illness patterns seen converging as equality grows between races," *Mental Health Scope*, 1[14], 1–3 (1967).

Volkart, E. H., and Michael, S. T., "Bereavement and mental health," in Leighton, A. H., et al., *Explorations in Social Psychiatry*. New York, Basic Books, 1957, pp. 281–307.

Watson, J. B., and Rayner, R., "Conditioned emotional reactions," *Journal of Experimental Psychology*, **3**, 1–4 (1920).

Wechsler, David, *The Measurement and Appraisal of Adult Intelligence*, Baltimore, Williams and Wilkins, 1958.

Weiner, Norbert, *The Human Use of Human Beings*, New York, Avon Books, 1967.

Winch, Robert F., *Mate Selection: A Study of Complementary Needs*, New York, Harper and Brothers, 1958.

Wittreich, W. J., "Visual perception and personality," *Scientific American*, April, 1959, pp. 56–60.

Wooldridge, Dean E., *Mechanical Man*, New York, McGraw-Hill, 1968.

Wright, Beatrice A., *Psychology and Rehabilitation*, Washington, D.C., American Psychological Association, 1959.

Zimmerman, William B., "Psychological and physiological differences between light and deep sleepers," *Psychophysiology*, **4**, 387 (1968).

Author Index

Subject Index

About the Authors

IDELLA M. EVANS is the Supervisory Clinical Psychologist at the Saratoga County (New York) Mental Health Center. She is a graduate of the University of Washington and has an M.S. and Ph.D. in clinical psychology from the University of Oregon. Her clinical psychology internship was served at the Community Child Guidance Clinic in Portland, Oregon, and her additional academic background includes post-doctoral training at the Center for Training in Community Psychiatry and Mental Health Administration, Berkeley, California. Dr. Evans has engaged in the private practice of clinical psychology for several years, and she has served on the staffs of Northern State Hospital (Washington), the Santa Clara County (California) Mental Health Department, and the Santa Clara Valley Medical Center. She has taught psychology in the Oregon state system of higher education and at San Jose State College.

PATRICIA A. SMITH is a Counseling Psychologist with the San Jose State College Foundation (California). She holds degrees in social work and psychology from the University of Wisconsin and a Ph.D. degree in counseling psychology from the University of Oregon. She was a clinical psychology trainee with the Veterans Administration and the Oregon State Home for the Retarded. She served a counseling internship with the student Counseling Center at the University of Oregon. She was a staff counselor at Oregon State University and the University of Oregon. Her post-doctoral experience includes assignments as a Community Mental Health Consultant for the San Jose Health Department, Lecturer in U.S. Employment Service Counselor Workshops, and Field Assessment Officer for the Peace Corps. She has held teaching positions with Southern Oregon College, the College of San Mateo, San Jose State College, and Ohlone College. She is the author of several publications in the areas of motor skills and family life.